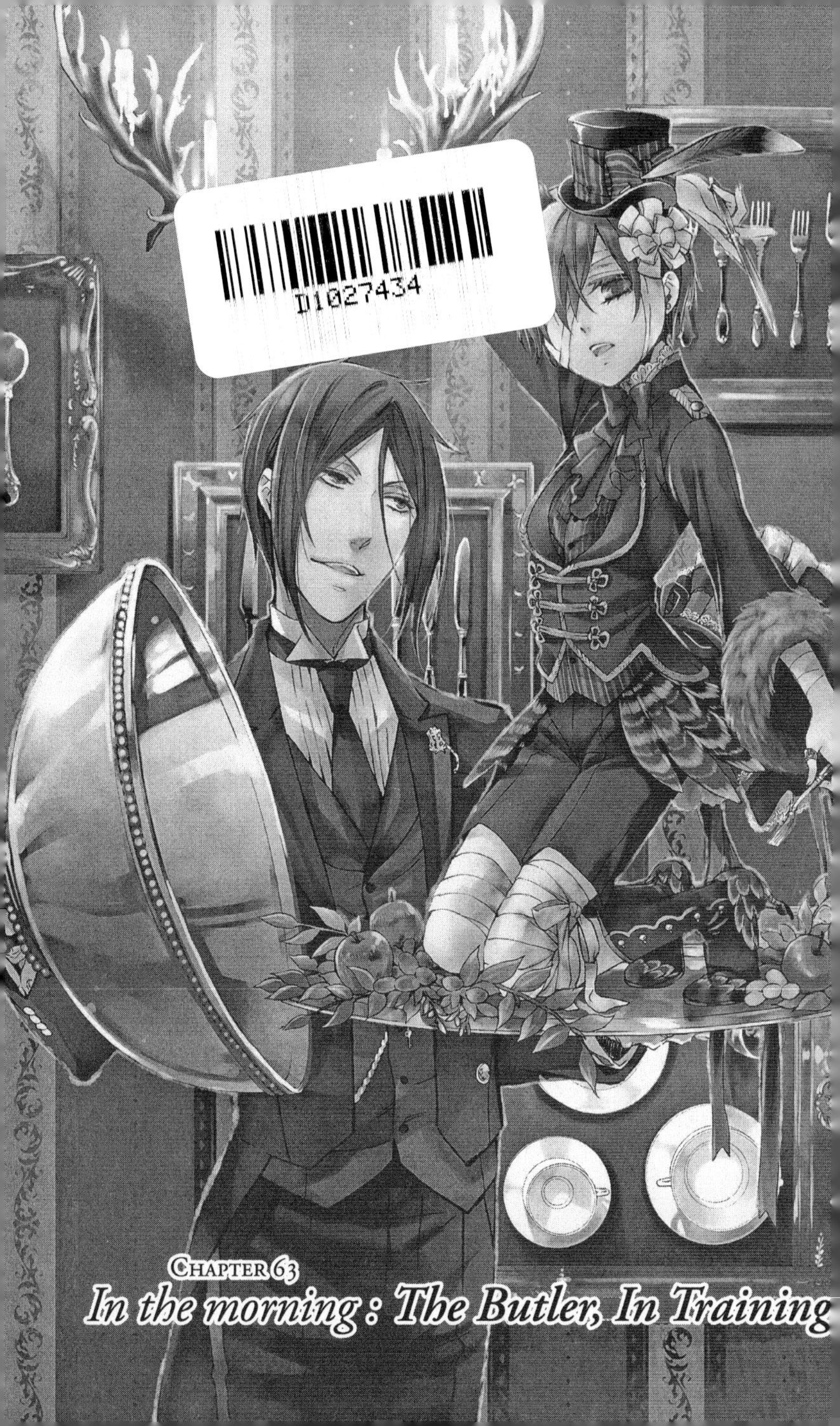

Chapter 63

In the morning : The Butler, In Training

Black Butler

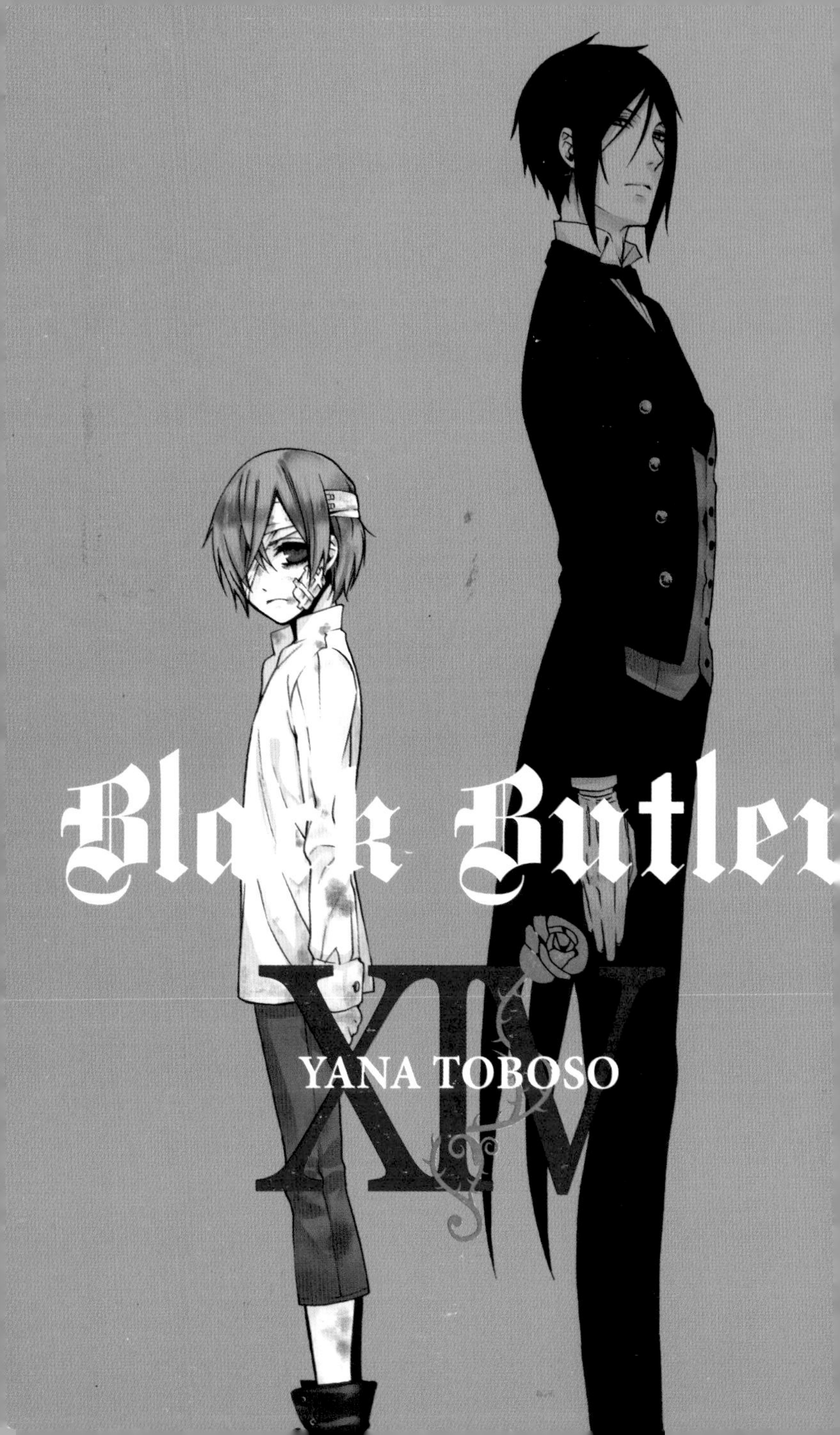
Black Butler
XIV
YANA TOBOSO

Contents

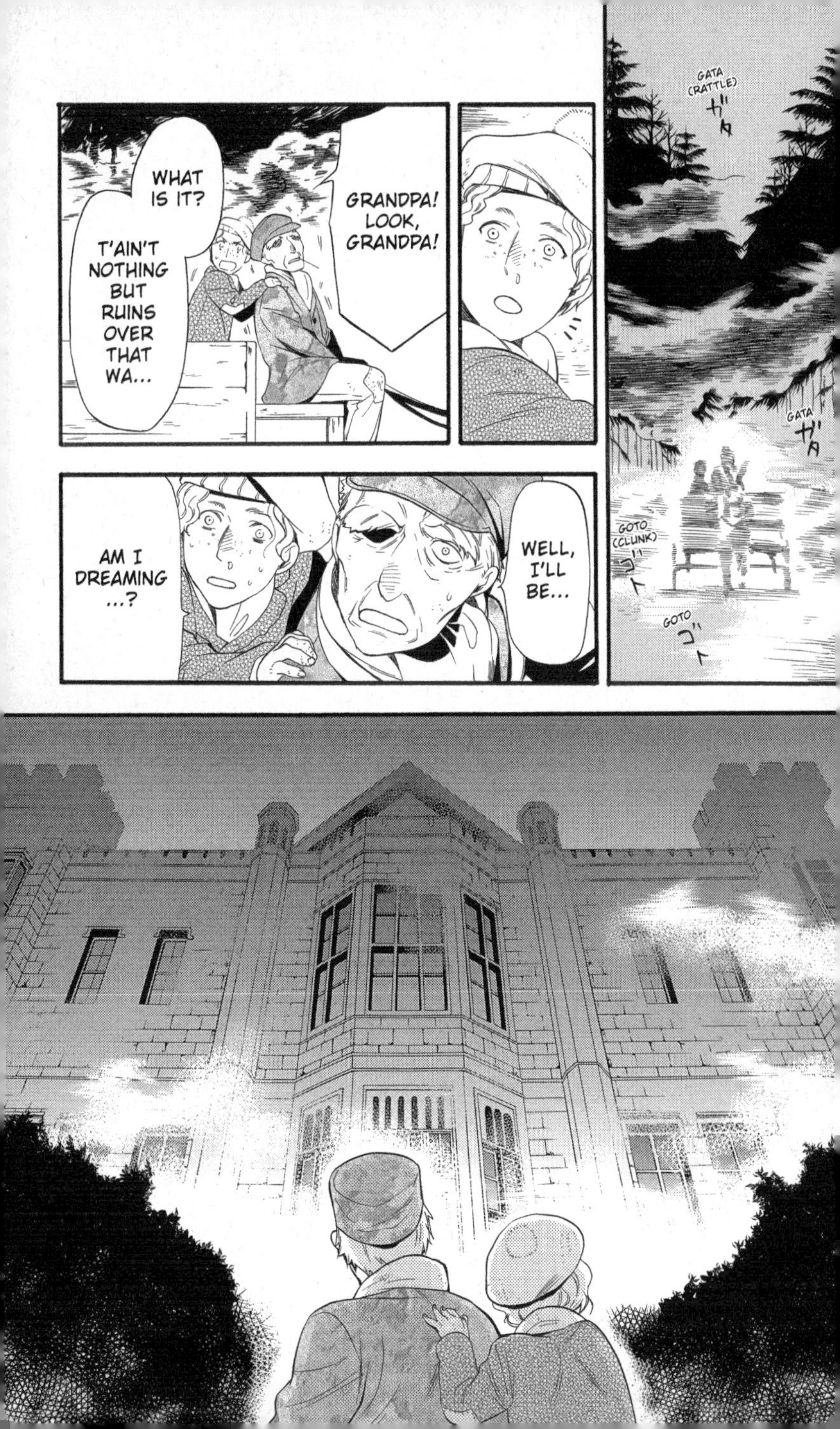
GATA (RATTLE)
GATA
GOTO (CLUNK)
GOTO
GRANDPA! LOOK, GRANDPA!
WHAT IS IT?
T'AIN'T NOTHING BUT RUINS OVER THAT WA...
WELL, I'LL BE...
AM I DREAMING ...?

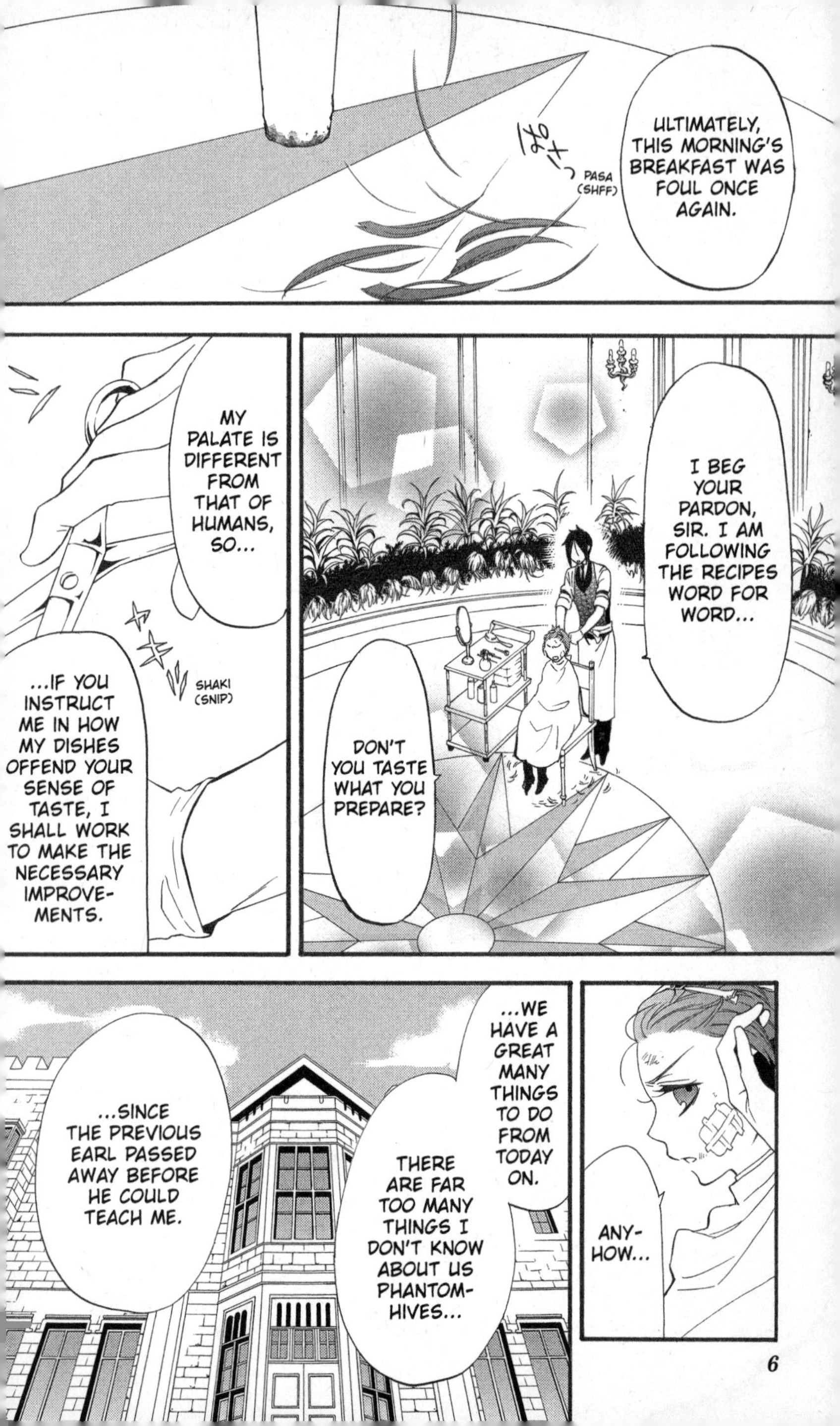
ULTIMATELY, THIS MORNING'S BREAKFAST WAS FOUL ONCE AGAIN.
PASA (SHFF)
I BEG YOUR PARDON, SIR. I AM FOLLOWING THE RECIPES WORD FOR WORD...
DON'T YOU TASTE WHAT YOU PREPARE?
MY PALATE IS DIFFERENT FROM THAT OF HUMANS, SO...
SHAKI (SNIP)
...IF YOU INSTRUCT ME IN HOW MY DISHES OFFEND YOUR SENSE OF TASTE, I SHALL WORK TO MAKE THE NECESSARY IMPROVE-MENTS.
ANY-HOW...
...WE HAVE A GREAT MANY THINGS TO DO FROM TODAY ON.
THERE ARE FAR TOO MANY THINGS I DON'T KNOW ABOUT US PHANTOM-HIVES...
...SINCE THE PREVIOUS EARL PASSED AWAY BEFORE HE COULD TEACH ME.

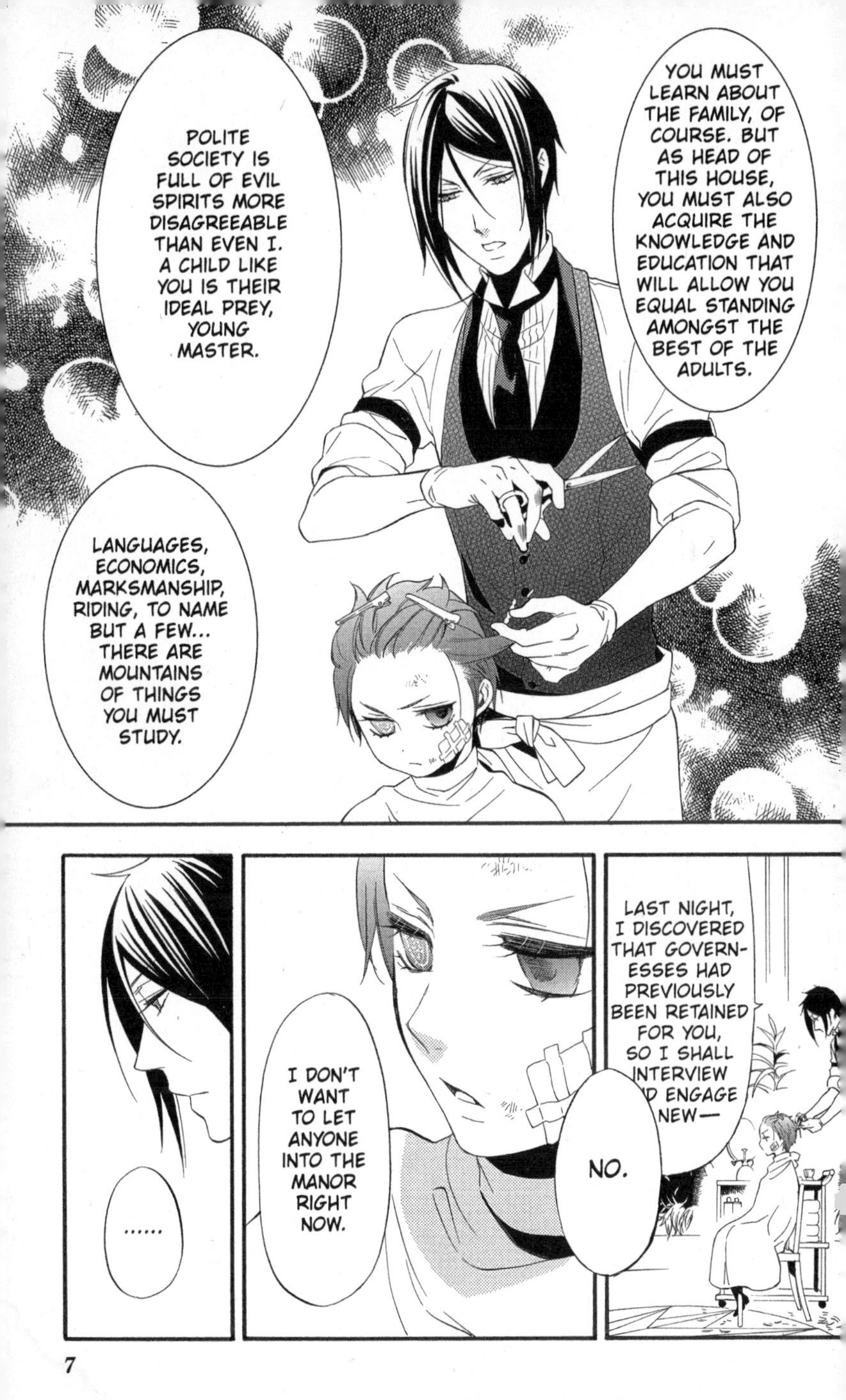
YOU MUST LEARN ABOUT THE FAMILY, OF COURSE. BUT AS HEAD OF THIS HOUSE, YOU MUST ALSO ACQUIRE THE KNOWLEDGE AND EDUCATION THAT WILL ALLOW YOU EQUAL STANDING AMONGST THE BEST OF THE ADULTS.
POLITE SOCIETY IS FULL OF EVIL SPIRITS MORE DISAGREEABLE THAN EVEN I. A CHILD LIKE YOU IS THEIR IDEAL PREY, YOUNG MASTER.
LANGUAGES, ECONOMICS, MARKSMANSHIP, RIDING, TO NAME BUT A FEW... THERE ARE MOUNTAINS OF THINGS YOU MUST STUDY.
LAST NIGHT, I DISCOVERED THAT GOVERNESSES HAD PREVIOUSLY BEEN RETAINED FOR YOU, SO I SHALL INTERVIEW D ENGAGE NEW—
NO.
I DON'T WANT TO LET ANYONE INTO THE MANOR RIGHT NOW.
......

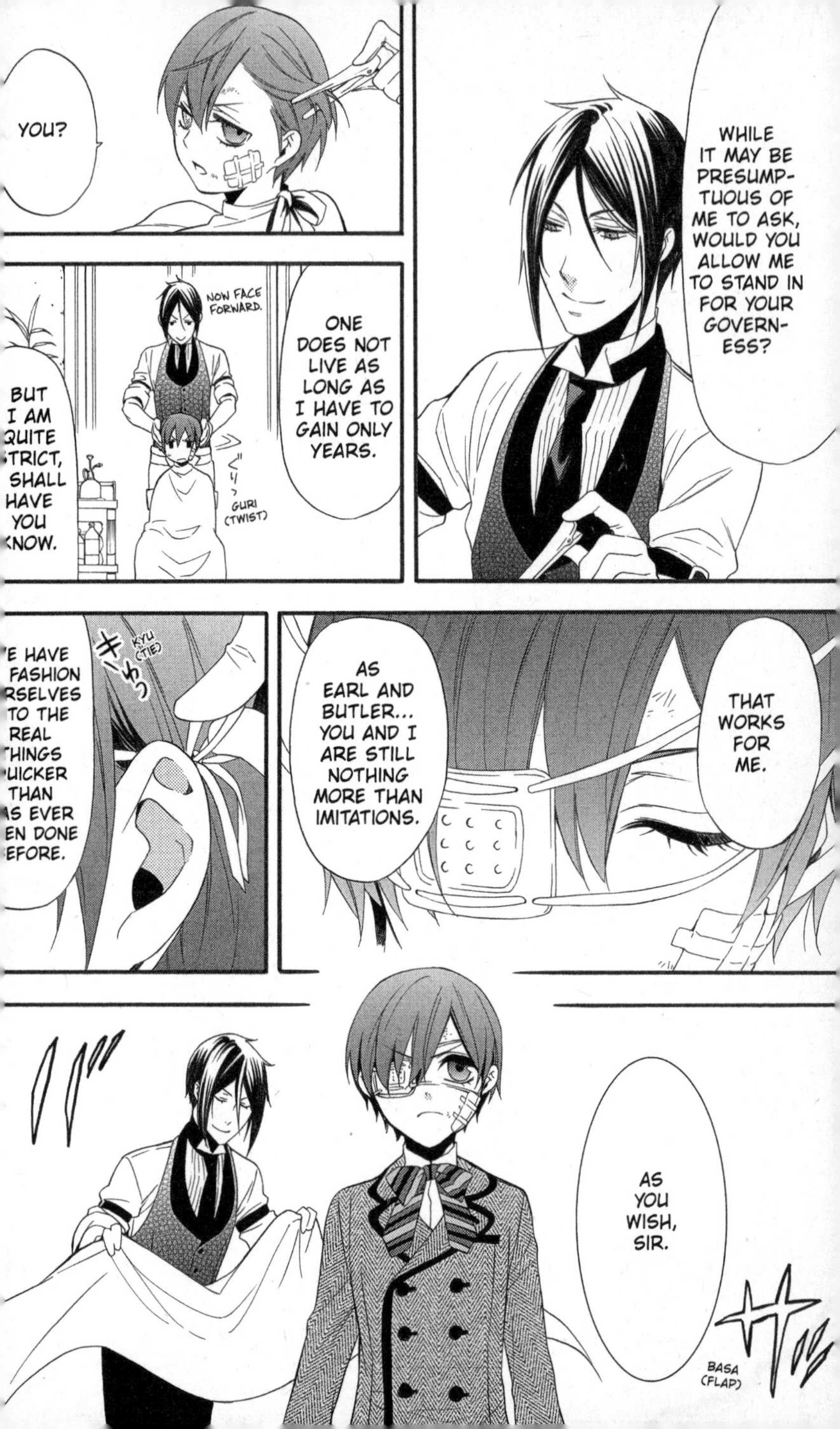
WHILE IT MAY BE PRESUMPTUOUS OF ME TO ASK, WOULD YOU ALLOW ME TO STAND IN FOR YOUR GOVERNESS?
YOU?
ONE DOES NOT LIVE AS LONG AS I HAVE TO GAIN ONLY YEARS.
NOW FACE FORWARD.
GURI (TWIST)
BUT I AM QUITE TRICT, SHALL HAVE YOU NOW.
THAT WORKS FOR ME.
AS EARL AND BUTLER... YOU AND I ARE STILL NOTHING MORE THAN IMITATIONS.
KYU (TIE)
E HAVE FASHION RSELVES TO THE REAL THINGS UICKER THAN AS EVER EN DONE EFORE.
AS YOU WISH, SIR.
BASA (FLAP)

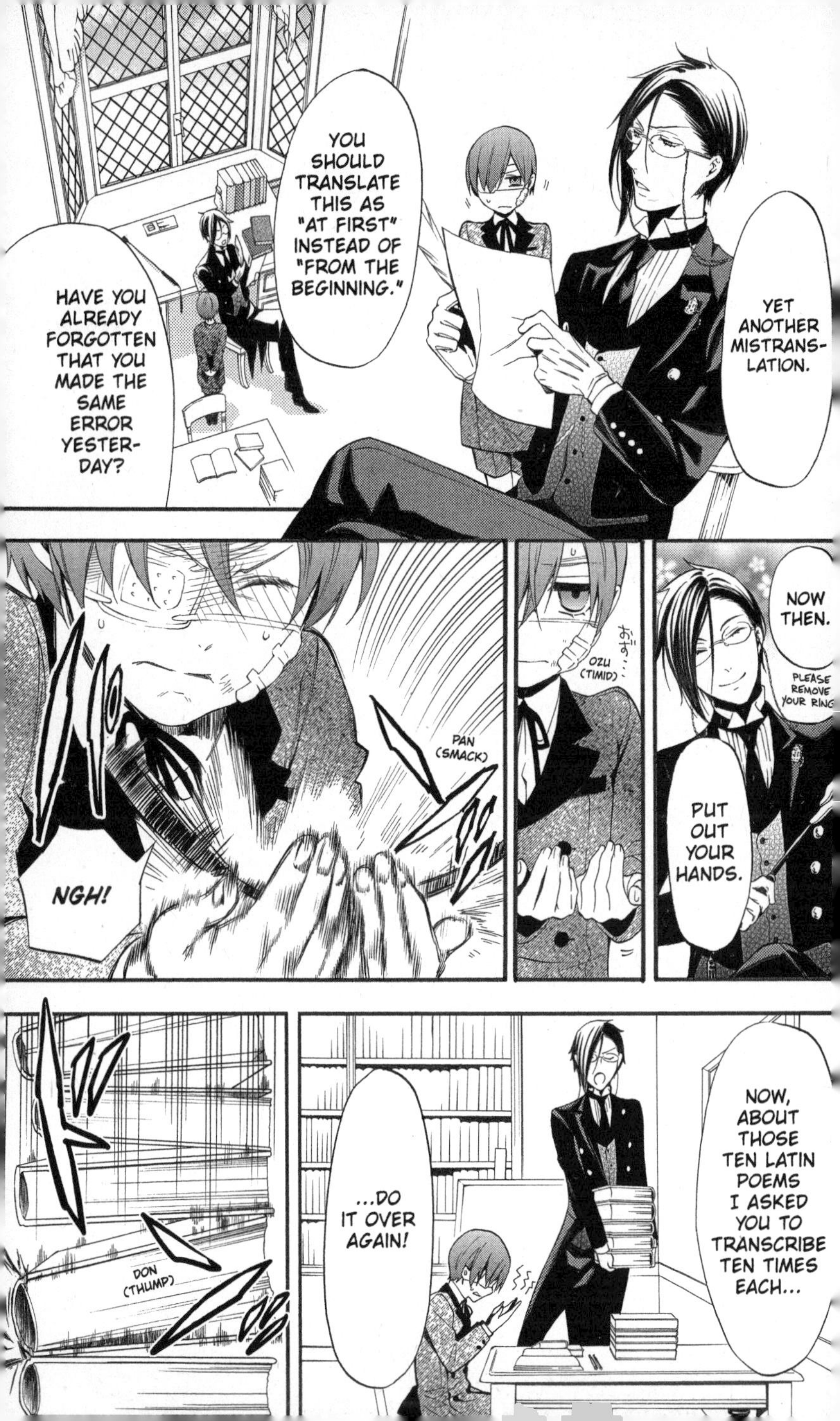
YET ANOTHER MISTRANSLATION.
YOU SHOULD TRANSLATE THIS AS "AT FIRST" INSTEAD OF "FROM THE BEGINNING."
HAVE YOU ALREADY FORGOTTEN THAT YOU MADE THE SAME ERROR YESTERDAY?
NOW THEN.
PLEASE REMOVE YOUR RING
PUT OUT YOUR HANDS.
おず…
OZU (TIMID)
PAN (SMACK)
NGH!
NOW, ABOUT THOSE TEN LATIN POEMS I ASKED YOU TO TRANSCRIBE TEN TIMES EACH…
…DO IT OVER AGAIN!
DON (THUMP)

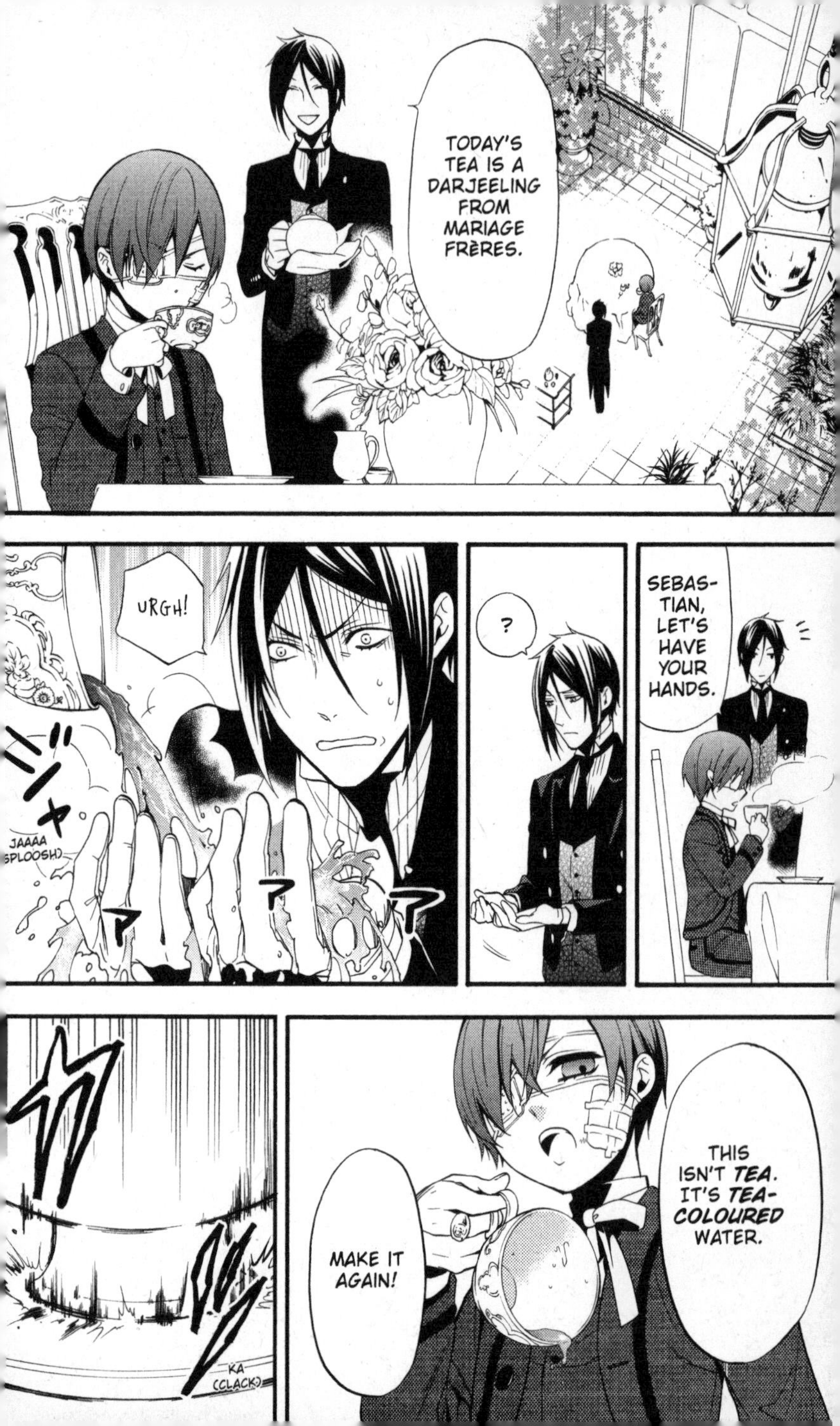
TODAY'S TEA IS A DARJEELING FROM MARIAGE FRÈRES.
SEBAS-TIAN, LET'S HAVE YOUR HANDS.
?
URGH!
JAAAA (SPLOOSH)
THIS ISN'T *TEA*. IT'S *TEA-COLOURED* WATER.
MAKE IT AGAIN!
KA (CLACK)

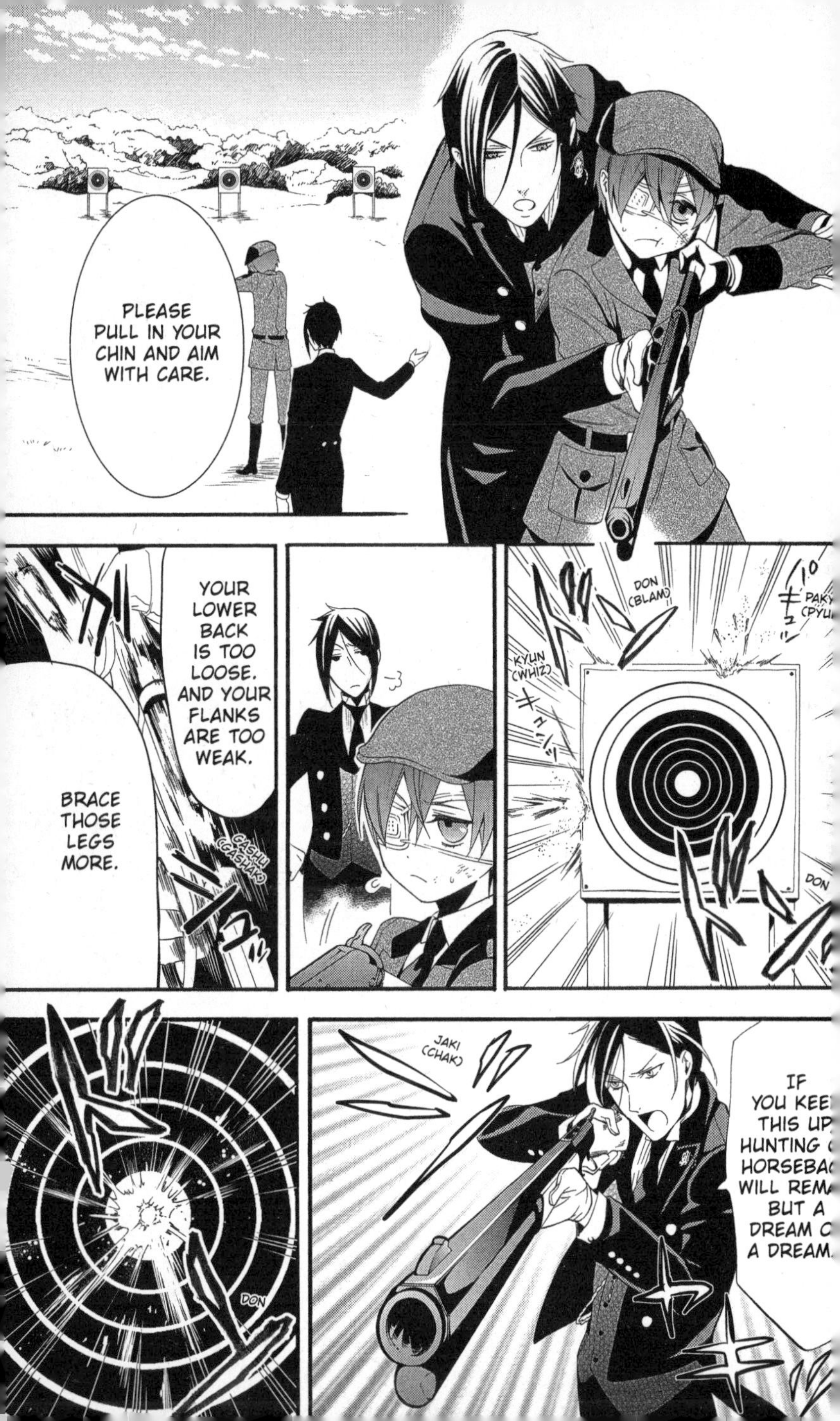
PLEASE PULL IN YOUR CHIN AND AIM WITH CARE.
DON (BLAM)
PAKY (PYU
KYUN (WHIZ)
DON
YOUR LOWER BACK IS TOO LOOSE. AND YOUR FLANKS ARE TOO WEAK.
GASHU (GASHAK)
BRACE THOSE LEGS MORE.
JAKI (CHAK)
IF YOU KEE THIS UP HUNTING HORSEBAC WILL REMA BUT A DREAM O A DREAM.
DON

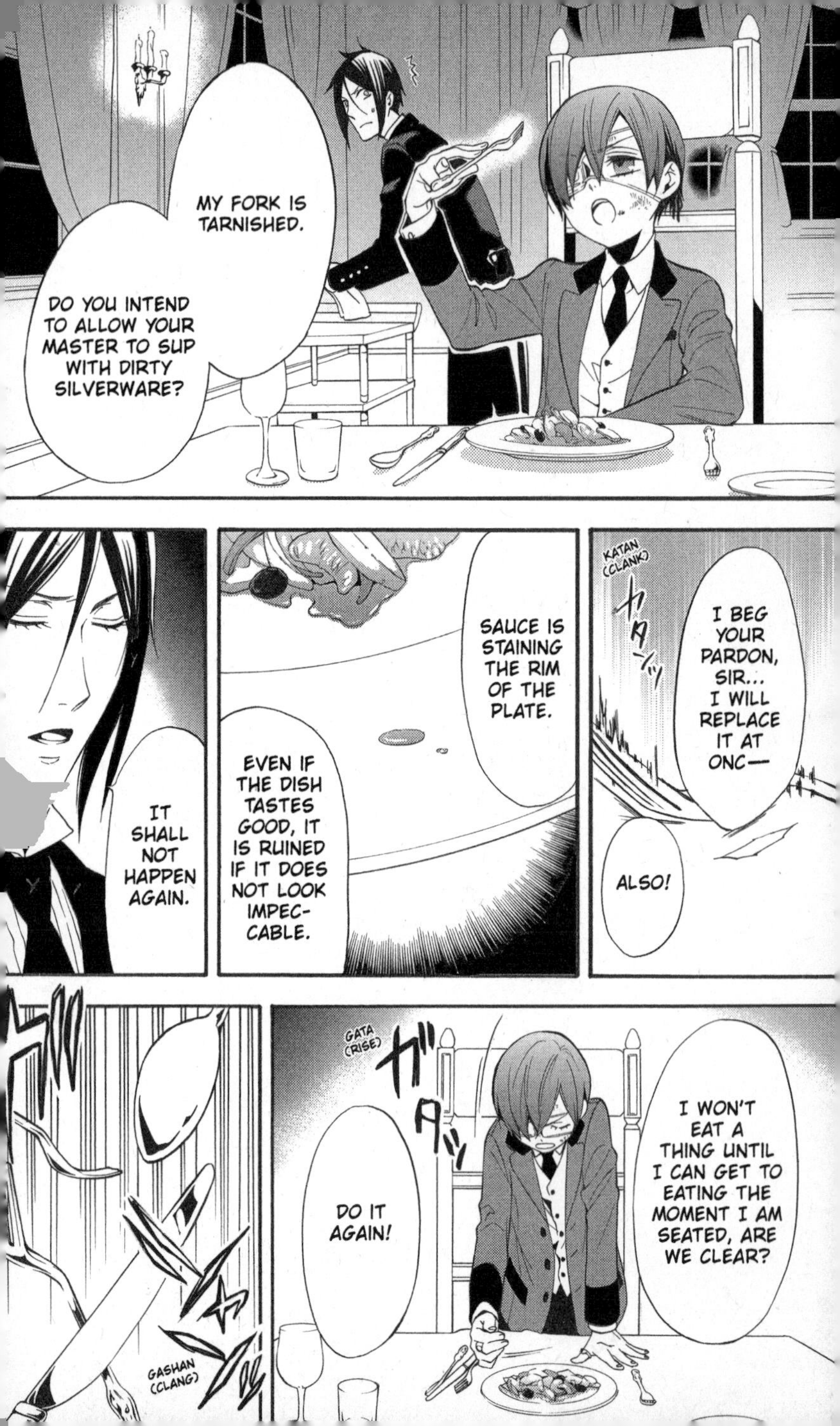
MY FORK IS TARNISHED.
DO YOU INTEND TO ALLOW YOUR MASTER TO SUP WITH DIRTY SILVERWARE?
KATAN (CLANK)
I BEG YOUR PARDON, SIR... I WILL REPLACE IT AT ONC—
ALSO!
SAUCE IS STAINING THE RIM OF THE PLATE.
EVEN IF THE DISH TASTES GOOD, IT IS RUINED IF IT DOES NOT LOOK IMPEC-CABLE.
IT SHALL NOT HAPPEN AGAIN.
GATA (RISE)
I WON'T EAT A THING UNTIL I CAN GET TO EATING THE MOMENT I AM SEATED, ARE WE CLEAR?
DO IT AGAIN!
GASHAN (CLANG)

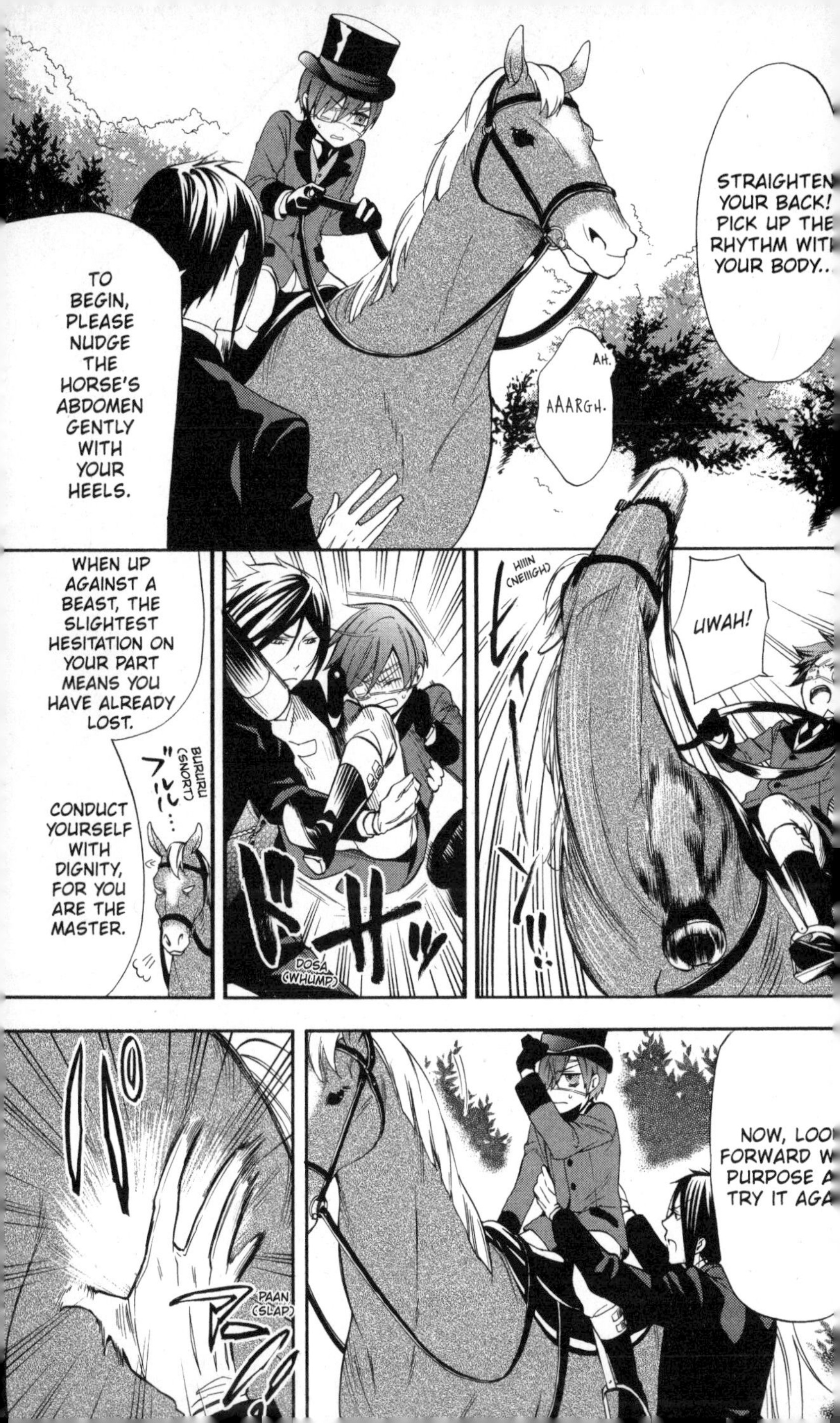
STRAIGHTEN YOUR BACK! PICK UP THE RHYTHM WIT YOUR BODY..
AH.
AAARGH.
TO BEGIN, PLEASE NUDGE THE HORSE'S ABDOMEN GENTLY WITH YOUR HEELS.
HIIIN (NEIIIGH)
UWAH!
!!
DOSA (WHUMP)
WHEN UP AGAINST A BEAST, THE SLIGHTEST HESITATION ON YOUR PART MEANS YOU HAVE ALREADY LOST.
BURURU (SNORT)
CONDUCT YOURSELF WITH DIGNITY, FOR YOU ARE THE MASTER.
NOW, LOO FORWARD W PURPOSE A TRY IT AGA
PAAN (SLAP)

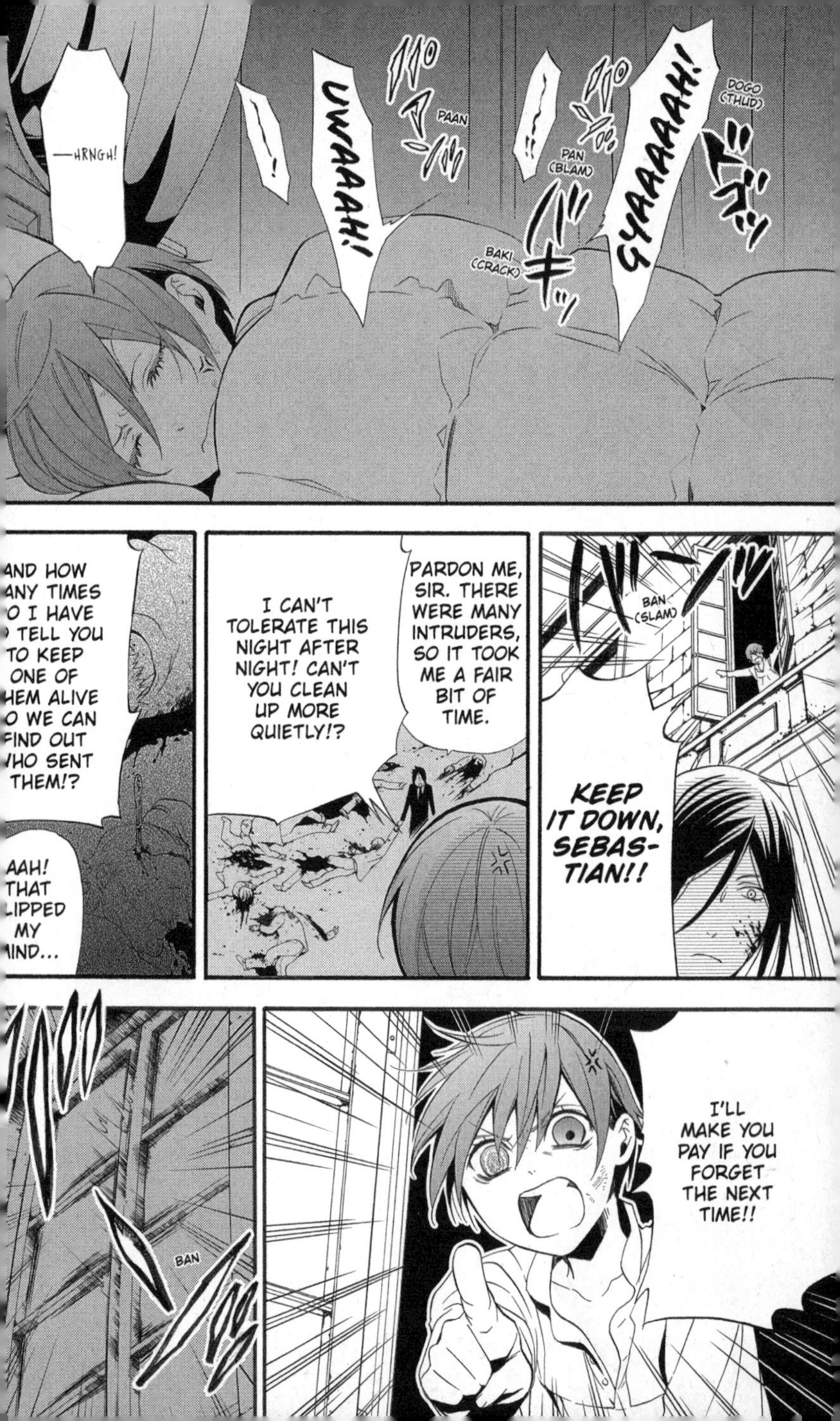
DOGO (THUD)
GYAAAAAH!
PAN (BLAM)
BAKI (CRACK)
—!!
UWAAAAH!
PAAN
—!
—HRNGH!
BAN (SLAM)
KEEP IT DOWN, SEBASTIAN!!
PARDON ME, SIR. THERE WERE MANY INTRUDERS, SO IT TOOK ME A FAIR BIT OF TIME.
I CAN'T TOLERATE THIS NIGHT AFTER NIGHT! CAN'T YOU CLEAN UP MORE QUIETLY!?
AND HOW ANY TIMES O I HAVE TELL YOU TO KEEP ONE OF HEM ALIVE O WE CAN FIND OUT HO SENT THEM!?
AAH! THAT LIPPED MY IND...
I'LL MAKE YOU PAY IF YOU FORGET THE NEXT TIME!!
BAN

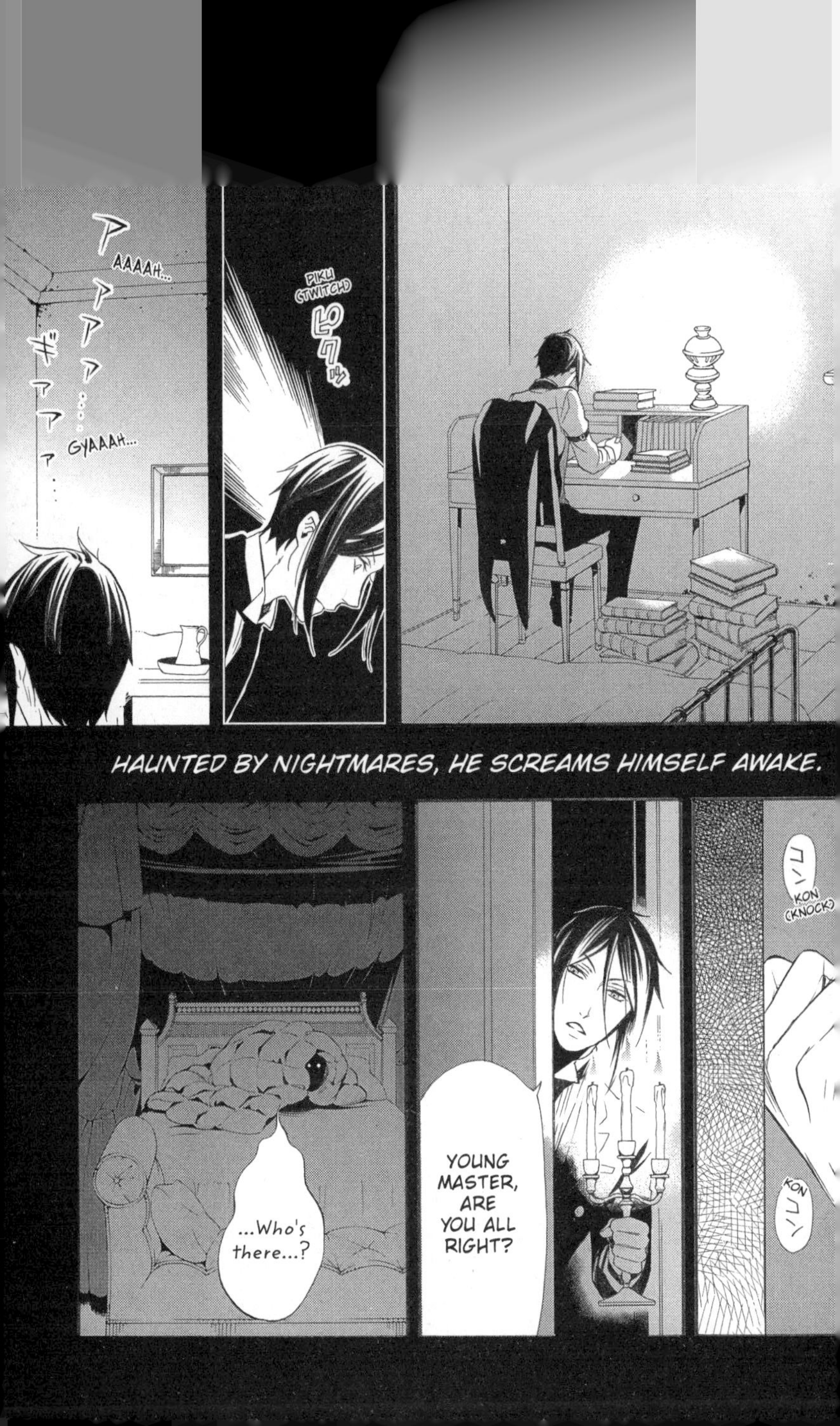
PIKU (TWITCH)
ピクッ
アアアア…
AAAAH...
ギァァァ…
GYAAAH...
HAUNTED BY NIGHTMARES, HE SCREAMS HIMSELF AWAKE.
コン
KON (KNOCK)
コン
KON
YOUNG MASTER, ARE YOU ALL RIGHT?
...Who's there...?

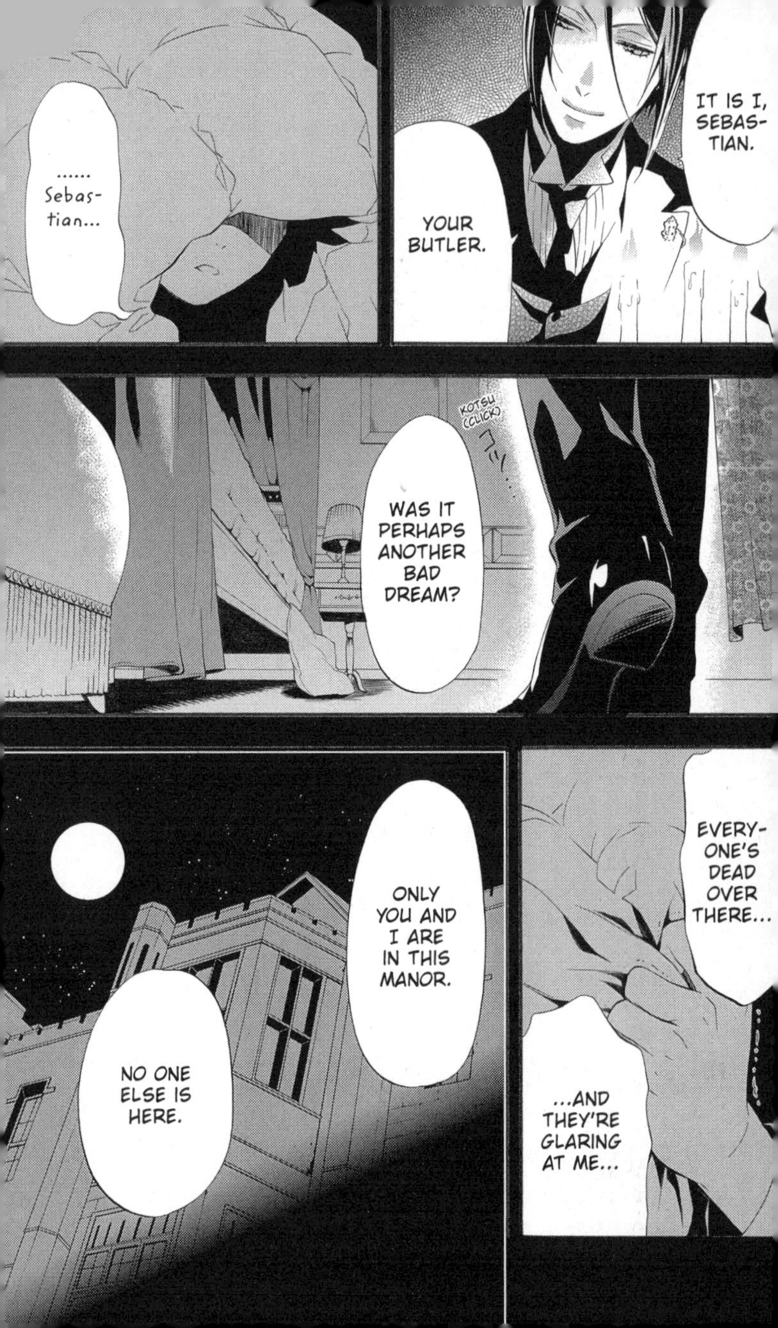
IT IS I, SEBASTIAN.
YOUR BUTLER.
...... Sebastian...
KOTSU (CLICK)
WAS IT PERHAPS ANOTHER BAD DREAM?
EVERYONE'S DEAD OVER THERE...
...AND THEY'RE GLARING AT ME...
ONLY YOU AND I ARE IN THIS MANOR.
NO ONE ELSE IS HERE.

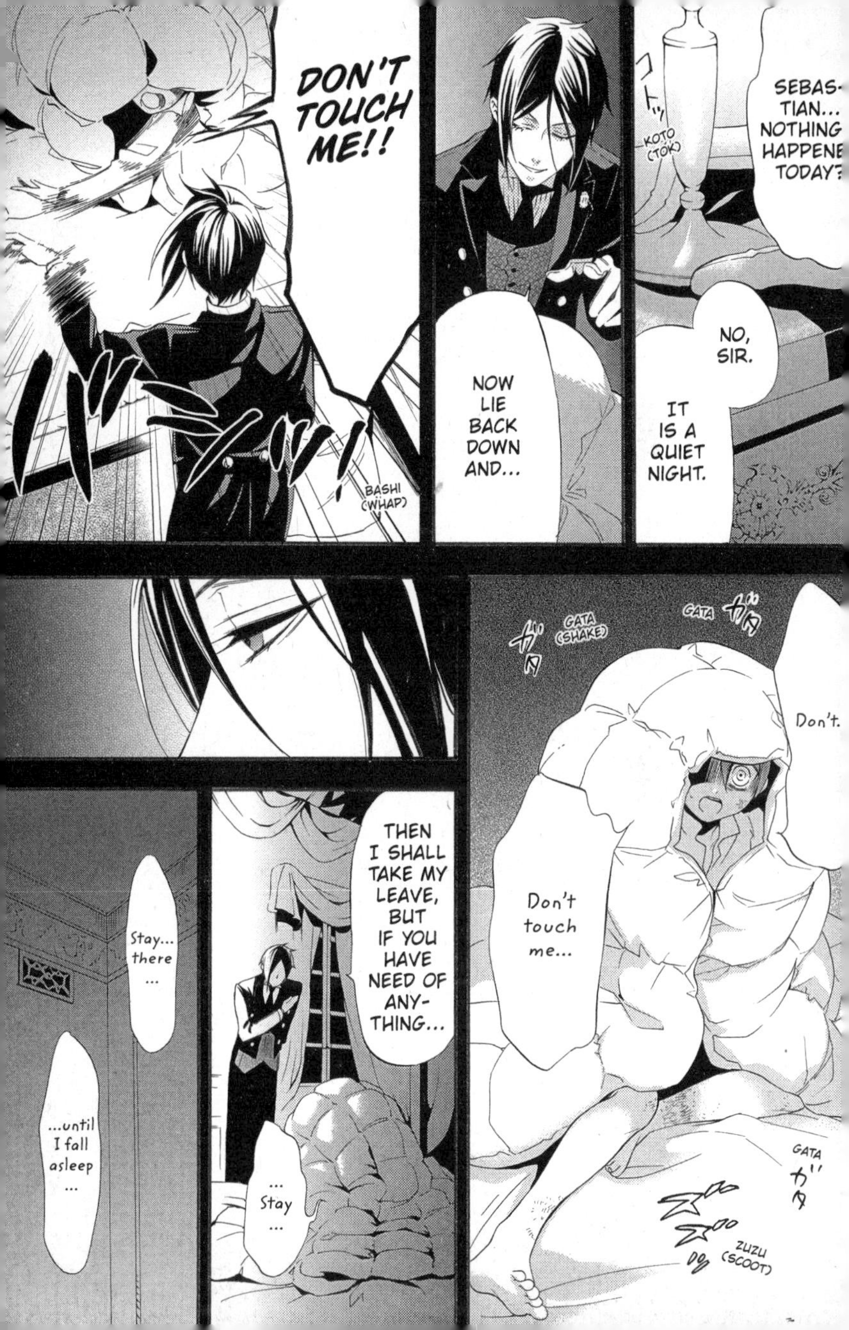
SEBAS-TIAN… NOTHING HAPPENE TODAY?
KOTO (TOK)
NO, SIR.
IT IS A QUIET NIGHT.
NOW LIE BACK DOWN AND…
DON'T TOUCH ME!!
BASHI (WHAP)
GATA
GATA (SHAKE)
Don't.
Don't touch me…
GATA
ZUZU (SCOOT)
THEN I SHALL TAKE MY LEAVE, BUT IF YOU HAVE NEED OF ANY-THING…
…Stay…
Stay… there …
…until I fall asleep …

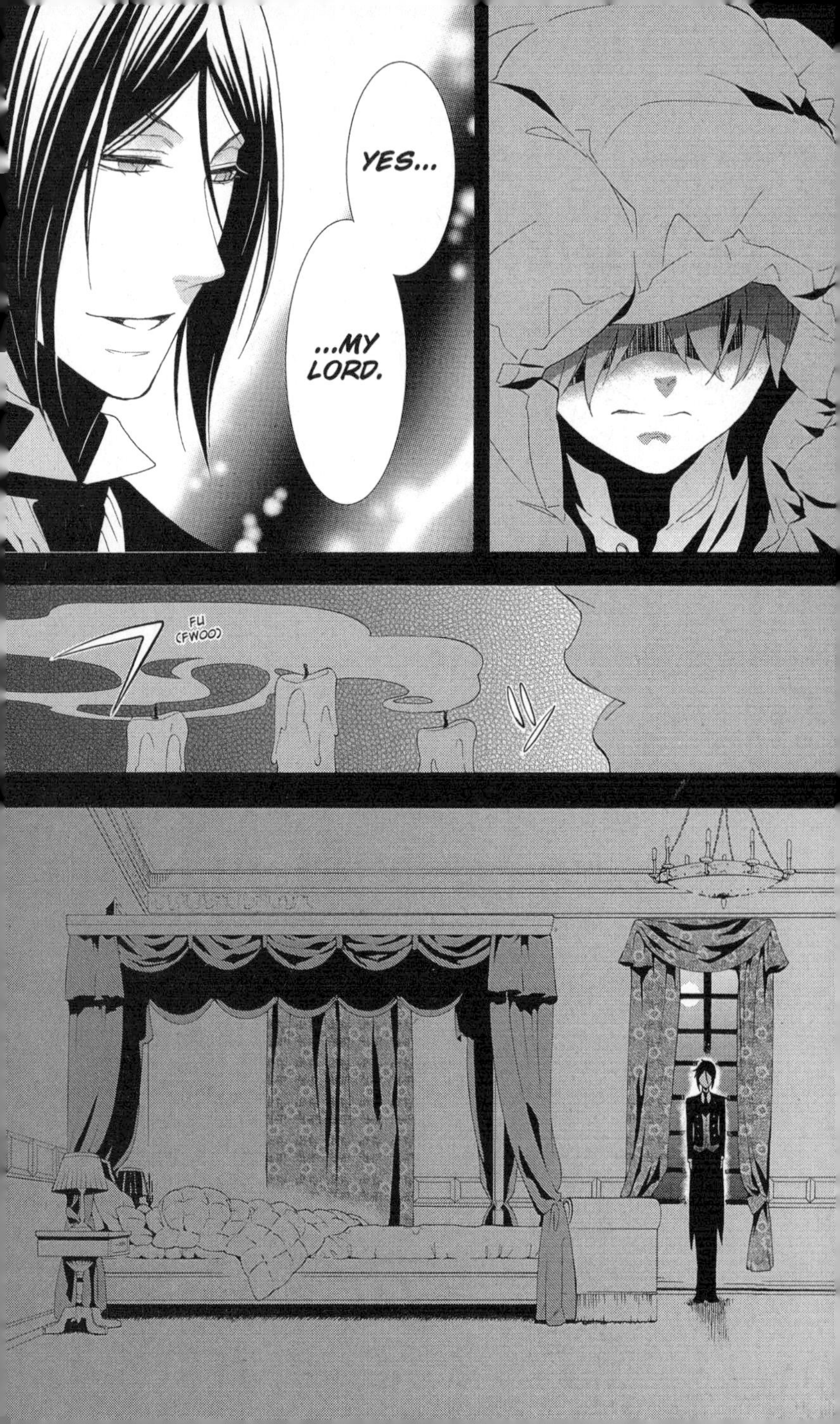
YES...
...MY LORD.
FU (FWOO)

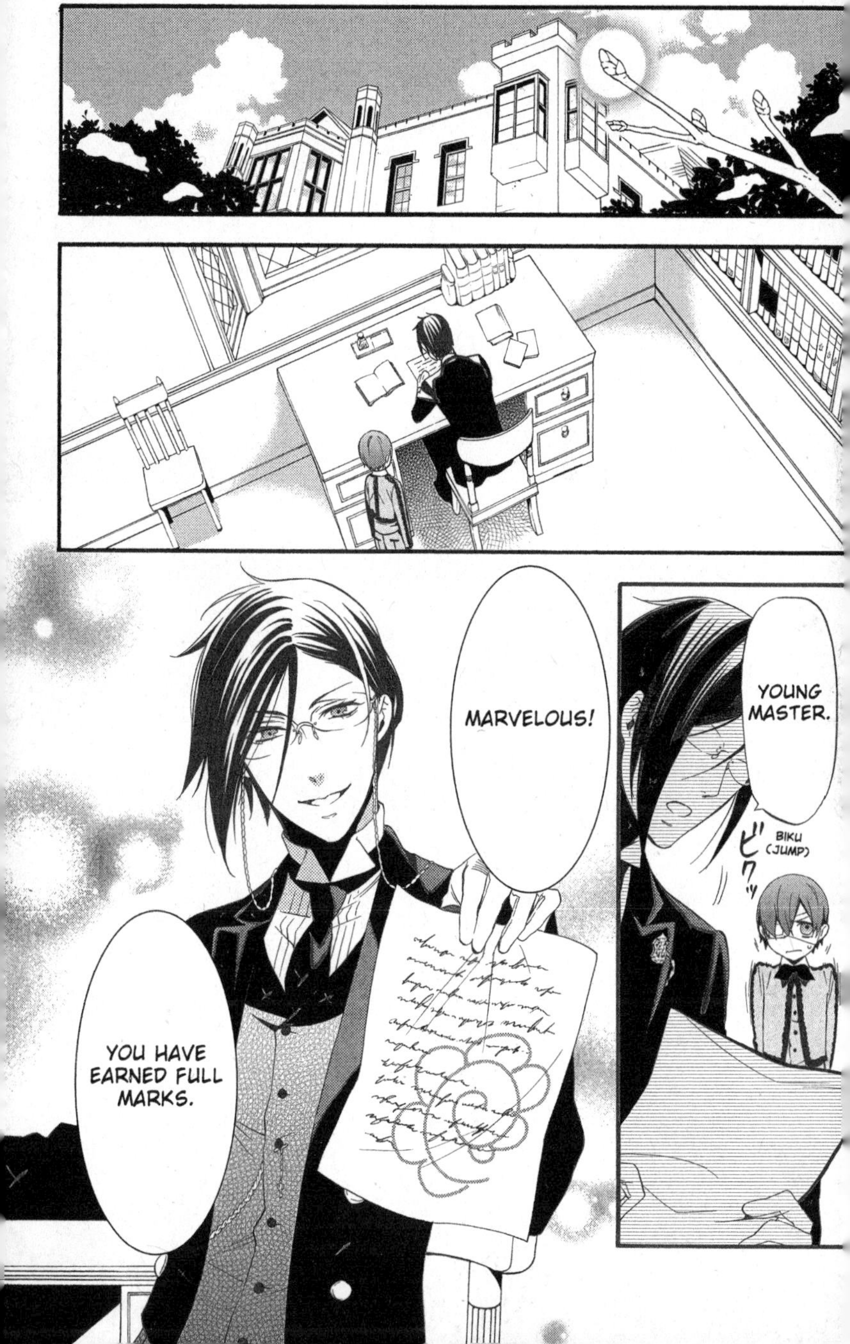
YOUNG MASTER.
BIKU (JUMP)
MARVELOUS!
YOU HAVE EARNED FULL MARKS.

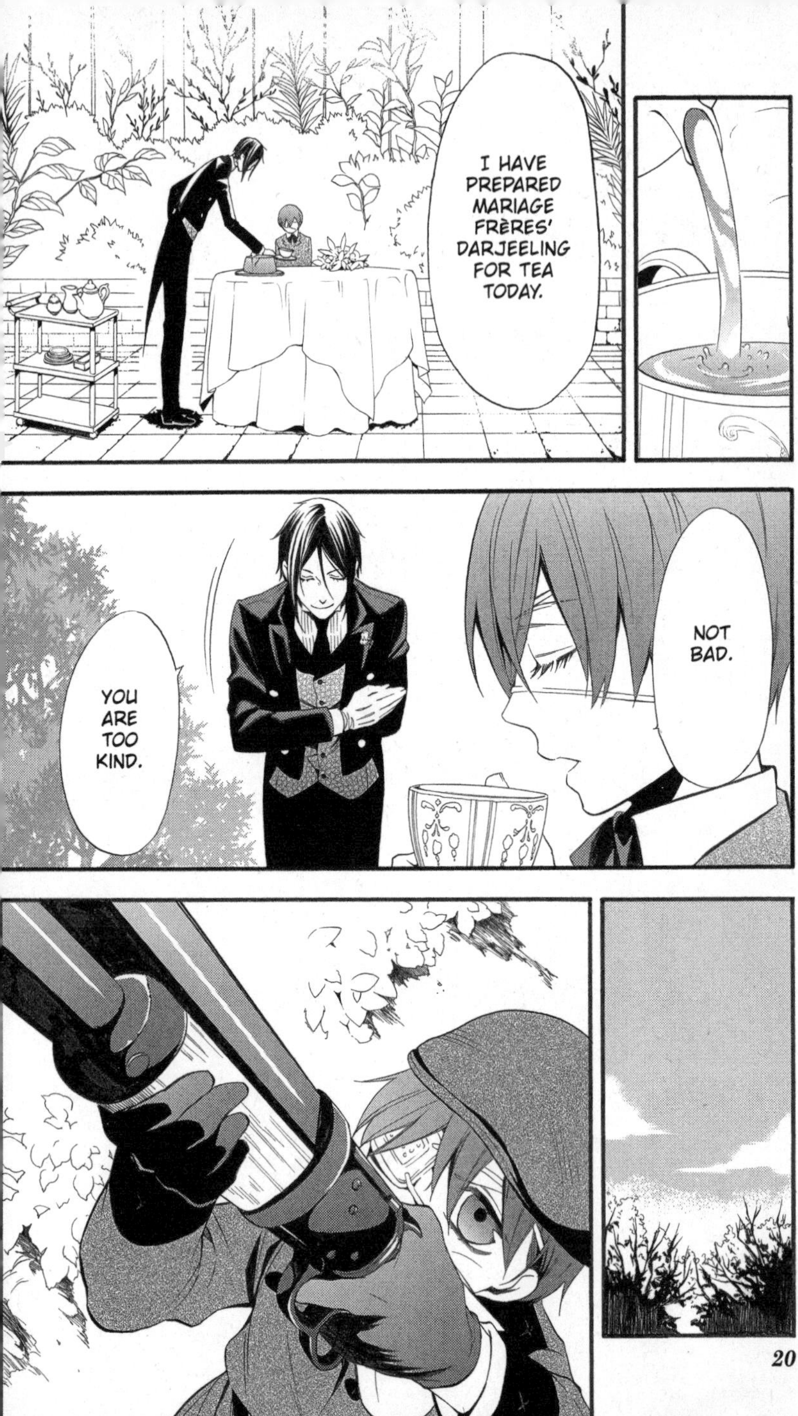
I HAVE PREPARED MARIAGE FRÈRES' DARJEELING FOR TEA TODAY.
NOT BAD.
YOU ARE TOO KIND.

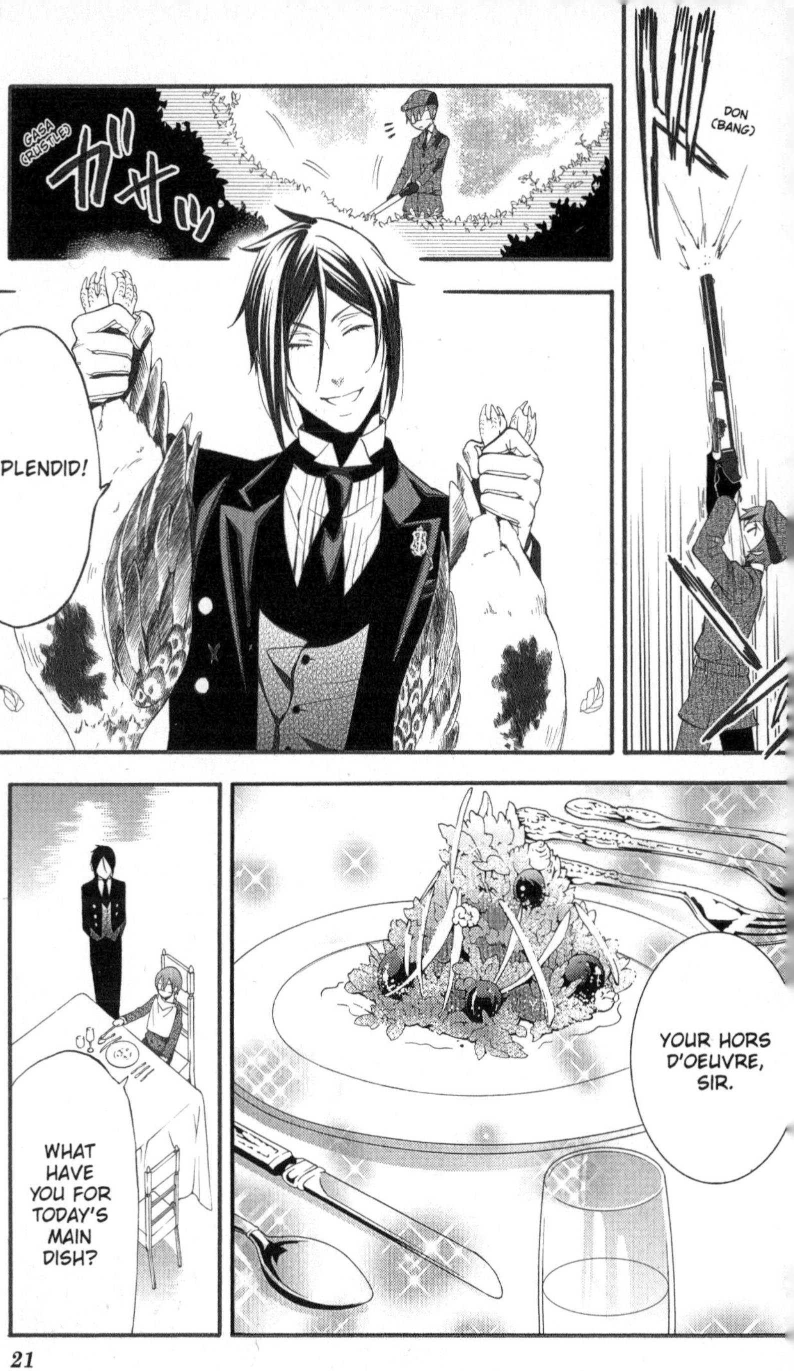
DON (BANG)
GASA (RUSTLE)
ガサッ
SPLENDID!
YOUR HORS D'OEUVRE, SIR.
WHAT HAVE YOU FOR TODAY'S MAIN DISH?

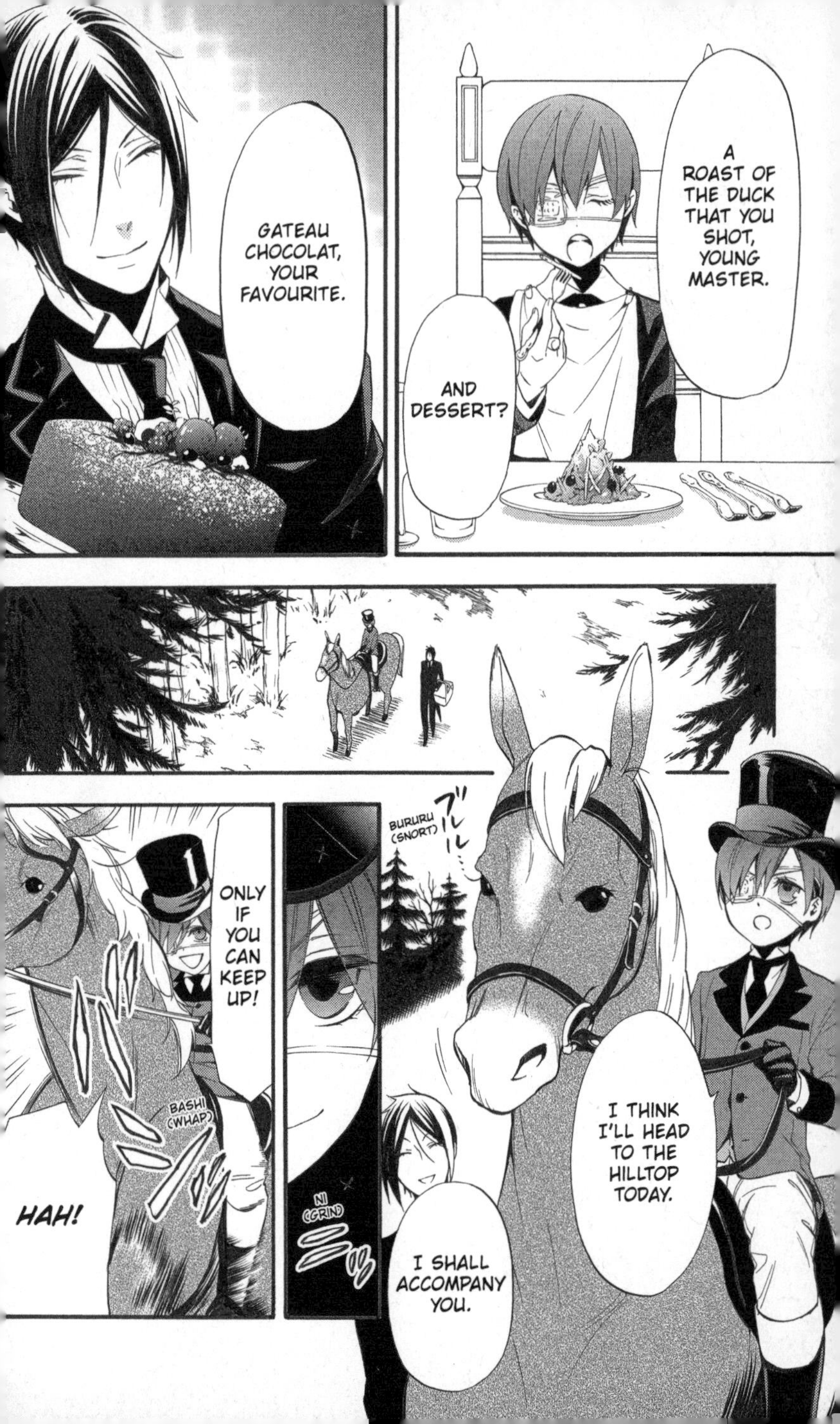
A ROAST OF THE DUCK THAT YOU SHOT, YOUNG MASTER.
AND DESSERT?
GATEAU CHOCOLAT, YOUR FAVOURITE.
ブルル…
BURURU (SNORT)
I THINK I'LL HEAD TO THE HILLTOP TODAY.
I SHALL ACCOMPANY YOU.
NI (GRIN)
ONLY IF YOU CAN KEEP UP!
BASHI (WHAP)
HAH!

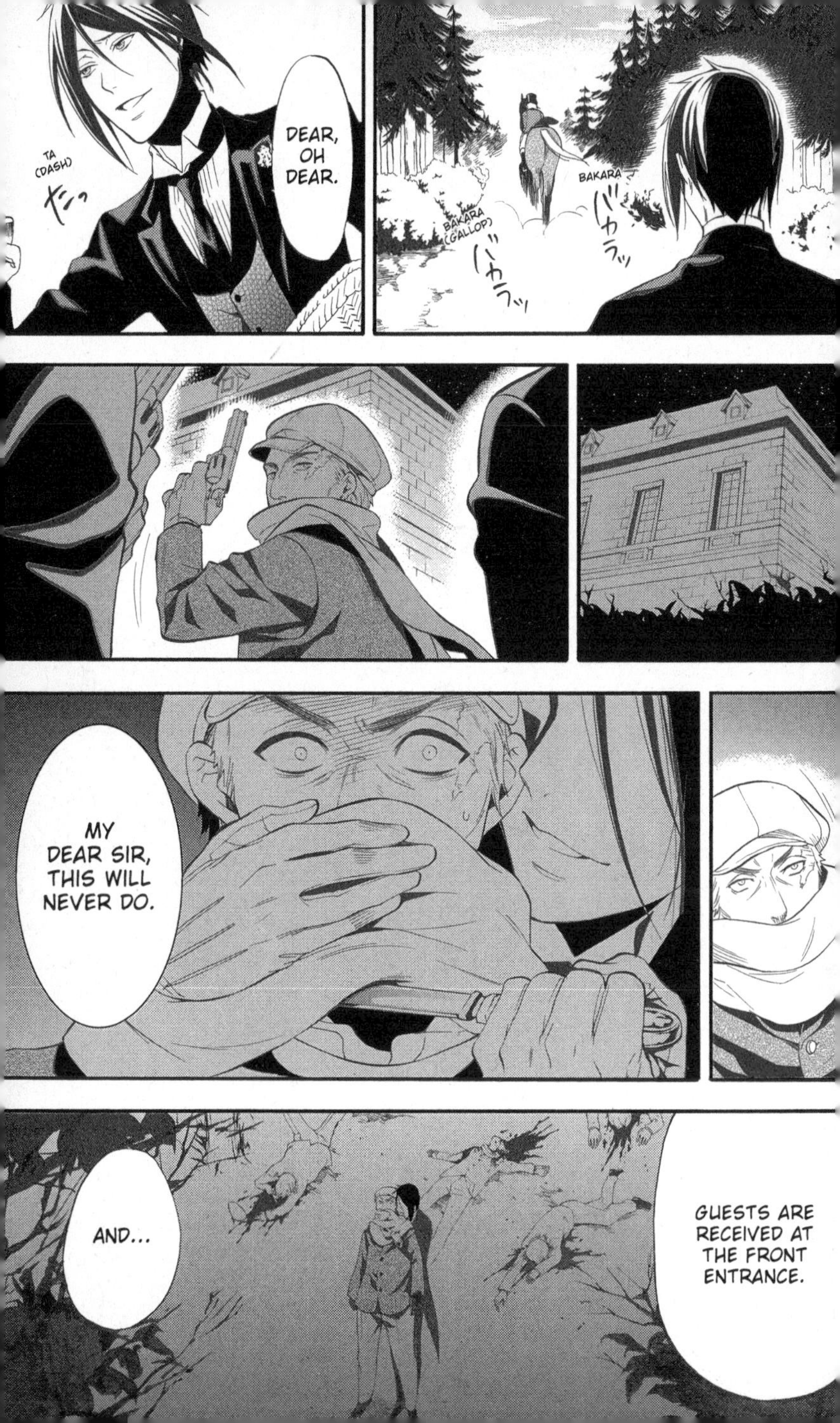
BAKARA
バカラッ
BAKARA (GALLOP)
バカラッ
DEAR, OH DEAR.
TA (DASH)
タッ
MY DEAR SIR, THIS WILL NEVER DO.
GUESTS ARE RECEIVED AT THE FRONT ENTRANCE.
AND...

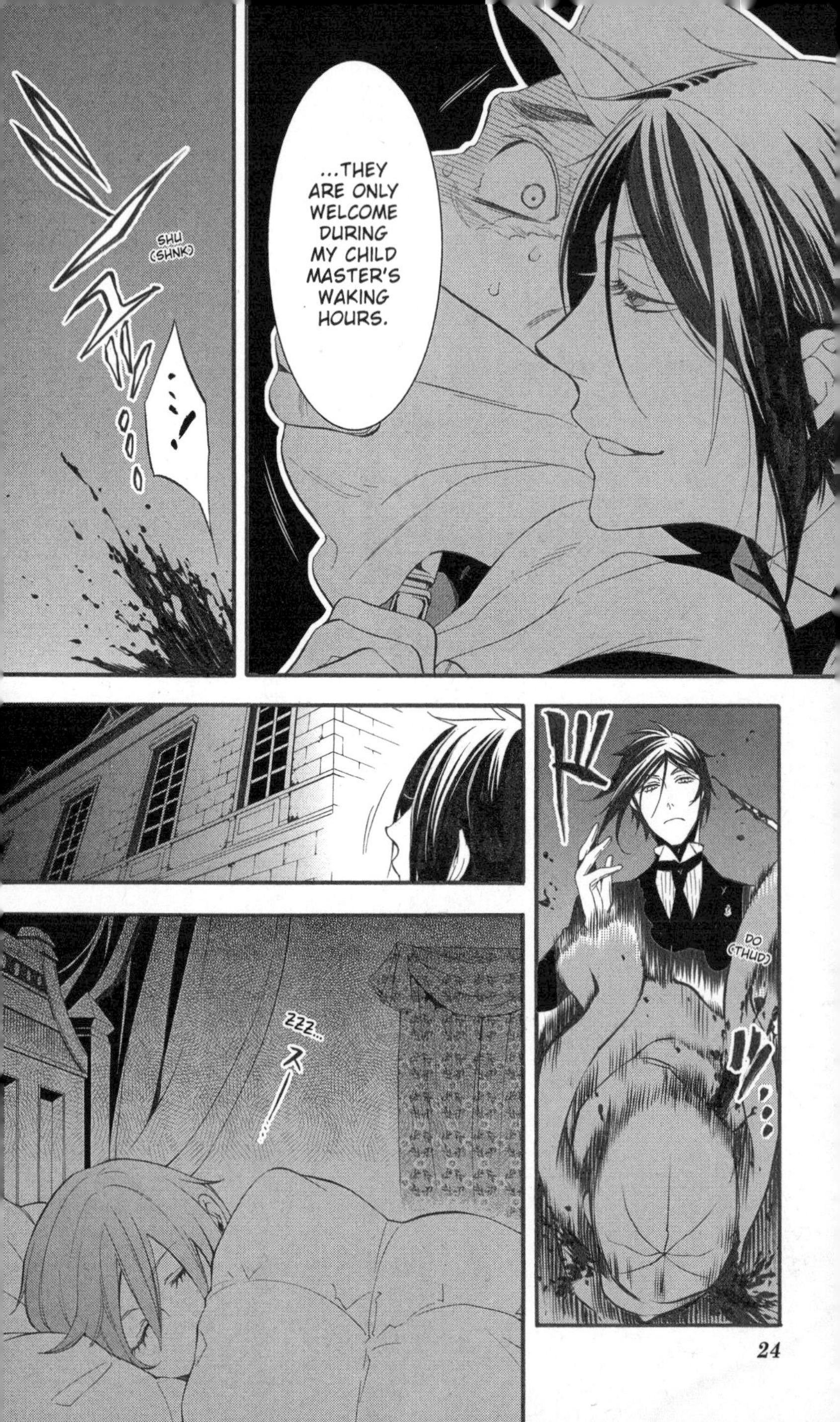
...THEY ARE ONLY WELCOME DURING MY CHILD MASTER'S WAKING HOURS.
SHU (SHNK)
...!
DO (THUD)
ZZZ...

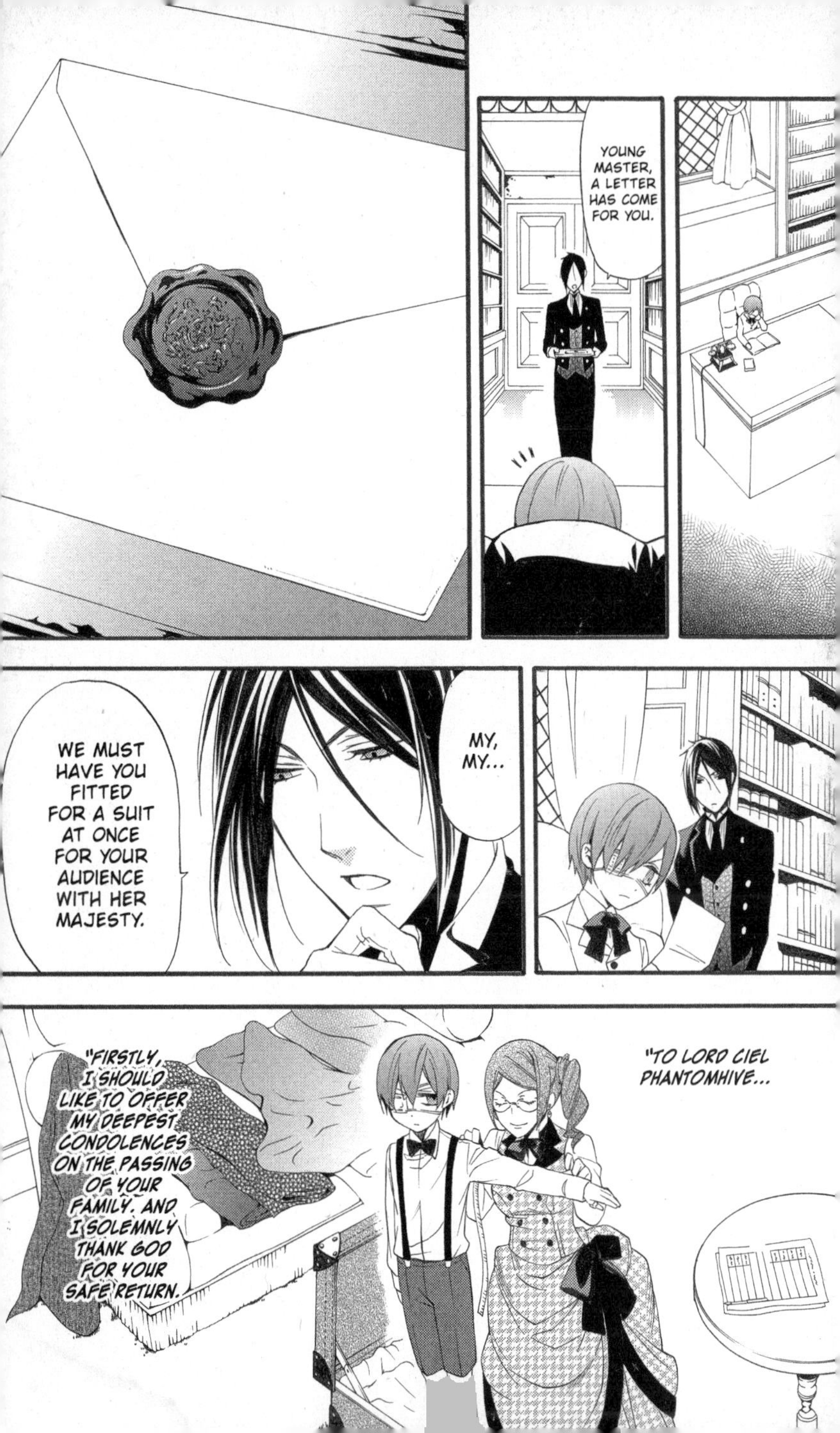
YOUNG MASTER, A LETTER HAS COME FOR YOU.
MY, MY...
WE MUST HAVE YOU FITTED FOR A SUIT AT ONCE FOR YOUR AUDIENCE WITH HER MAJESTY.
"TO LORD CIEL PHANTOMHIVE...
"FIRSTLY, I SHOULD LIKE TO OFFER MY DEEPEST CONDOLENCES ON THE PASSING OF YOUR FAMILY. AND I SOLEMNLY THANK GOD FOR YOUR SAFE RETURN.

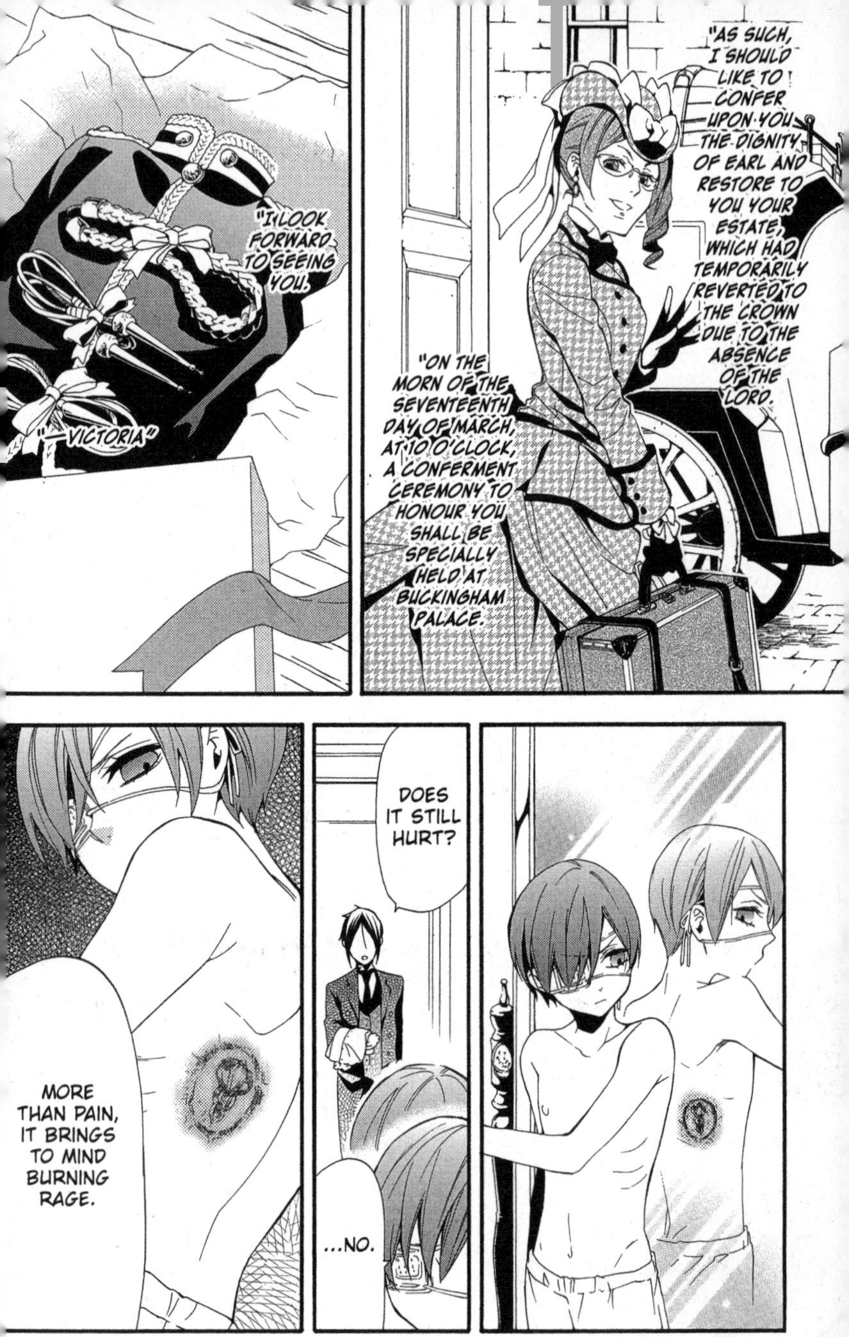
"AS SUCH, I SHOULD LIKE TO CONFER UPON YOU THE DIGNITY OF EARL AND RESTORE TO YOU YOUR ESTATE, WHICH HAD TEMPORARILY REVERTED TO THE CROWN DUE TO THE ABSENCE OF THE LORD.
"ON THE MORN OF THE SEVENTEENTH DAY OF MARCH, AT 10 O'CLOCK, A CONFERMENT CEREMONY TO HONOUR YOU SHALL BE SPECIALLY HELD AT BUCKINGHAM PALACE.
"I LOOK FORWARD TO SEEING YOU.
"—VICTORIA"
DOES IT STILL HURT?
...NO.
MORE THAN PAIN, IT BRINGS TO MIND BURNING RAGE.

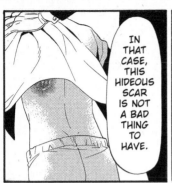

SO IT IS EVERLASTING FURY THAT HAS BEEN SEARED INTO YOU... IS THAT IT?
FU-FU.
IN THAT CASE, THIS HIDEOUS SCAR IS NOT A BAD THING TO HAVE.

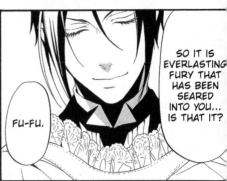

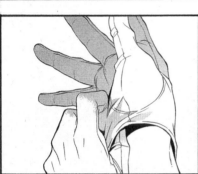

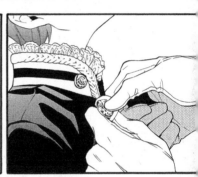

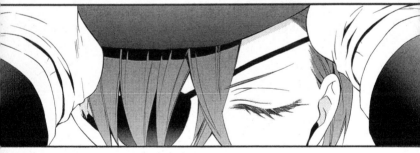

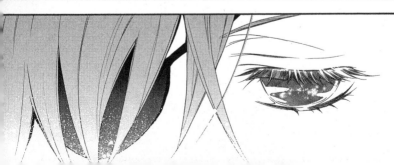

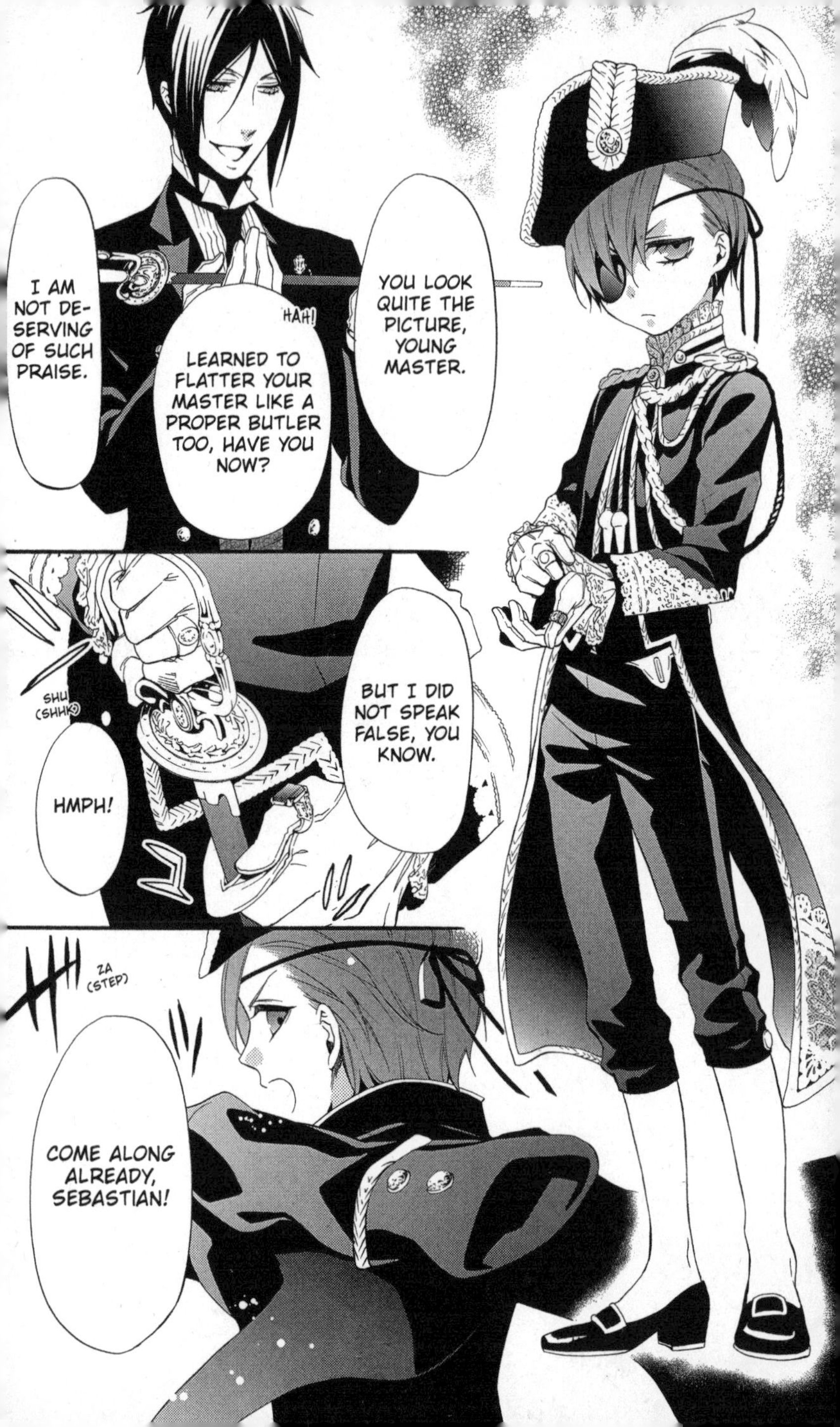
YOU LOOK QUITE THE PICTURE, YOUNG MASTER.
HAH!
LEARNED TO FLATTER YOUR MASTER LIKE A PROPER BUTLER TOO, HAVE YOU NOW?
I AM NOT DE-SERVING OF SUCH PRAISE.
BUT I DID NOT SPEAK FALSE, YOU KNOW.
SHU (SHHK)
HMPH!
ZA (STEP)
COME ALONG ALREADY, SEBASTIAN!

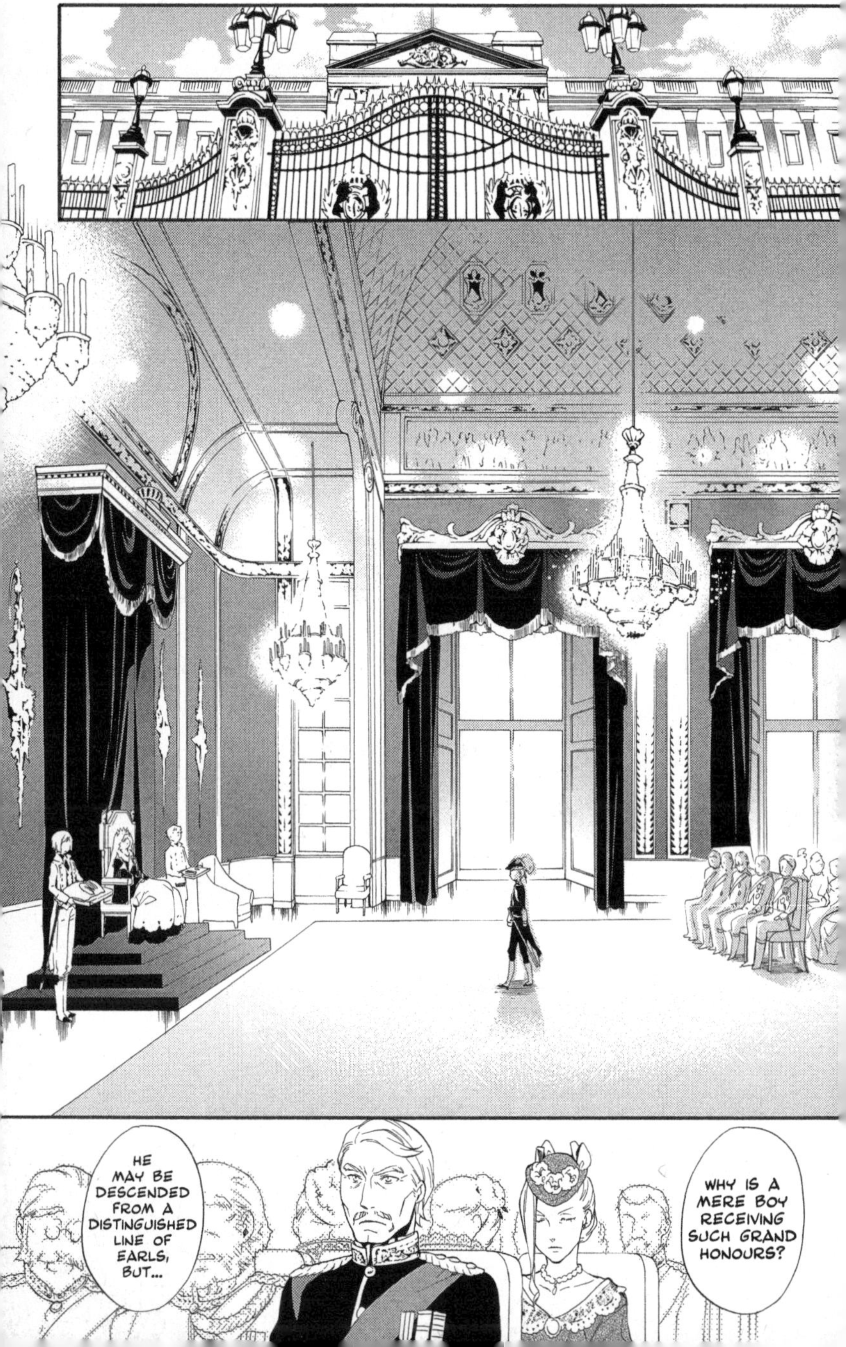
WHY IS A MERE BOY RECEIVING SUCH GRAND HONOURS?
HE MAY BE DESCENDED FROM A DISTINGUISHED LINE OF EARLS, BUT...

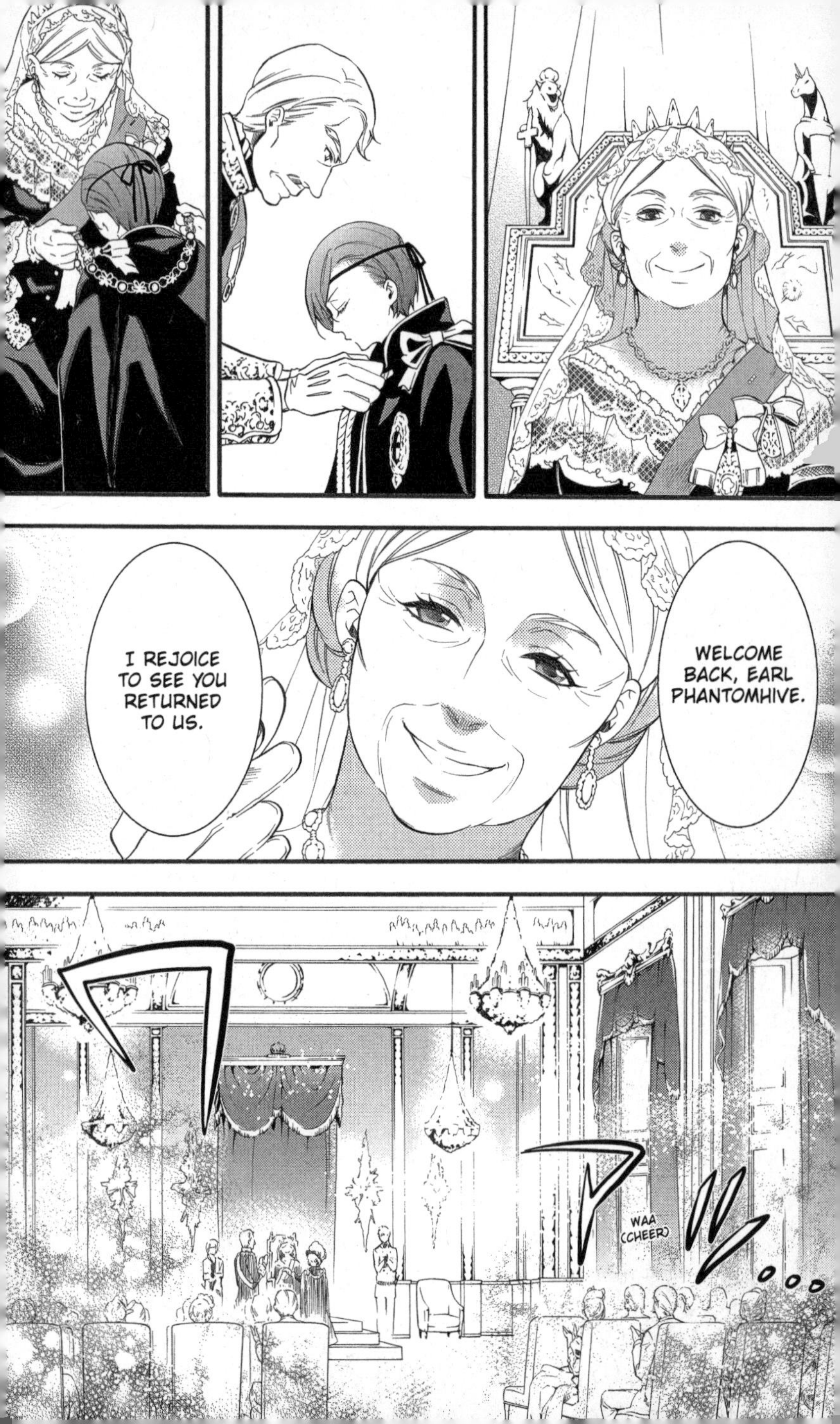
WELCOME BACK, EARL PHANTOMHIVE.
I REJOICE TO SEE YOU RETURNED TO US.
WAA (CHEER)

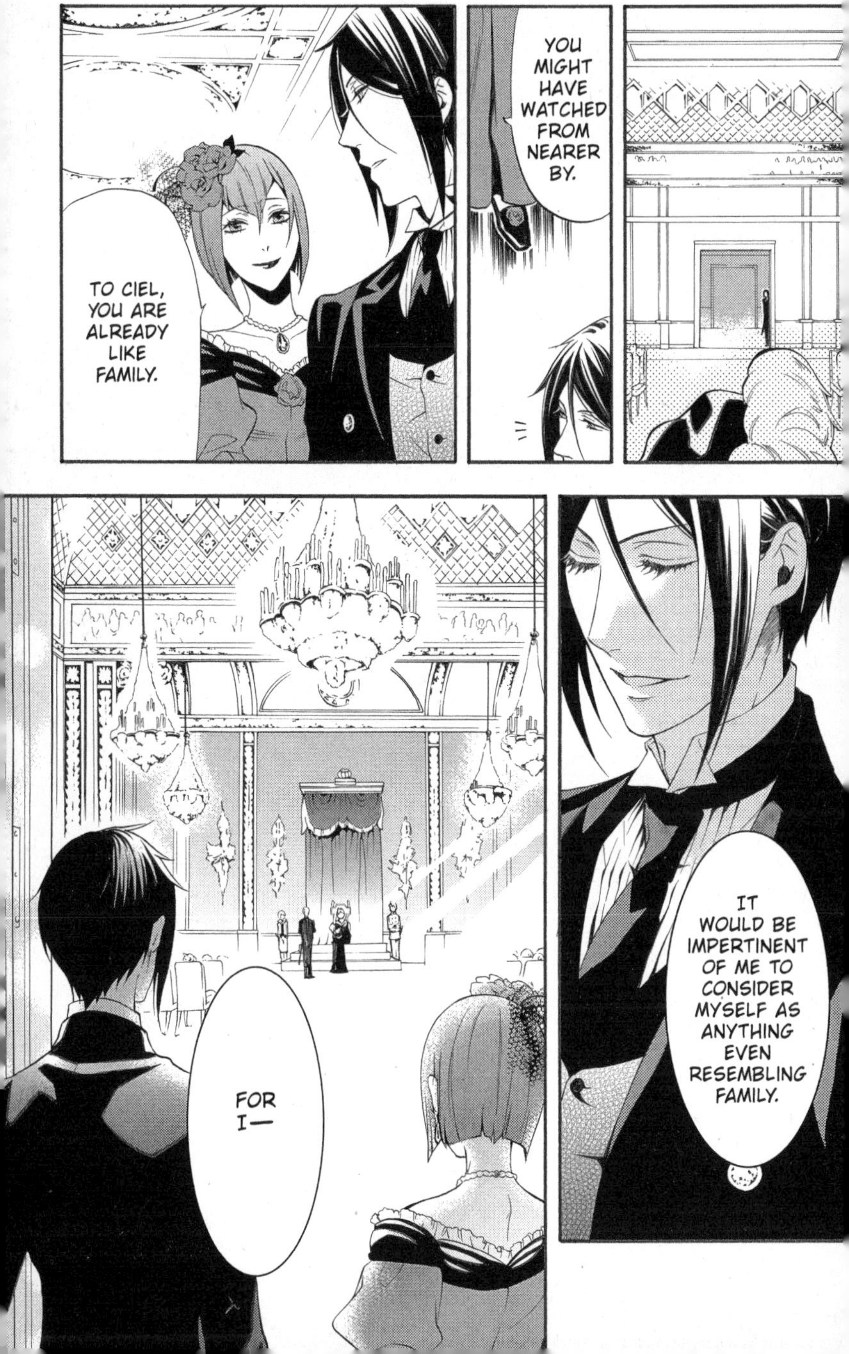
YOU MIGHT HAVE WATCHED FROM NEARER BY.
TO CIEL, YOU ARE ALREADY LIKE FAMILY.
IT WOULD BE IMPERTINENT OF ME TO CONSIDER MYSELF AS ANYTHING EVEN RESEMBLING FAMILY.
FOR I—

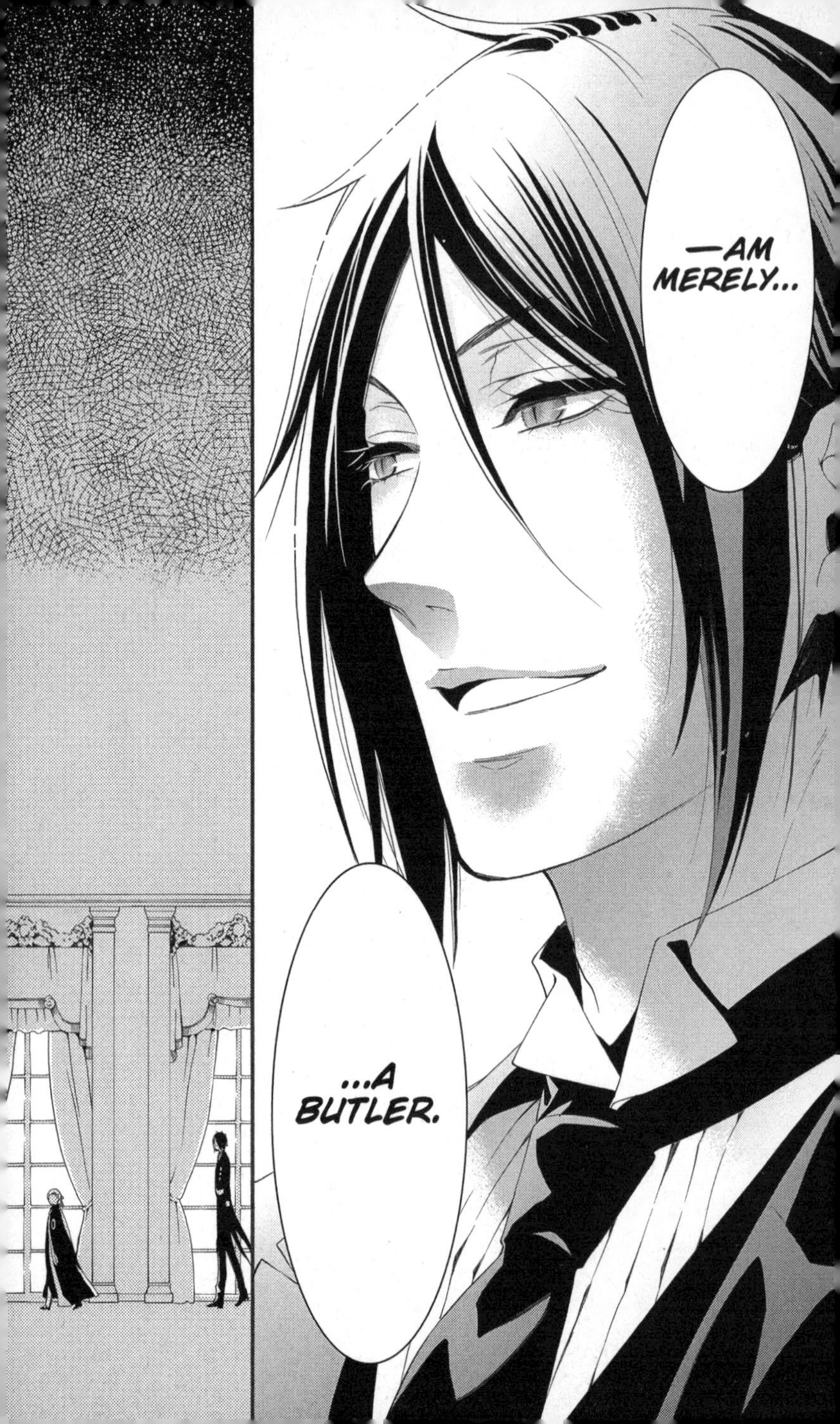
—AM MERELY...
...A BUTLER.

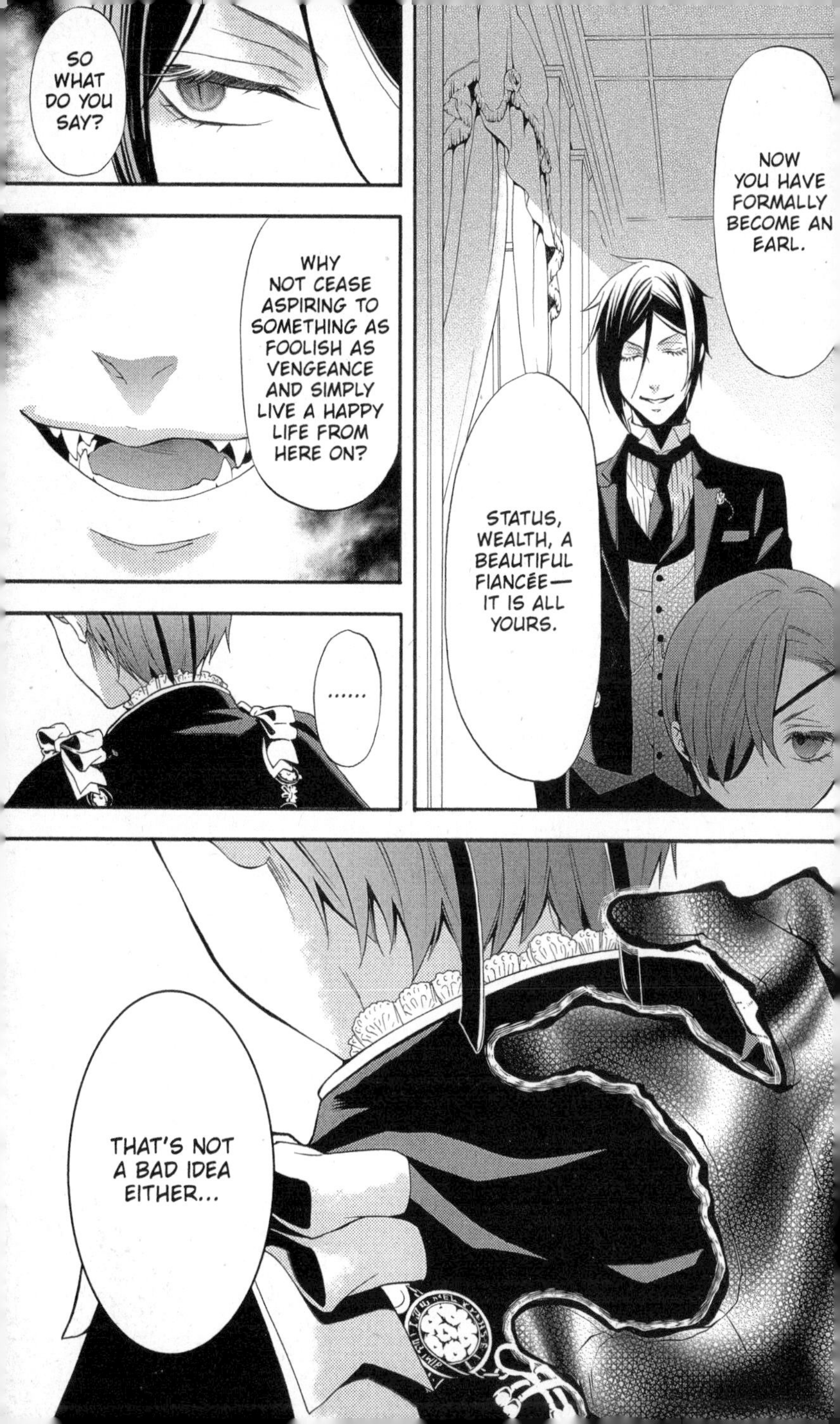
NOW YOU HAVE FORMALLY BECOME AN EARL.
STATUS, WEALTH, A BEAUTIFUL FIANCÉE—IT IS ALL YOURS.
SO WHAT DO YOU SAY?
WHY NOT CEASE ASPIRING TO SOMETHING AS FOOLISH AS VENGEANCE AND SIMPLY LIVE A HAPPY LIFE FROM HERE ON?
......
THAT'S NOT A BAD IDEA EITHER...

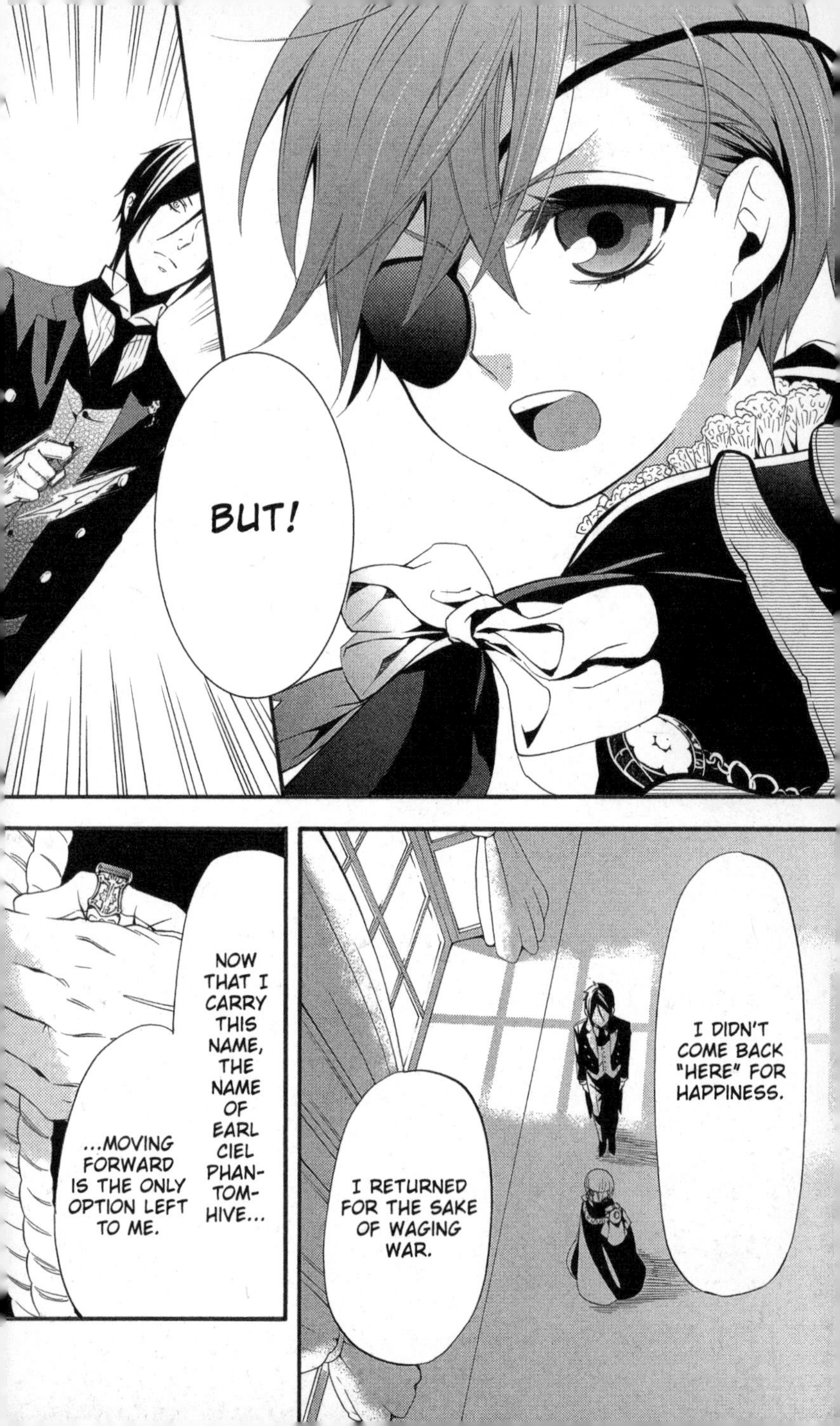
BUT!
I DIDN'T COME BACK "HERE" FOR HAPPINESS.
I RETURNED FOR THE SAKE OF WAGING WAR.
NOW THAT I CARRY THIS NAME, THE NAME OF EARL CIEL PHAN-TOM-HIVE...
...MOVING FORWARD IS THE ONLY OPTION LEFT TO ME.

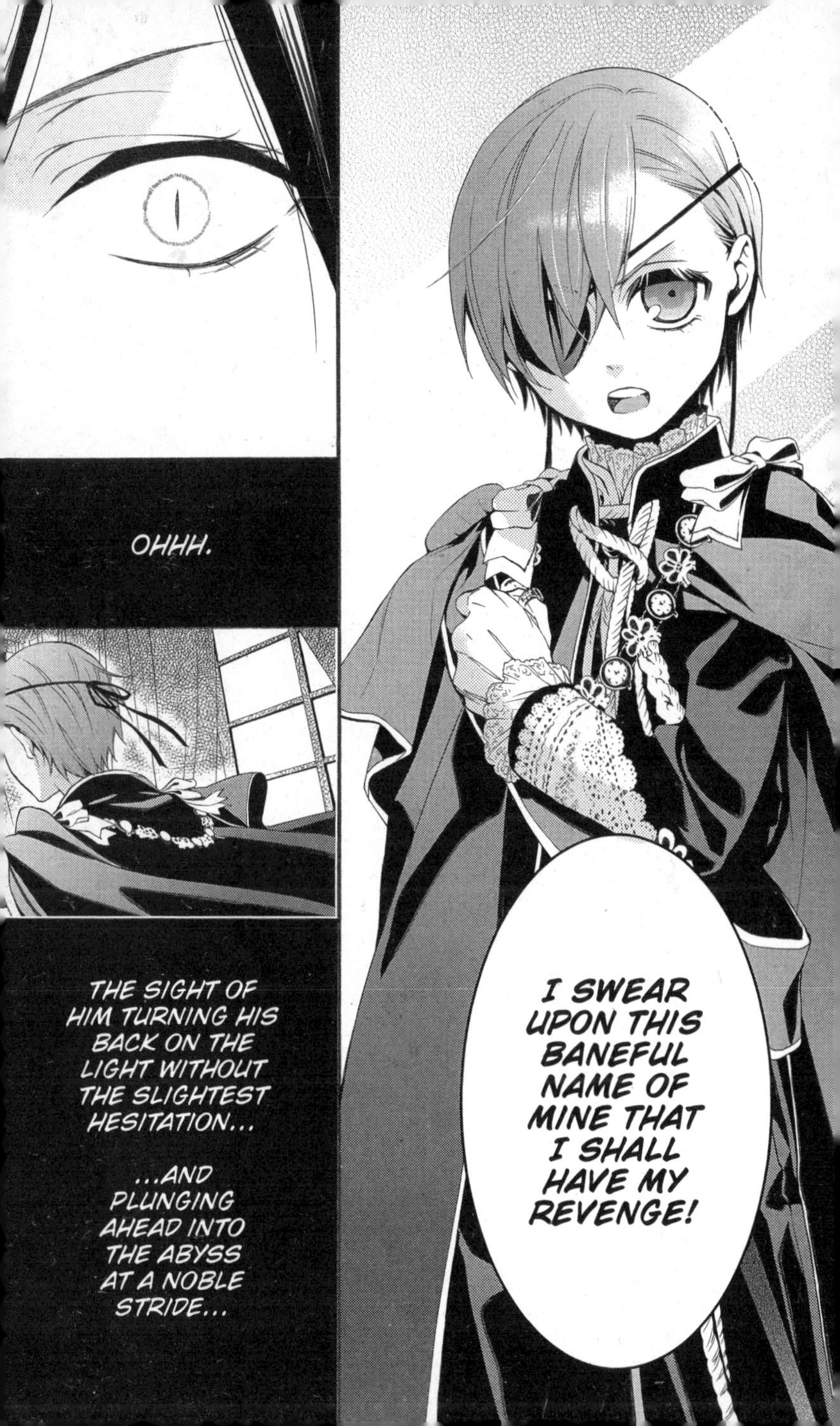
I SWEAR UPON THIS BANEFUL NAME OF MINE THAT I SHALL HAVE MY REVENGE!
OHHH.
THE SIGHT OF HIM TURNING HIS BACK ON THE LIGHT WITHOUT THE SLIGHTEST HESITATION...
...AND PLUNGING AHEAD INTO THE ABYSS AT A NOBLE STRIDE...

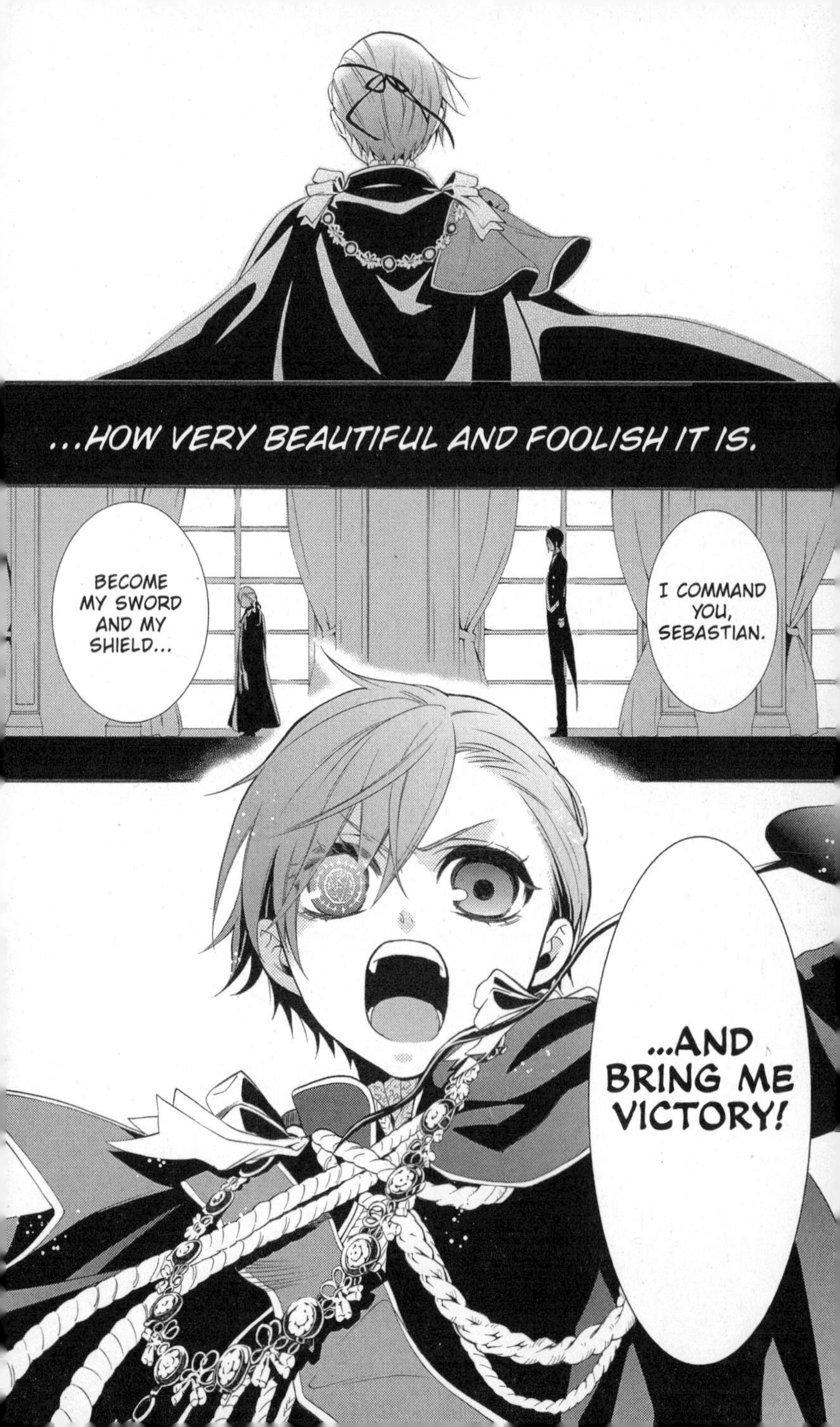
...HOW VERY BEAUTIFUL AND FOOLISH IT IS.
I COMMAND YOU, SEBASTIAN.
BECOME MY SWORD AND MY SHIELD...
...AND BRING ME VICTORY!

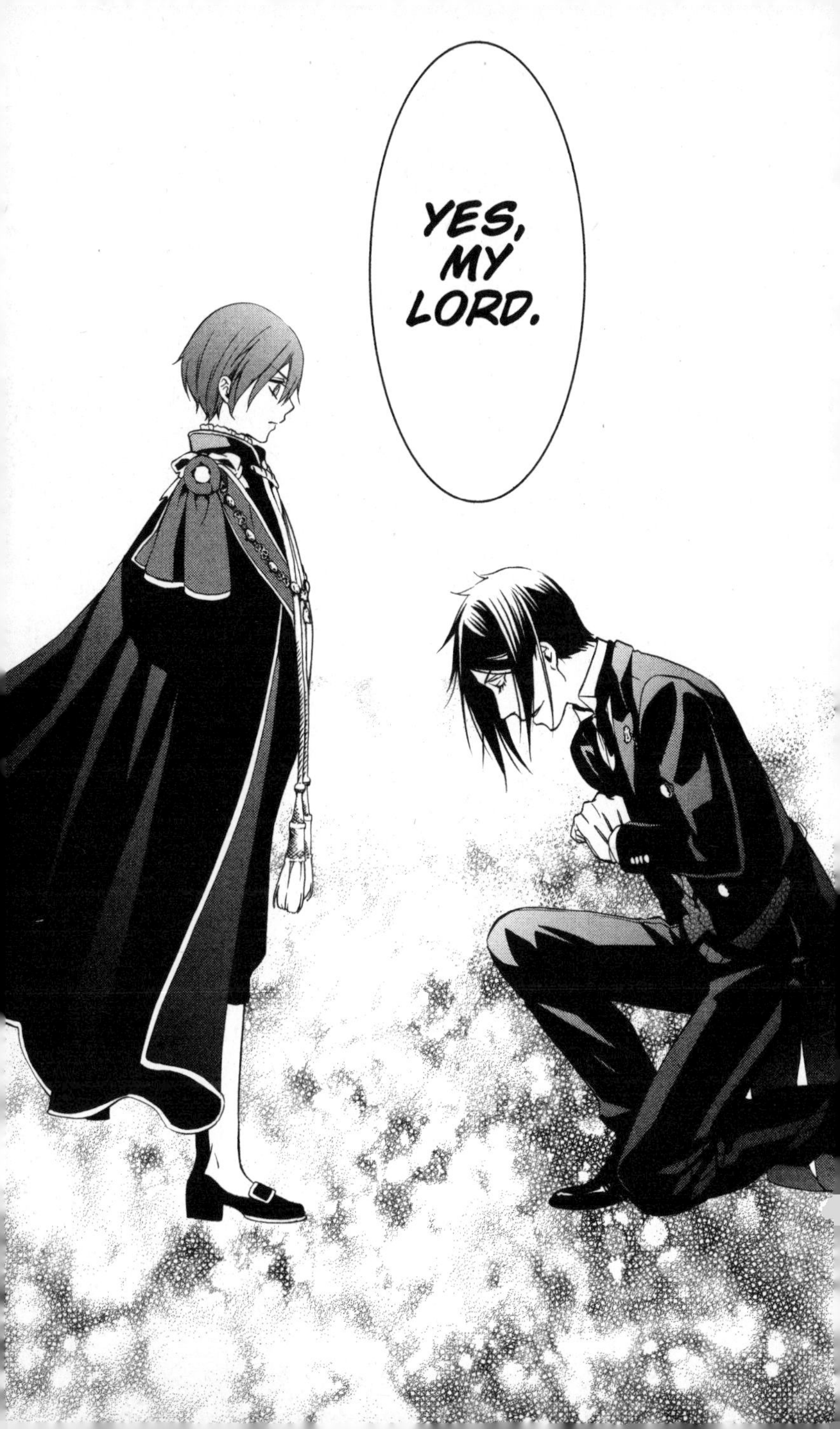
YES, MY LORD.

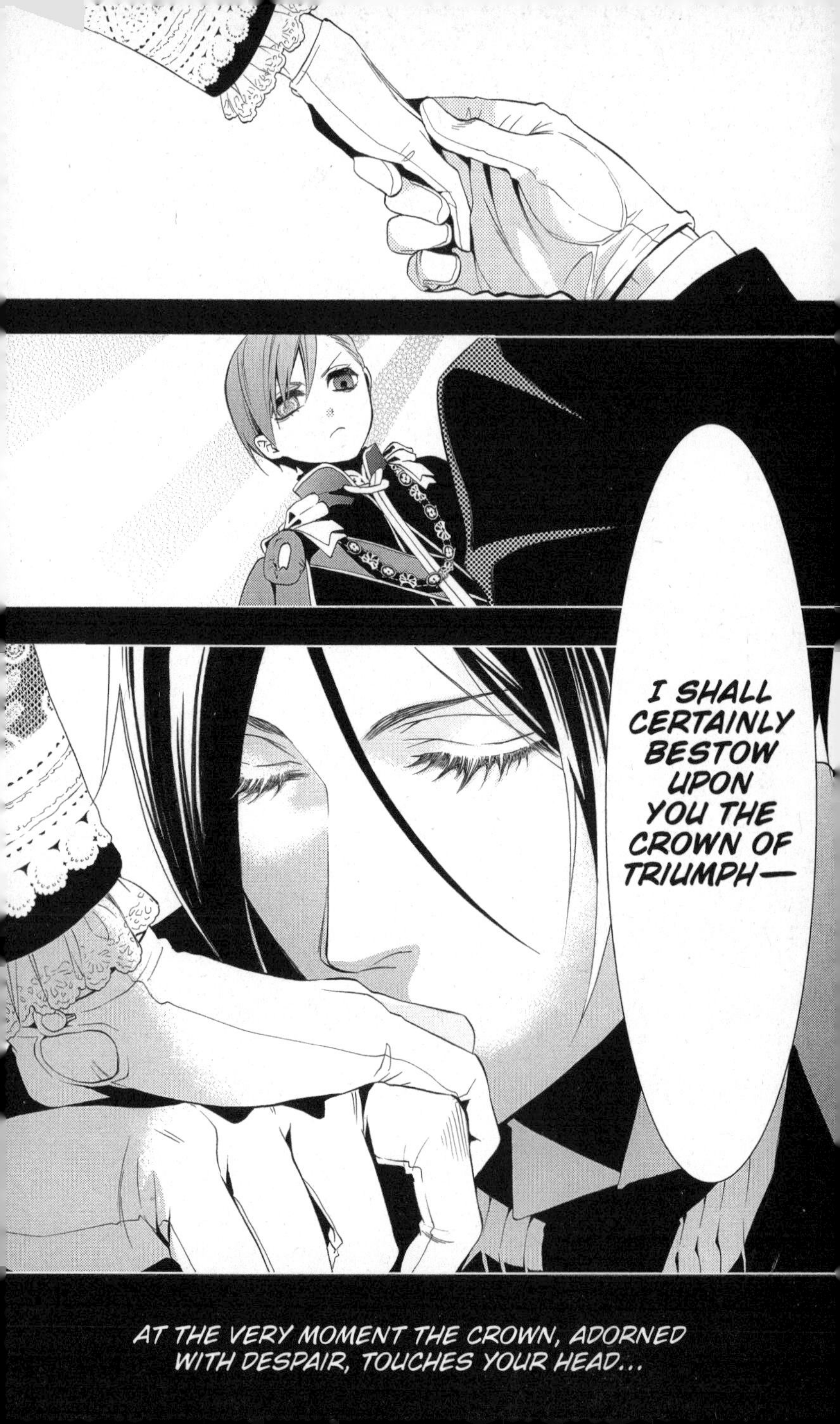

I SHALL CERTAINLY BESTOW UPON YOU THE CROWN OF TRIUMPH—
AT THE VERY MOMENT THE CROWN, ADORNED WITH DESPAIR, TOUCHES YOUR HEAD...

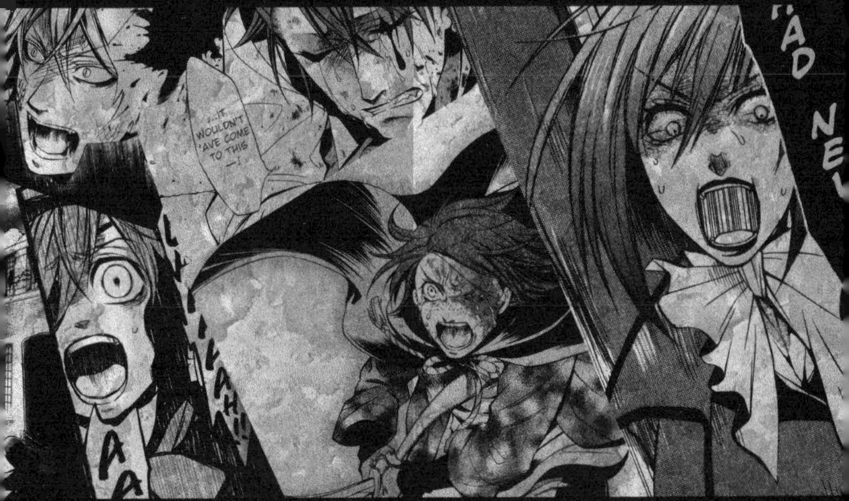
'AD NE
...IT WOULDN'T 'AVE COME TO THIS —!

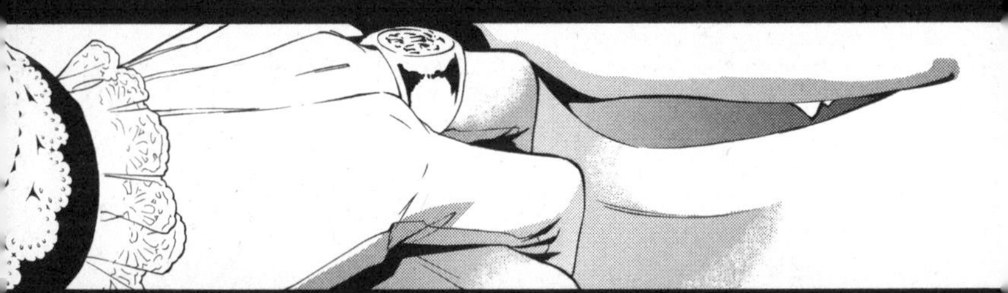

...AT ITS MOST MOUTHWATERINGLY DELECTABLE.

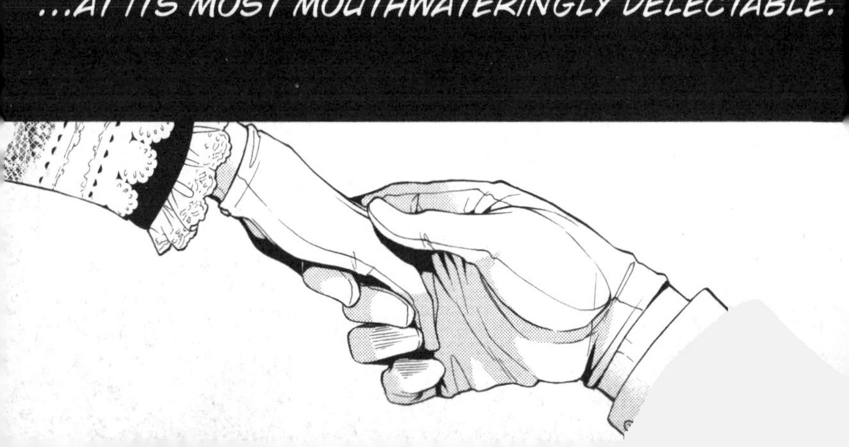

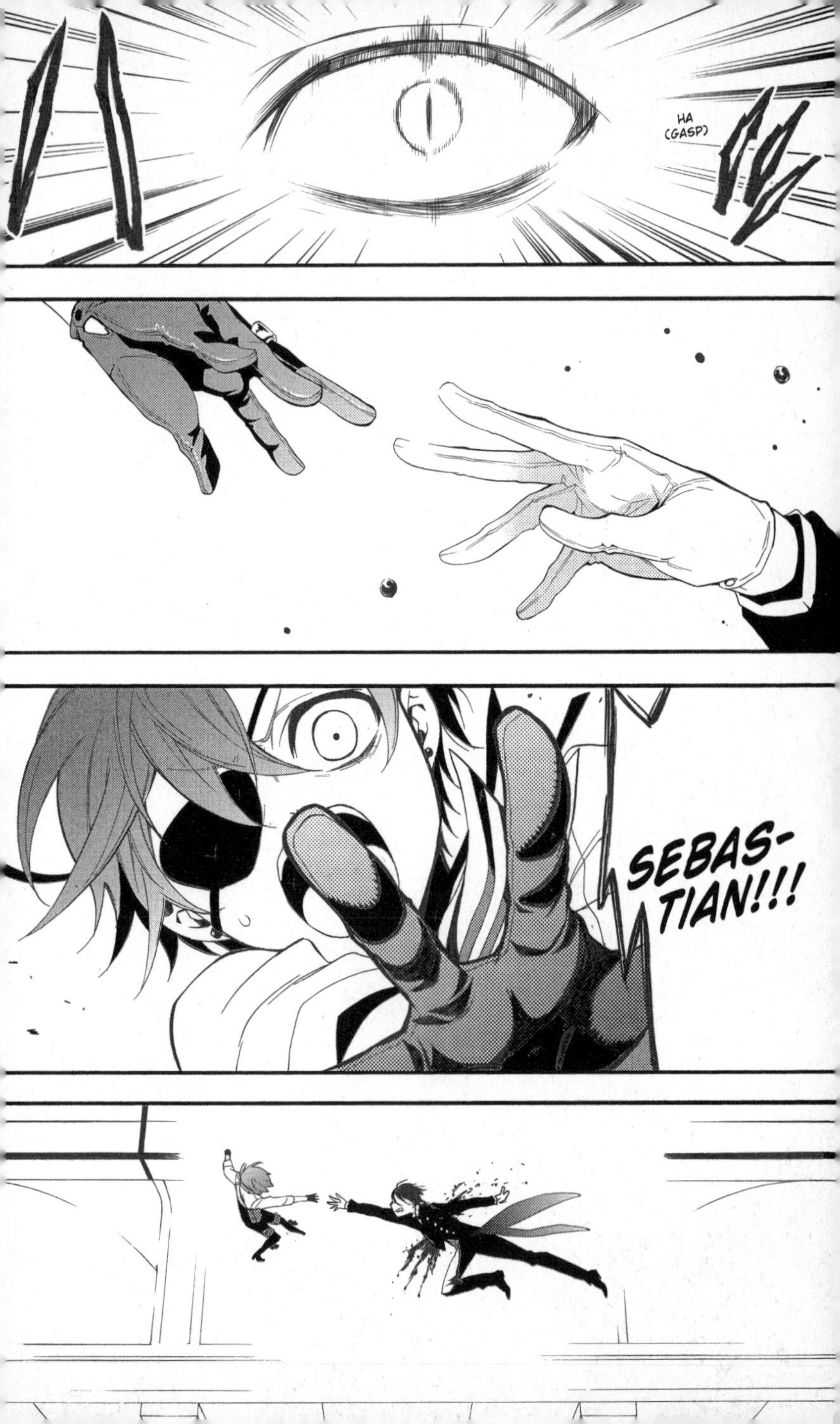
HA
(GASP)
SEBAS-
TIAN!!!

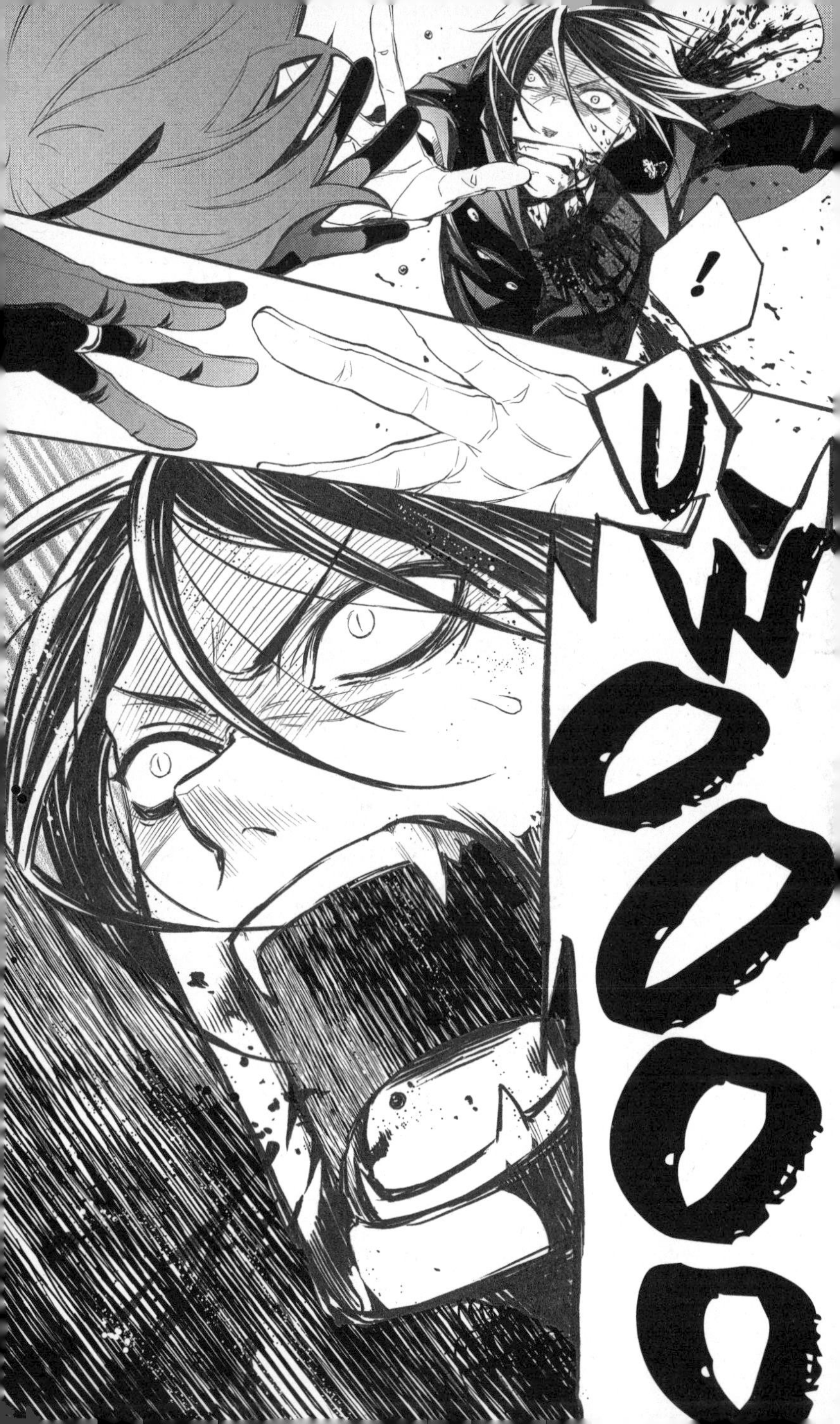
!
UWOOOOO

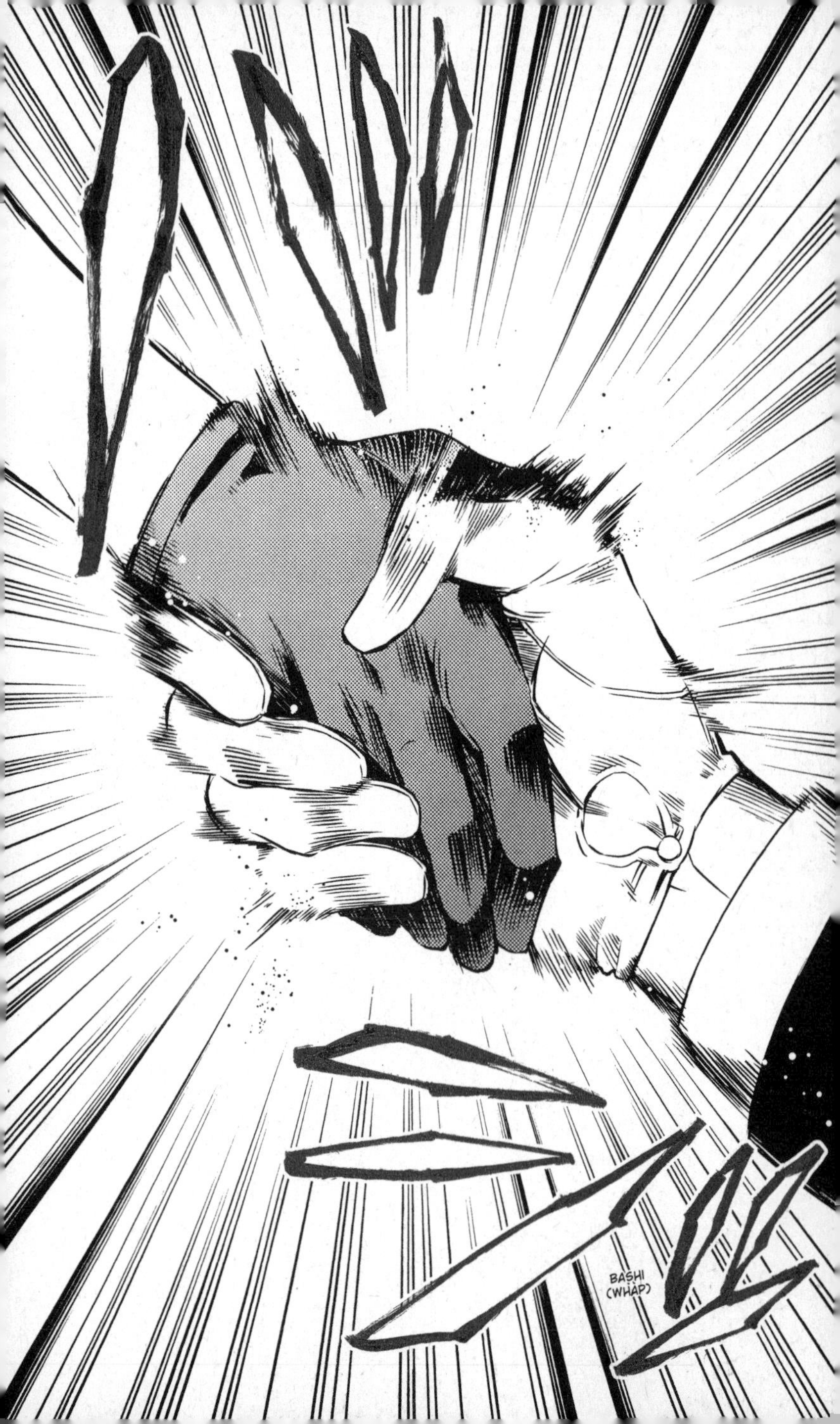
BASHI
(WHAP)

Black Butler

Chapter 64

At noon : The Butler, Gravely Wounded

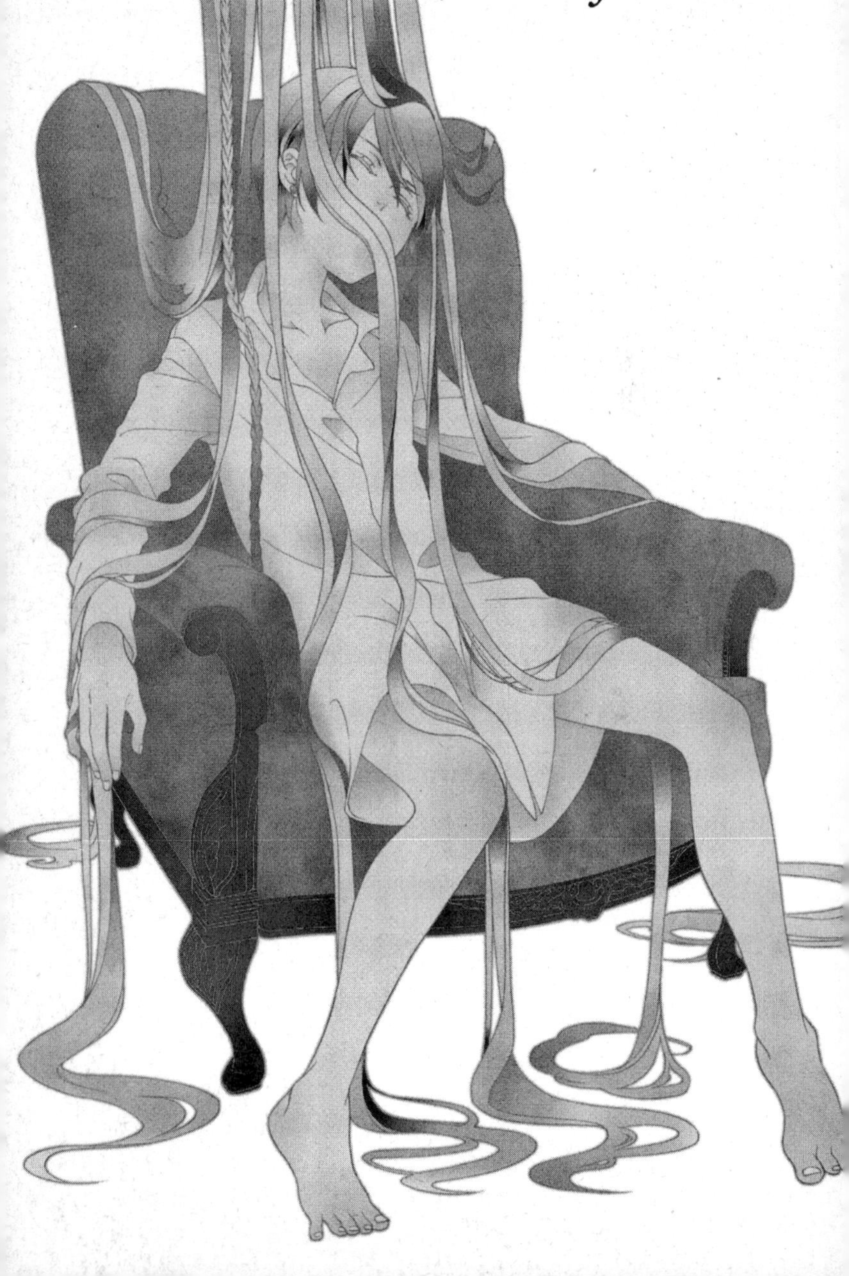

Black Butler

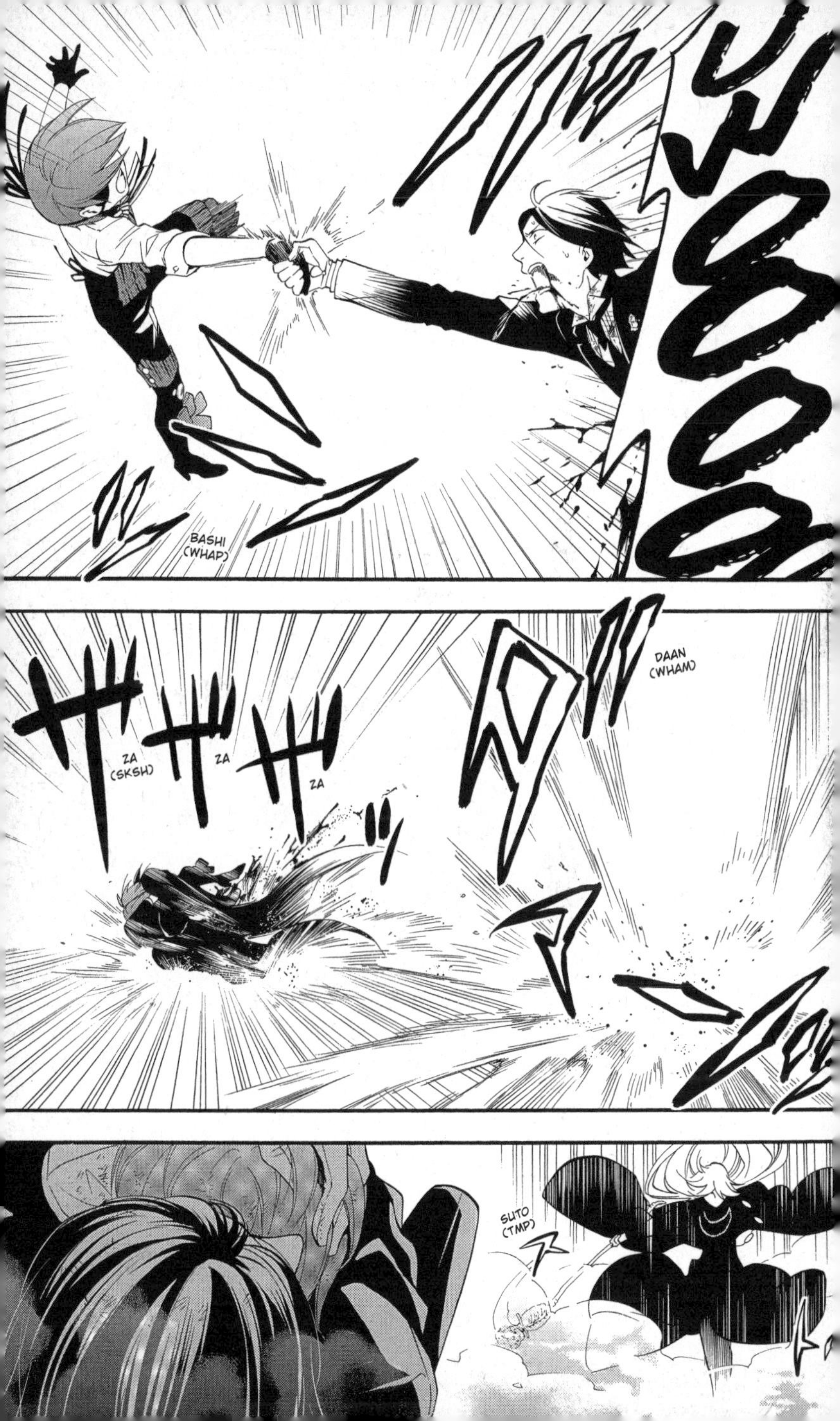
BASHI (WHAP)
DAAN (WHAM)
ZA (SKSH)
ZA
ZA
SUTO (TMP)

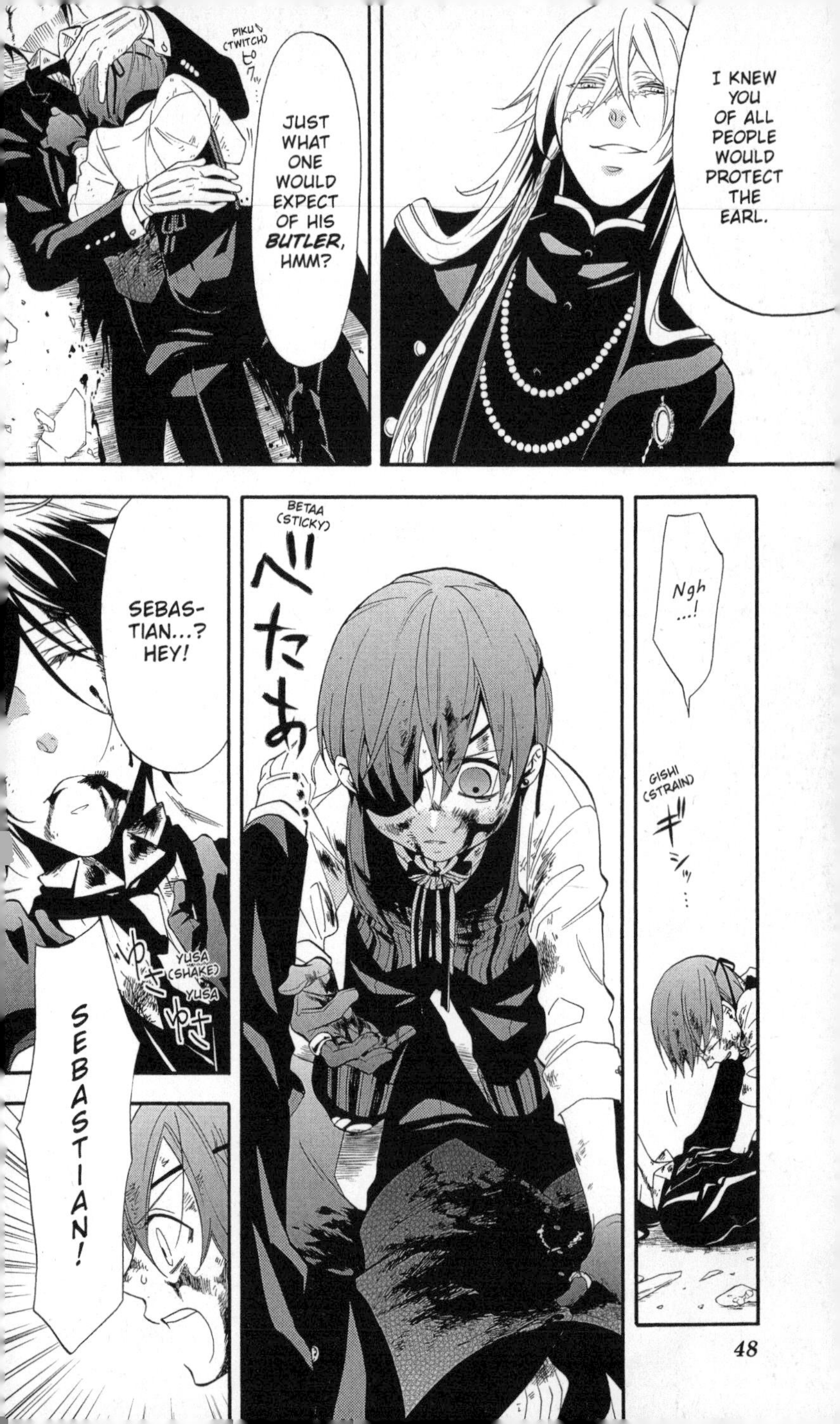
I KNEW YOU OF ALL PEOPLE WOULD PROTECT THE EARL.
PIKU (TWITCH)
ピク
JUST WHAT ONE WOULD EXPECT OF HIS *BUTLER*, HMM?
Ngh ...!
GISHI (STRAIN)
ギシッ
BETAA (STICKY)
べたあ
SEBAS-TIAN...? HEY!
YUSA (SHAKE) YUSA
ゆさゆさ
SEBASTIAN!

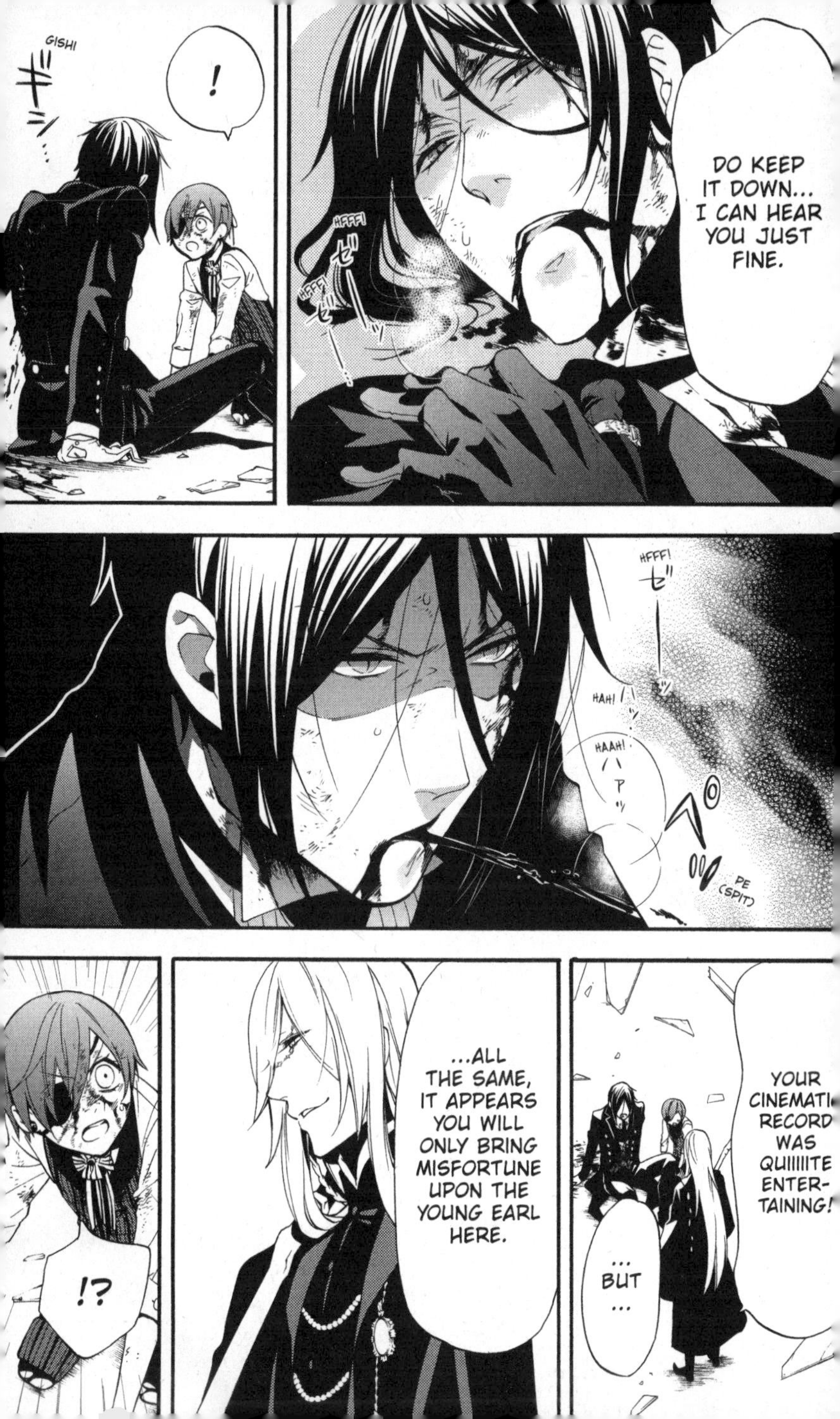
HFFF!
HFFF!
DO KEEP IT DOWN... I CAN HEAR YOU JUST FINE.
GISHI
!
HFFF!
HAH!
HAAH!
PE (SPIT)
YOUR CINEMATI RECORD WAS QUIIIIITE ENTER-TAINING!
... BUT ...
...ALL THE SAME, IT APPEARS YOU WILL ONLY BRING MISFORTUNE UPON THE YOUNG EARL HERE.
!?

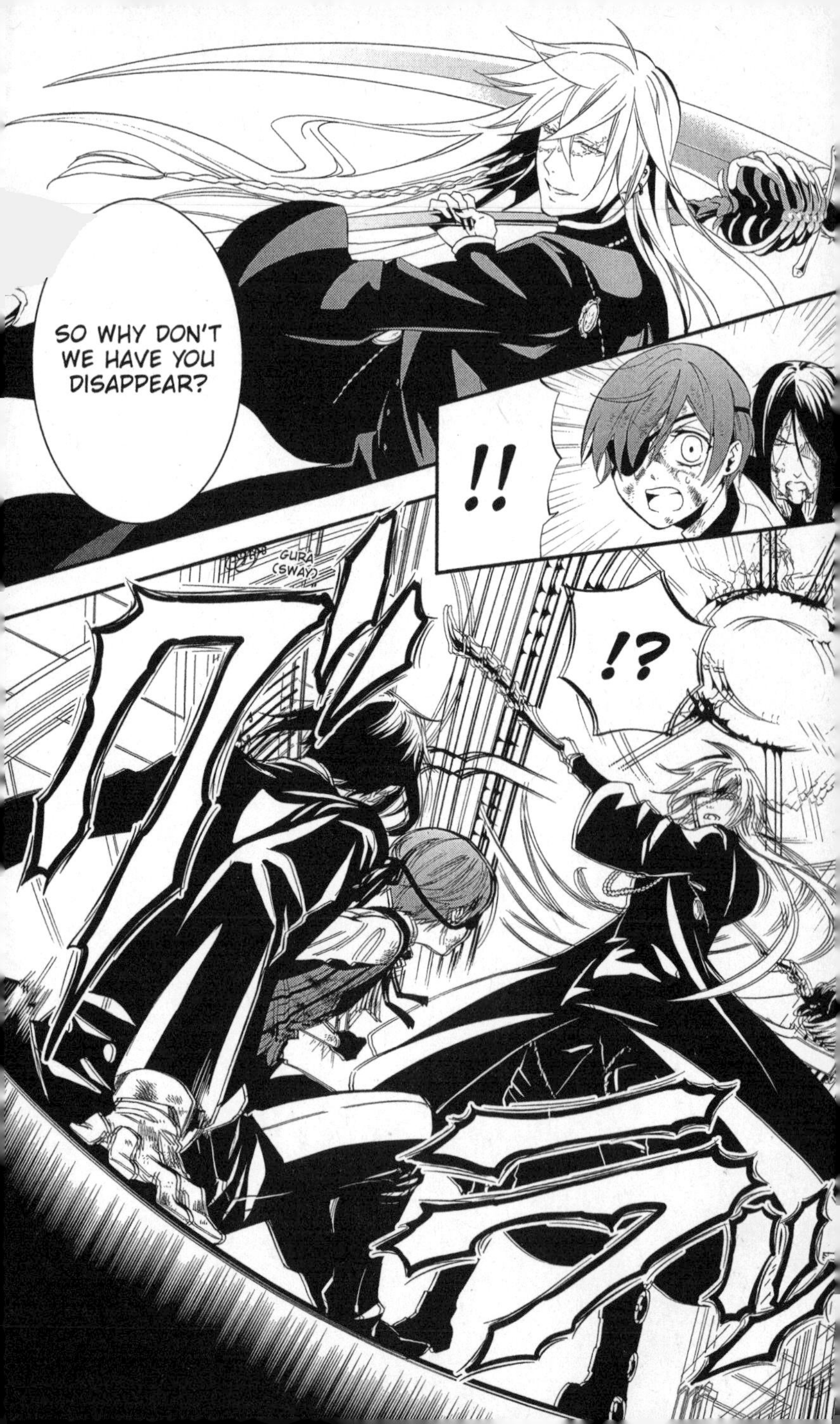
SO WHY DON'T WE HAVE YOU DISAPPEAR?
!!
GURA (SWAY)
!?

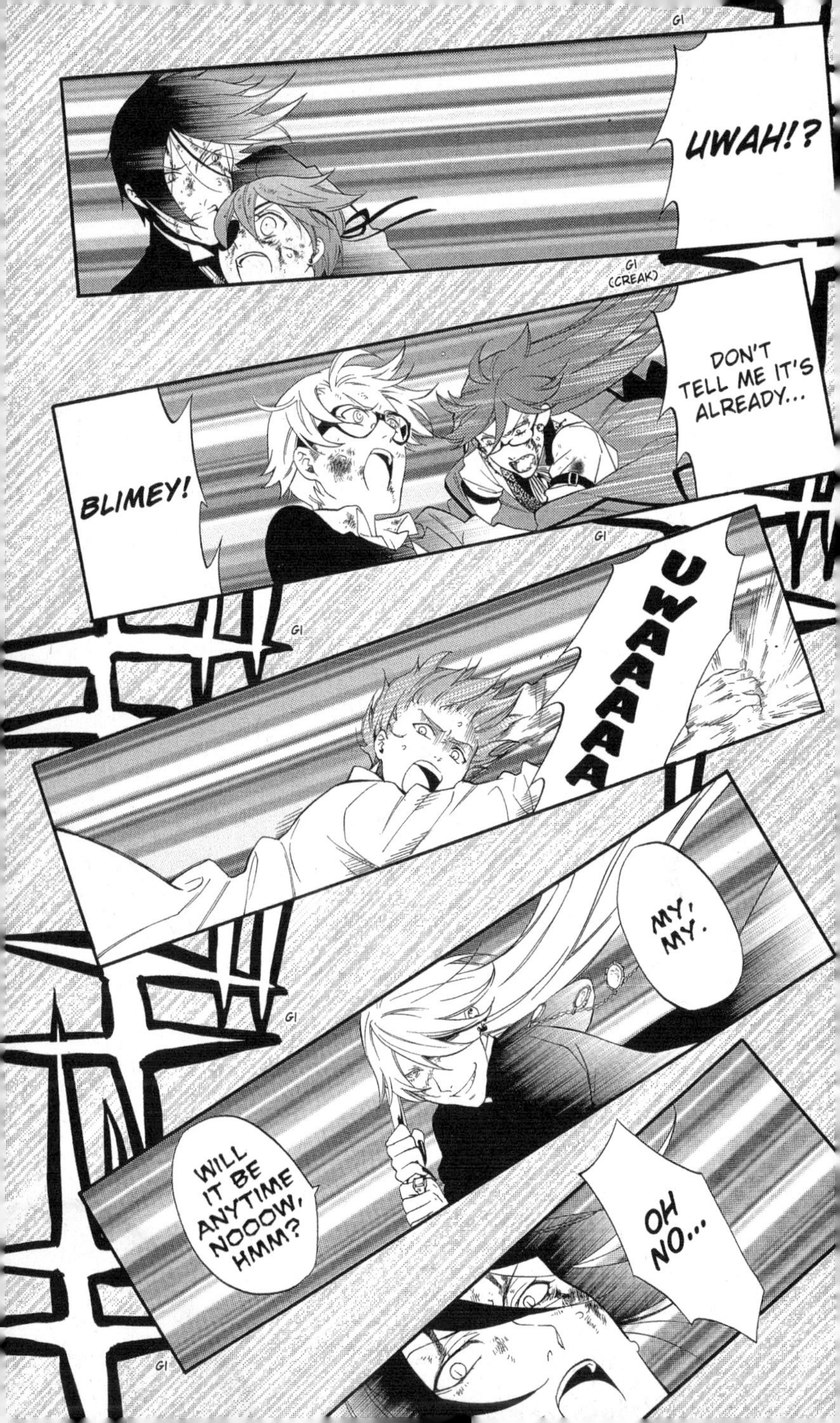
GI
UWAH!?
GI
(CREAK)
DON'T TELL ME IT'S ALREADY...
BLIMEY!
GI
UWAAAAA
GI
MY, MY.
GI
WILL IT BE ANYTIME NOOOW, HMM?
OH NO...
GI

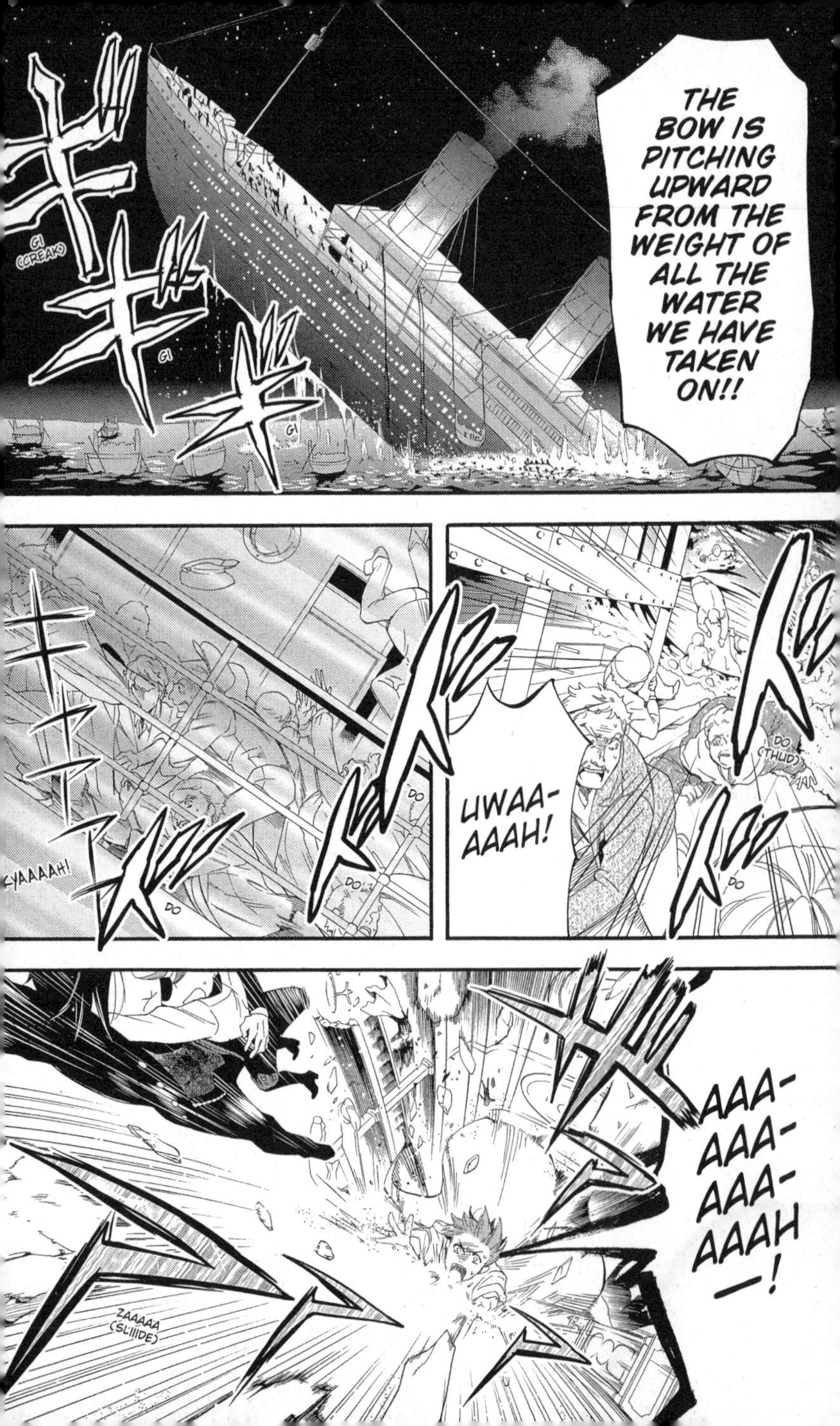
THE BOW IS PITCHING UPWARD FROM THE WEIGHT OF ALL THE WATER WE HAVE TAKEN ON!!
GI (CREAK)
GI
GI
DO (THUD)
UWAA-AAAH!
DO
DO
DO
DO
KYAAAAH!
AAA-AAA-AAA-AAAH—!
ZAAAAA (SL'IIIDE)

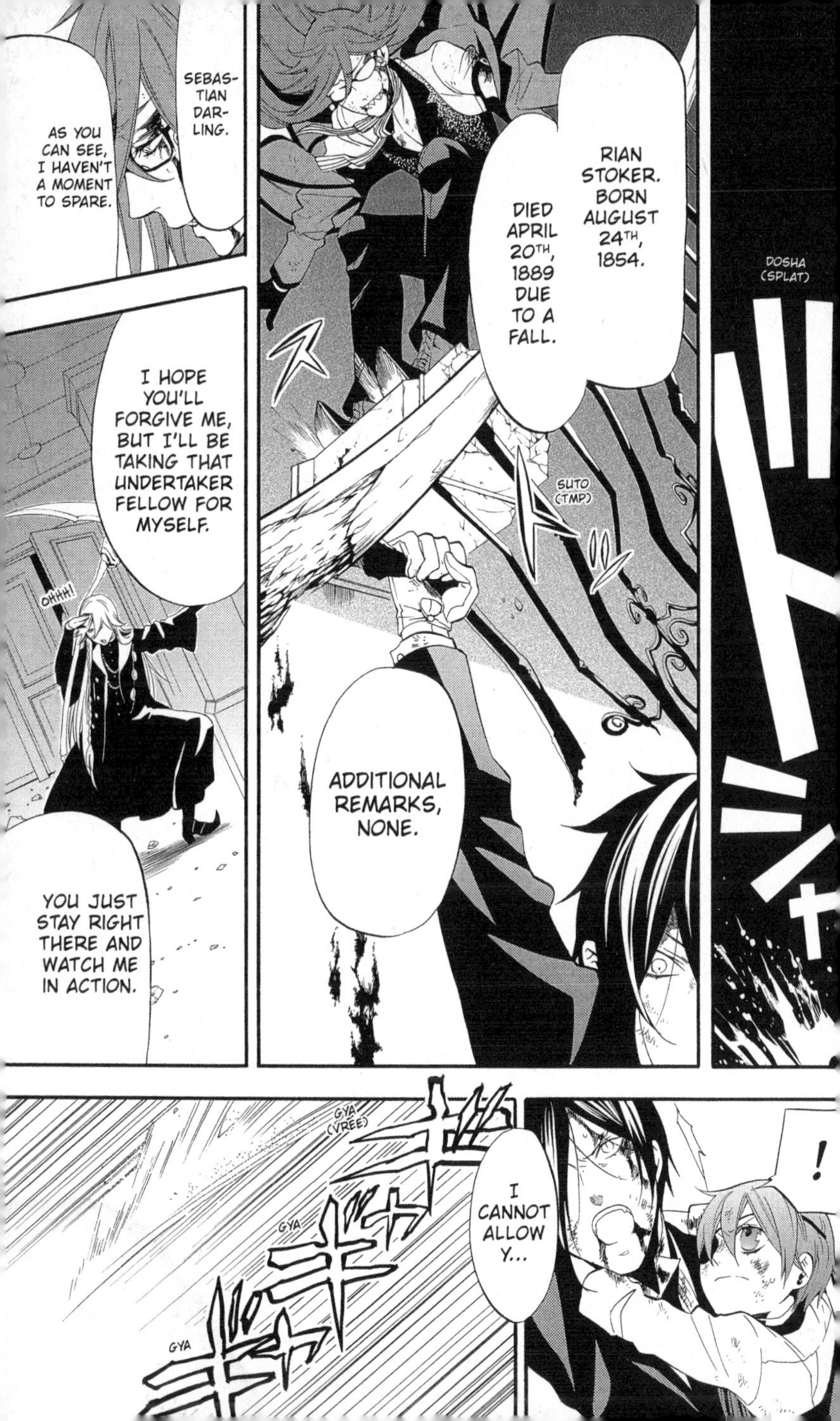
DOSHA (SPLAT)
RIAN STOKER. BORN AUGUST 24TH, 1854.
DIED APRIL 20TH, 1889 DUE TO A FALL.
SUTO (TMP)
ADDITIONAL REMARKS, NONE.
SEBASTIAN DARLING.
AS YOU CAN SEE, I HAVEN'T A MOMENT TO SPARE.
I HOPE YOU'LL FORGIVE ME, BUT I'LL BE TAKING THAT UNDERTAKER FELLOW FOR MYSELF.
OHHH!
YOU JUST STAY RIGHT THERE AND WATCH ME IN ACTION.
!
I CANNOT ALLOW Y...
GYA (VREE)
GYA
GYA

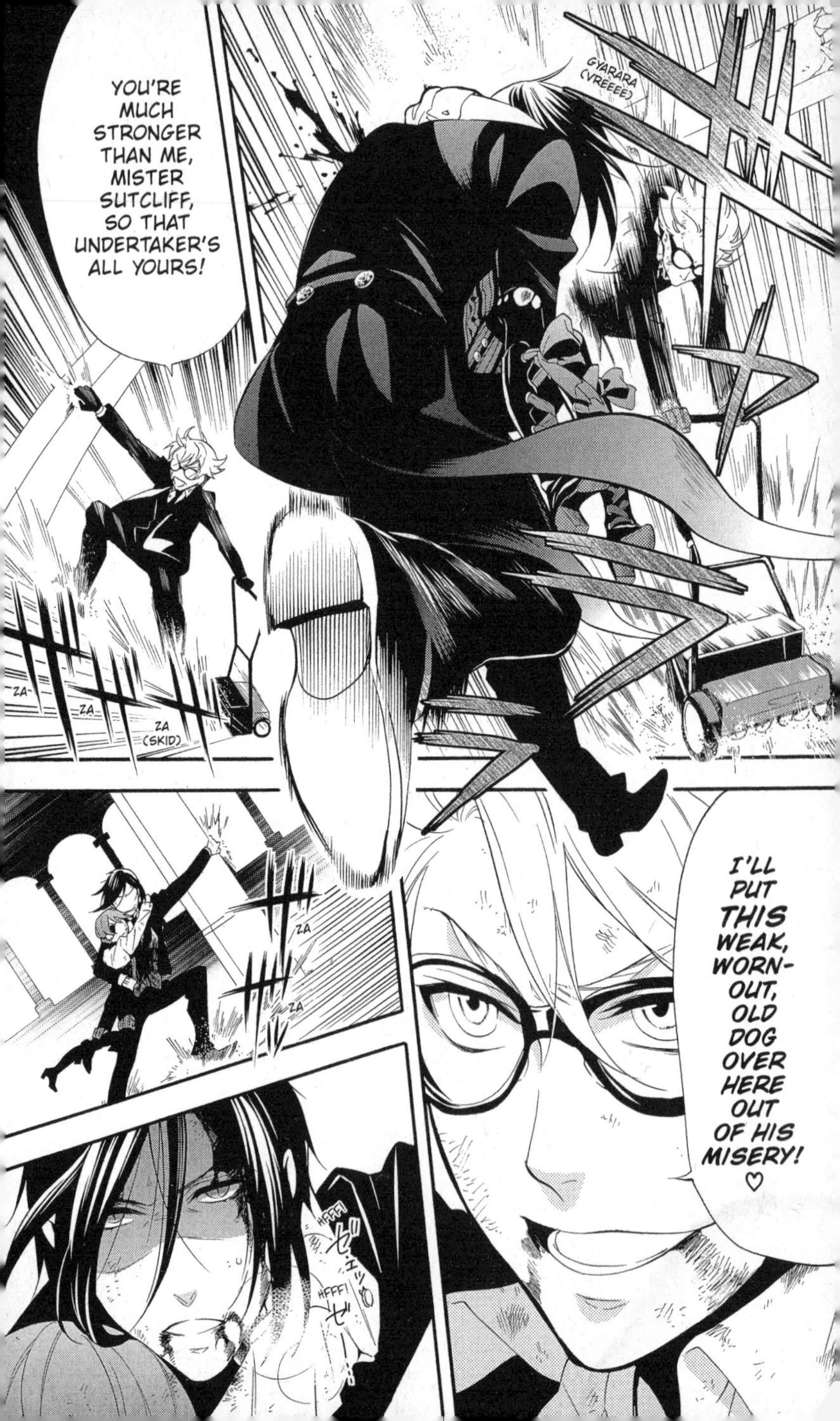
GYARARA (VREEEE)
YOU'RE MUCH STRONGER THAN ME, MISTER SUTCLIFF, SO THAT UNDERTAKER'S ALL YOURS!
ZA- ZA- ZA (SKID)
I'LL PUT THIS WEAK, WORN-OUT, OLD DOG OVER HERE OUT OF HIS MISERY! ♡
ZA
ZA
HFFF!
HFFF!

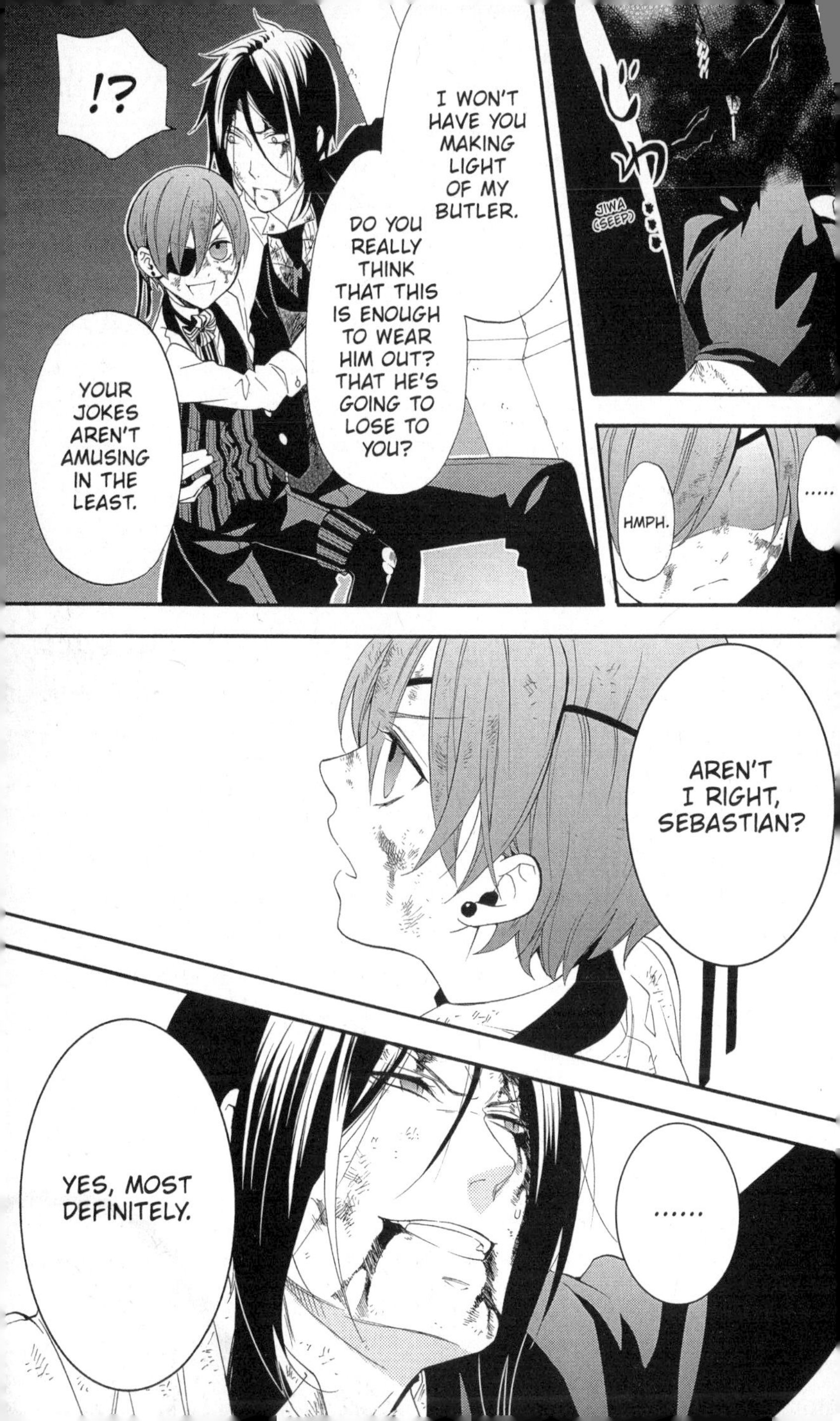
JIWA (SEEP)
......
HMPH.
I WON'T HAVE YOU MAKING LIGHT OF MY BUTLER.
!?
DO YOU REALLY THINK THAT THIS IS ENOUGH TO WEAR HIM OUT? THAT HE'S GOING TO LOSE TO YOU?
YOUR JOKES AREN'T AMUSING IN THE LEAST.
AREN'T I RIGHT, SEBASTIAN?
......
YES, MOST DEFINITELY.

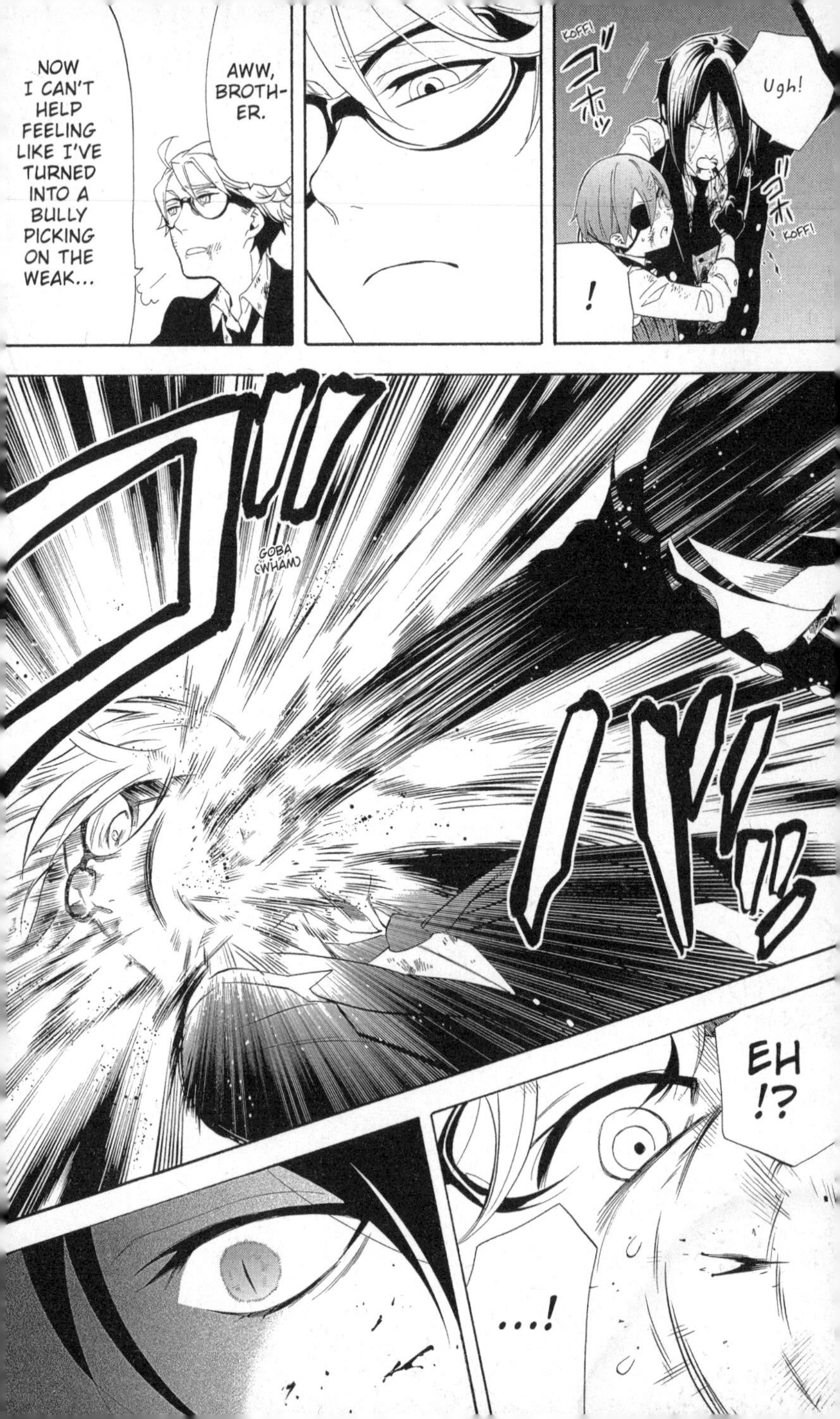

KOFF!
Ugh!
KOFF!
!
AWW, BROTHER-ER.
NOW I CAN'T HELP FEELING LIKE I'VE TURNED INTO A BULLY PICKING ON THE WEAK...
GOBA (WHAM)
EH !?
...!

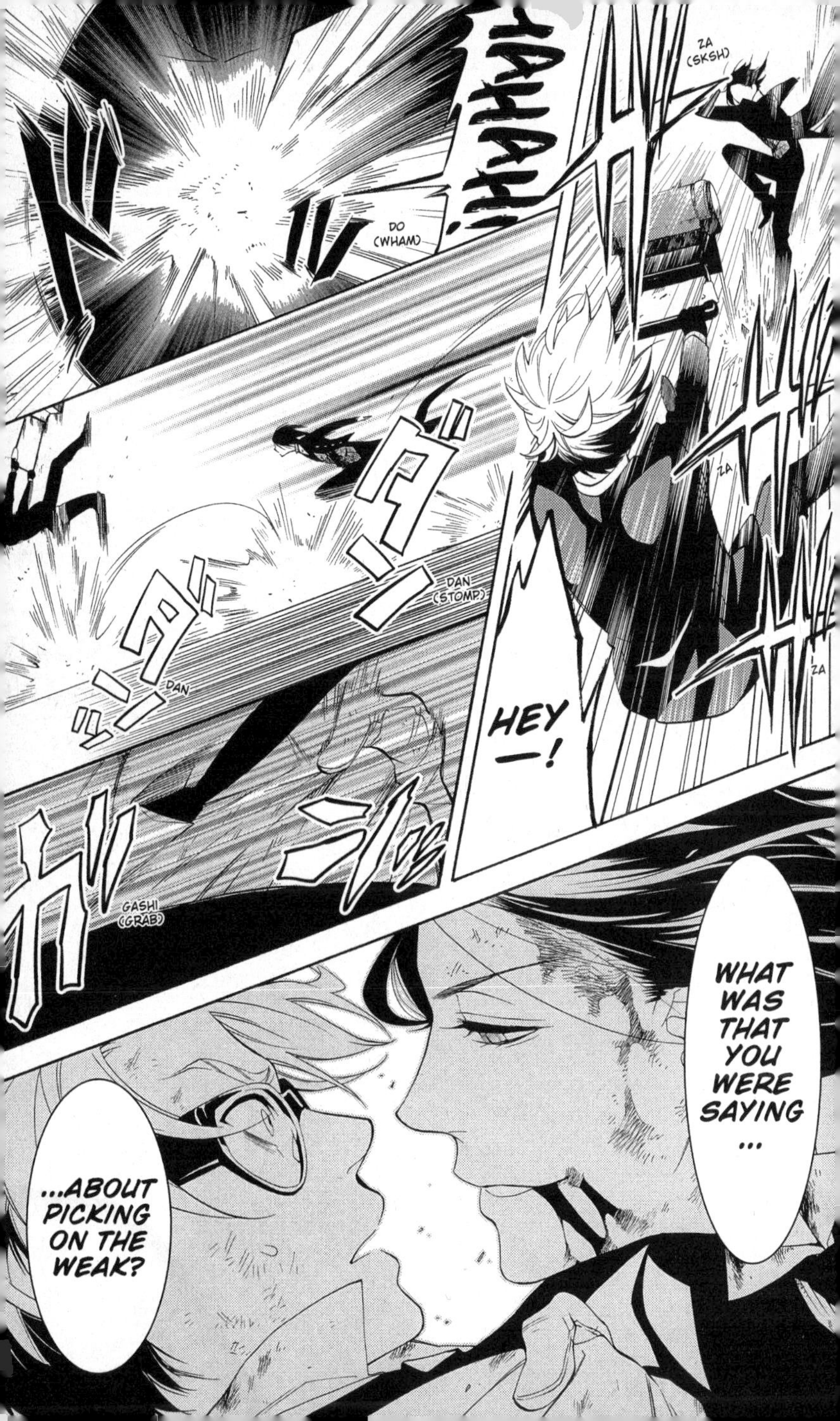
ZA (SKSH)
DO (WHAM)
ZA
ZA
DAN (STOMP)
DAN
HEY—!
GASHI (GRAB)
WHAT WAS THAT YOU WERE SAYING...
...ABOUT PICKING ON THE WEAK?

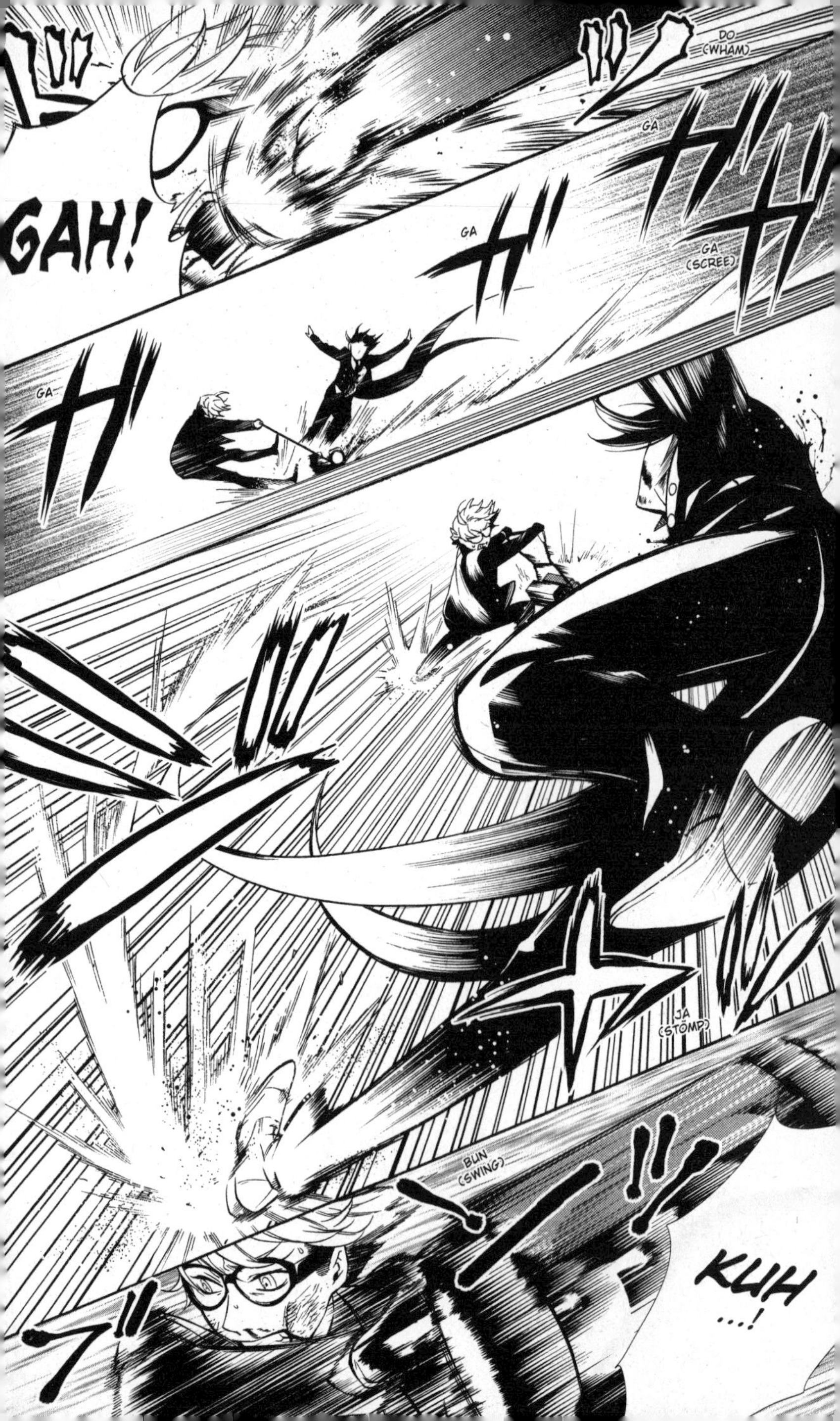
DO (WHAM)
GAH!
GA
GA (SCREE)
GA
GA
JA (STOMP)
BUN (SWING)
KUH ...!

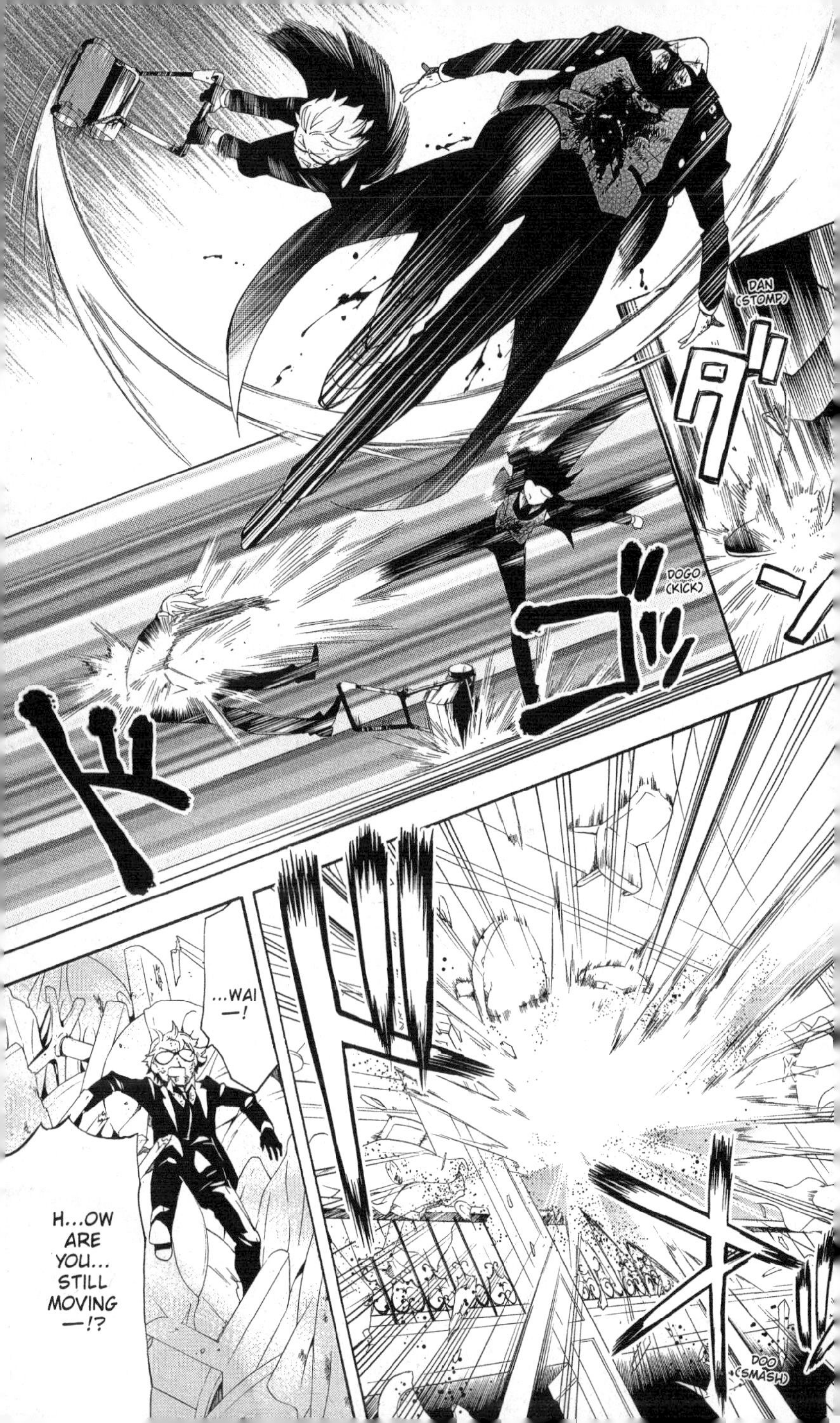
DAN (STOMP)
DOGO (KICK)
...WAI —!
H...OW ARE YOU... STILL MOVING —!?
DOO (SMASH)

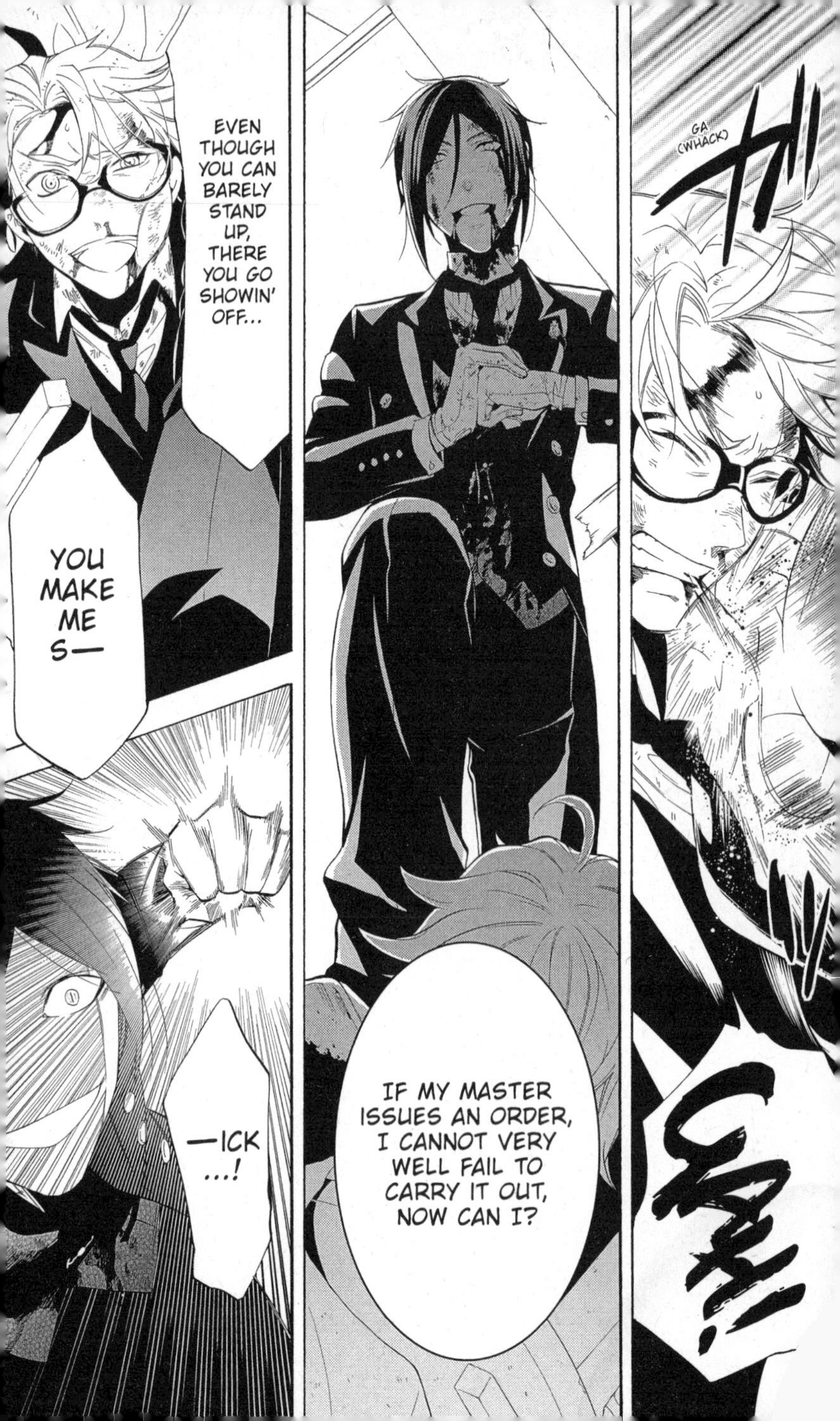

GA (WHACK)
IF MY MASTER ISSUES AN ORDER, I CANNOT VERY WELL FAIL TO CARRY IT OUT, NOW CAN I?
EVEN THOUGH YOU CAN BARELY STAND UP, THERE YOU GO SHOWIN' OFF...
YOU MAKE ME S—
—ICK ...!

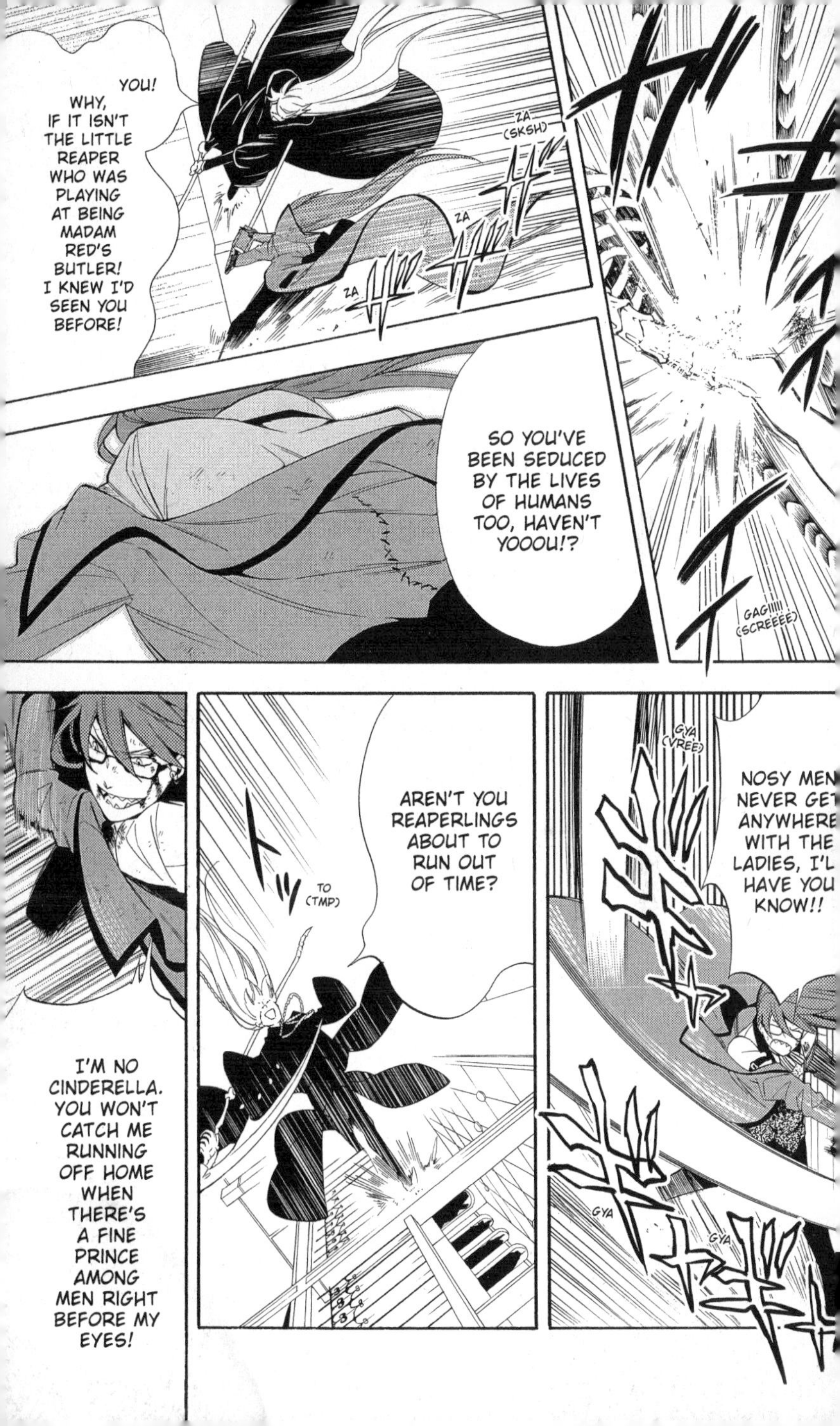
GAGIIII (SCREEEE)
ZA (SKSH)
ZA
ZA
YOU! WHY, IF IT ISN'T THE LITTLE REAPER WHO WAS PLAYING AT BEING MADAM RED'S BUTLER! I KNEW I'D SEEN YOU BEFORE!
SO YOU'VE BEEN SEDUCED BY THE LIVES OF HUMANS TOO, HAVEN'T YOOOU!?
GYA (VREE)
NOSY MEN NEVER GE ANYWHERE WITH THE LADIES, I'L HAVE YOU KNOW!!
GYA
GYA
AREN'T YOU REAPERLINGS ABOUT TO RUN OUT OF TIME?
TO (TMP)
I'M NO CINDERELLA. YOU WON'T CATCH ME RUNNING OFF HOME WHEN THERE'S A FINE PRINCE AMONG MEN RIGHT BEFORE MY EYES!

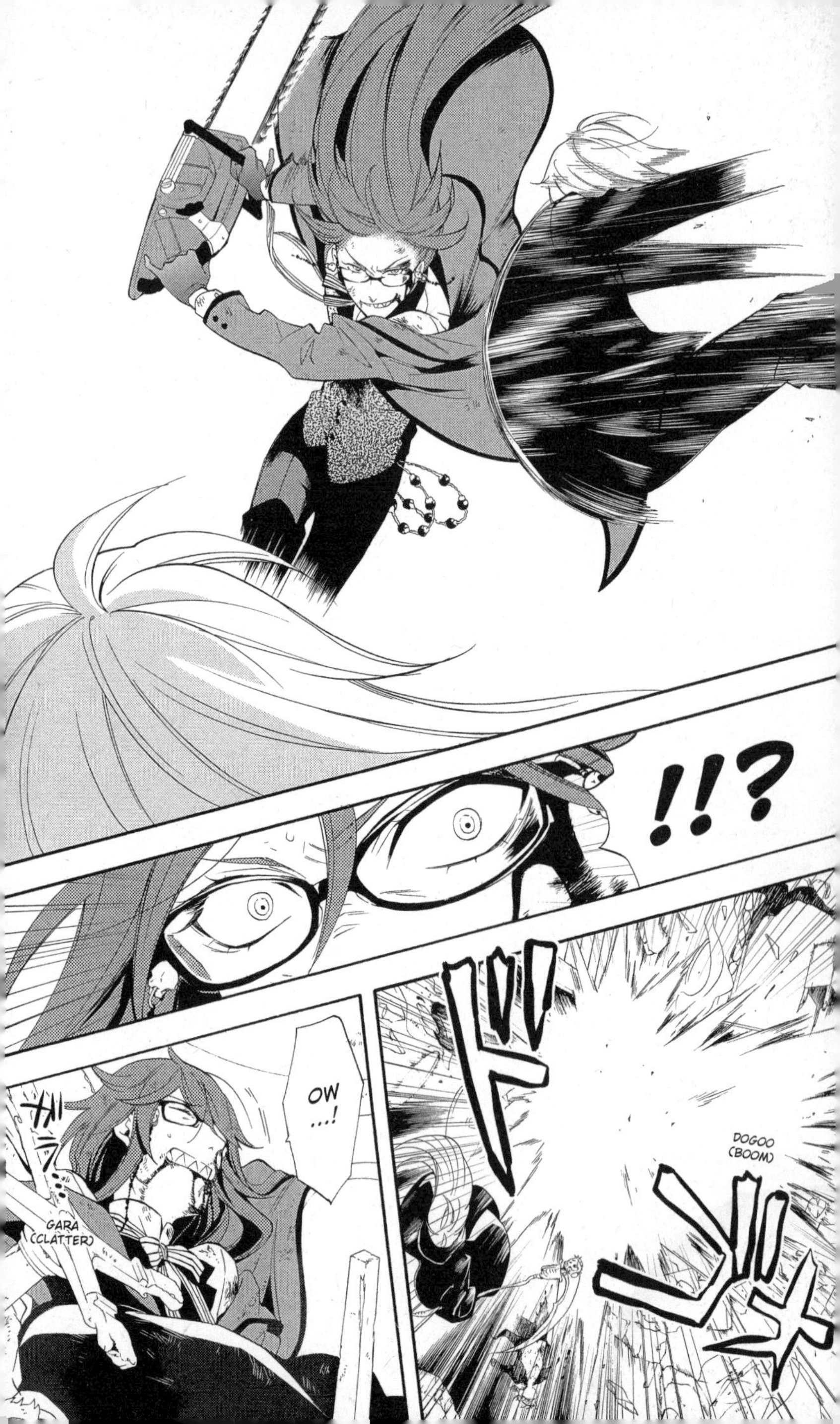
!!?
DOGOO (BOOM)
OW ...!
GARA (CLATTER)

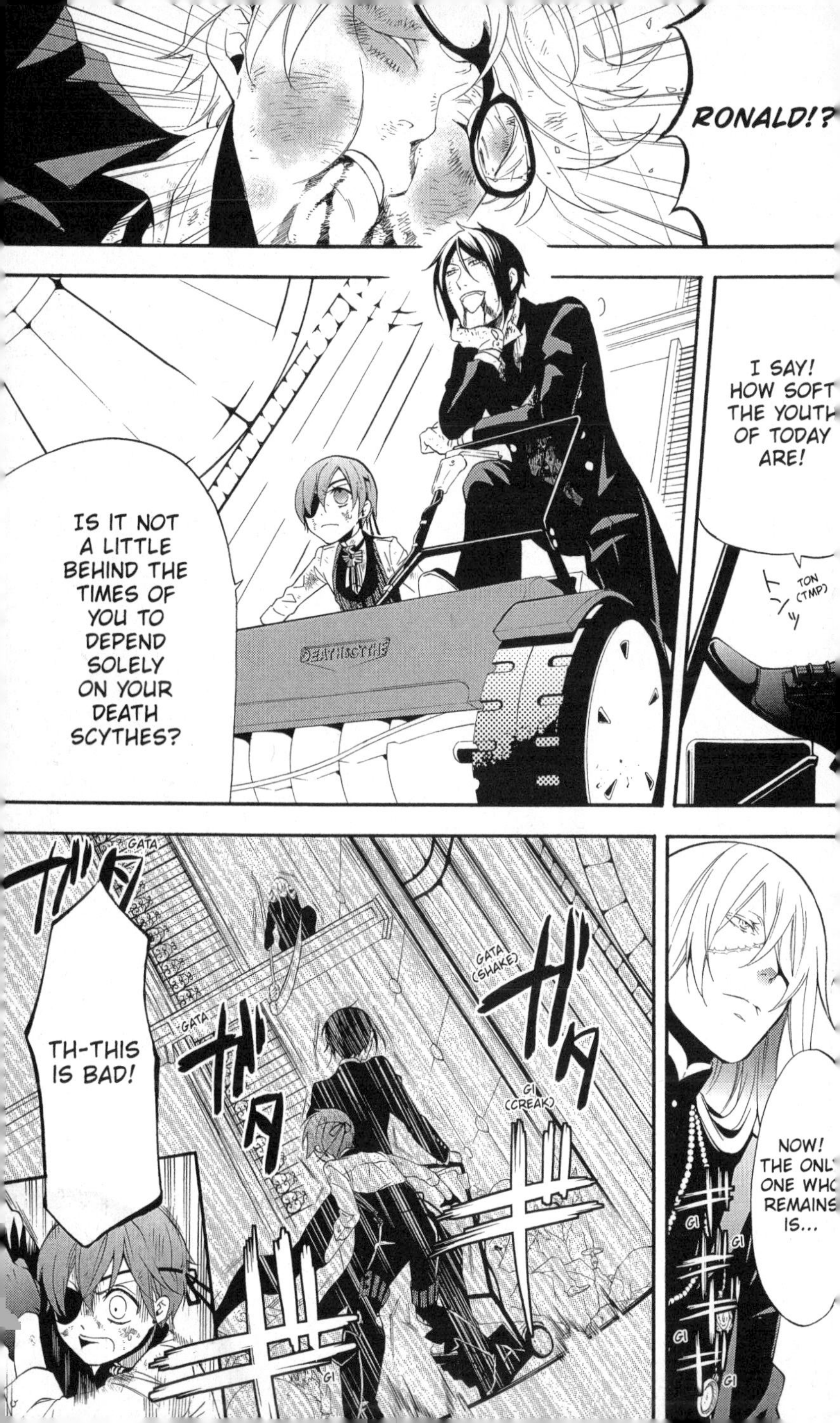
RONALD!?
I SAY! HOW SOFT THE YOUTH OF TODAY ARE!
TON (TMP)
IS IT NOT A LITTLE BEHIND THE TIMES OF YOU TO DEPEND SOLELY ON YOUR DEATH SCYTHES?
NOW! THE ONL ONE WHO REMAINS IS...
GI
GI
GI
GI
GATA
GATA (SHAKE)
GATA
GI (CREAK)
TH-THIS IS BAD!
GI

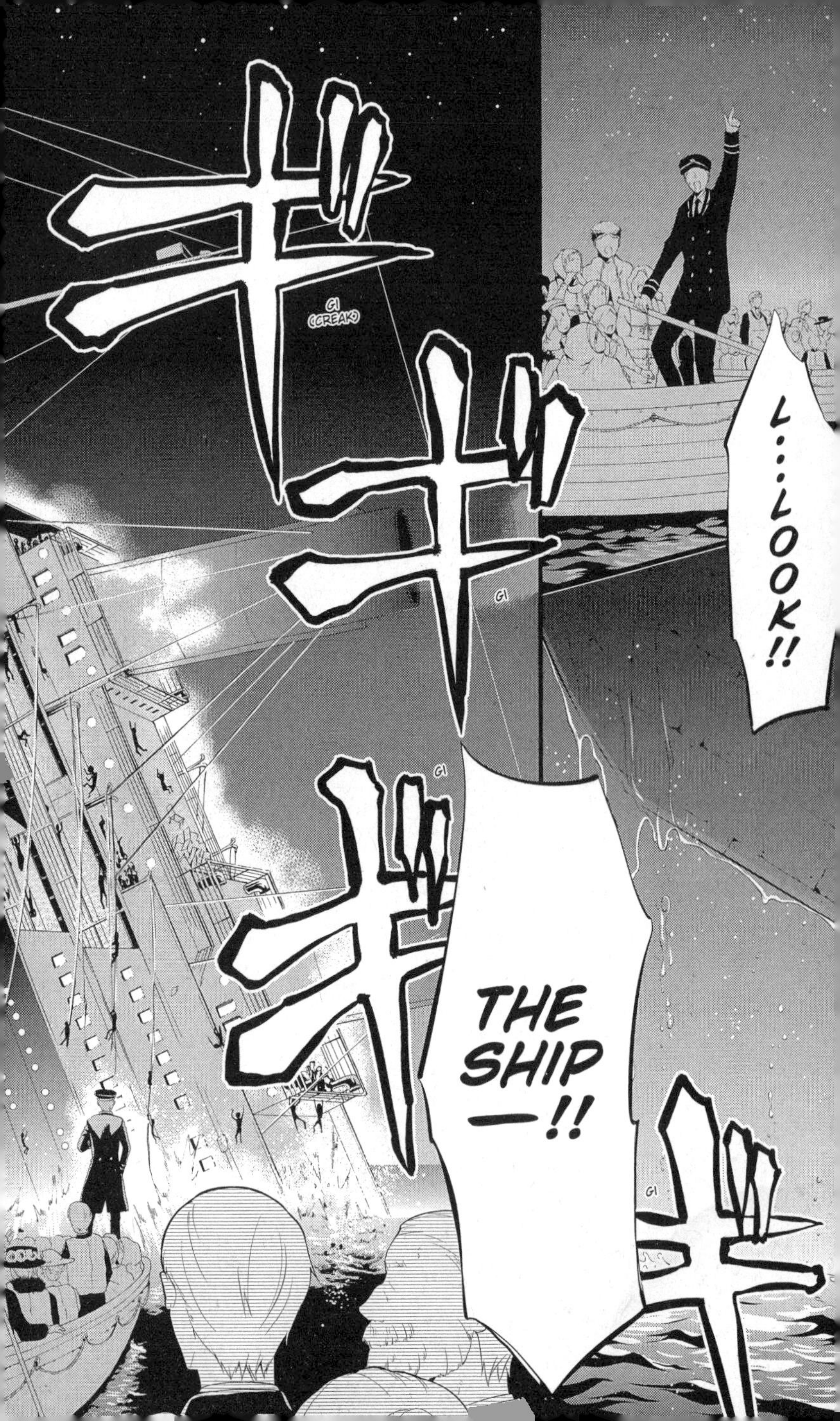
L...LOOOK!!
GI
(CREAK)
GI
GI
THE SHIP—!!
GI

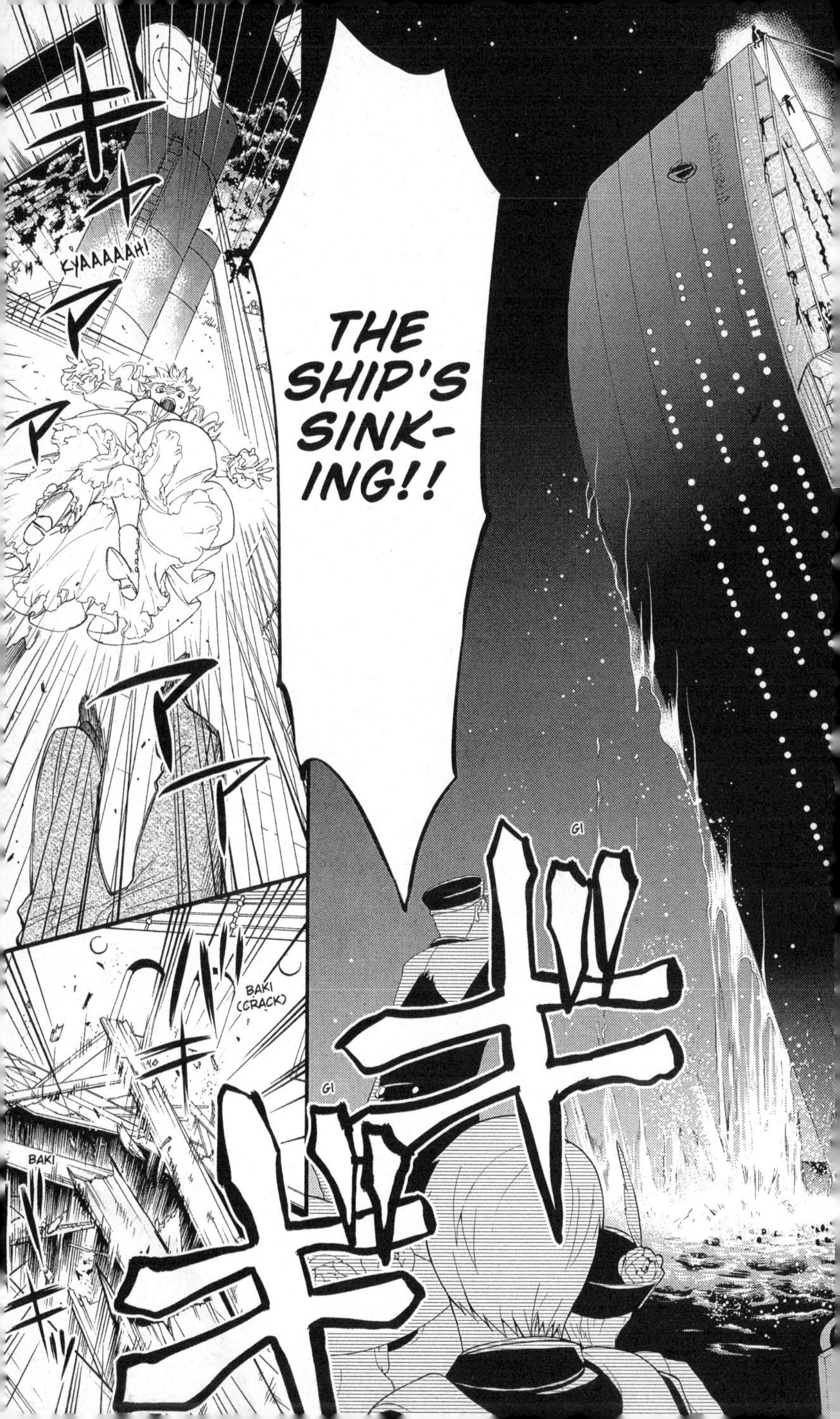
THE SHIP'S SINK-ING!!
GI
GI
KYAAAAAH!
BAKI (CRACK)
BAKI

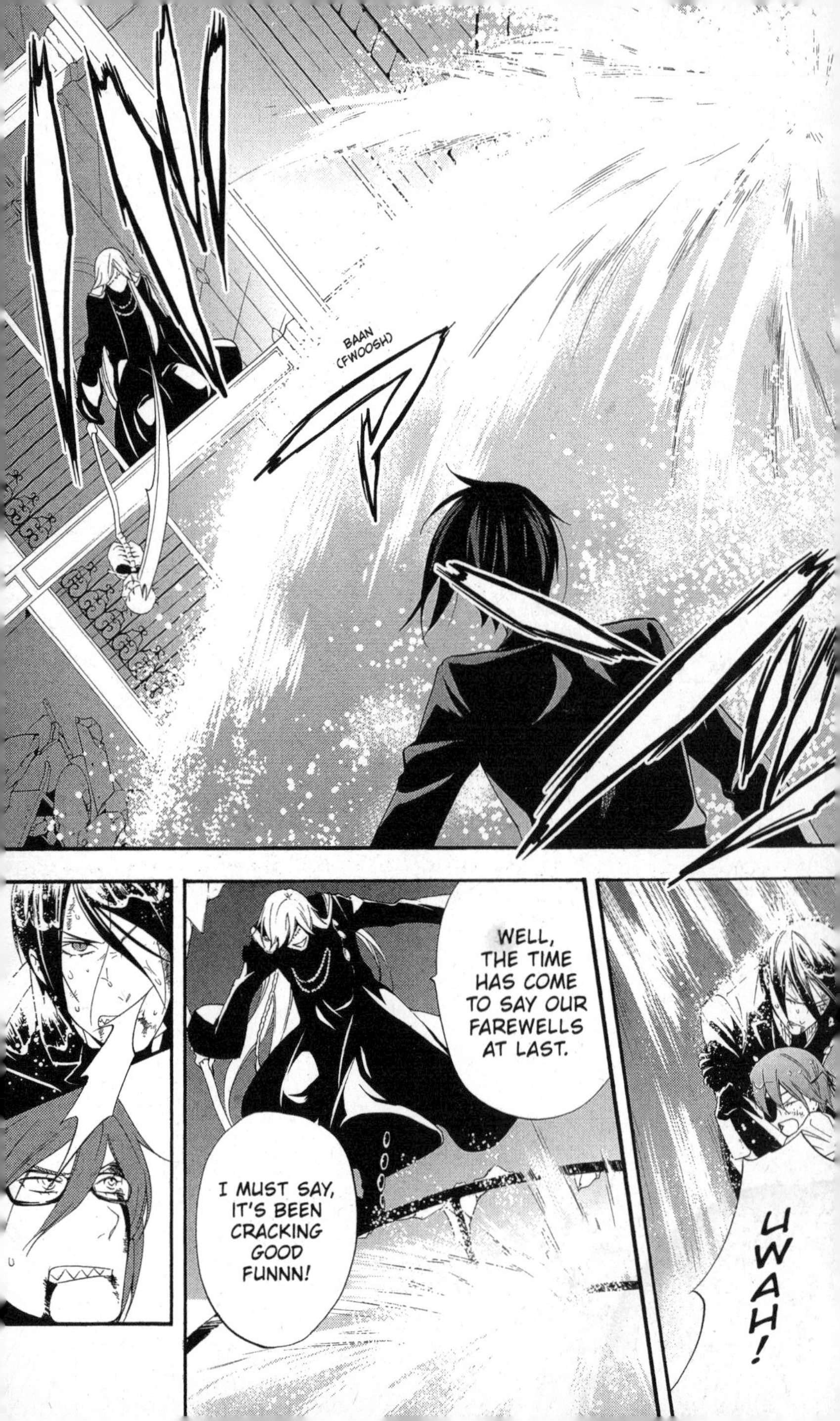
BAAN (FWOOSH)
UWAH!
WELL, THE TIME HAS COME TO SAY OUR FAREWELLS AT LAST.
I MUST SAY, IT'S BEEN CRACKING GOOD FUNNN!

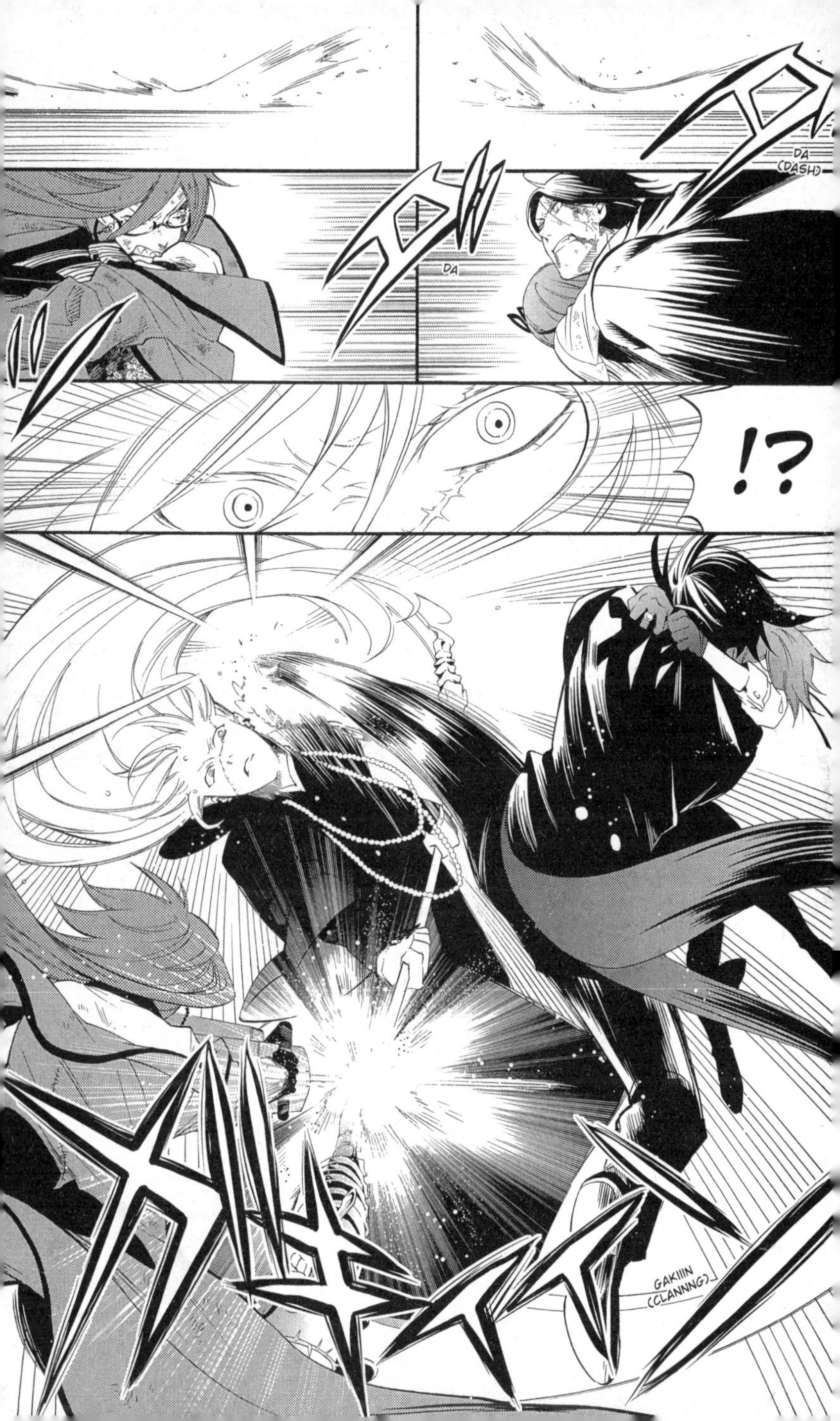
DA
(DASH)
DA
!?
GAKIIN
(CLANNNG)

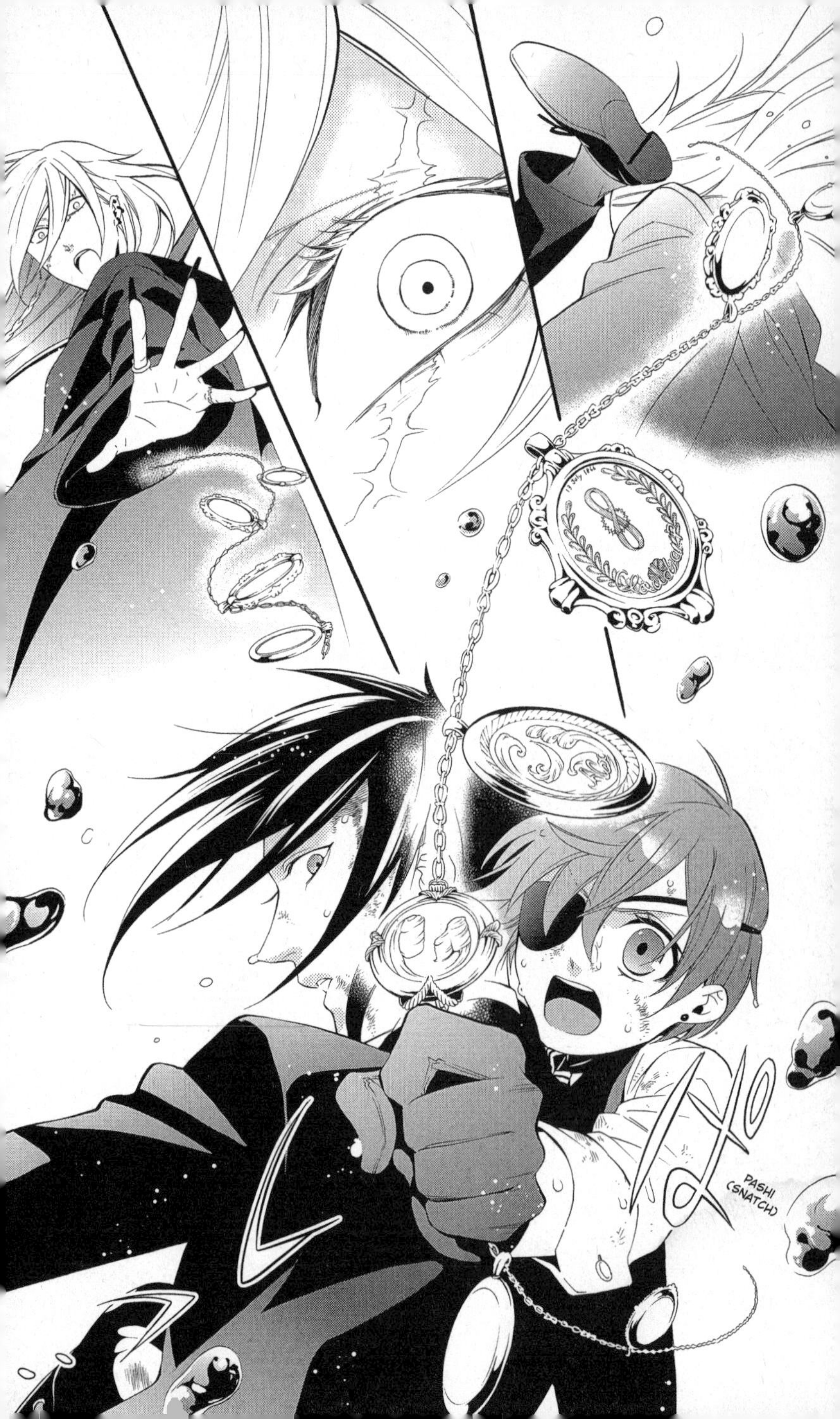
PASHI
(SNATCH)

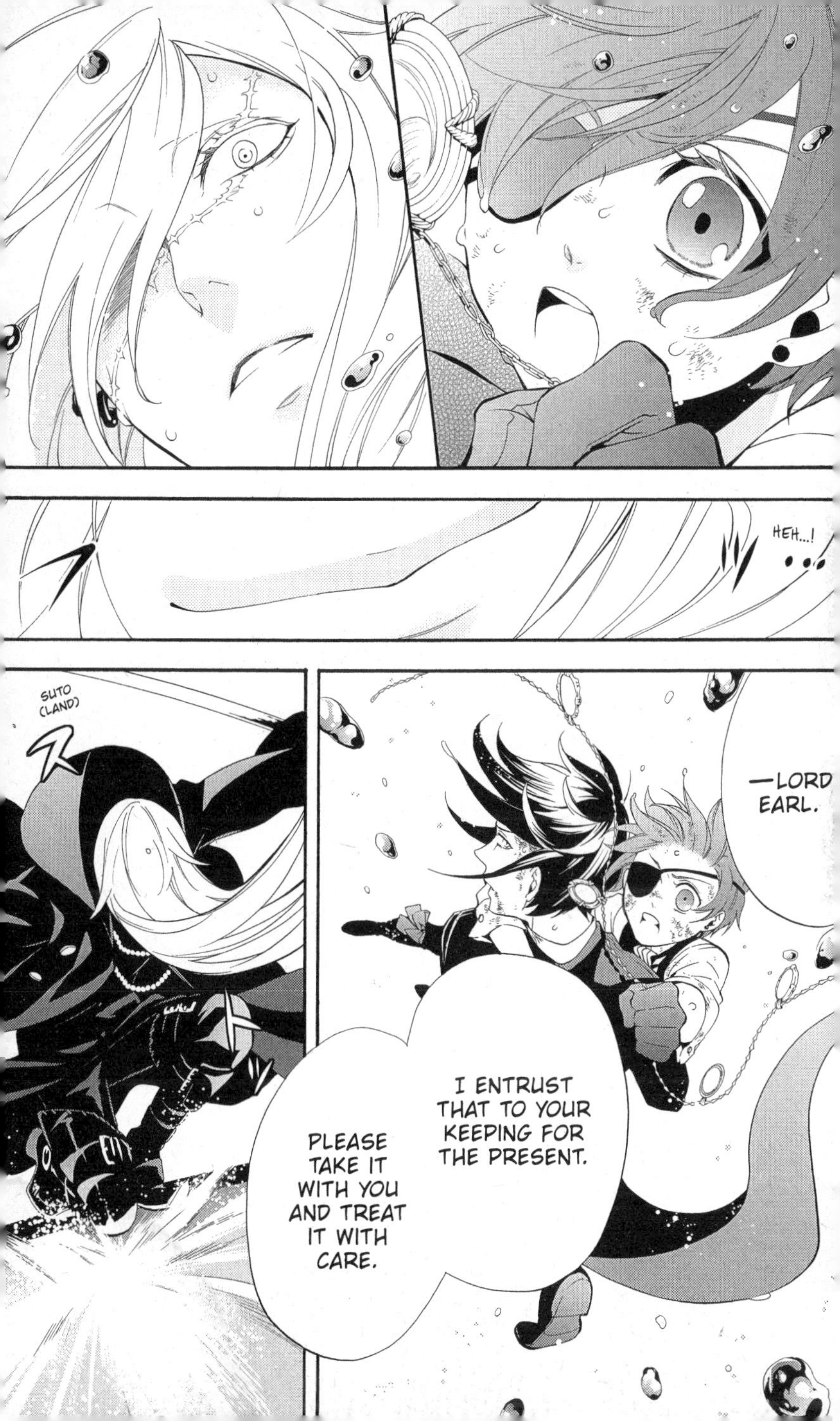
HEH...!
...
—LORD EARL.
I ENTRUST THAT TO YOUR KEEPING FOR THE PRESENT.
PLEASE TAKE IT WITH YOU AND TREAT IT WITH CARE.
SUTO (LAND)

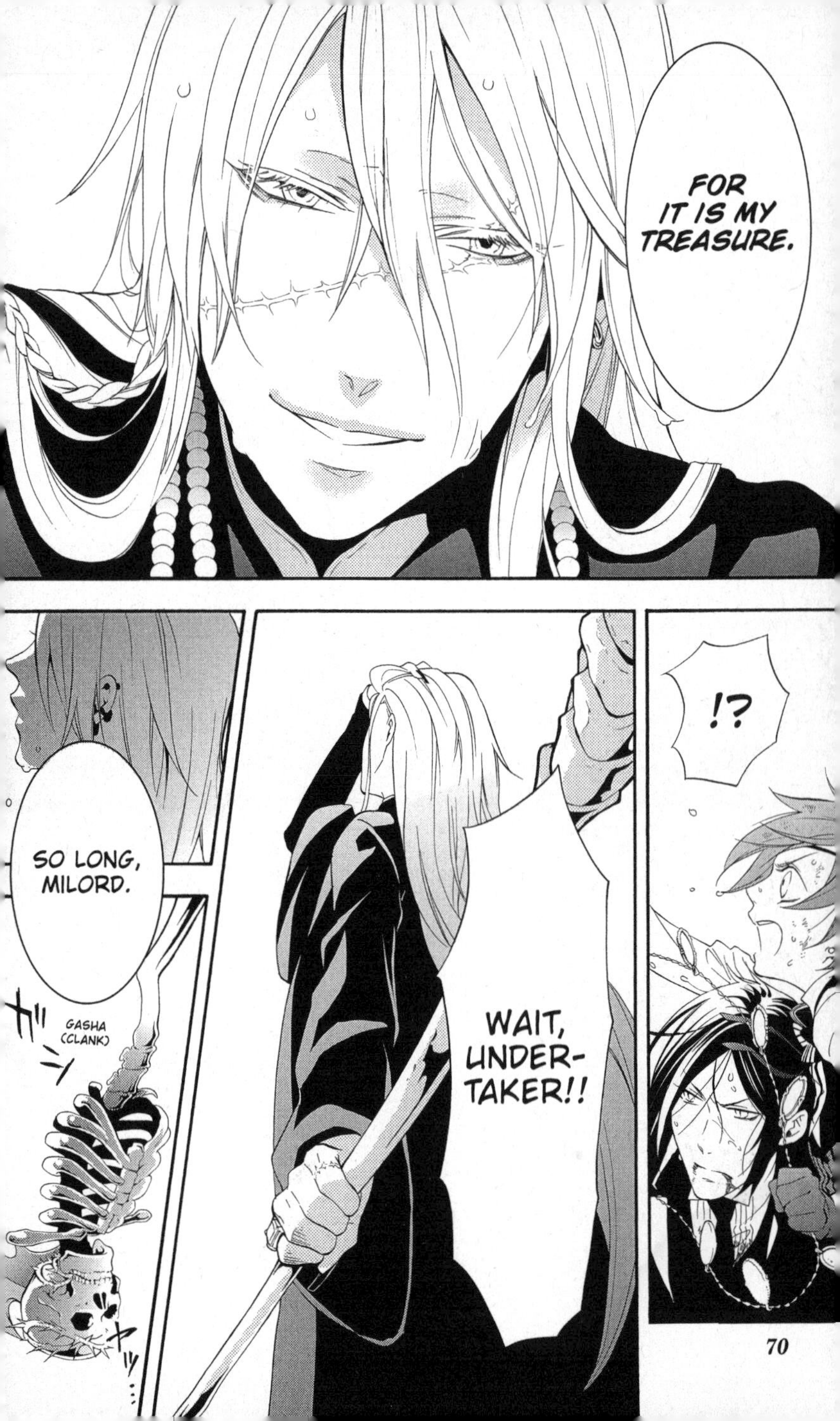
FOR IT IS MY TREASURE.
!?
WAIT, UNDER-TAKER!!
SO LONG, MILORD.
GASHA (CLANK)

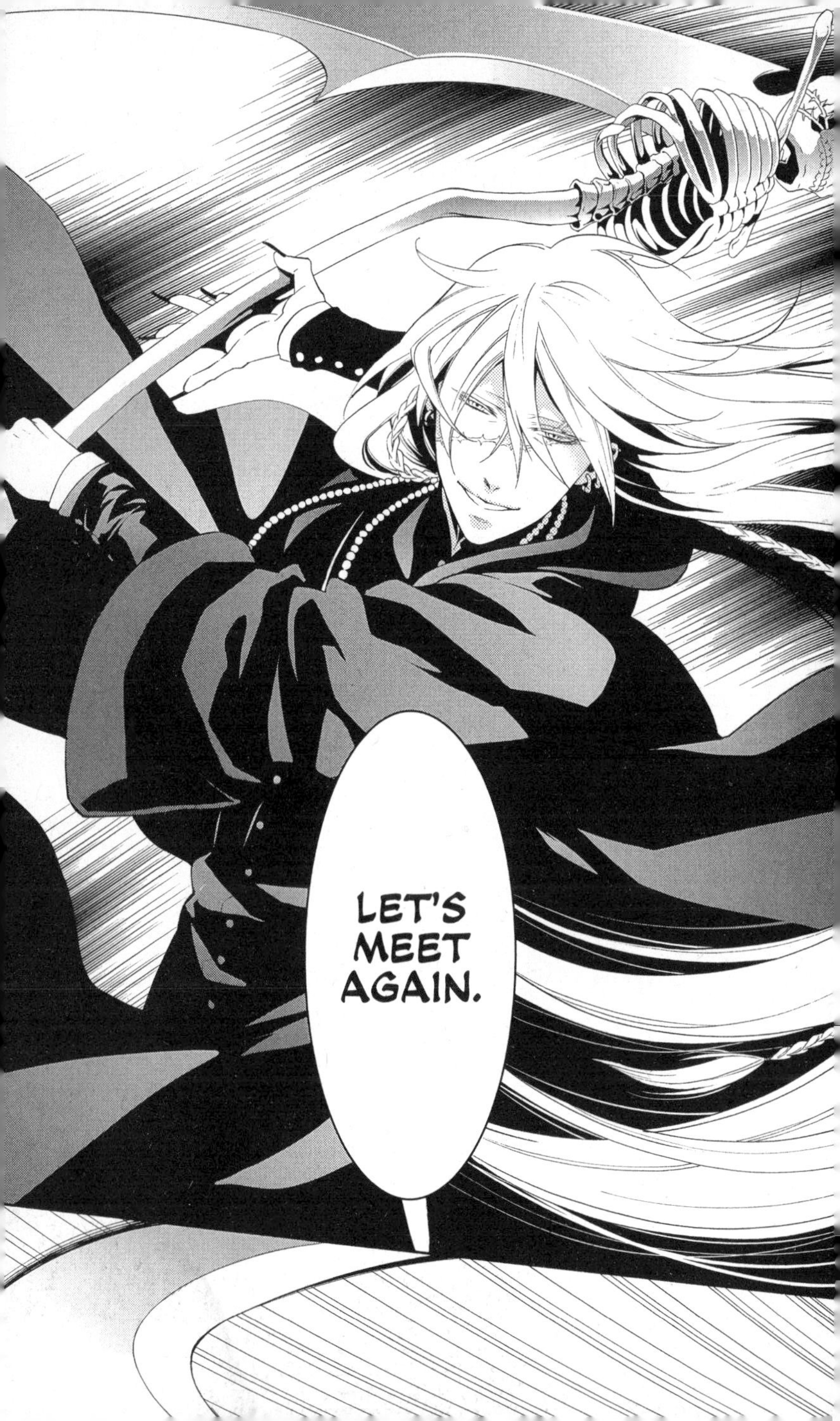
LET'S MEET AGAIN.

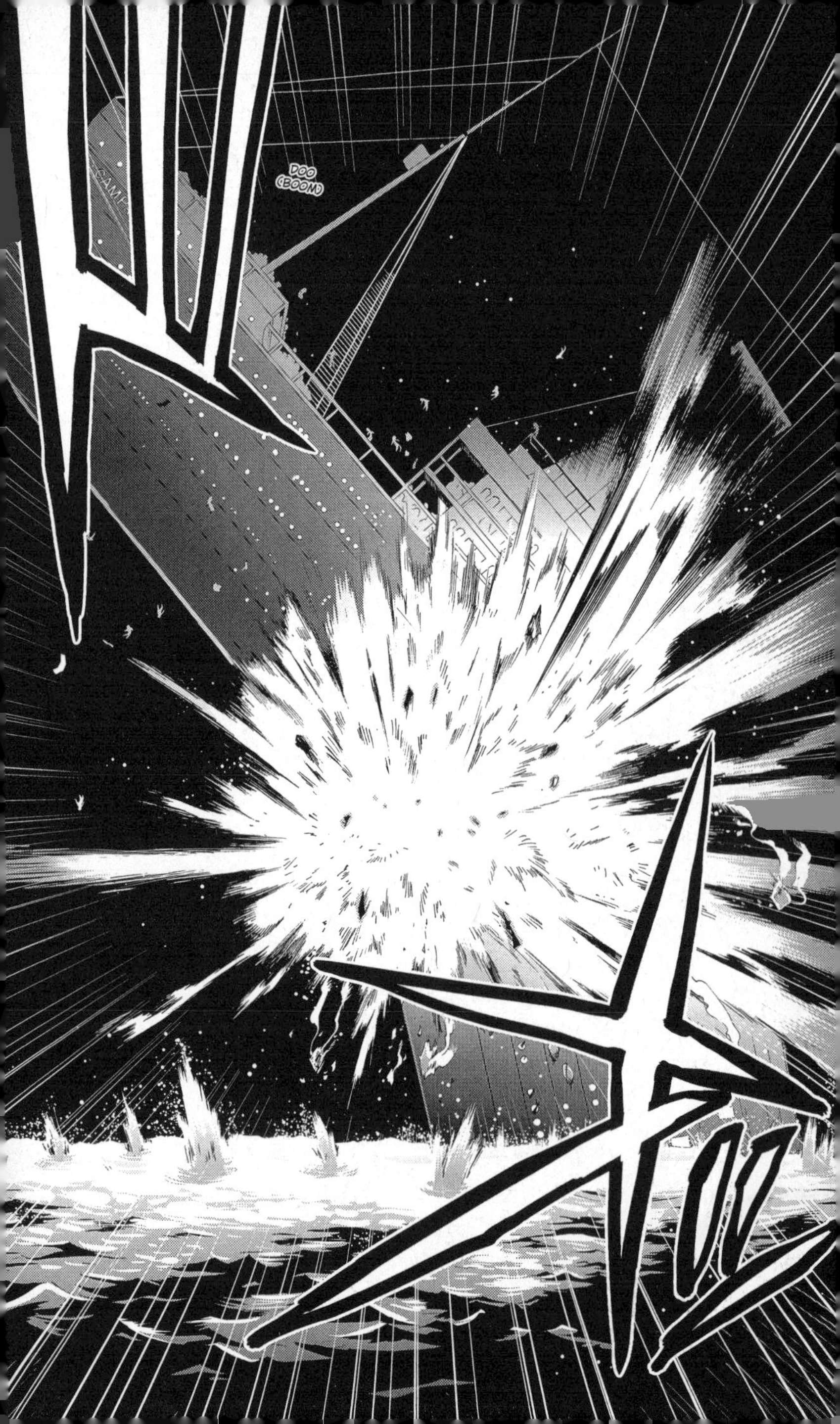
DOO
(BOOM)
CAMP

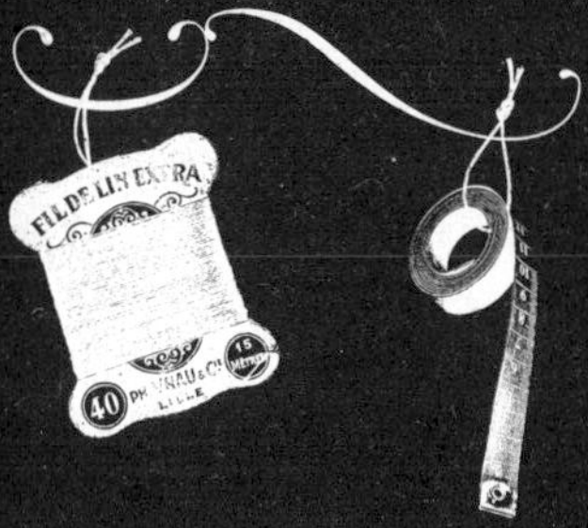
FIL DE LIN EXTRA
40
LILLE

Black Butler

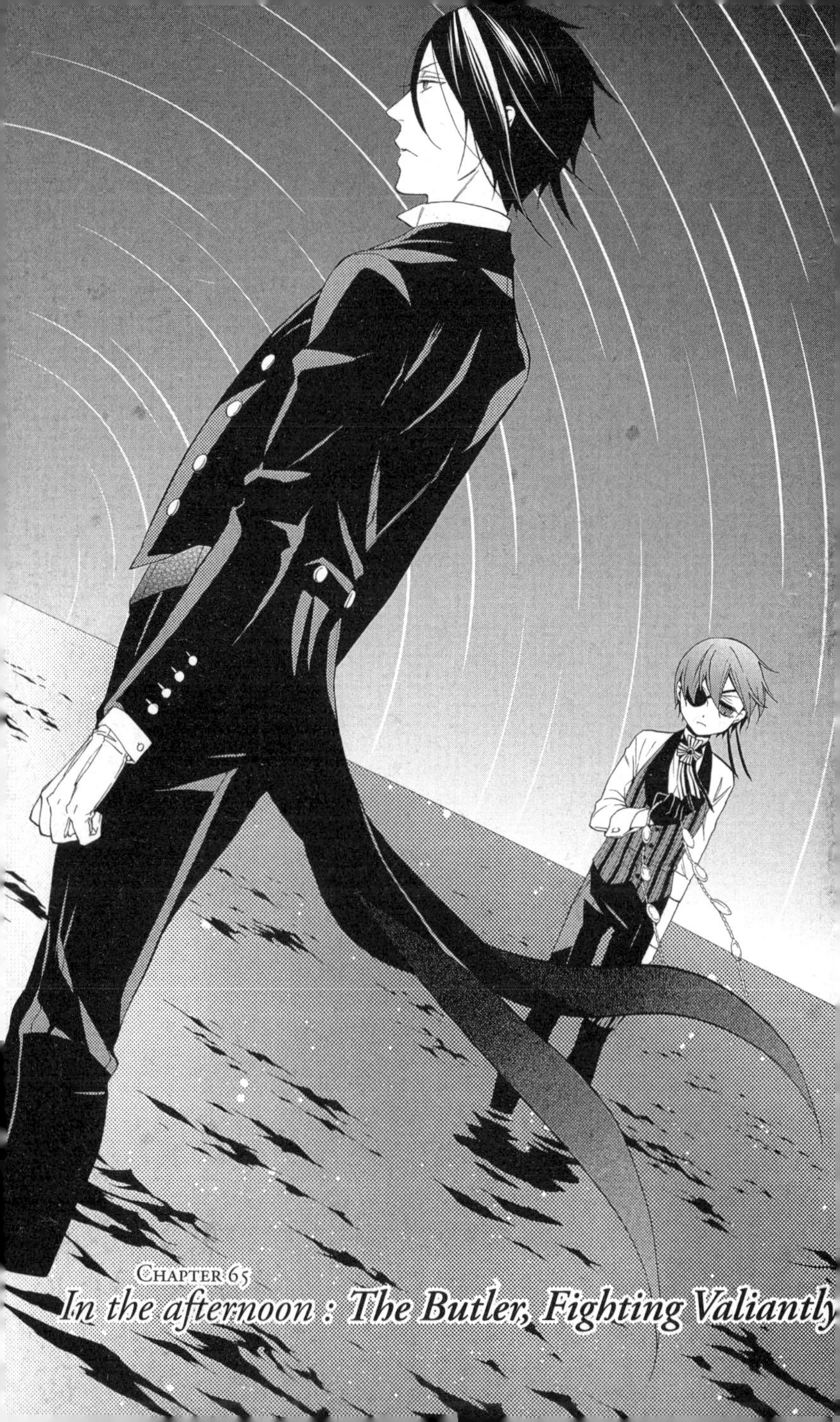
Chapter 65
In the afternoon : The Butler, Fighting Valiantly

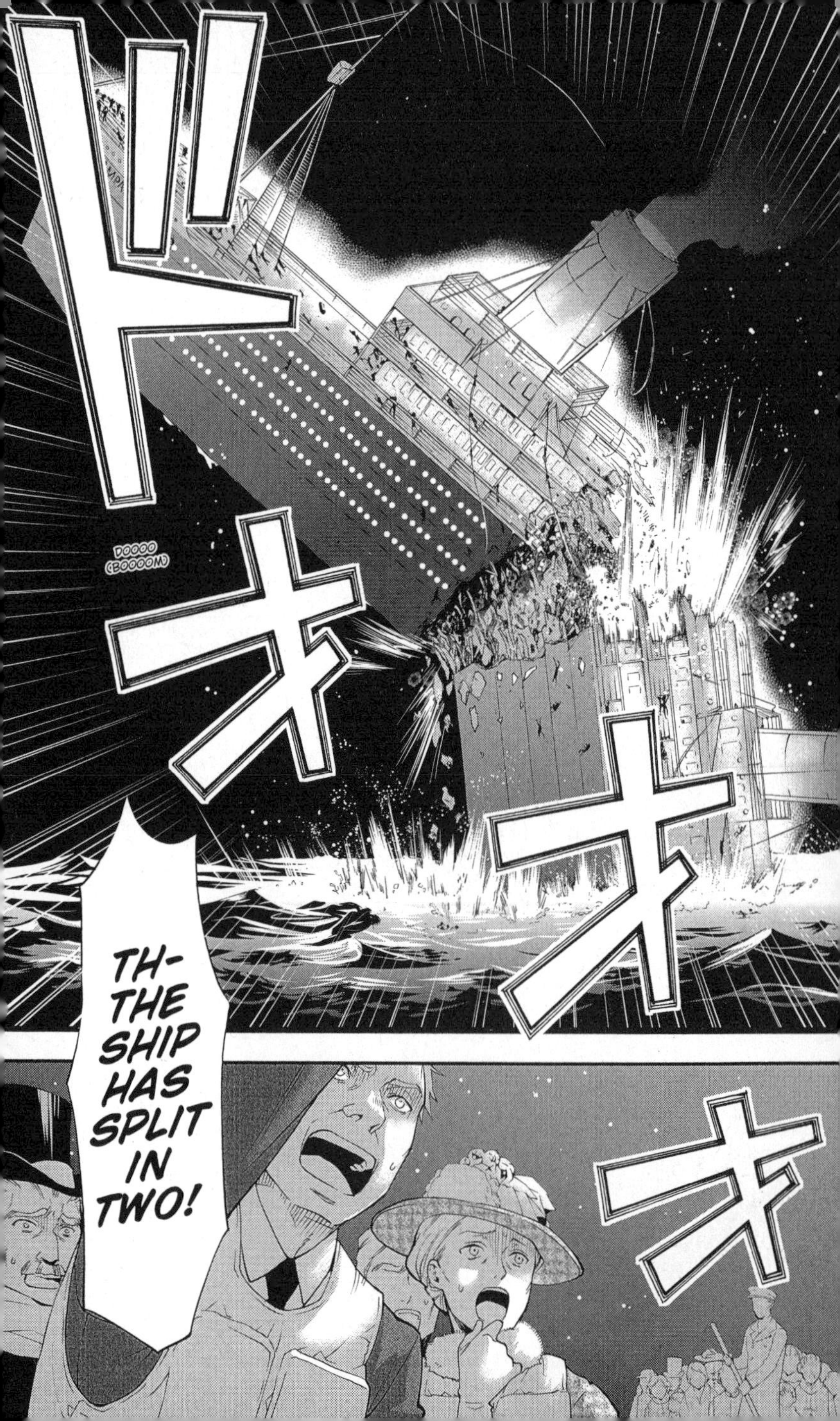
ドオオオ
DOOOO
(BOOOOM)
TH-THE SHIP HAS SPLIT IN TWO!

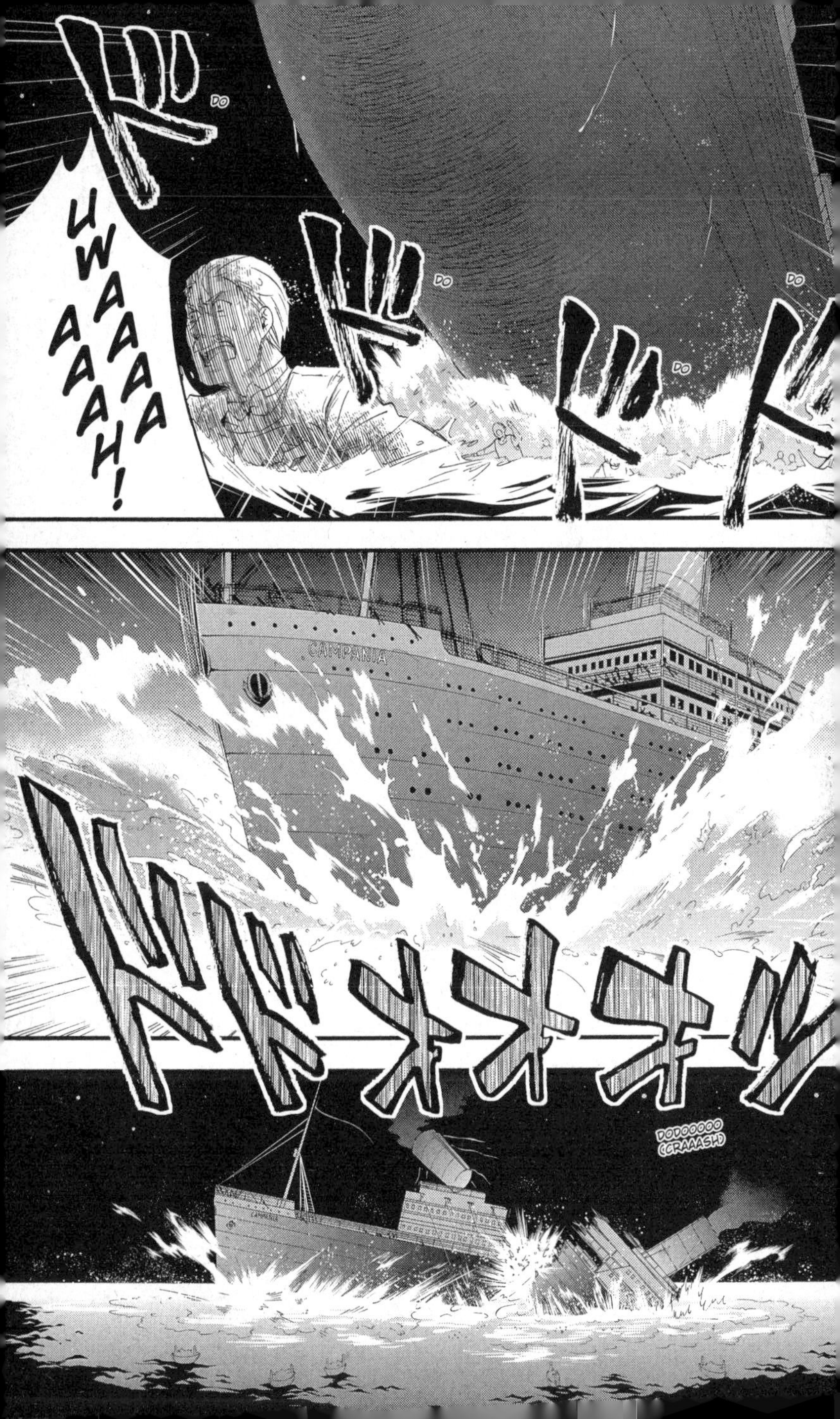
DO
DO
DO
DO
UWAAAAAAAH!
DODOOOOO (CRAAASH)

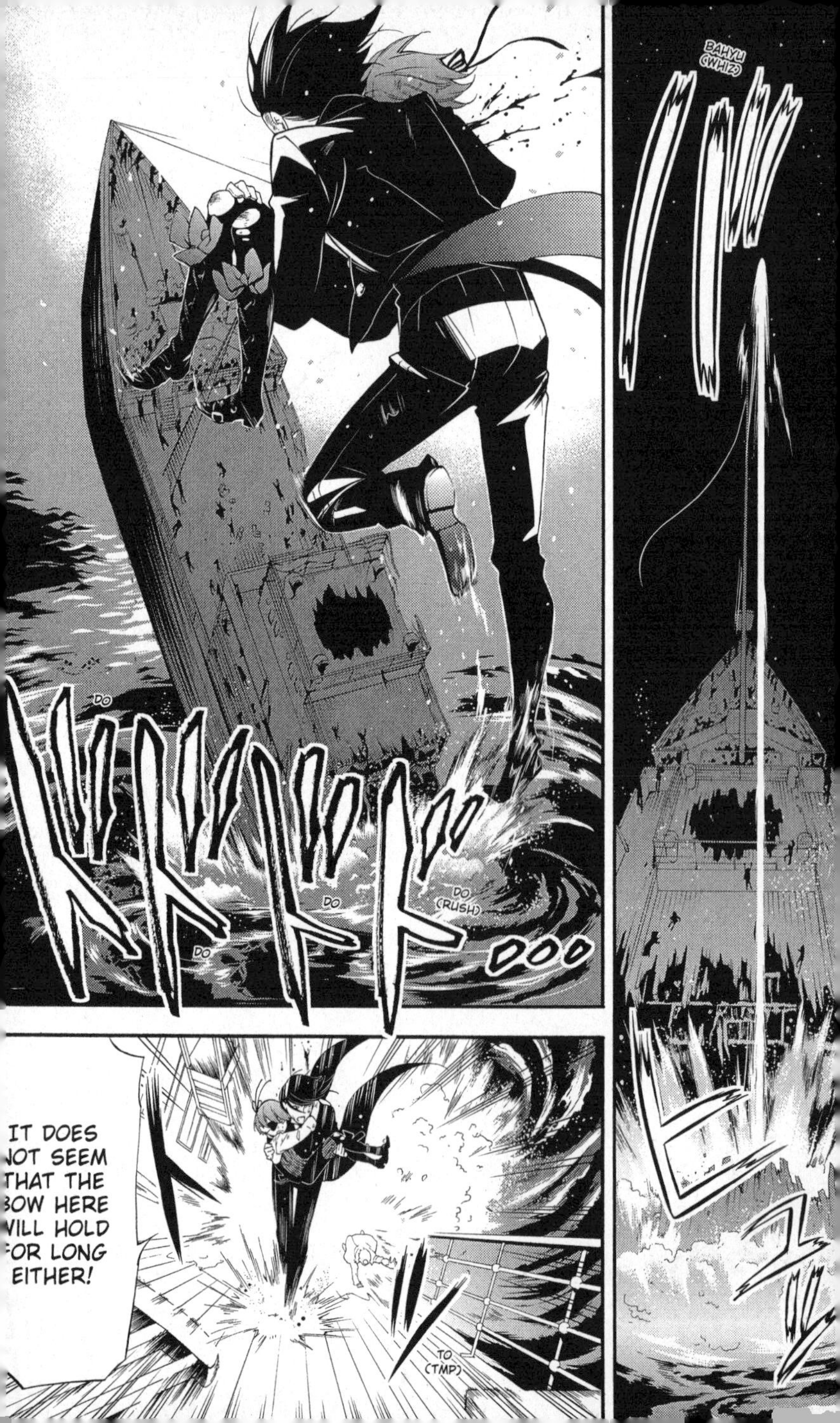
BAHYU (WHIZ)
DO
DO (RUSH)
DO
DO
DOO
IT DOES NOT SEEM THAT THE BOW HERE WILL HOLD FOR LONG EITHER!
TO (TMP)

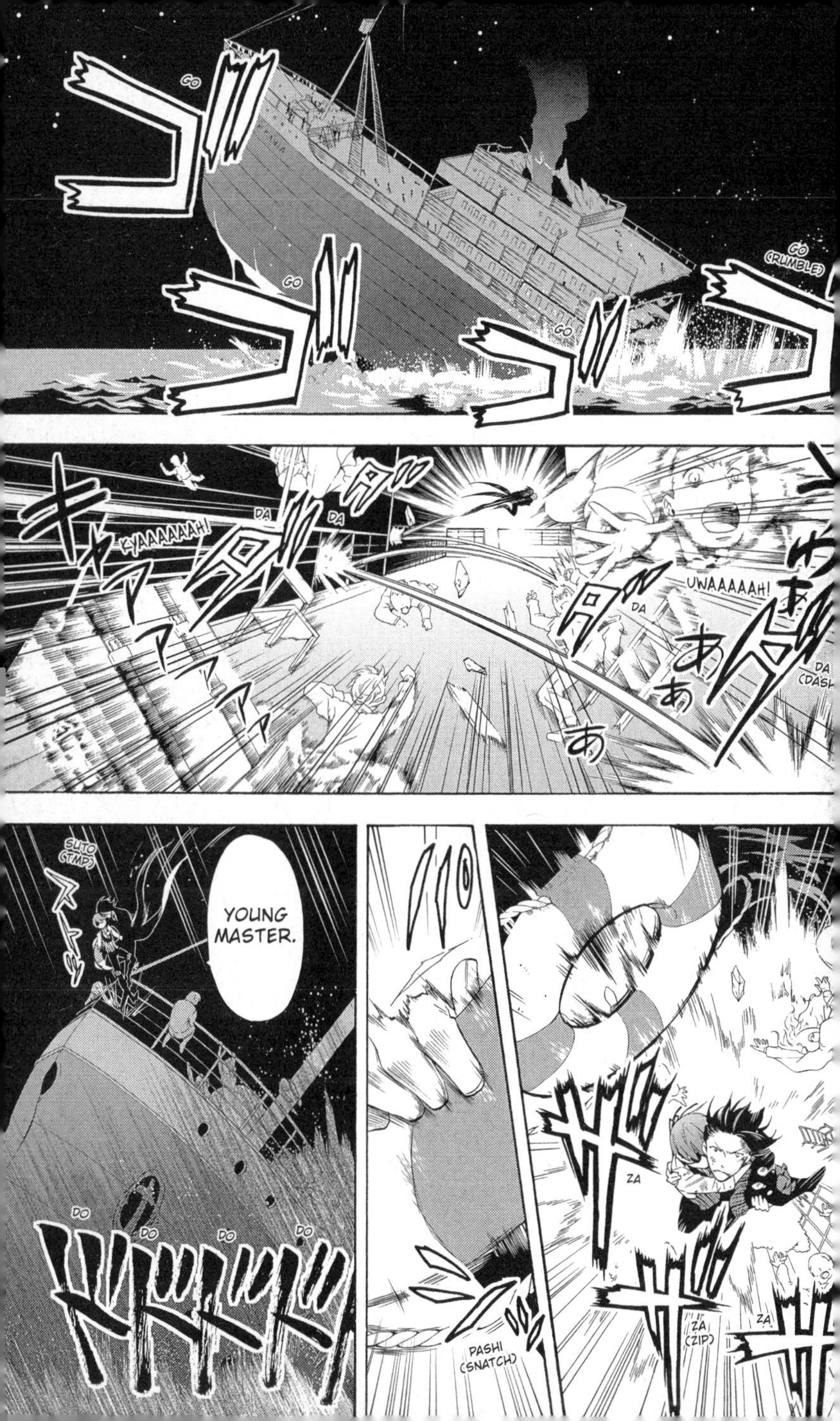
GO (RUMBLE)
GO
GO
GO
DA (DASH)
UWAAAAAH!
DA
DA
DA
KYAAAAAAH!
ZA
ZA (ZIP)
ZA
PASHI (SNATCH)
SUTO (TMP)
YOUNG MASTER.
DO
DO
DO
DO

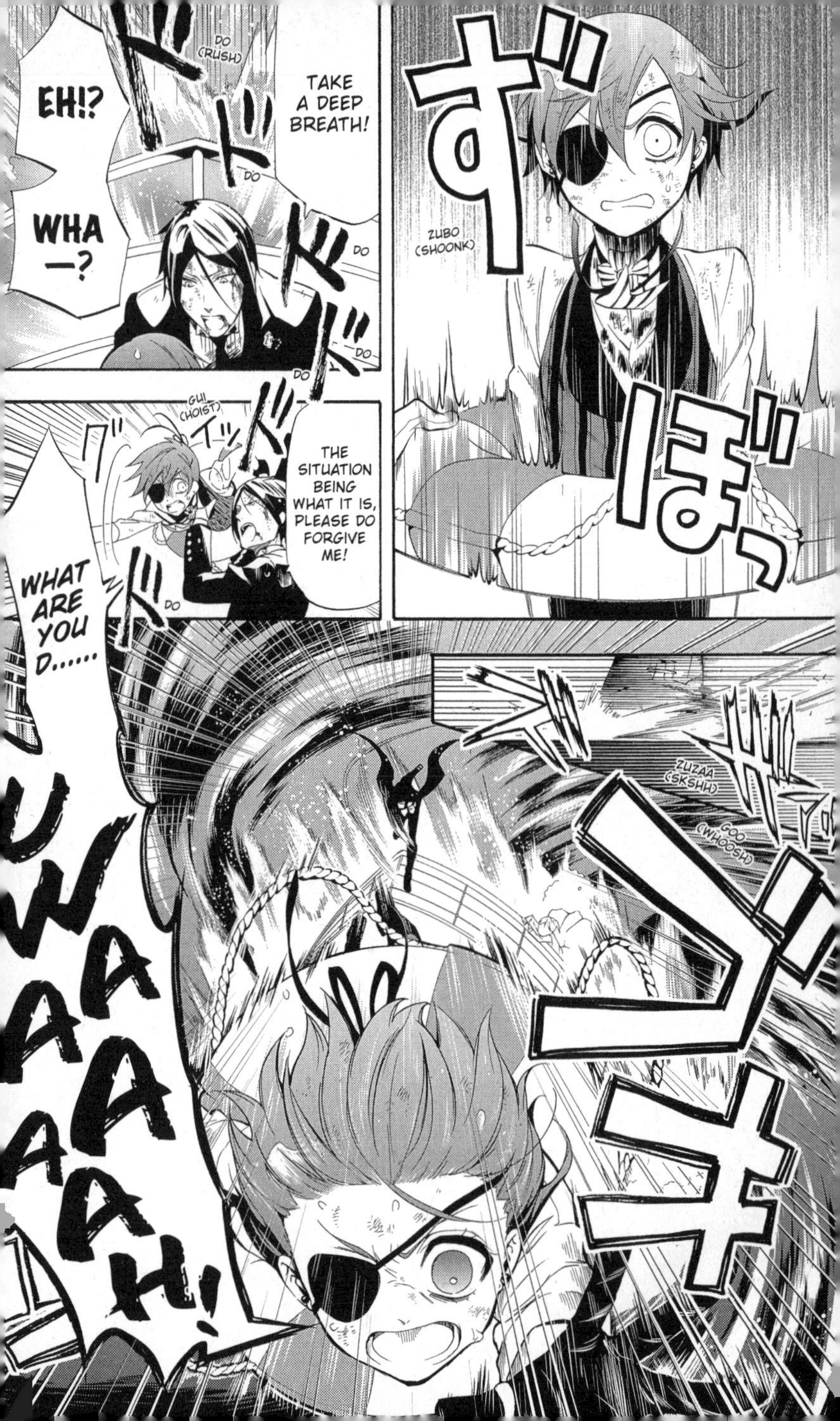
ZUBO (SHOONK)
DO (RUSH)
TAKE A DEEP BREATH!
EH!?
DO
WHA—?
DO
DO
DO
GUI (HOIST)
THE SITUATION BEING WHAT IT IS, PLEASE DO FORGIVE ME!
WHAT ARE YOU D......
DO
ZUZAA (SKSHH)
GOO (WHOOSH)
UWAAAAAH!

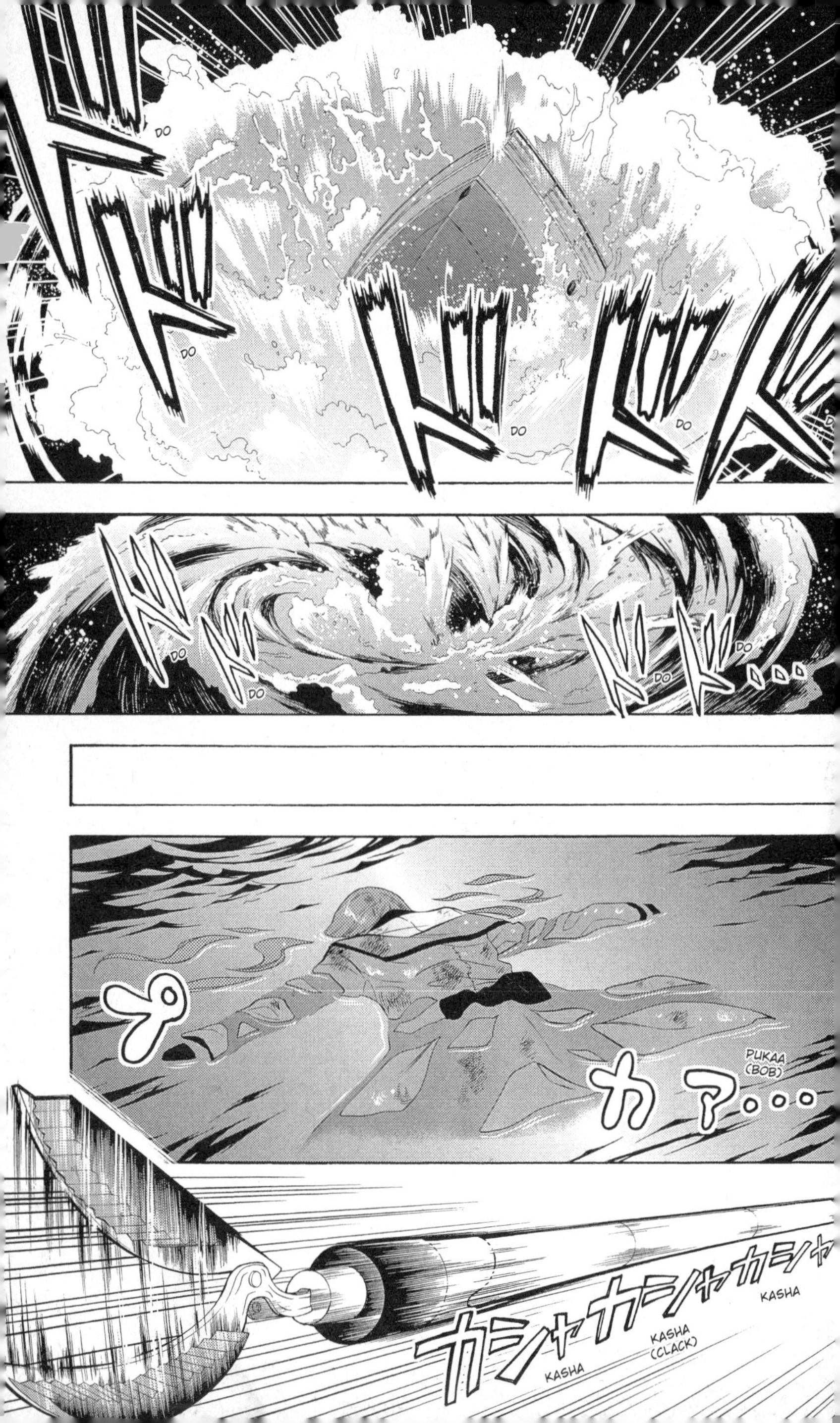
DO
DO
DO
DO
DO
DO
DO
DO
PUKAA (BOB)
KASHA
KASHA (CLACK)
KASHA

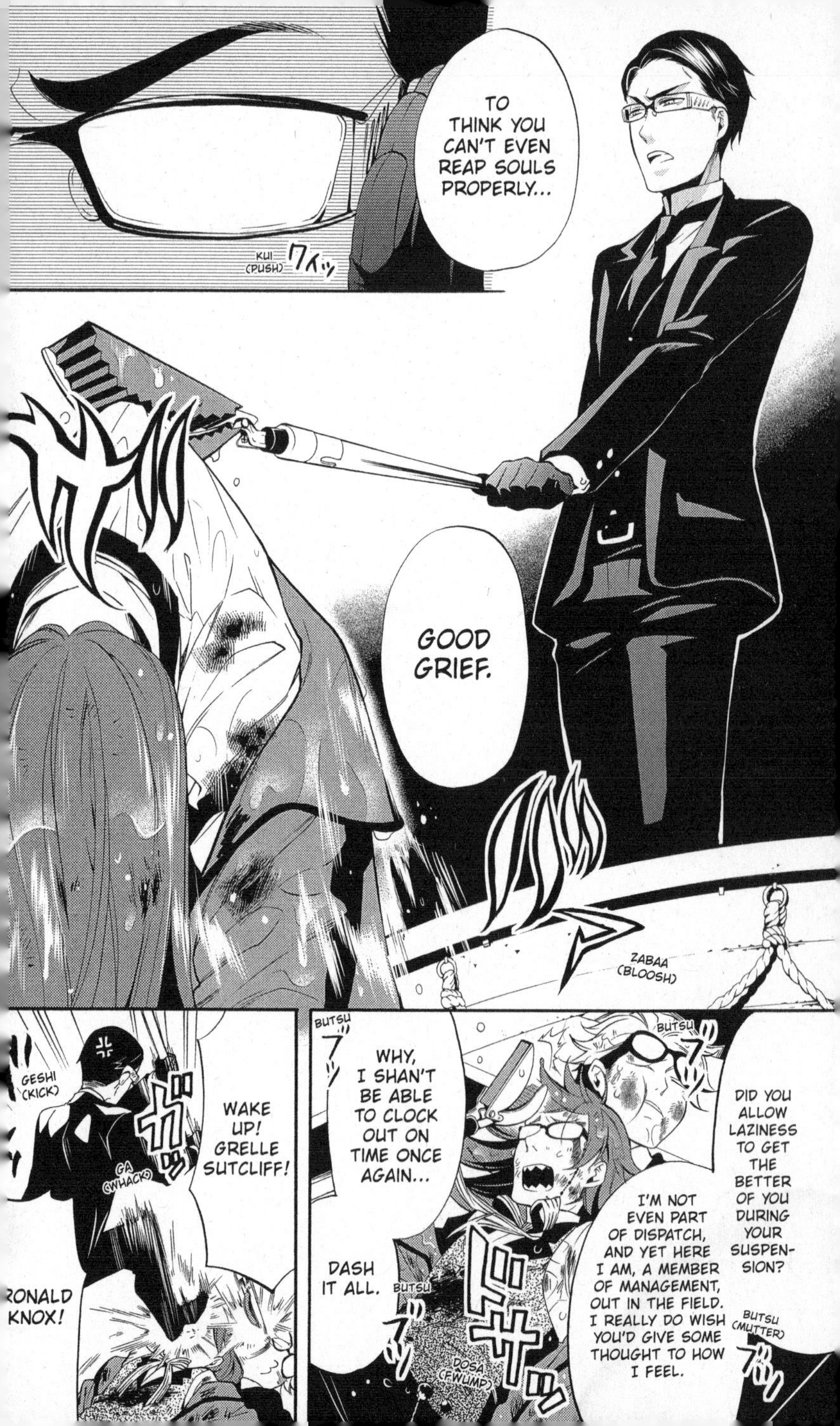
TO THINK YOU CAN'T EVEN REAP SOULS PROPERLY...
KUI (PUSH)
GOOD GRIEF.
ZABAA (BLOOSH)
BUTSU
DID YOU ALLOW LAZINESS TO GET THE BETTER OF YOU DURING YOUR SUSPEN-SION?
I'M NOT EVEN PART OF DISPATCH, AND YET HERE I AM, A MEMBER OF MANAGEMENT, OUT IN THE FIELD. I REALLY DO WISH YOU'D GIVE SOME THOUGHT TO HOW I FEEL.
BUTSU (MUTTER)
BUTSU
WHY, I SHAN'T BE ABLE TO CLOCK OUT ON TIME ONCE AGAIN...
DASH IT ALL.
BUTSU
DOSA (FWUMP)
WAKE UP! GRELLE SUTCLIFF!
GESHI (KICK)
GA (WHACK)
RONALD KNOX!

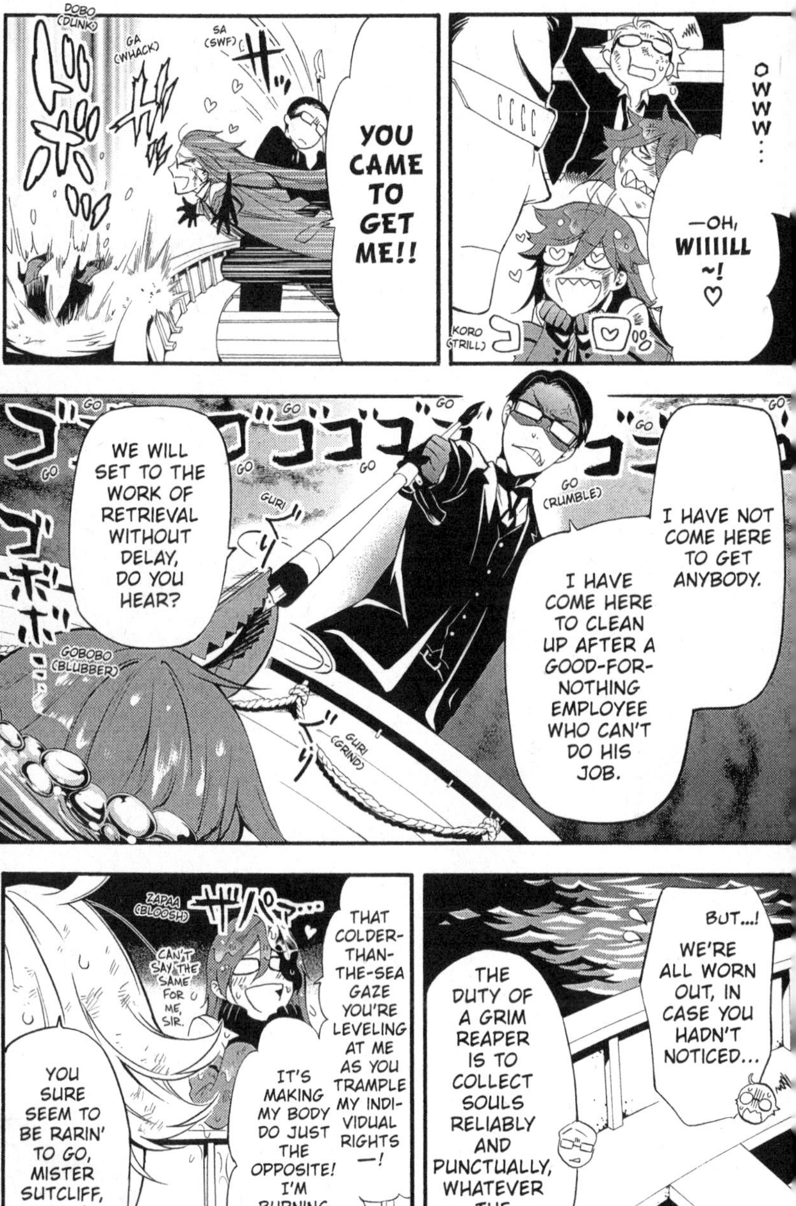
OWWW...
—OH, WIIIILL ~! ♡
KORO (TRILL)
YOU CAME TO GET ME!!
SA (SWF)
GA (WHACK)
DOBO (DUNK)
I HAVE NOT COME HERE TO GET ANYBODY.
I HAVE COME HERE TO CLEAN UP AFTER A GOOD-FOR-NOTHING EMPLOYEE WHO CAN'T DO HIS JOB.
GO (RUMBLE)
WE WILL SET TO THE WORK OF RETRIEVAL WITHOUT DELAY, DO YOU HEAR?
GURI
GOBOBO (BLUBBER)
GURI (GRIND)
BUT...! WE'RE ALL WORN OUT, IN CASE YOU HADN'T NOTICED...
THE DUTY OF A GRIM REAPER IS TO COLLECT SOULS RELIABLY AND PUNCTUALLY, WHATEVER THE SITUATION.
THAT COLDER-THAN-THE-SEA GAZE YOU'RE LEVELING AT ME AS YOU TRAMPLE MY INDIVIDUAL RIGHTS—!
IT'S MAKING MY BODY DO JUST THE OPPOSITE! I'M BURNING UP!
ZAPAA (BLOOSH)
CAN'T SAY THE SAME FOR ME, SIR.
YOU SURE SEEM TO BE RARIN' TO GO, MISTER SUTCLIFF, SIR~!

ZABAA
(BLOOSH)

I WILL REQUIRE YOU TO RETURN TO HEAD-QUARTERS AND SUBMIT YOUR REPORT IMMEDIATELY AFTER WE'VE FINISHED OUR COLLECTIONS HERE.

KUI
(PUSH)

YOUR REPORT ON THE TRANS-GRESSOR, THAT IS.

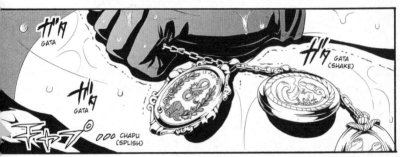

GATA

GATA (SHAKE)

GATA

CHAPU (SPLISH)

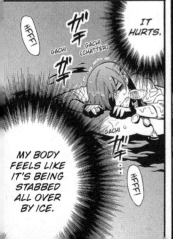

HFF!

GACHI

GACHI (CHATTER)

IT HURTS.

GACHI

HFF!

MY BODY FEELS LIKE IT'S BEING STABBED ALL OVER BY ICE.

WAAAh...

WAAAh...

Ugh......

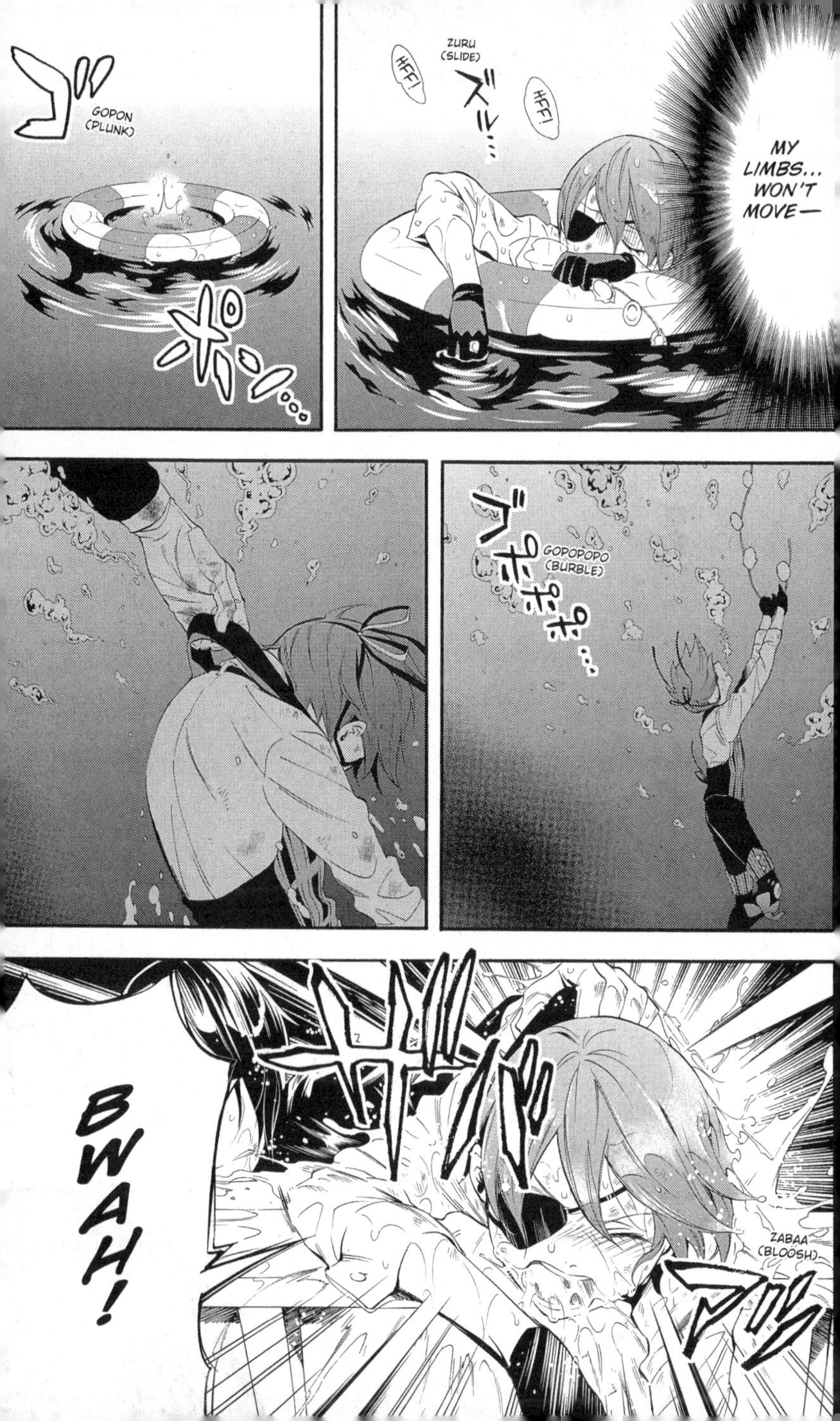
MY LIMBS... WON'T MOVE—
HFF!
ZURU (SLIDE)
HFF!
GOPON (PLUNK)
GOPOPOPO (BURBLE)
ZABAA (BLOOSH)
BWAH!

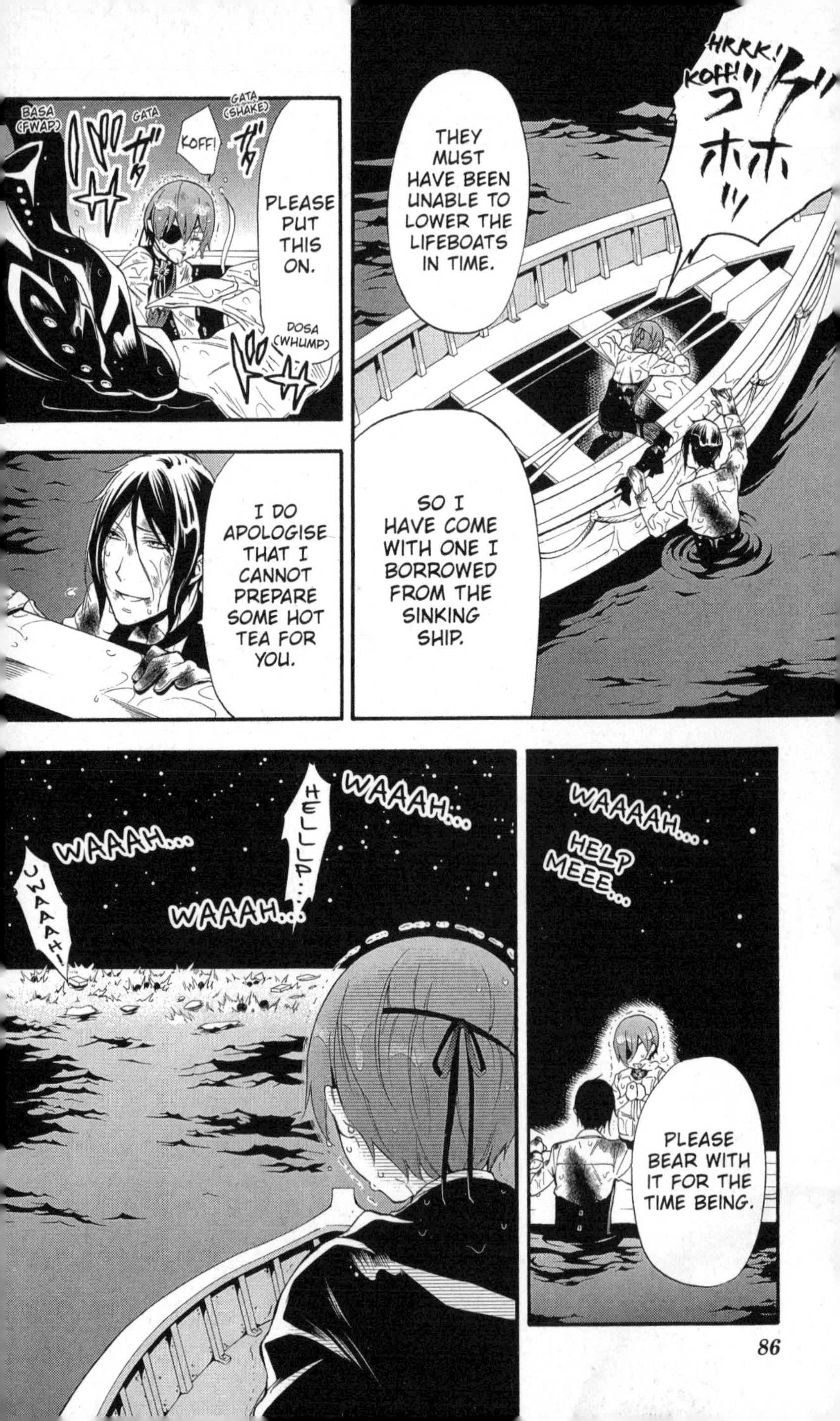
HRRK!
KOFF!
THEY MUST HAVE BEEN UNABLE TO LOWER THE LIFEBOATS IN TIME.
SO I HAVE COME WITH ONE I BORROWED FROM THE SINKING SHIP.
PLEASE PUT THIS ON.
GATA (SHAKE)
KOFF!
GATA
BASA (FWAP)
DOSA (WHUMP)
I DO APOLOGISE THAT I CANNOT PREPARE SOME HOT TEA FOR YOU.
WAAAAH...
HELP MEEE...
PLEASE BEAR WITH IT FOR THE TIME BEING.
WAAAH...
HELLLP...
WAAAH...
WAAAH...
UWAAAH!

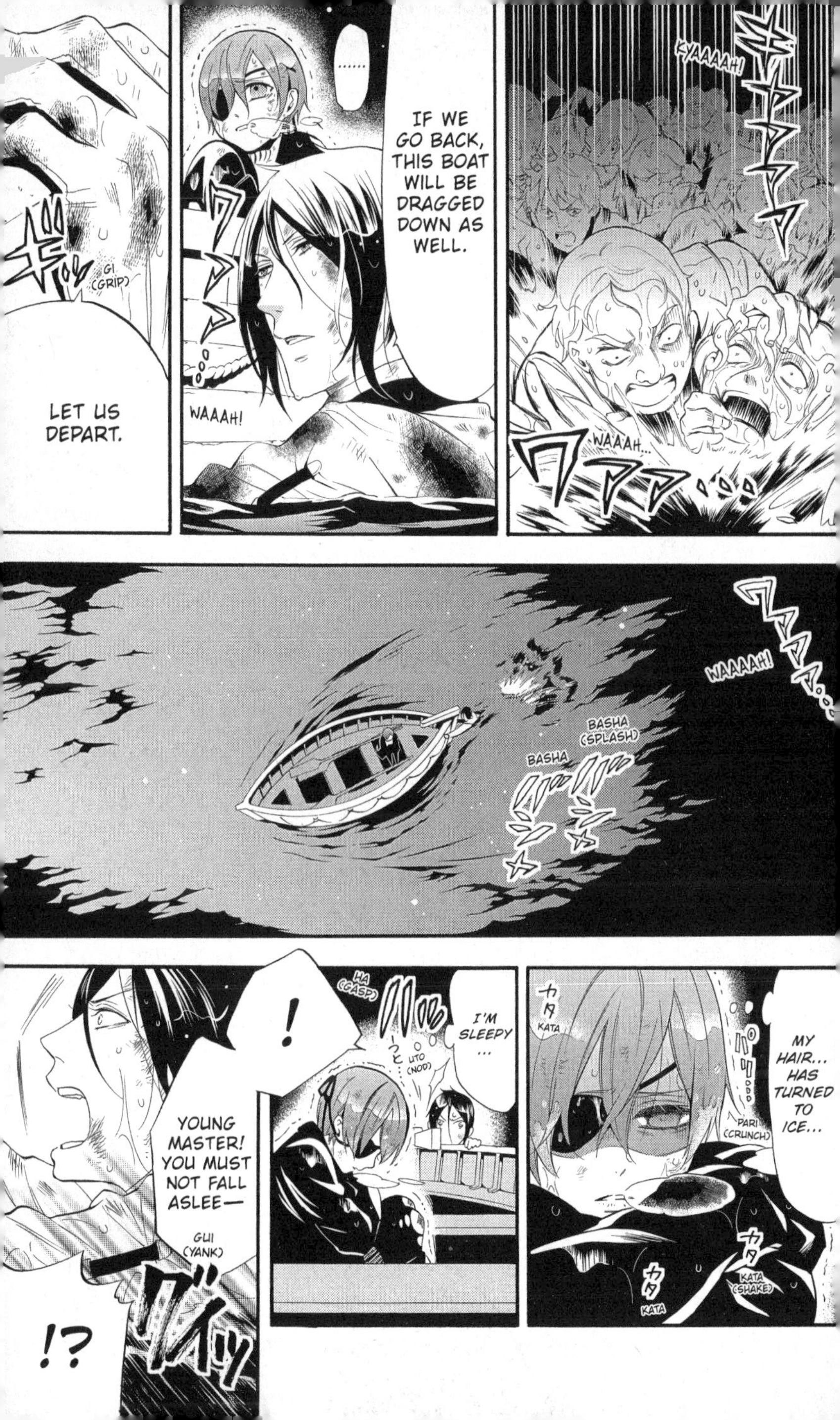
KYAAAAH!
WAAAH...
......
IF WE GO BACK, THIS BOAT WILL BE DRAGGED DOWN AS WELL.
WAAAH!
GI (GRIP)
LET US DEPART.
WAAAAH!
BASHA (SPLASH)
BASHA
MY HAIR... HAS TURNED TO ICE...
PARI (CRUNCH)
KATA
KATA (SHAKE)
KATA
I'M SLEEPY...
HA (GASP)
UTO (NOD)
!
YOUNG MASTER! YOU MUST NOT FALL ASLEE—
GUI (YANK)
!?

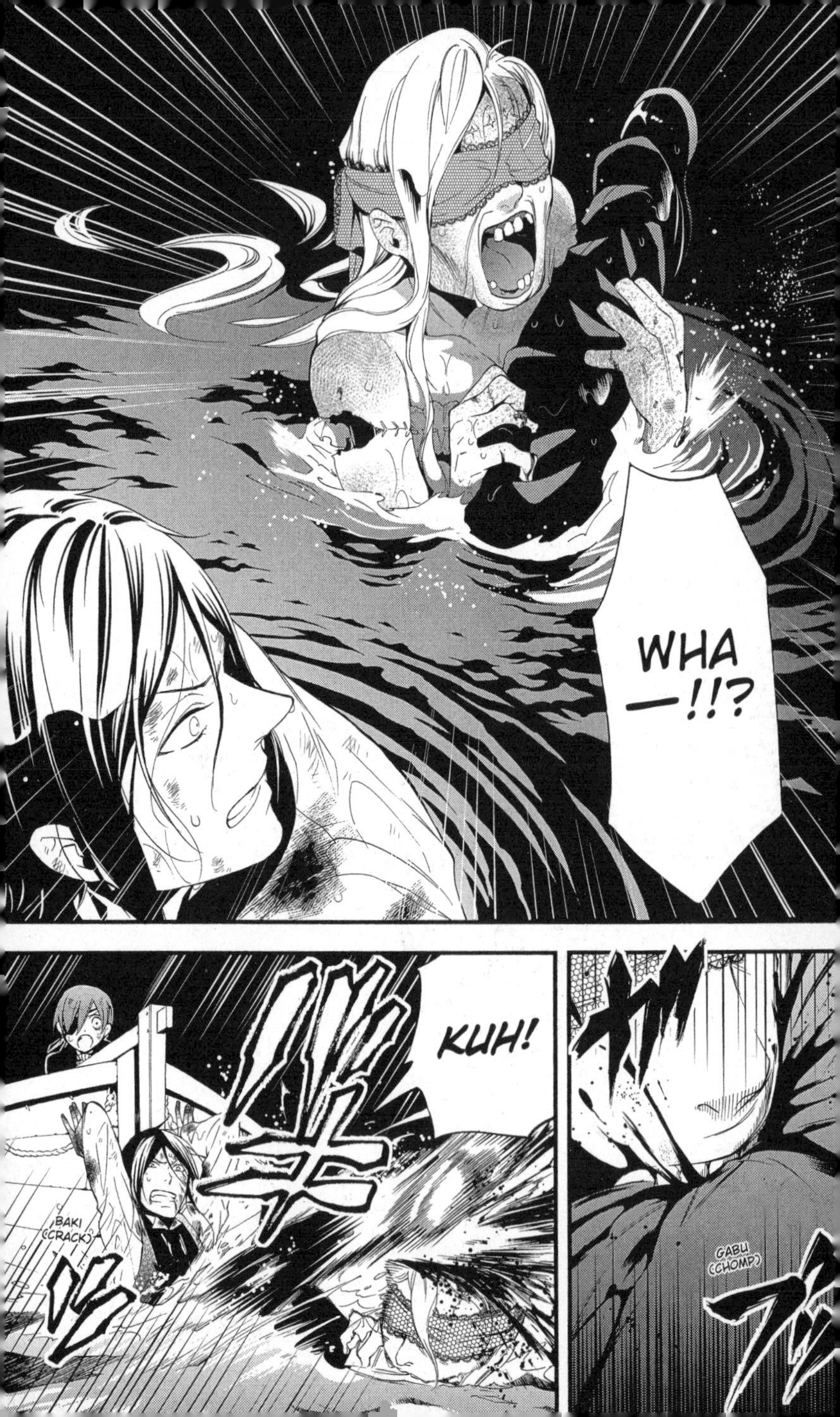
WHA—!!?
GABU (CHOMP)
KUH!
BAKI (CRACK)

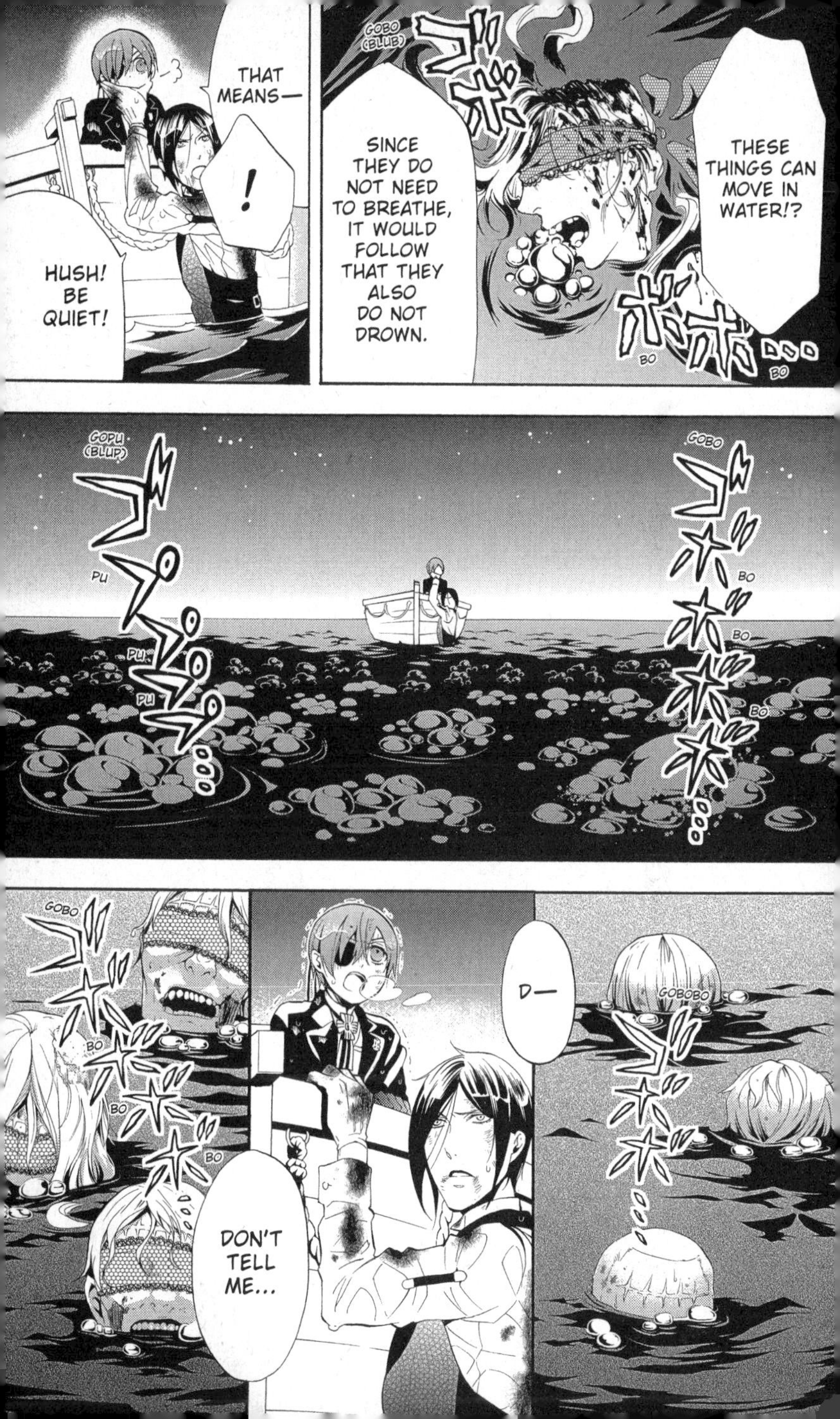
GOBO (BLUB)
THESE THINGS CAN MOVE IN WATER!?
SINCE THEY DO NOT NEED TO BREATHE, IT WOULD FOLLOW THAT THEY ALSO DO NOT DROWN.
BO
BO
THAT MEANS—
!
HUSH! BE QUIET!
GOBO
BO
BO
BO
GOPU (BLUP)
PU
PU
PU
GOBOBO
D—
DON'T TELL ME...
GOBO
BO
BO
BO

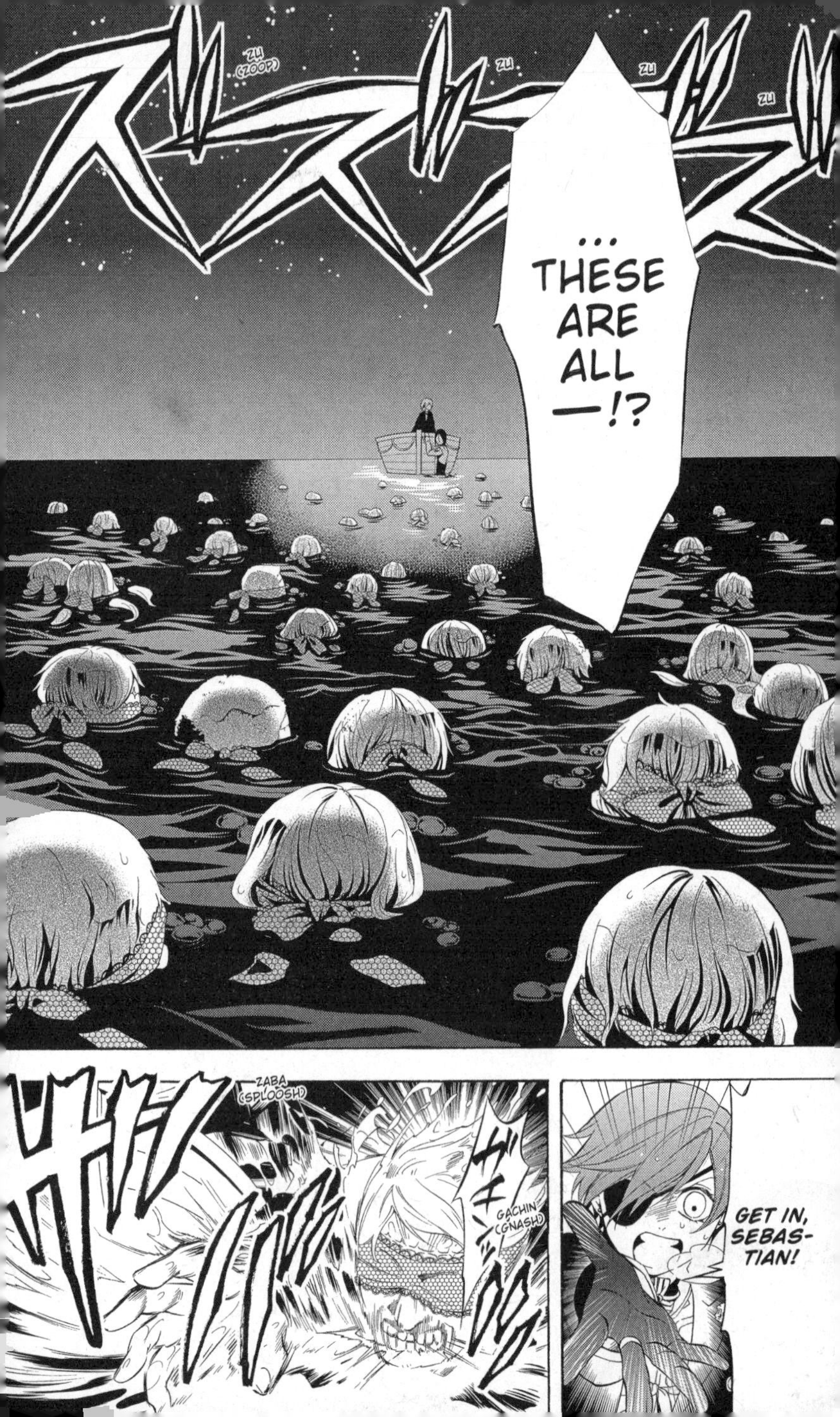
ZU
ZU
ZU
ZU (ZOOP)
... THESE ARE ALL —!?
GET IN, SEBAS- TIAN!
GACHIN (GNASH)
ZABA (SPLOOSH)

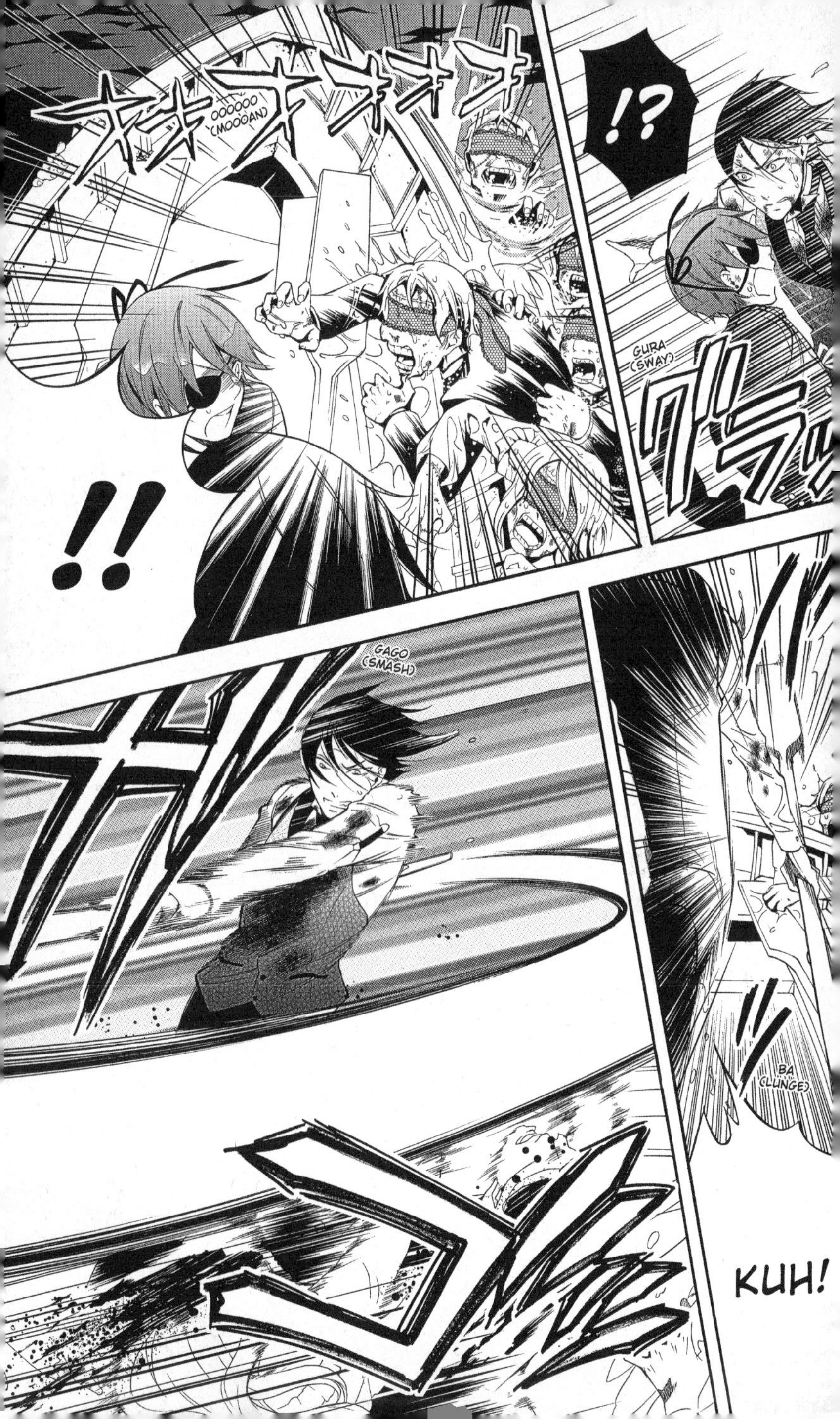
!?
GURA (SWAY)
OOOOOO (MOOOAN)
!!
BA (LUNGE)
KUH!
GAGO (SMASH)

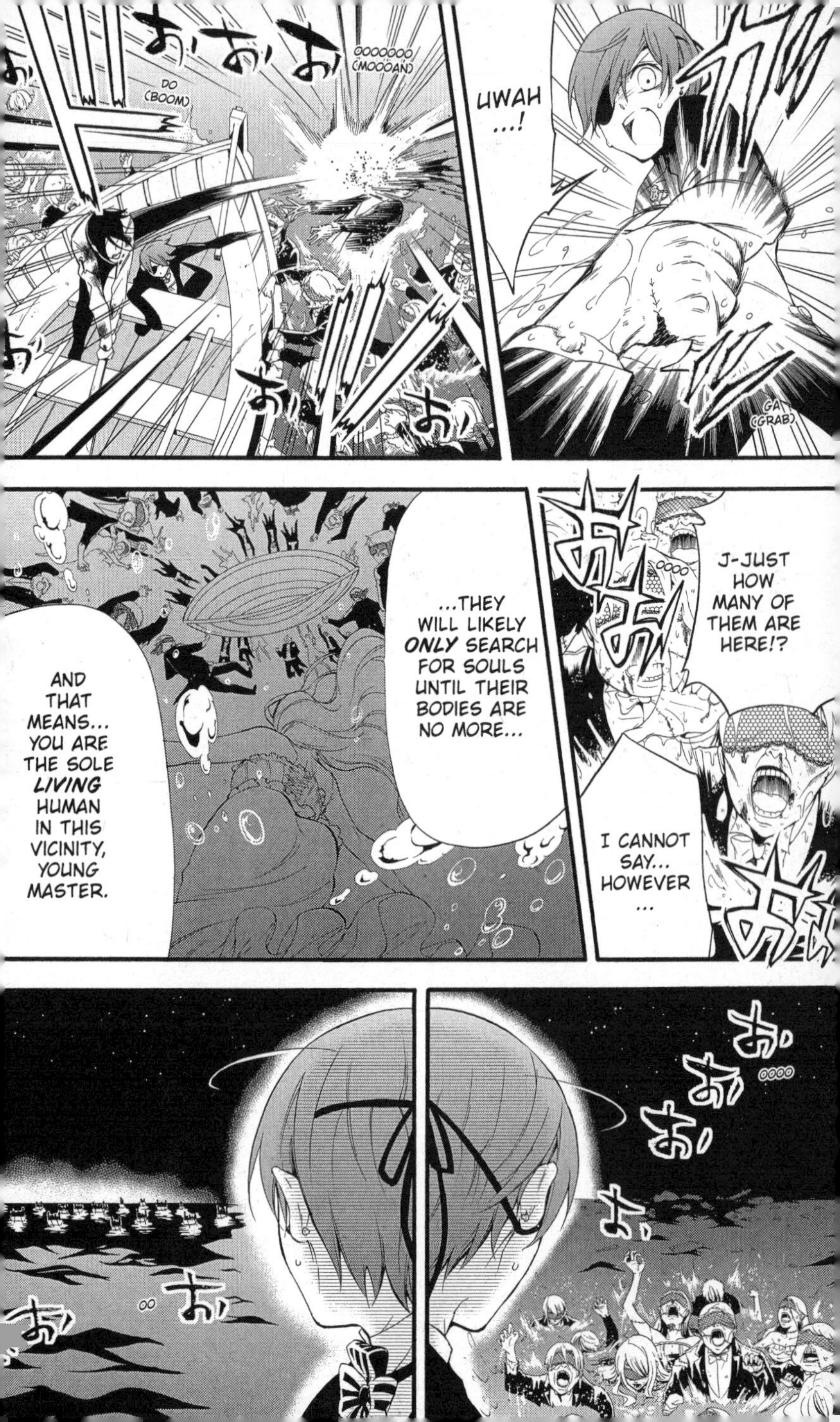
UWAH ...!
GA (GRAB)
OOOOOOO (MOOOAN)
DO (BOOM)
J-JUST HOW MANY OF THEM ARE HERE!?
OOOO
I CANNOT SAY... HOWEVER ...
...THEY WILL LIKELY ONLY SEARCH FOR SOULS UNTIL THEIR BODIES ARE NO MORE...
AND THAT MEANS... YOU ARE THE SOLE LIVING HUMAN IN THIS VICINITY, YOUNG MASTER.
OOOO
OO

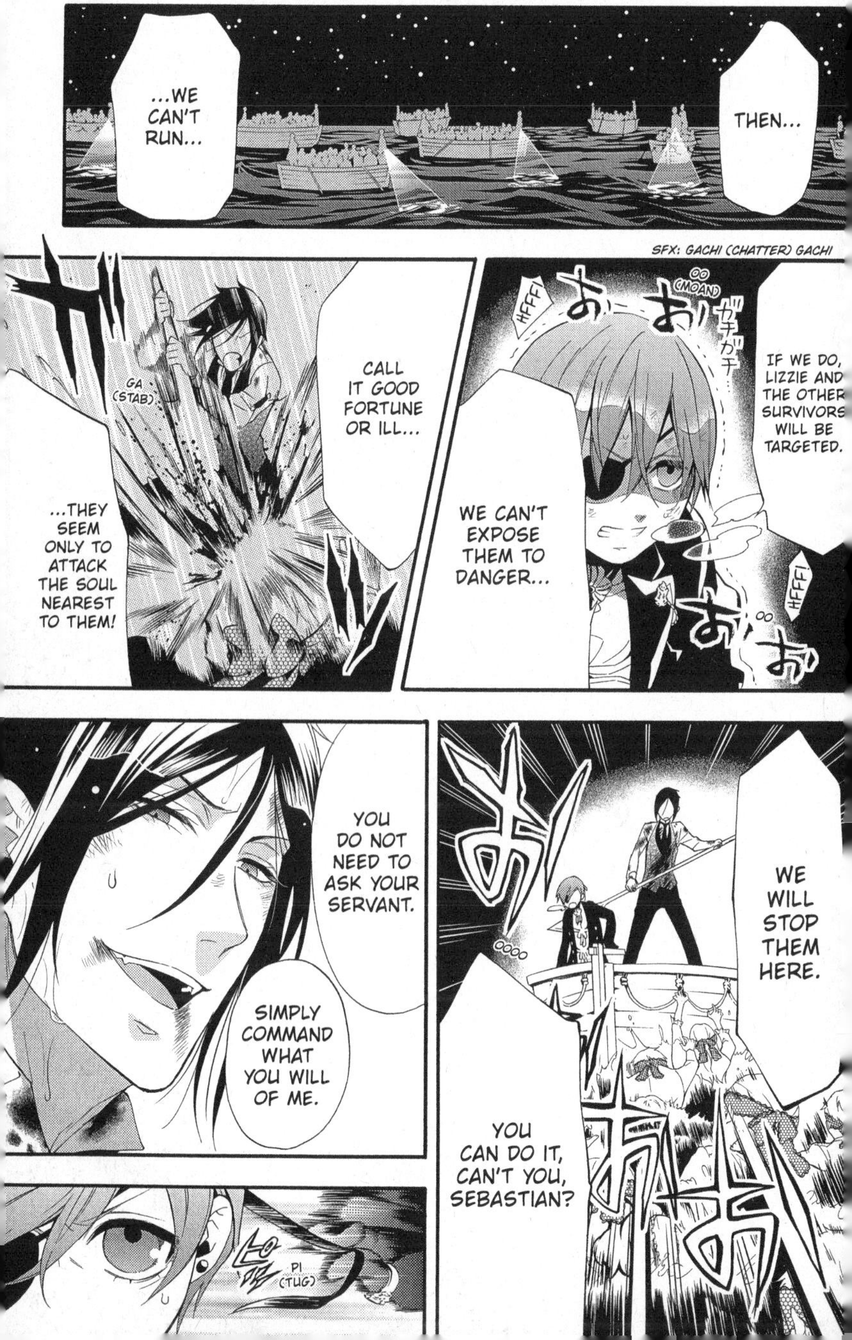
THEN...
...WE CAN'T RUN...
SFX: GACHI (CHATTER) GACHI
OO (MOAN)
HEFF!
IF WE DO, LIZZIE AND THE OTHER SURVIVORS WILL BE TARGETED.
WE CAN'T EXPOSE THEM TO DANGER...
HEFF!
CALL IT GOOD FORTUNE OR ILL...
GA (STAB)
...THEY SEEM ONLY TO ATTACK THE SOUL NEAREST TO THEM!
WE WILL STOP THEM HERE.
OOOO
YOU CAN DO IT, CAN'T YOU, SEBASTIAN?
YOU DO NOT NEED TO ASK YOUR SERVANT.
SIMPLY COMMAND WHAT YOU WILL OF ME.
PI (TUG)

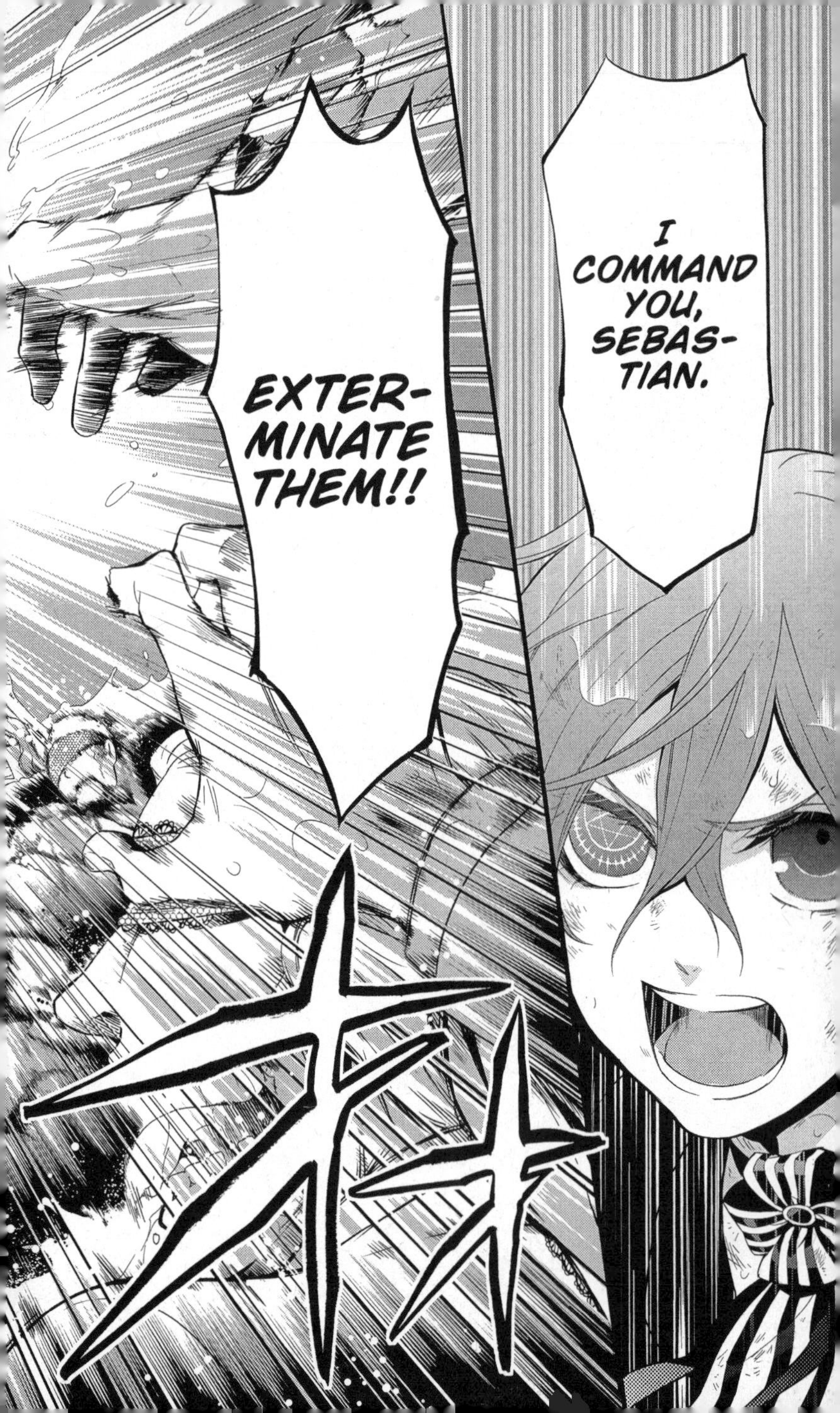
I COMMAND YOU, SEBAS-TIAN.
EXTER-MINATE THEM!!

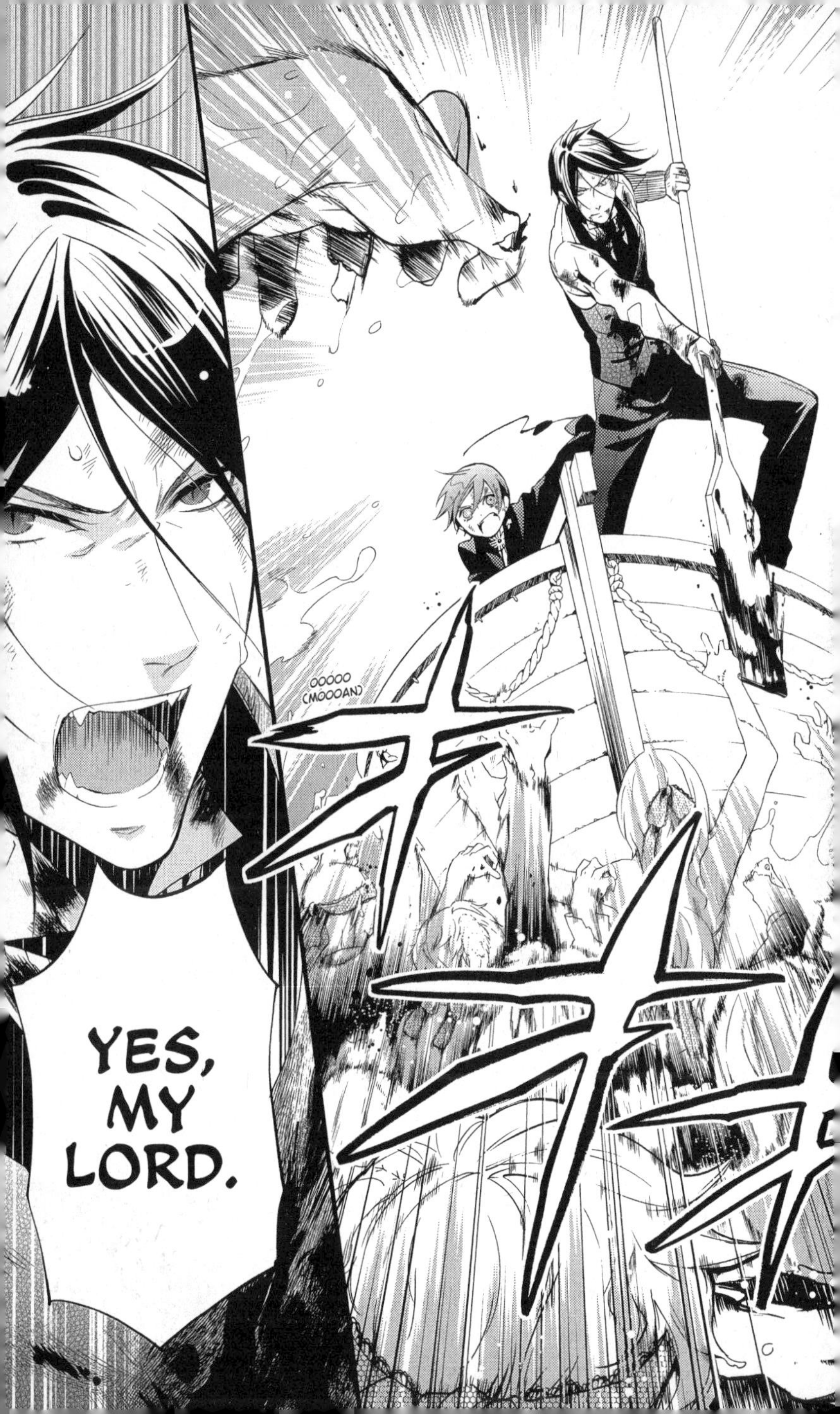
OOOOO
(MOOOAN)
YES, MY LORD.

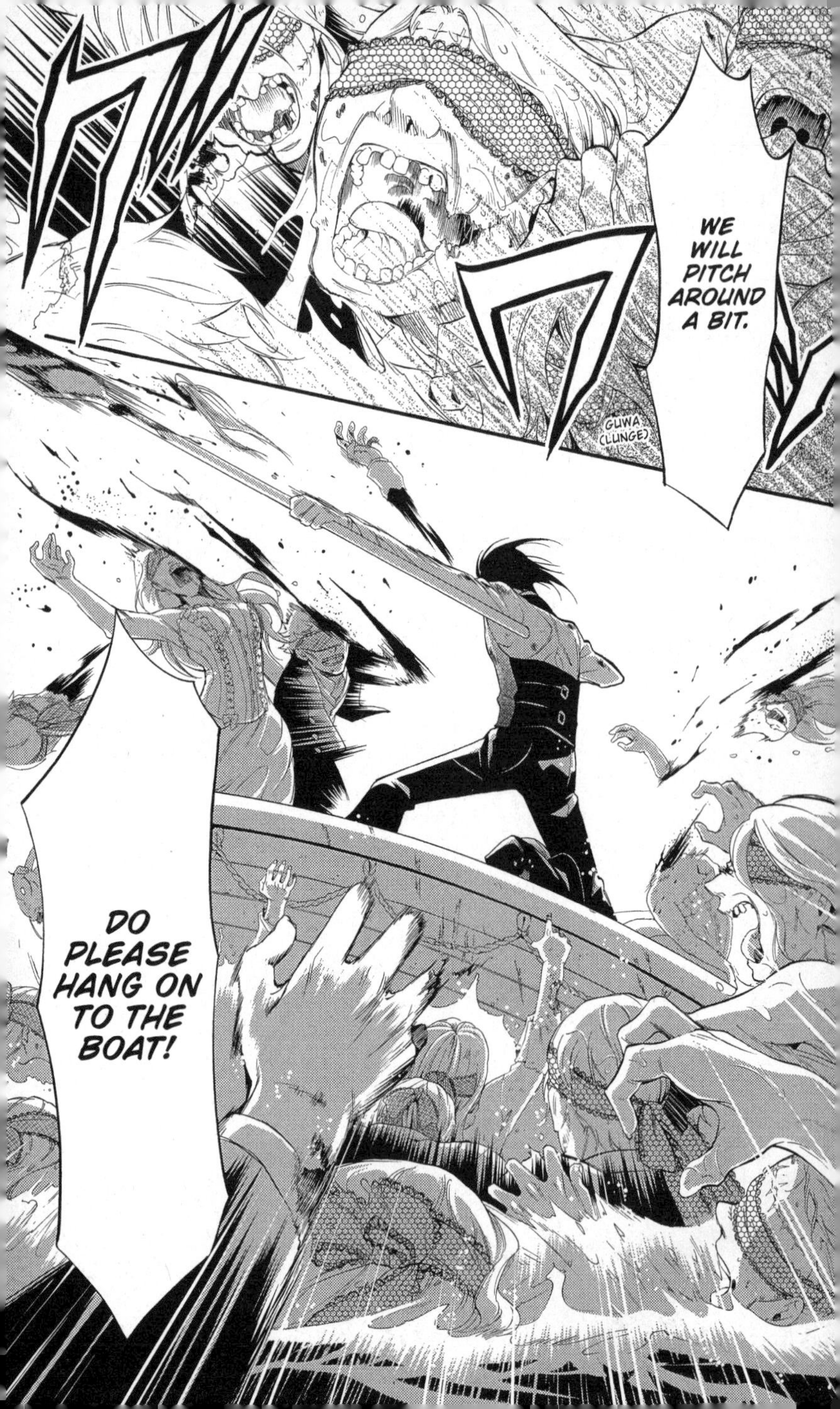
WE WILL PITCH AROUND A BIT.
GUWA (LUNGE)
DO PLEASE HANG ON TO THE BOAT!

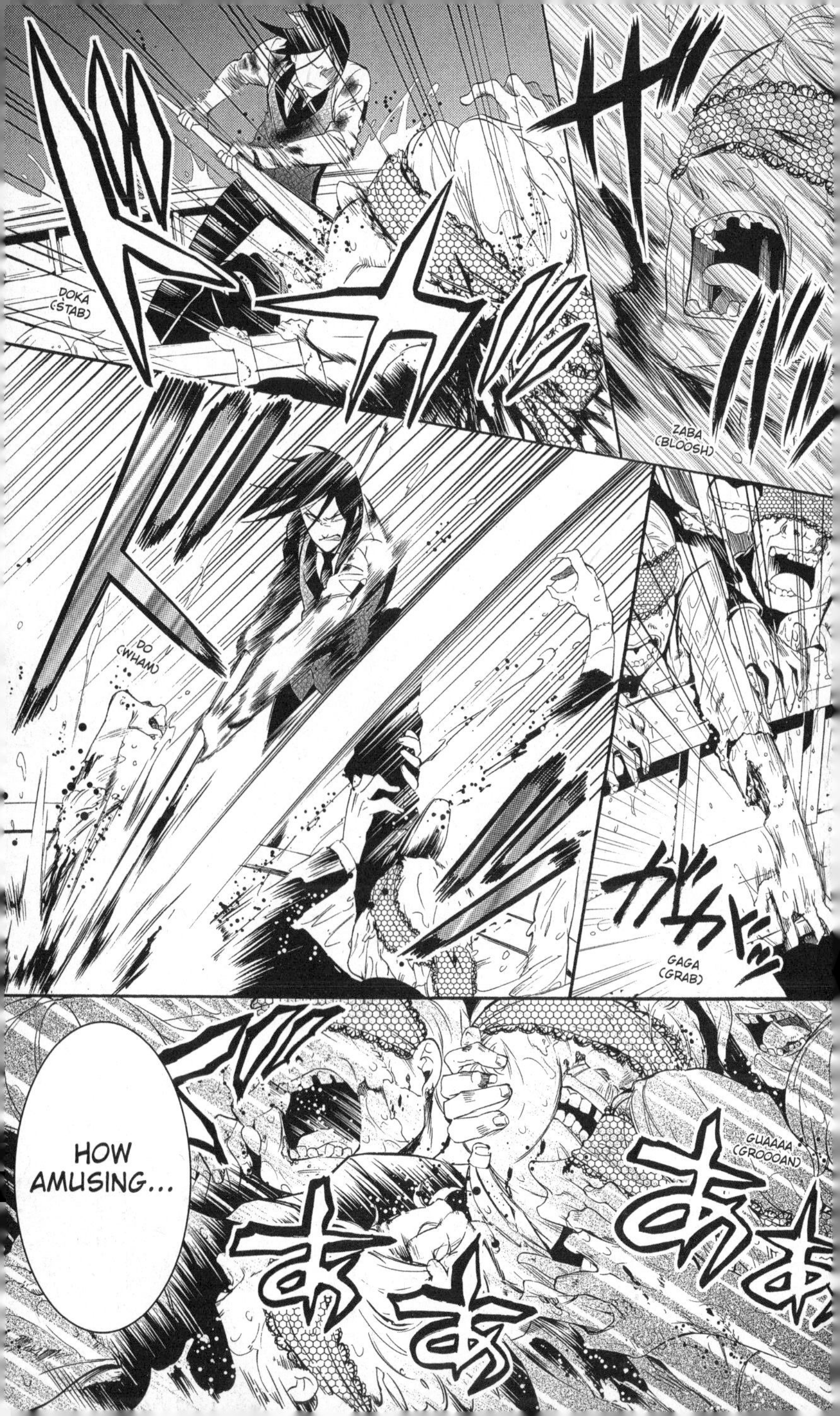
ZABA
(BLOOSH)
DOKA
(STAB)
GAGA
(GRAB)
DO
(WHAM)
GUAAAA
(GROOOAN)
HOW AMUSING...

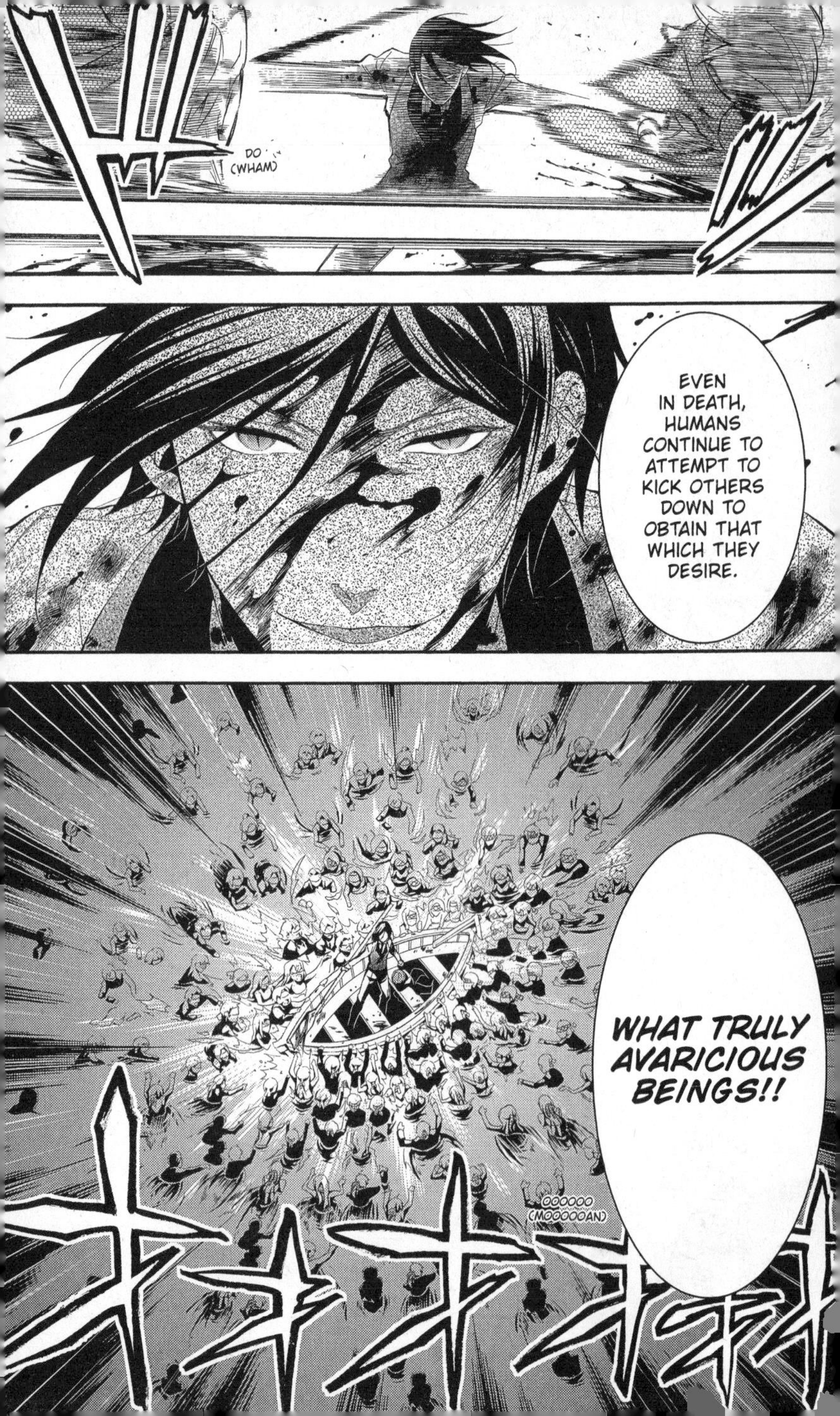
DO (WHAM)
EVEN IN DEATH, HUMANS CONTINUE TO ATTEMPT TO KICK OTHERS DOWN TO OBTAIN THAT WHICH THEY DESIRE.
WHAT TRULY AVARICIOUS BEINGS!!
OOOOOO (MOOOOOAN)

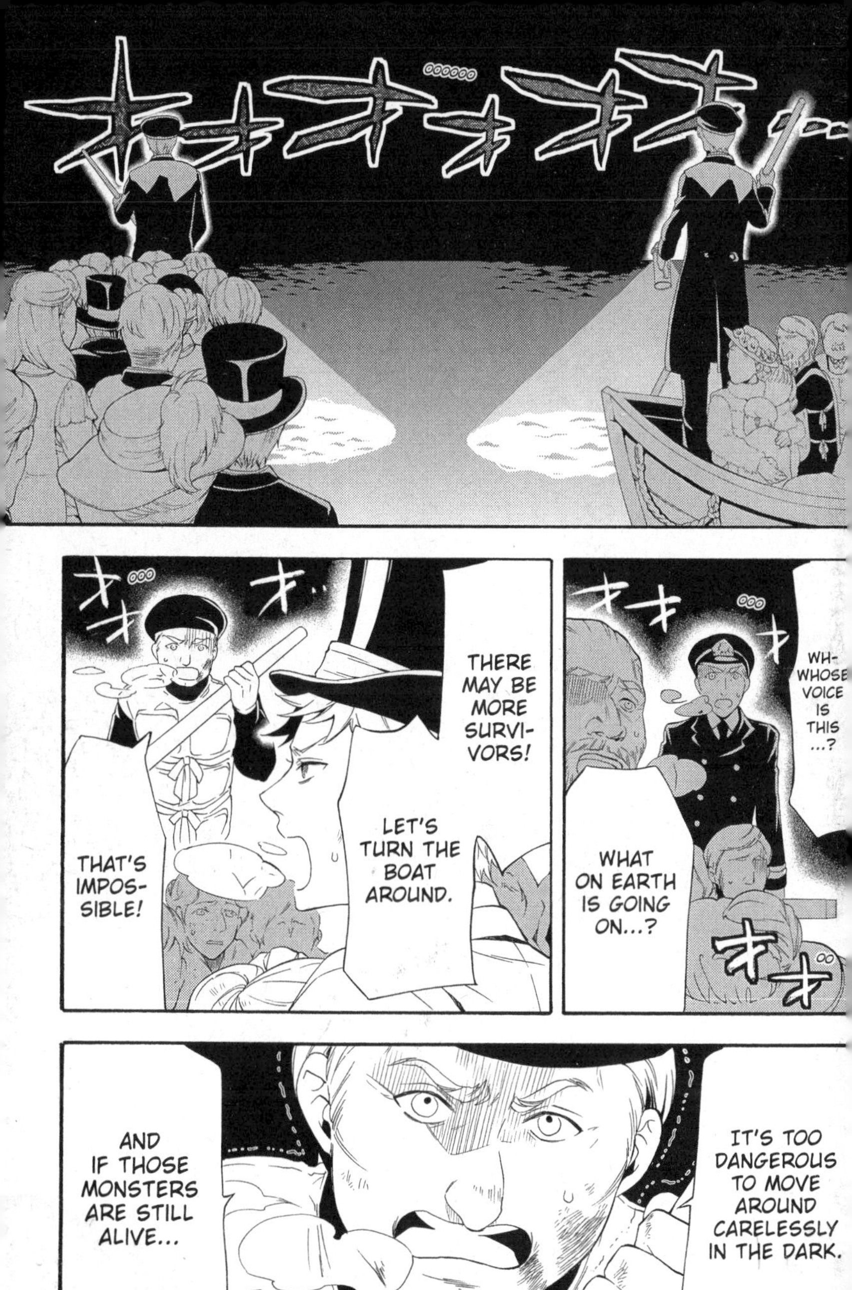
OOOOOO
OOO
WH-WHOSE VOICE IS THIS ...?
WHAT ON EARTH IS GOING ON...?
OO
THERE MAY BE MORE SURVI-VORS!
LET'S TURN THE BOAT AROUND.
OOO
THAT'S IMPOS-SIBLE!
IT'S TOO DANGEROUS TO MOVE AROUND CARELESSLY IN THE DARK.
AND IF THOSE MONSTERS ARE STILL ALIVE...

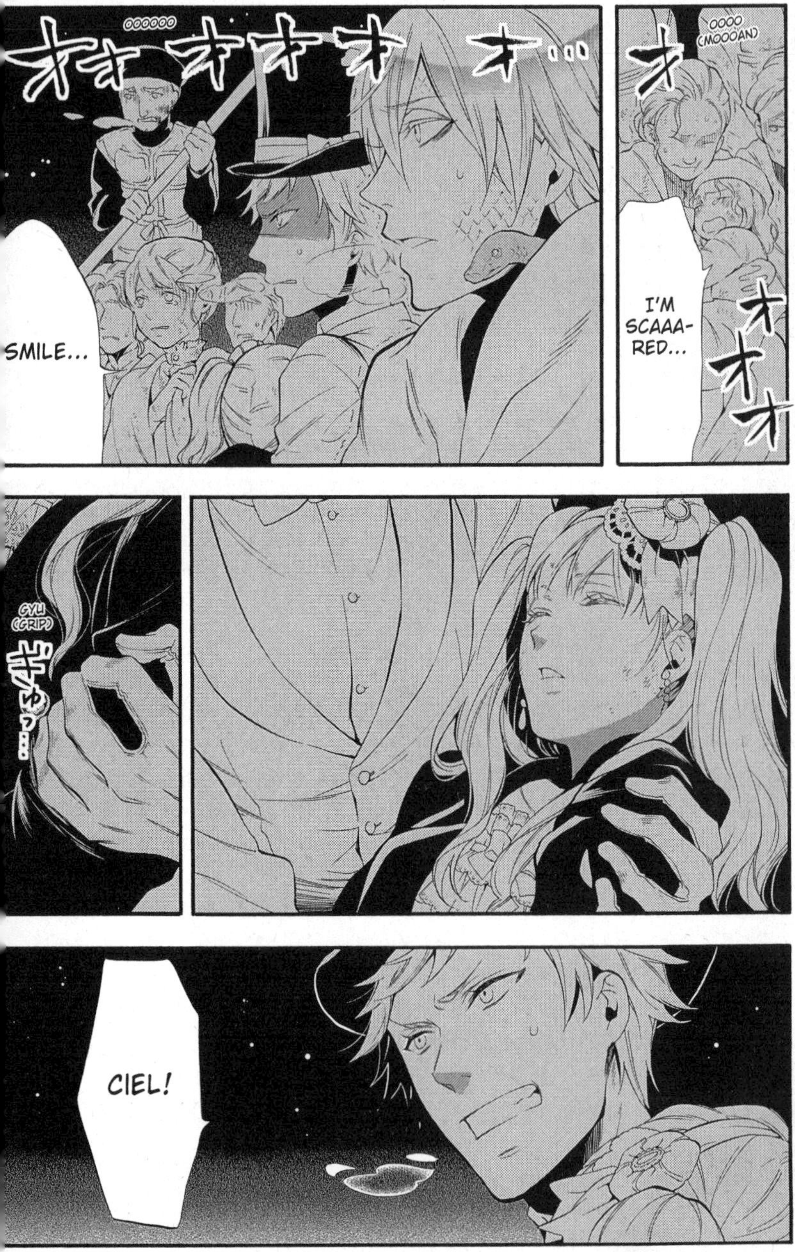
OOOO (MOOOAN)
I'M SCAAA-RED...
OOOOOO
SMILE...
GYU (GRIP)
CIEL!

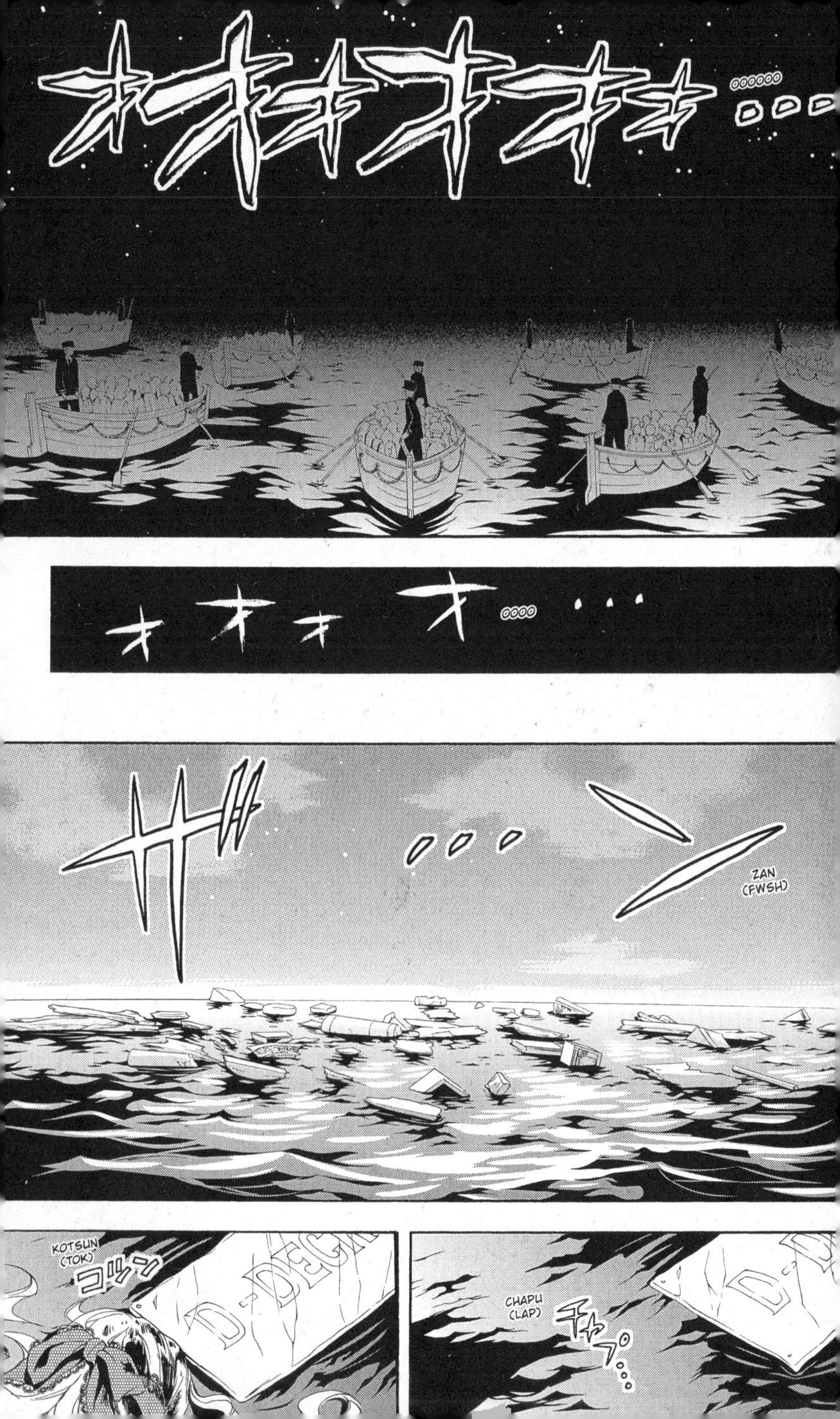
ZAN
(FWSH)
CHAPU
(LAP)
KOTSUN
(TOK)

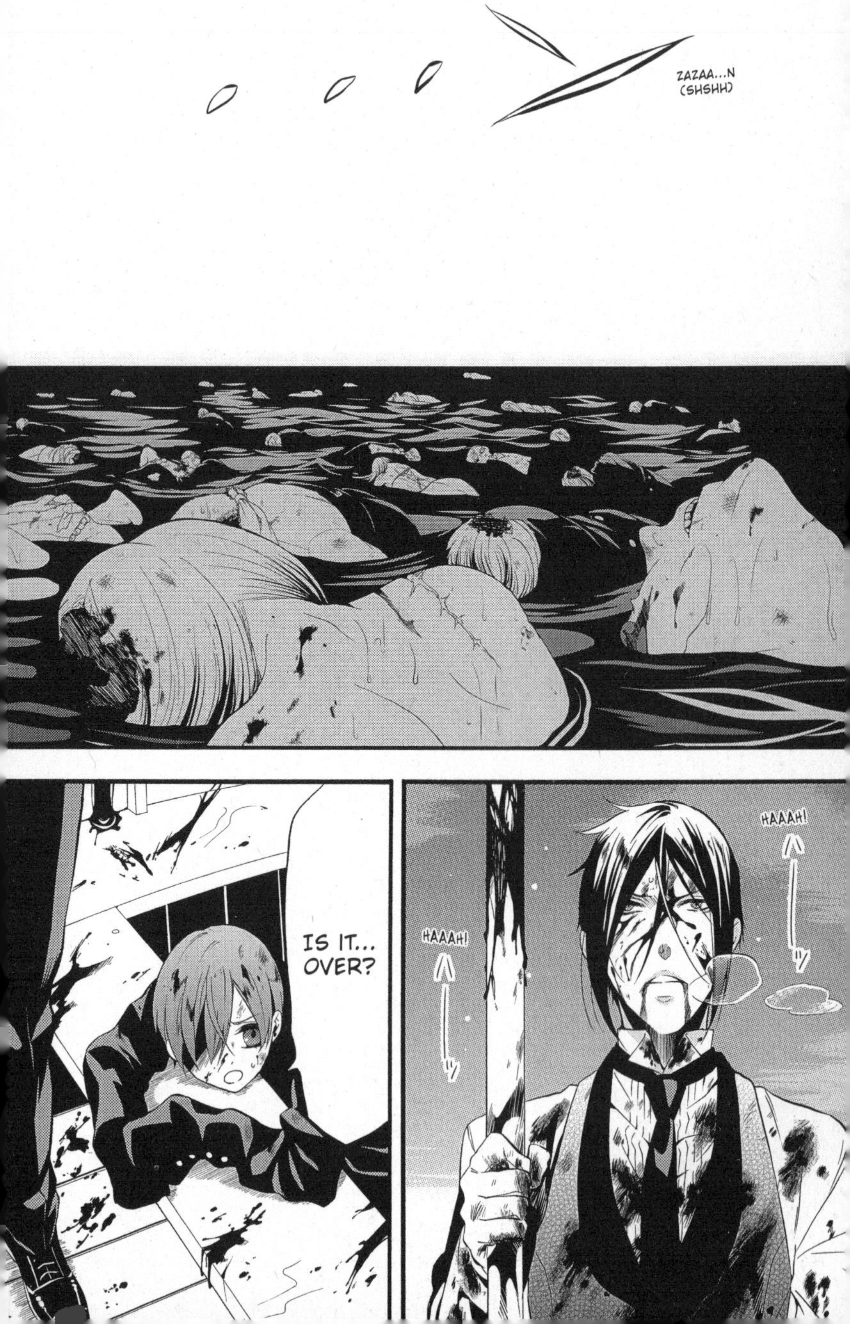
ZAZAA...N
(SHSHH)
HAAAH!
HAAAH!
IS IT... OVER?

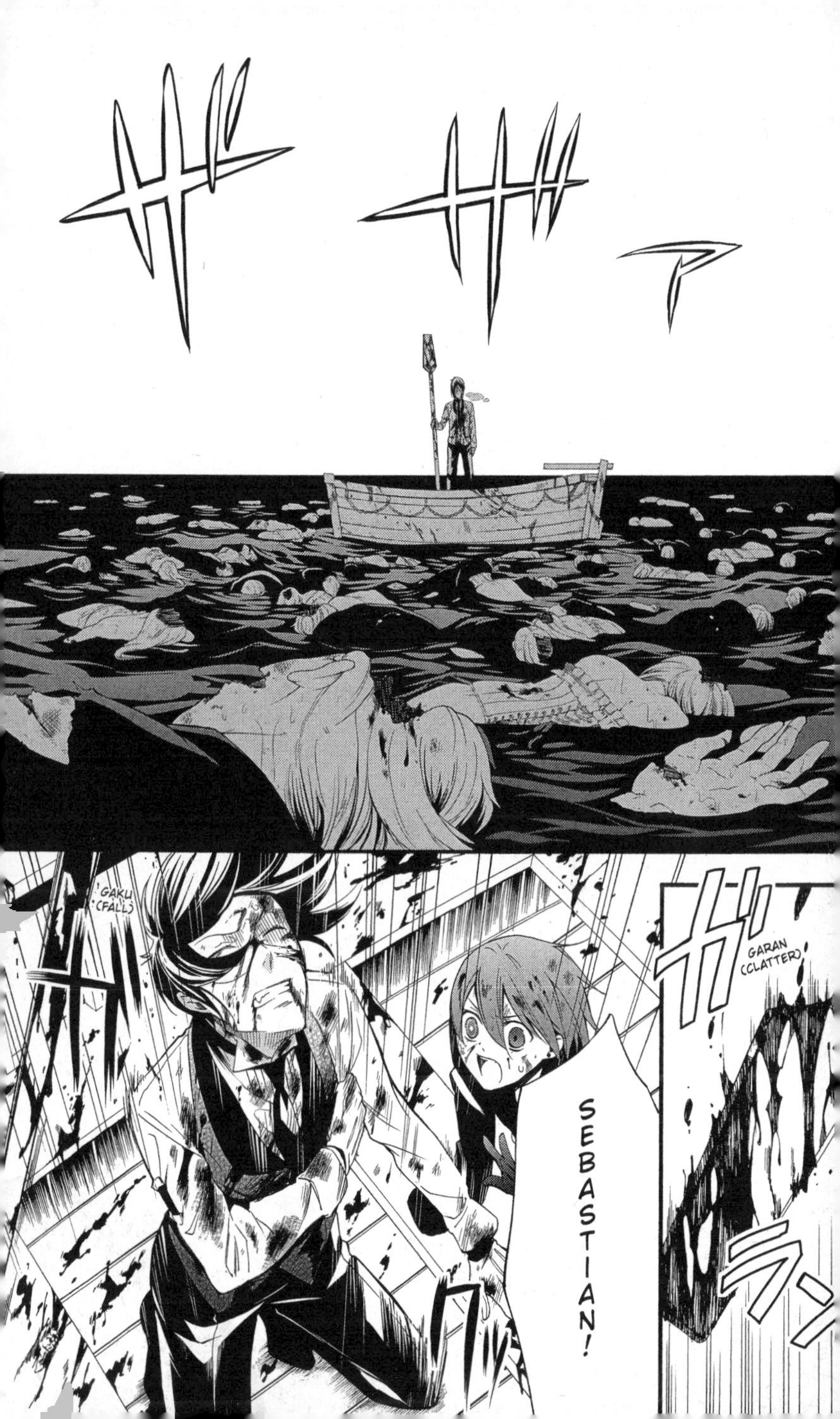
GARAN (CLATTER)
SEBASTIAN!
GAKU (FALL)

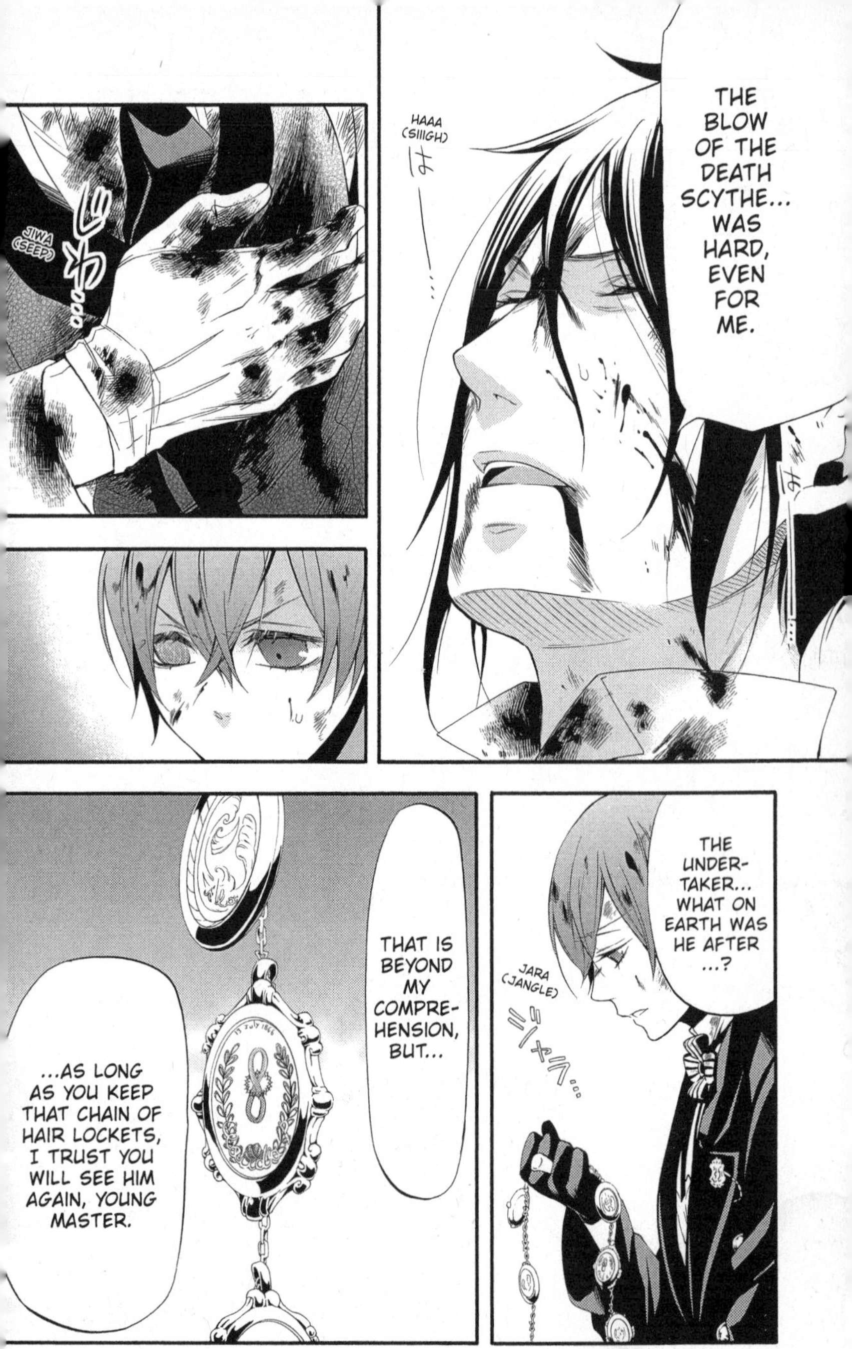
THE BLOW OF THE DEATH SCYTHE... WAS HARD, EVEN FOR ME.
HAAA (SIIGH)
は
JIWA (SEEP)
THE UNDER-TAKER... WHAT ON EARTH WAS HE AFTER ...?
JARA (JANGLE)
THAT IS BEYOND MY COMPRE-HENSION, BUT...
...AS LONG AS YOU KEEP THAT CHAIN OF HAIR LOCKETS, I TRUST YOU WILL SEE HIM AGAIN, YOUNG MASTER.

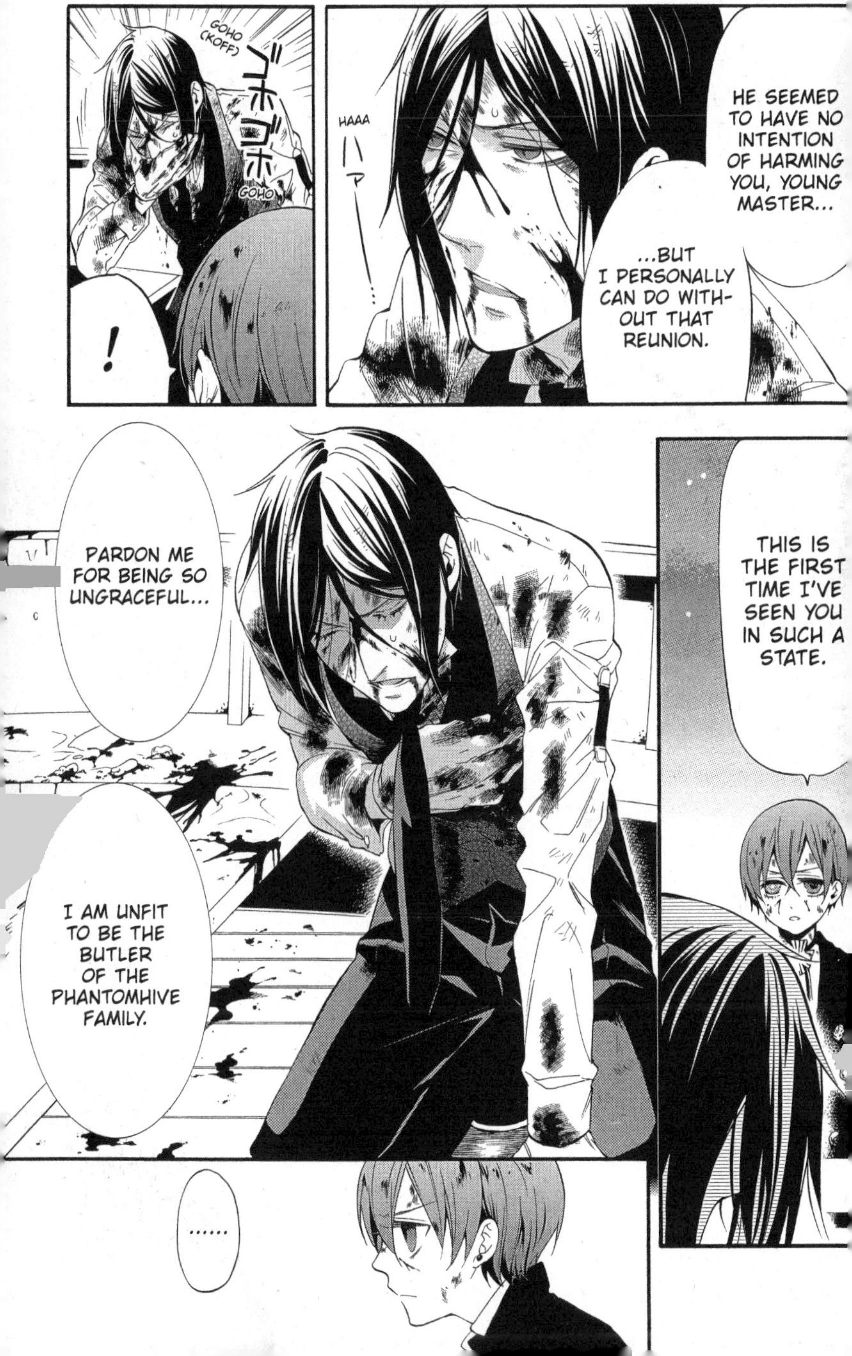
HE SEEMED TO HAVE NO INTENTION OF HARMING YOU, YOUNG MASTER...
...BUT I PERSONALLY CAN DO WITH-OUT THAT REUNION.
HAAA
ハァ
GOHO (KOFF)
ゴホゴホ
GOHO
!
THIS IS THE FIRST TIME I'VE SEEN YOU IN SUCH A STATE.
PARDON ME FOR BEING SO UNGRACEFUL...
I AM UNFIT TO BE THE BUTLER OF THE PHANTOMHIVE FAMILY.
......

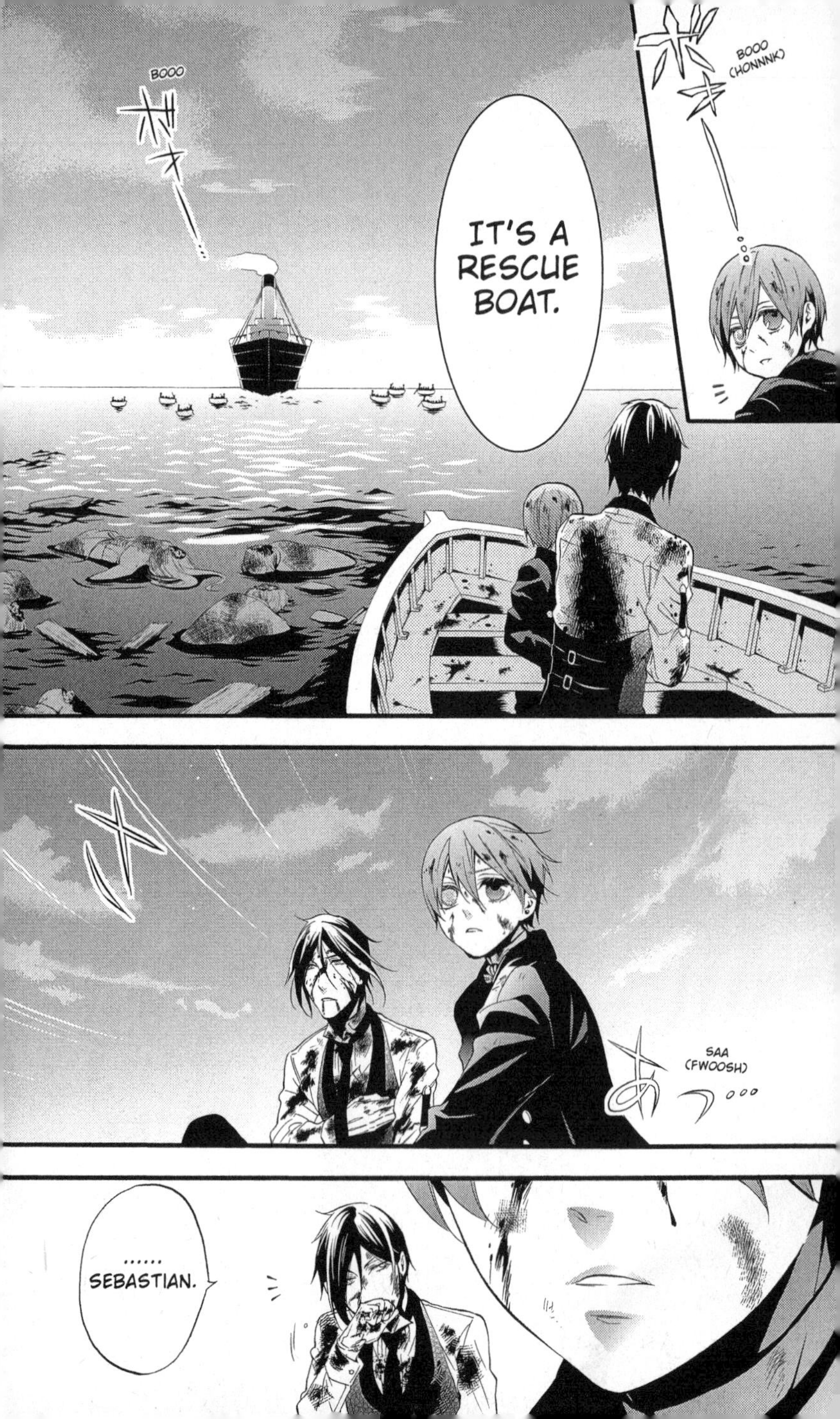
BOOO (HONNNK)
IT'S A RESCUE BOAT.
BOOO
SAA (FWOOSH)
...... SEBASTIAN.

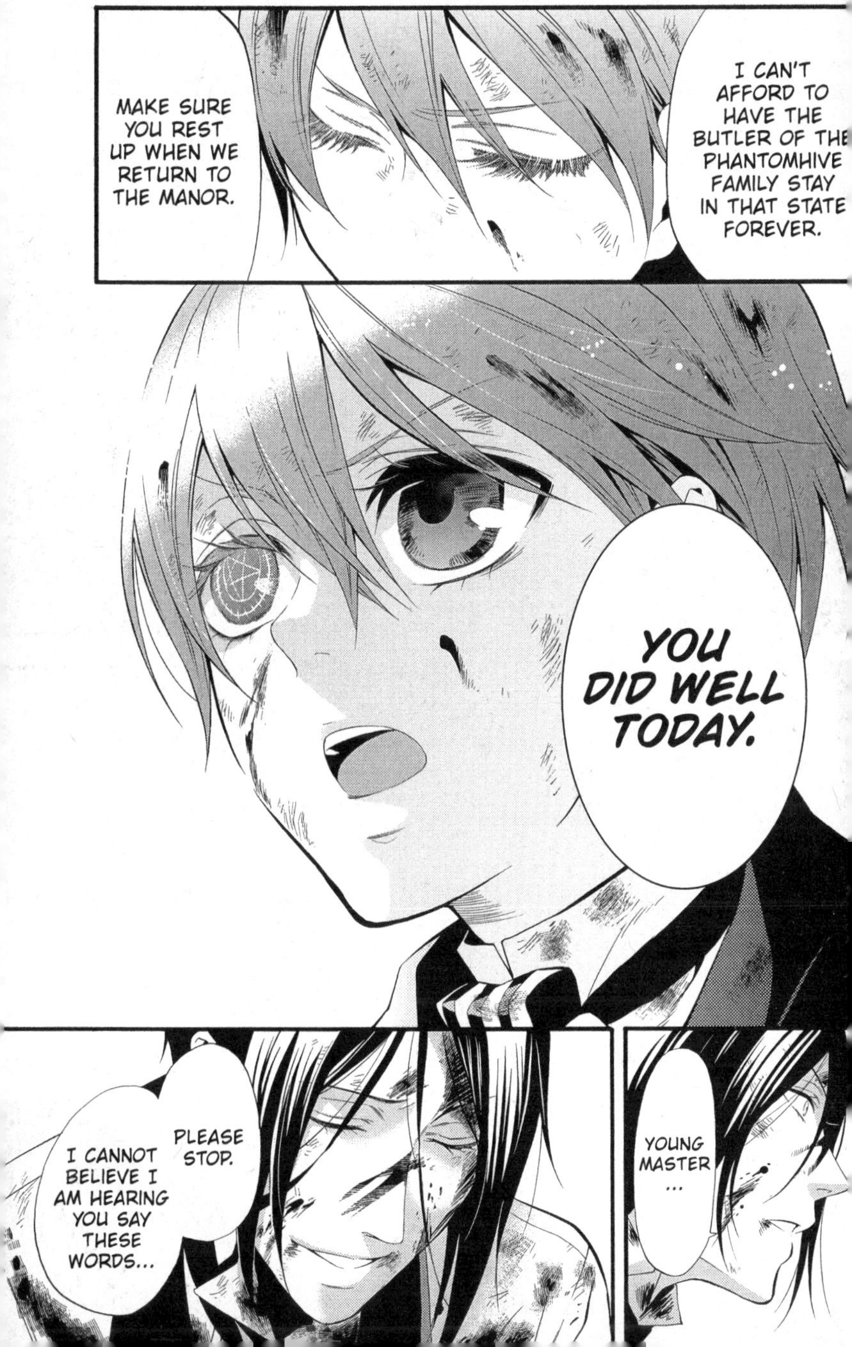
I CAN'T AFFORD TO HAVE THE BUTLER OF THE PHANTOMHIVE FAMILY STAY IN THAT STATE FOREVER.
MAKE SURE YOU REST UP WHEN WE RETURN TO THE MANOR.
YOU DID WELL TODAY.
YOUNG MASTER ...
PLEASE STOP.
I CANNOT BELIEVE I AM HEARING YOU SAY THESE WORDS...

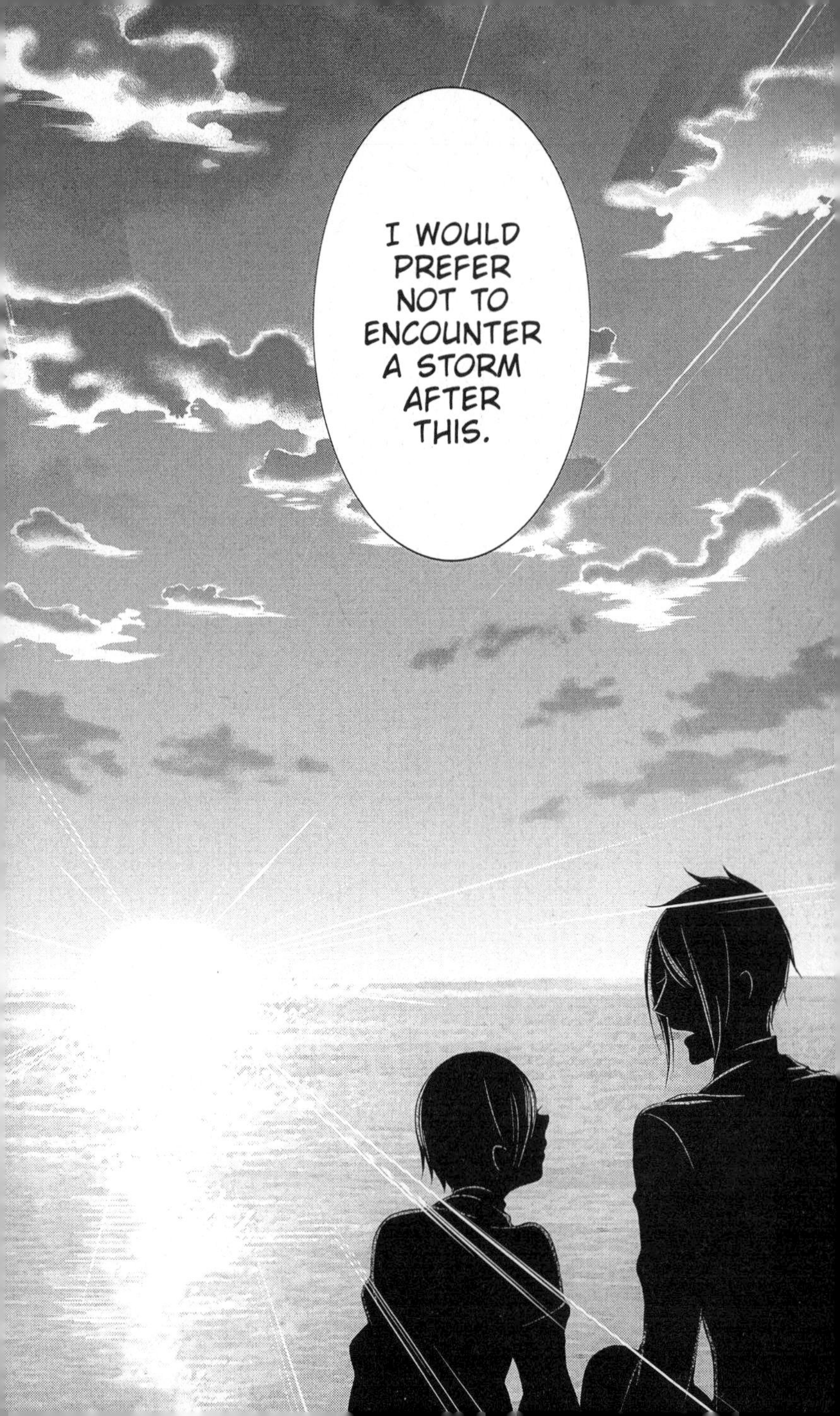
I WOULD PREFER NOT TO ENCOUNTER A STORM AFTER THIS.

Black Butler

Chapter 66

At night : The Butler, Frenzied

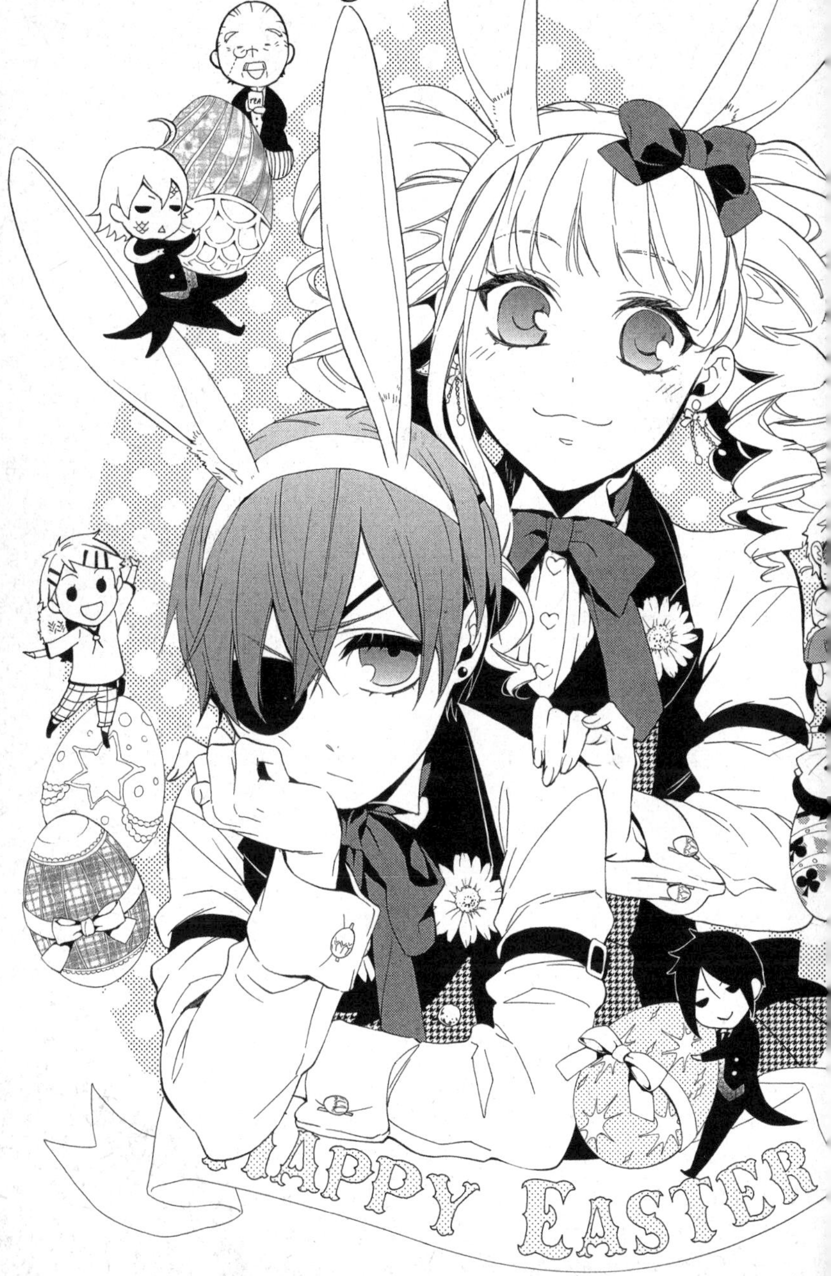
HAPPY EASTER

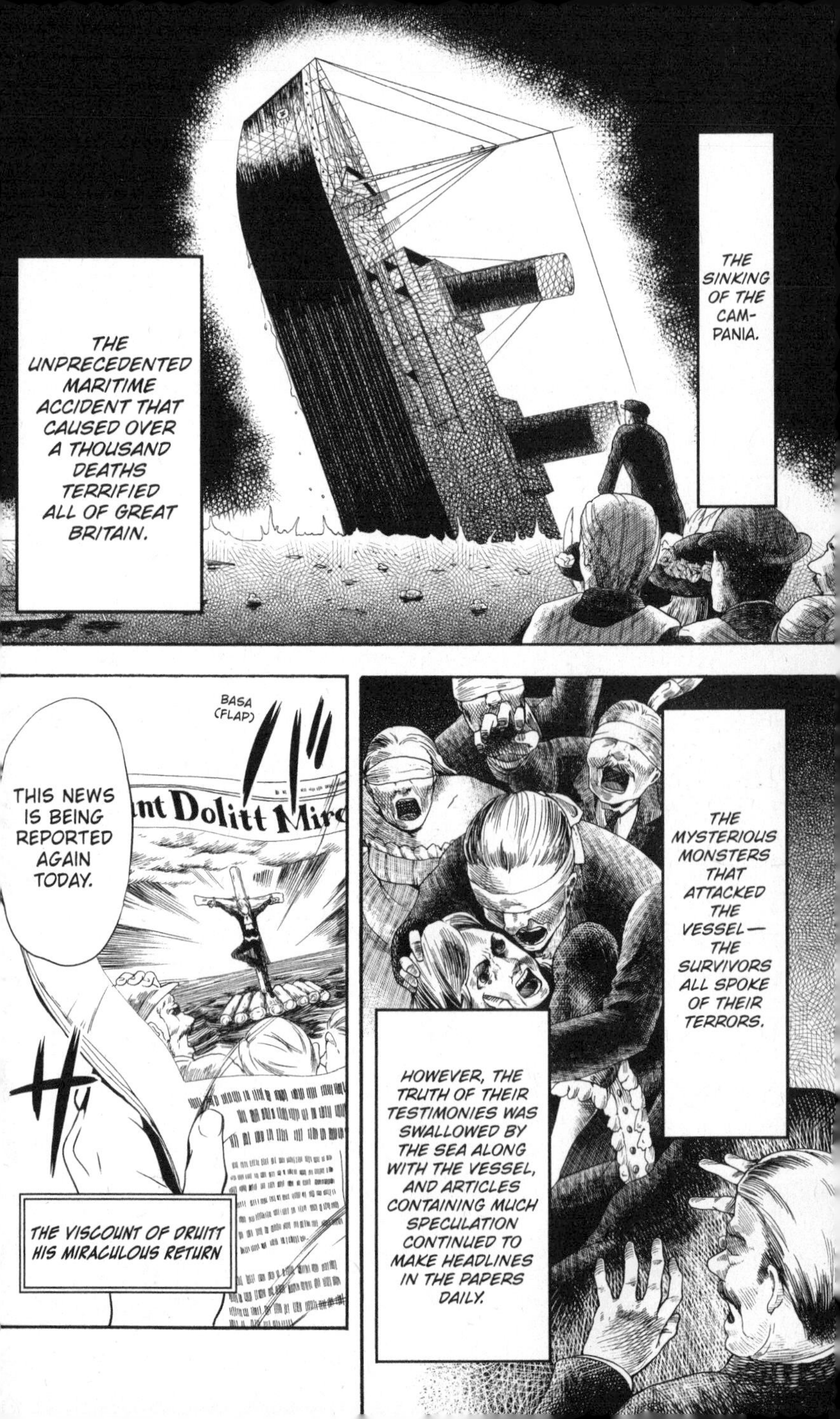
THE SINKING OF THE CAM-PANIA.
THE UNPRECEDENTED MARITIME ACCIDENT THAT CAUSED OVER A THOUSAND DEATHS TERRIFIED ALL OF GREAT BRITAIN.
THE MYSTERIOUS MONSTERS THAT ATTACKED THE VESSEL—THE SURVIVORS ALL SPOKE OF THEIR TERRORS.
HOWEVER, THE TRUTH OF THEIR TESTIMONIES WAS SWALLOWED BY THE SEA ALONG WITH THE VESSEL, AND ARTICLES CONTAINING MUCH SPECULATION CONTINUED TO MAKE HEADLINES IN THE PAPERS DAILY.
BASA (FLAP)
THIS NEWS IS BEING REPORTED AGAIN TODAY.
unt Dolitt Mirc
THE VISCOUNT OF DRUITT HIS MIRACULOUS RETURN

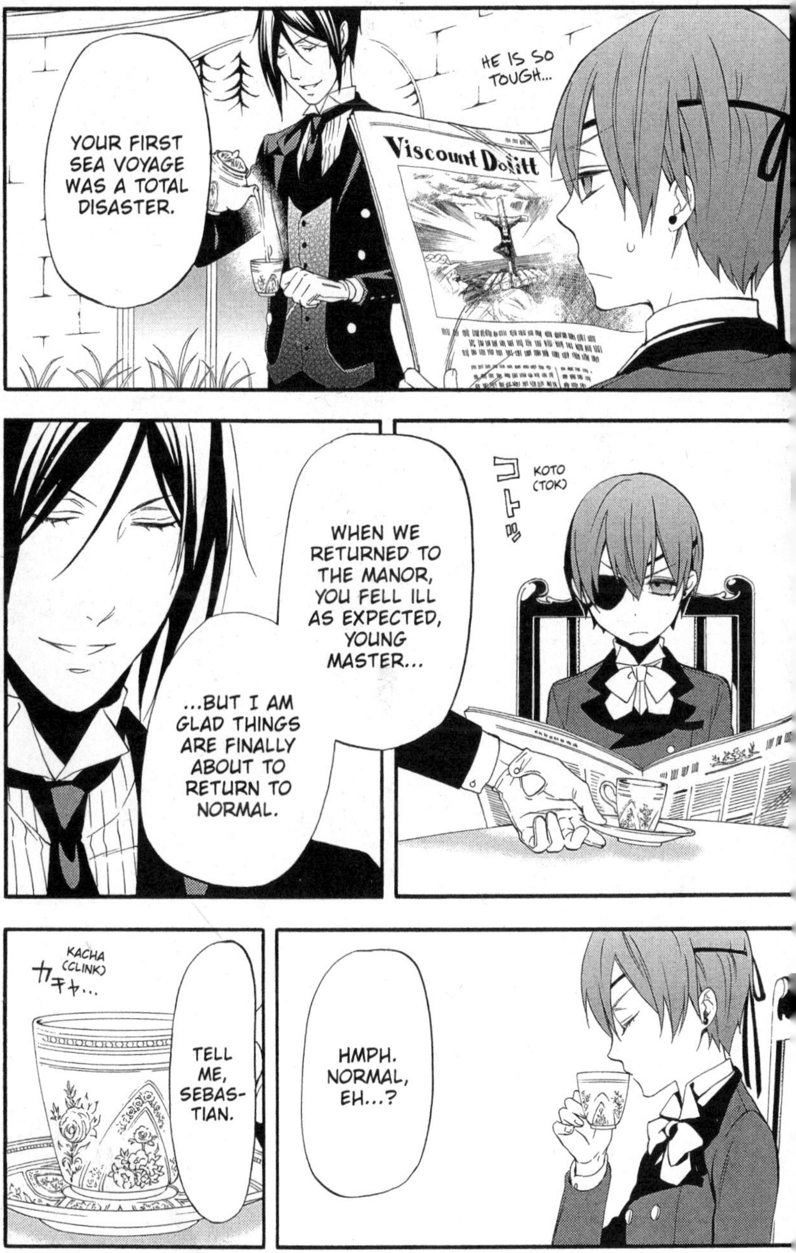
HE IS SO TOUGH...
YOUR FIRST SEA VOYAGE WAS A TOTAL DISASTER.
Viscount
コト
KOTO (TOK)
WHEN WE RETURNED TO THE MANOR, YOU FELL ILL AS EXPECTED, YOUNG MASTER...
...BUT I AM GLAD THINGS ARE FINALLY ABOUT TO RETURN TO NORMAL.
HMPH. NORMAL, EH...?
カチャ...
KACHA (CLINK)
TELL ME, SEBASTIAN.

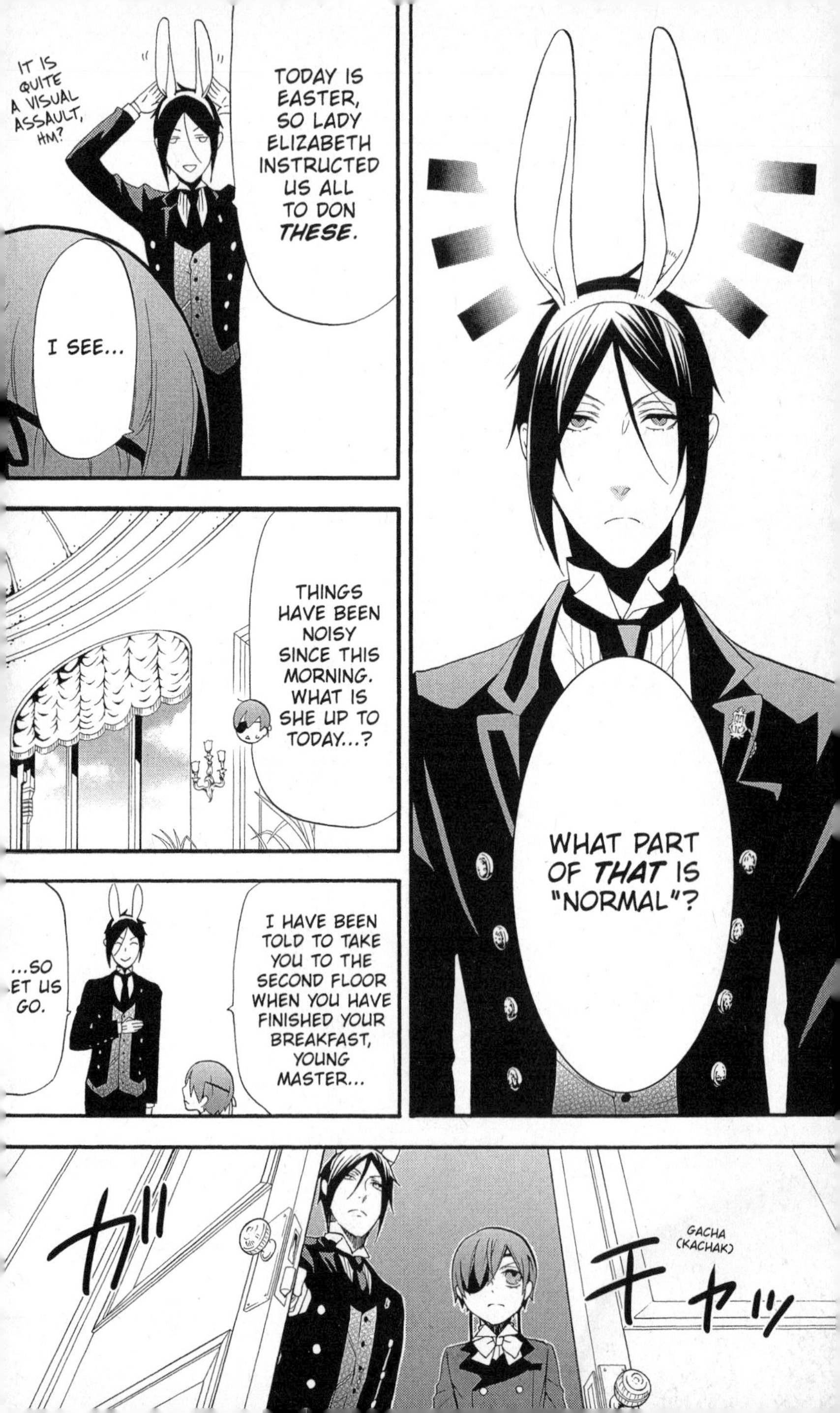
WHAT PART OF THAT IS "NORMAL"?
TODAY IS EASTER, SO LADY ELIZABETH INSTRUCTED US ALL TO DON THESE.
IT IS QUITE A VISUAL ASSAULT, HM?
I SEE...
THINGS HAVE BEEN NOISY SINCE THIS MORNING. WHAT IS SHE UP TO TODAY...?
I HAVE BEEN TOLD TO TAKE YOU TO THE SECOND FLOOR WHEN YOU HAVE FINISHED YOUR BREAKFAST, YOUNG MASTER...
...SO ET US GO.
ガチャッ
GACHA (KACHAK)

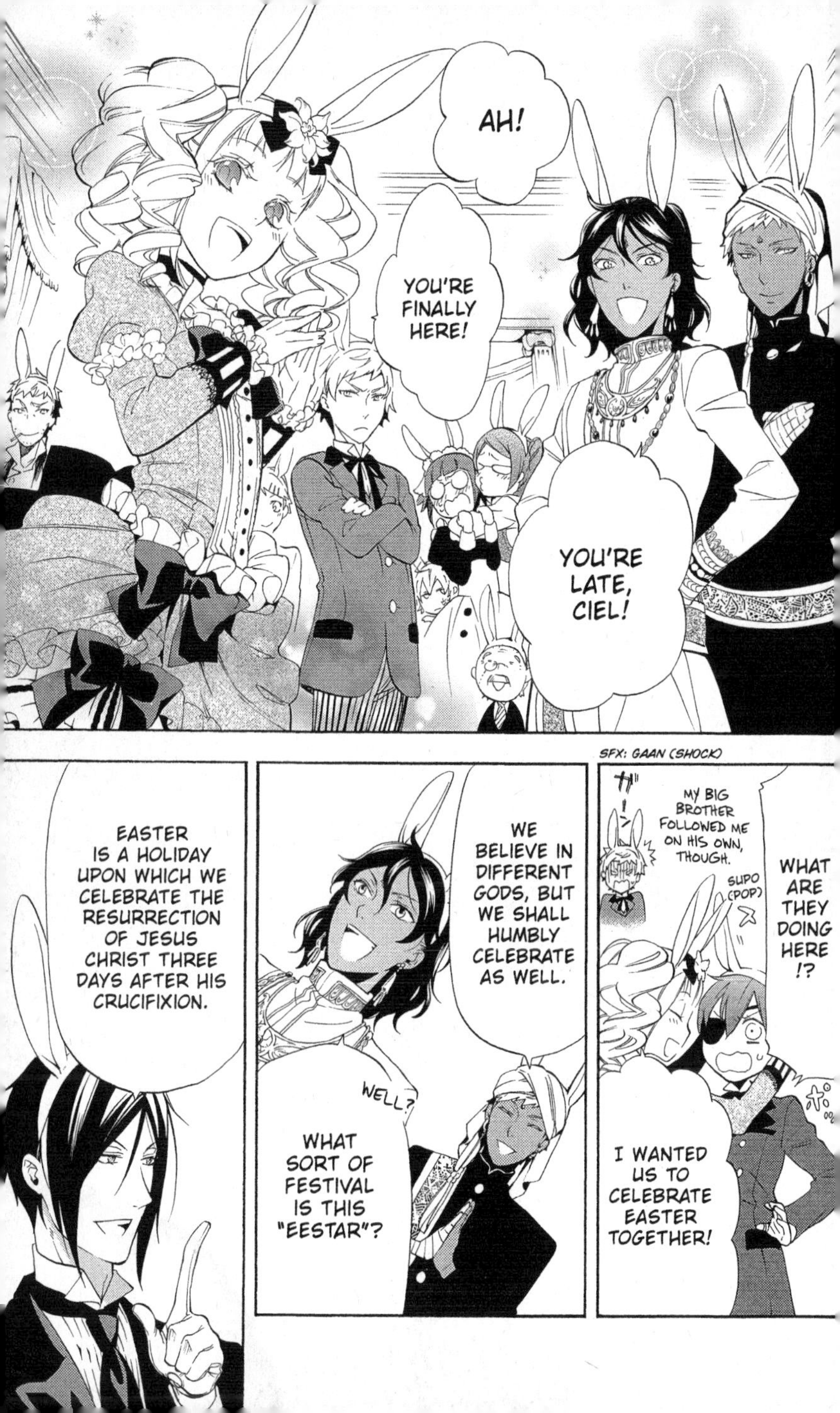
AH!
YOU'RE FINALLY HERE!
YOU'RE LATE, CIEL!
SFX: GAAN (SHOCK)
WHAT ARE THEY DOING HERE!?
MY BIG BROTHER FOLLOWED ME ON HIS OWN, THOUGH.
SUPO (POP)
I WANTED US TO CELEBRATE EASTER TOGETHER!
WE BELIEVE IN DIFFERENT GODS, BUT WE SHALL HUMBLY CELEBRATE AS WELL.
WELL?
WHAT SORT OF FESTIVAL IS THIS "EESTAR"?
EASTER IS A HOLIDAY UPON WHICH WE CELEBRATE THE RESURRECTION OF JESUS CHRIST THREE DAYS AFTER HIS CRUCIFIXION.

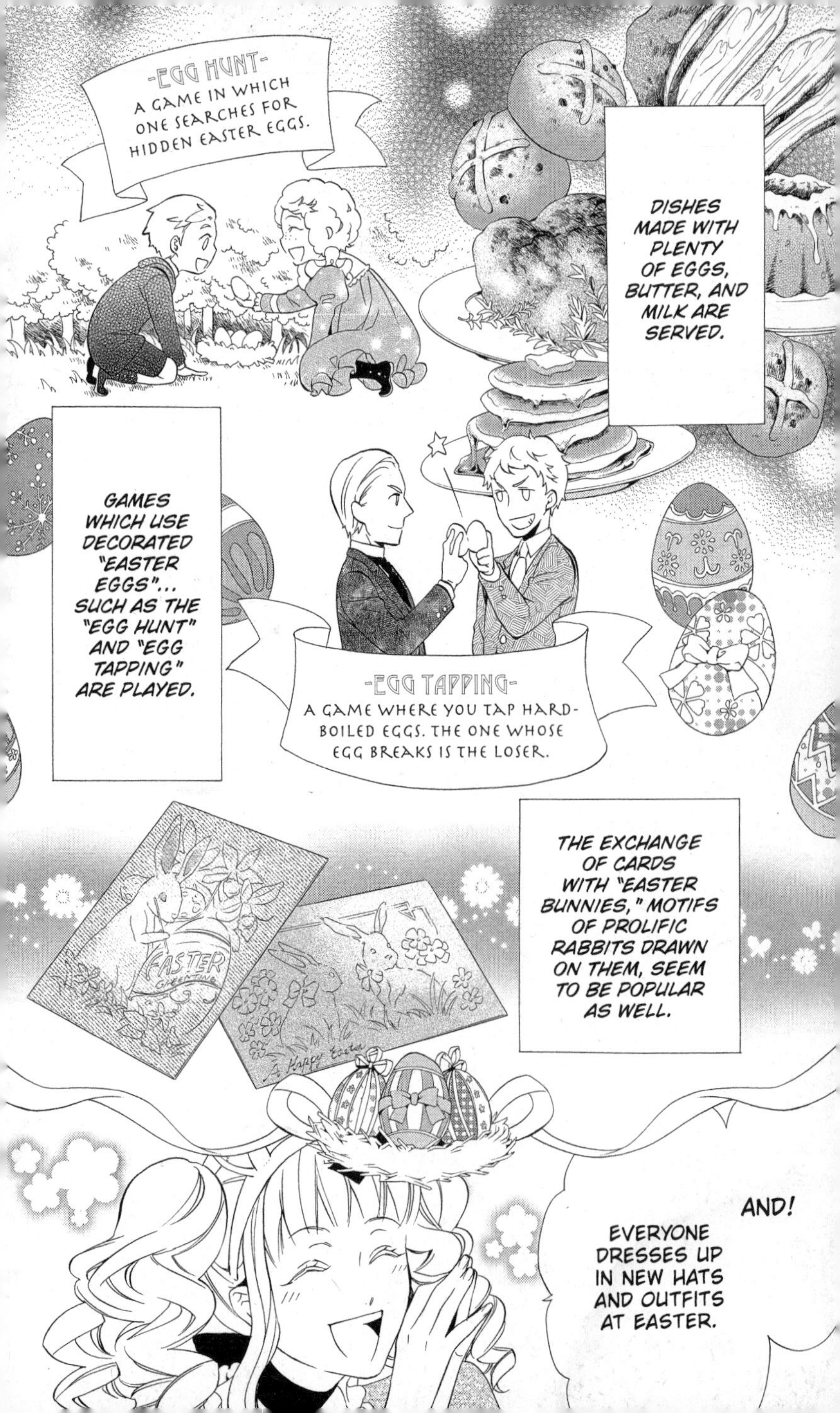
DISHES MADE WITH PLENTY OF EGGS, BUTTER, AND MILK ARE SERVED.
-EGG HUNT-
A GAME IN WHICH ONE SEARCHES FOR HIDDEN EASTER EGGS.
GAMES WHICH USE DECORATED "EASTER EGGS"... SUCH AS THE "EGG HUNT" AND "EGG TAPPING" ARE PLAYED.
-EGG TAPPING-
A GAME WHERE YOU TAP HARD-BOILED EGGS. THE ONE WHOSE EGG BREAKS IS THE LOSER.
THE EXCHANGE OF CARDS WITH "EASTER BUNNIES," MOTIFS OF PROLIFIC RABBITS DRAWN ON THEM, SEEM TO BE POPULAR AS WELL.
EASTER
AND!
EVERYONE DRESSES UP IN NEW HATS AND OUTFITS AT EASTER.

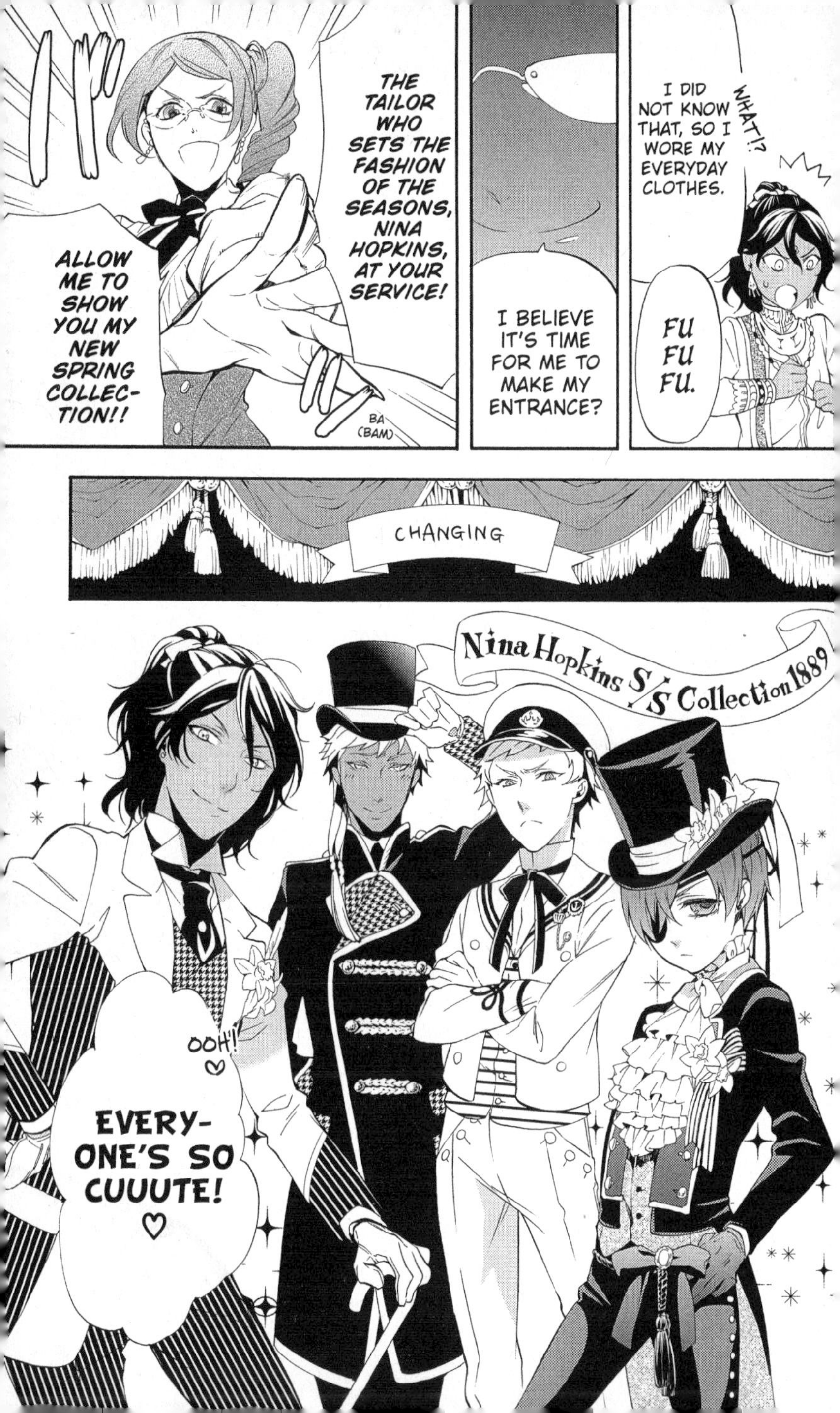

WHAT!?
I DID NOT KNOW THAT, SO I WORE MY EVERYDAY CLOTHES.
FU FU FU.
I BELIEVE IT'S TIME FOR ME TO MAKE MY ENTRANCE?
THE TAILOR WHO SETS THE FASHION OF THE SEASONS, NINA HOPKINS, AT YOUR SERVICE!
ALLOW ME TO SHOW YOU MY NEW SPRING COLLEC-TION!!
BA (BAM)
CHANGING
Nina Hopkins S/S Collection 1889
OOH!♡
EVERY-ONE'S SO CUUUTE! ♡

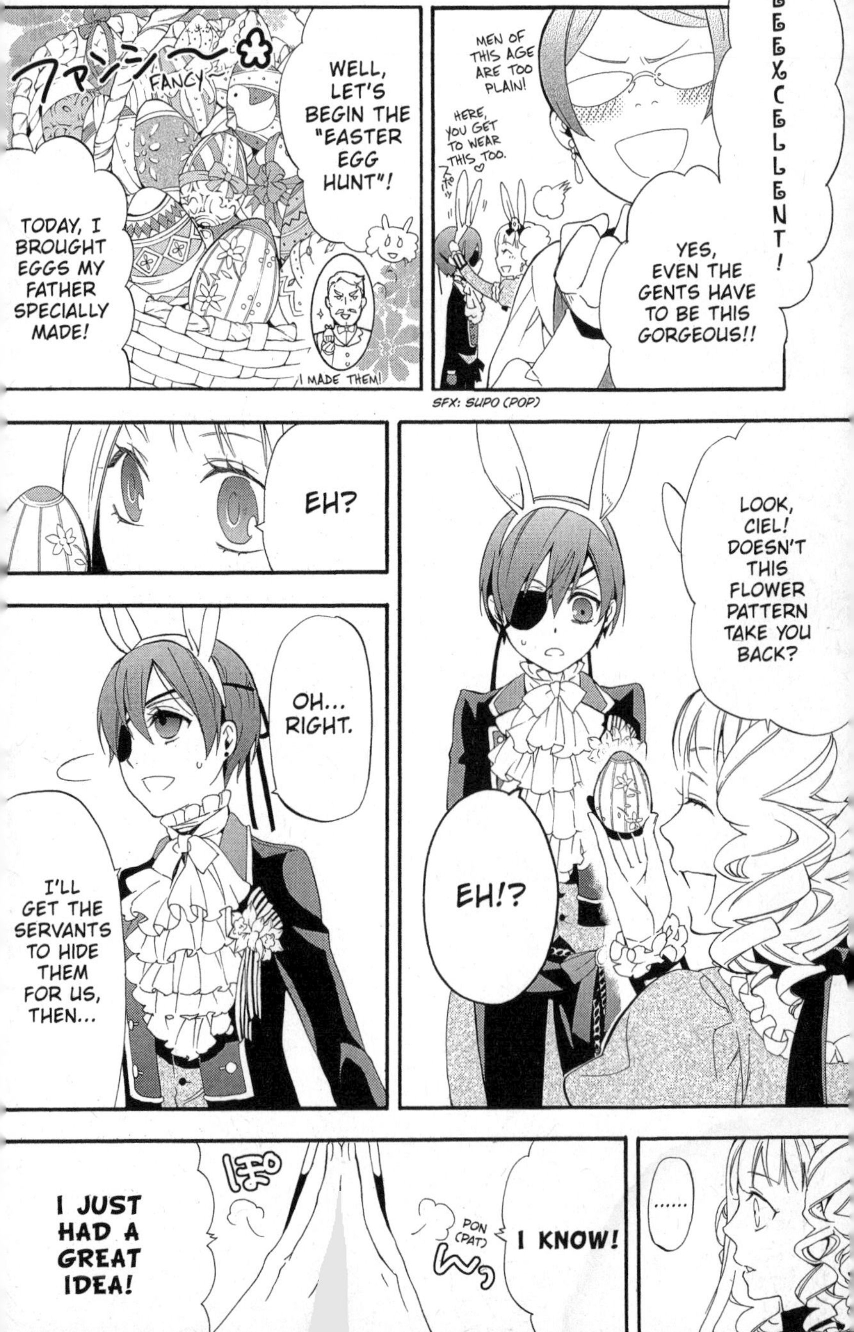
EEEXCELLENT!
YES, EVEN THE GENTS HAVE TO BE THIS GORGEOUS!!
MEN OF THIS AGE ARE TOO PLAIN!
HERE, YOU GET TO WEAR THIS, TOO. ♡
WELL, LET'S BEGIN THE "EASTER EGG HUNT"!
ファンシ～
FANCY
TODAY, I BROUGHT EGGS MY FATHER SPECIALLY MADE!
I MADE THEM!
SFX: SUPO (POP)
LOOK, CIEL! DOESN'T THIS FLOWER PATTERN TAKE YOU BACK?
EH!?
EH?
OH... RIGHT.
I'LL GET THE SERVANTS TO HIDE THEM FOR US, THEN...
......
I KNOW!
ぽん
PON (PAT)
I JUST HAD A GREAT IDEA!

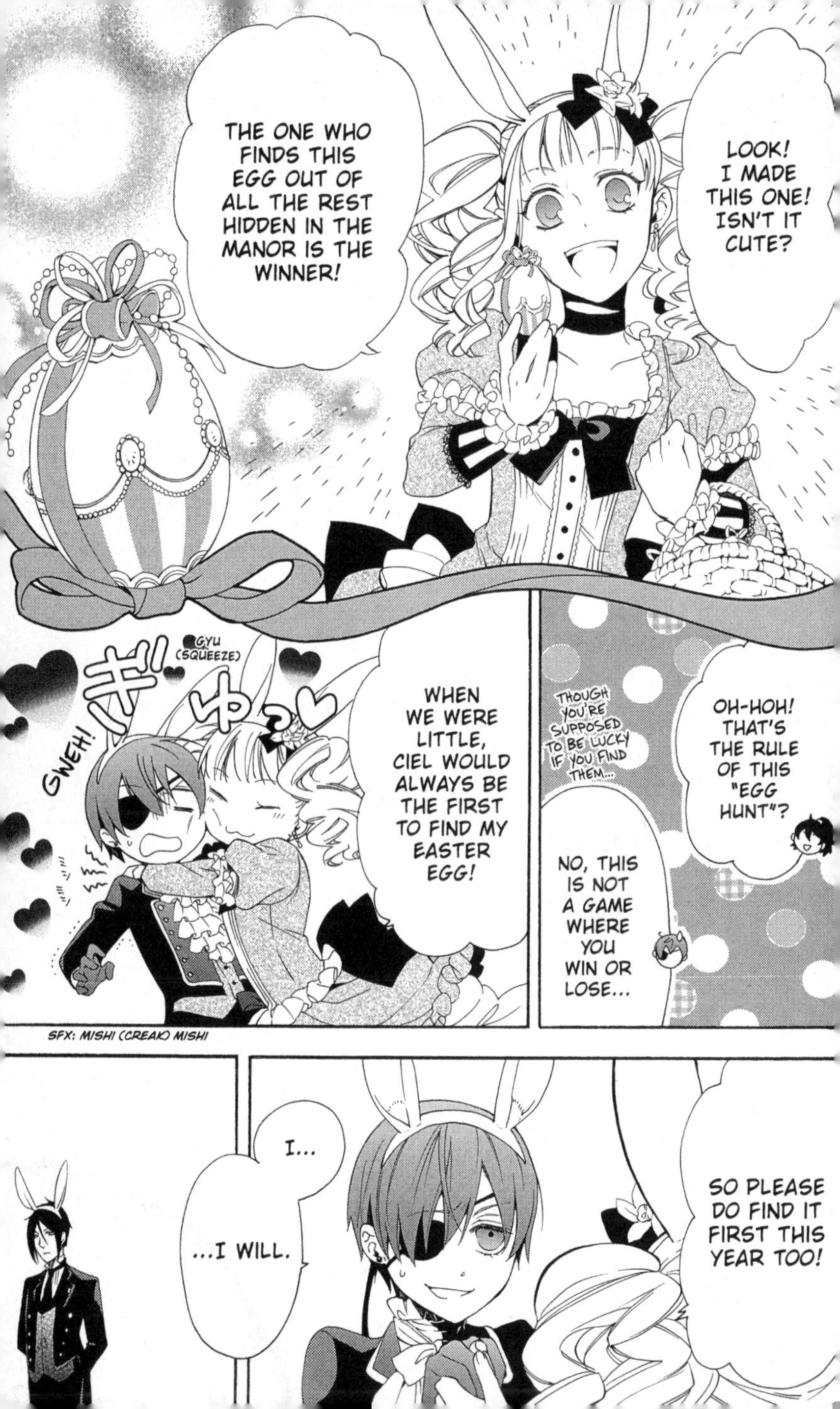
LOOK! I MADE THIS ONE! ISN'T IT CUTE?
THE ONE WHO FINDS THIS EGG OUT OF ALL THE REST HIDDEN IN THE MANOR IS THE WINNER!
OH-HOH! THAT'S THE RULE OF THIS "EGG HUNT"?
THOUGH YOU'RE SUPPOSED TO BE LUCKY IF YOU FIND THEM...
NO, THIS IS NOT A GAME WHERE YOU WIN OR LOSE...
WHEN WE WERE LITTLE, CIEL WOULD ALWAYS BE THE FIRST TO FIND MY EASTER EGG!
GYU (SQUEEZE)
GWEH!
SFX: MISHI (CREAK) MISHI
SO PLEASE DO FIND IT FIRST THIS YEAR TOO!
I...
...I WILL.

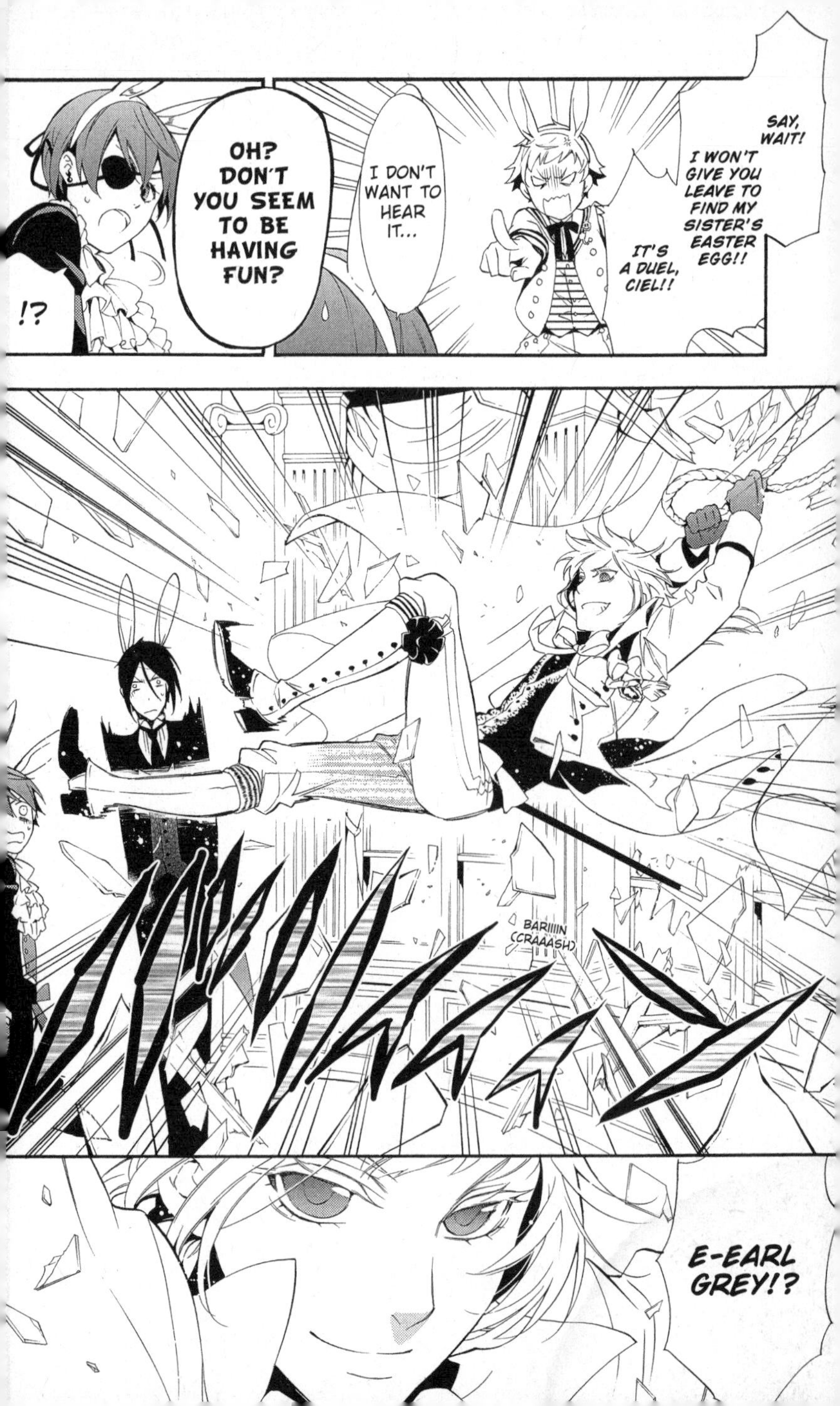

SAY, WAIT!
I WON'T GIVE YOU LEAVE TO FIND MY SISTER'S EASTER EGG!!
IT'S A DUEL, CIEL!!
I DON'T WANT TO HEAR IT...
OH? DON'T YOU SEEM TO BE HAVING FUN?
!?
BARIIIIN (CRAAASH)
E-EARL GREY!?

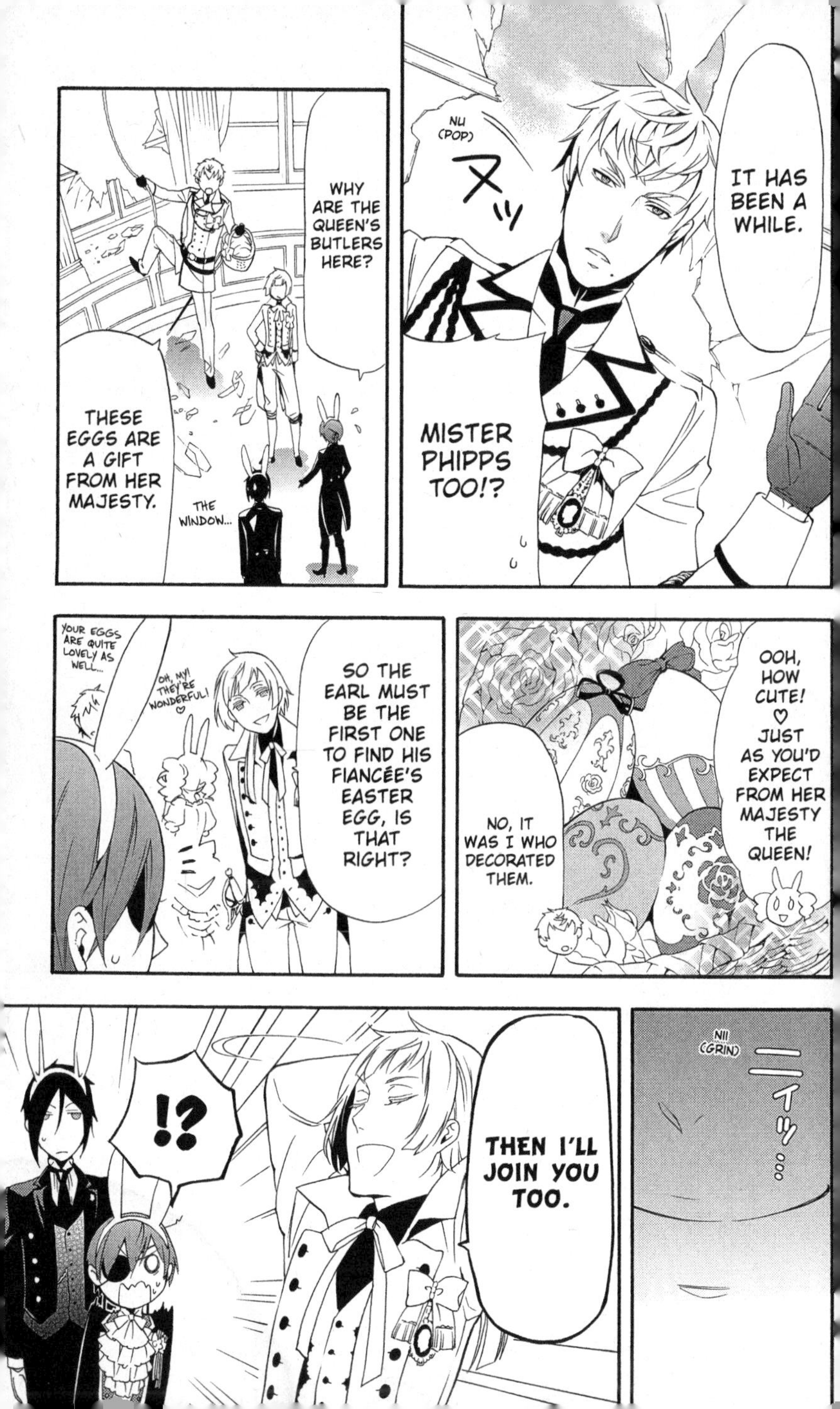
NU (POP)
ヌッ
IT HAS BEEN A WHILE.
MISTER PHIPPS TOO!?
WHY ARE THE QUEEN'S BUTLERS HERE?
THESE EGGS ARE A GIFT FROM HER MAJESTY.
THE WINDOW...
OOH, HOW CUTE! ♡ JUST AS YOU'D EXPECT FROM HER MAJESTY THE QUEEN!
NO, IT WAS I WHO DECORATED THEM.
SO THE EARL MUST BE THE FIRST ONE TO FIND HIS FIANCÉE'S EASTER EGG, IS THAT RIGHT?
OH, MY! THEY'RE WONDERFUL! ♡
YOUR EGGS ARE QUITE LOVELY AS WELL...
NII (GRIN)
ニーイッ…
THEN I'LL JOIN YOU TOO.
!?

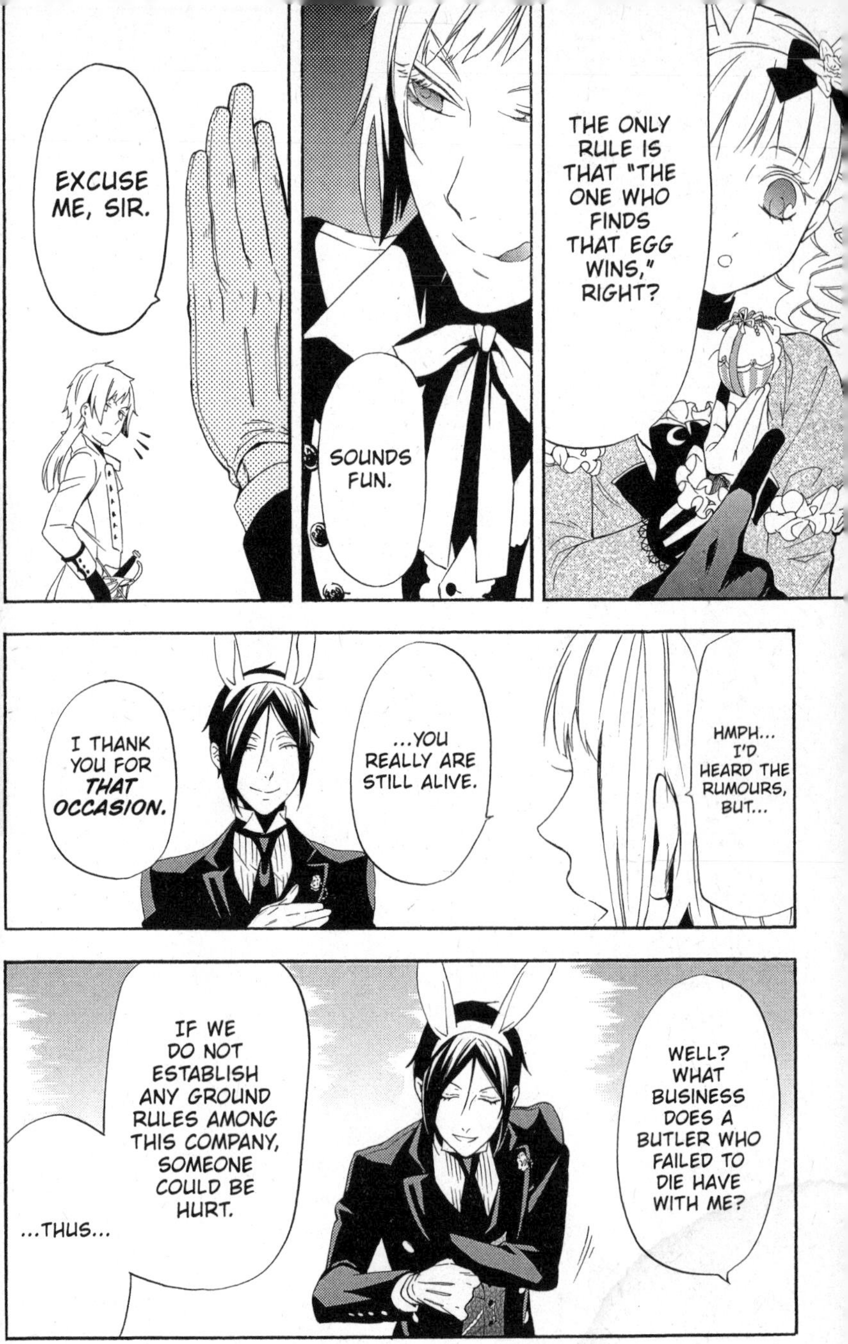
THE ONLY RULE IS THAT "THE ONE WHO FINDS THAT EGG WINS," RIGHT?
SOUNDS FUN.
EXCUSE ME, SIR.
HMPH... I'D HEARD THE RUMOURS, BUT...
...YOU REALLY ARE STILL ALIVE.
I THANK YOU FOR *THAT OCCASION.*
WELL? WHAT BUSINESS DOES A BUTLER WHO FAILED TO DIE HAVE WITH ME?
IF WE DO NOT ESTABLISH ANY GROUND RULES AMONG THIS COMPANY, SOMEONE COULD BE HURT.
...THUS...

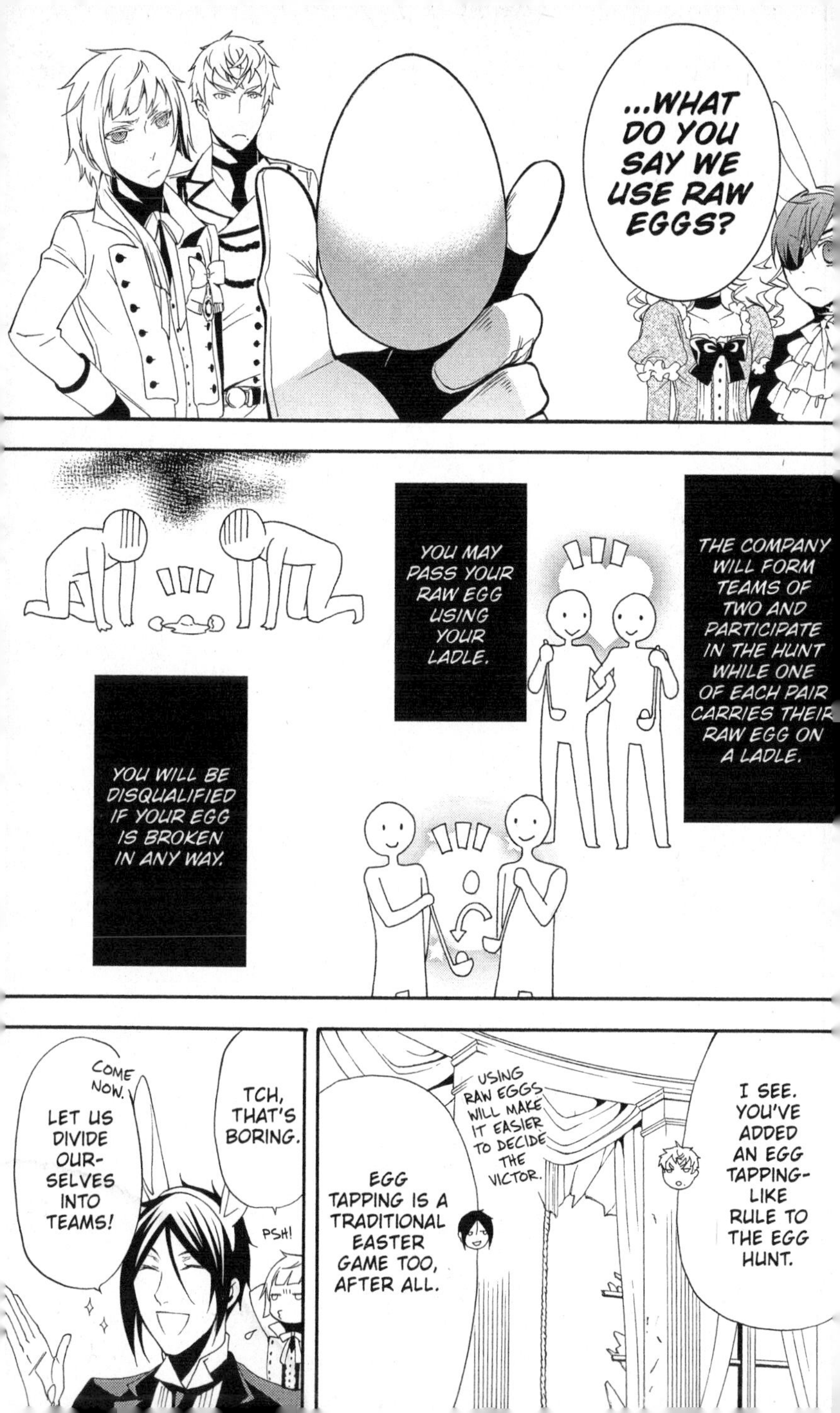
...WHAT DO YOU SAY WE USE RAW EGGS?
THE COMPANY WILL FORM TEAMS OF TWO AND PARTICIPATE IN THE HUNT WHILE ONE OF EACH PAIR CARRIES THEIR RAW EGG ON A LADLE.
YOU MAY PASS YOUR RAW EGG USING YOUR LADLE.
YOU WILL BE DISQUALIFIED IF YOUR EGG IS BROKEN IN ANY WAY.
I SEE. YOU'VE ADDED AN EGG TAPPING-LIKE RULE TO THE EGG HUNT.
USING RAW EGGS WILL MAKE IT EASIER TO DECIDE THE VICTOR.
EGG TAPPING IS A TRADITIONAL EASTER GAME TOO, AFTER ALL.
TCH, THAT'S BORING.
COME NOW.
LET US DIVIDE OURSELVES INTO TEAMS!
PSH!

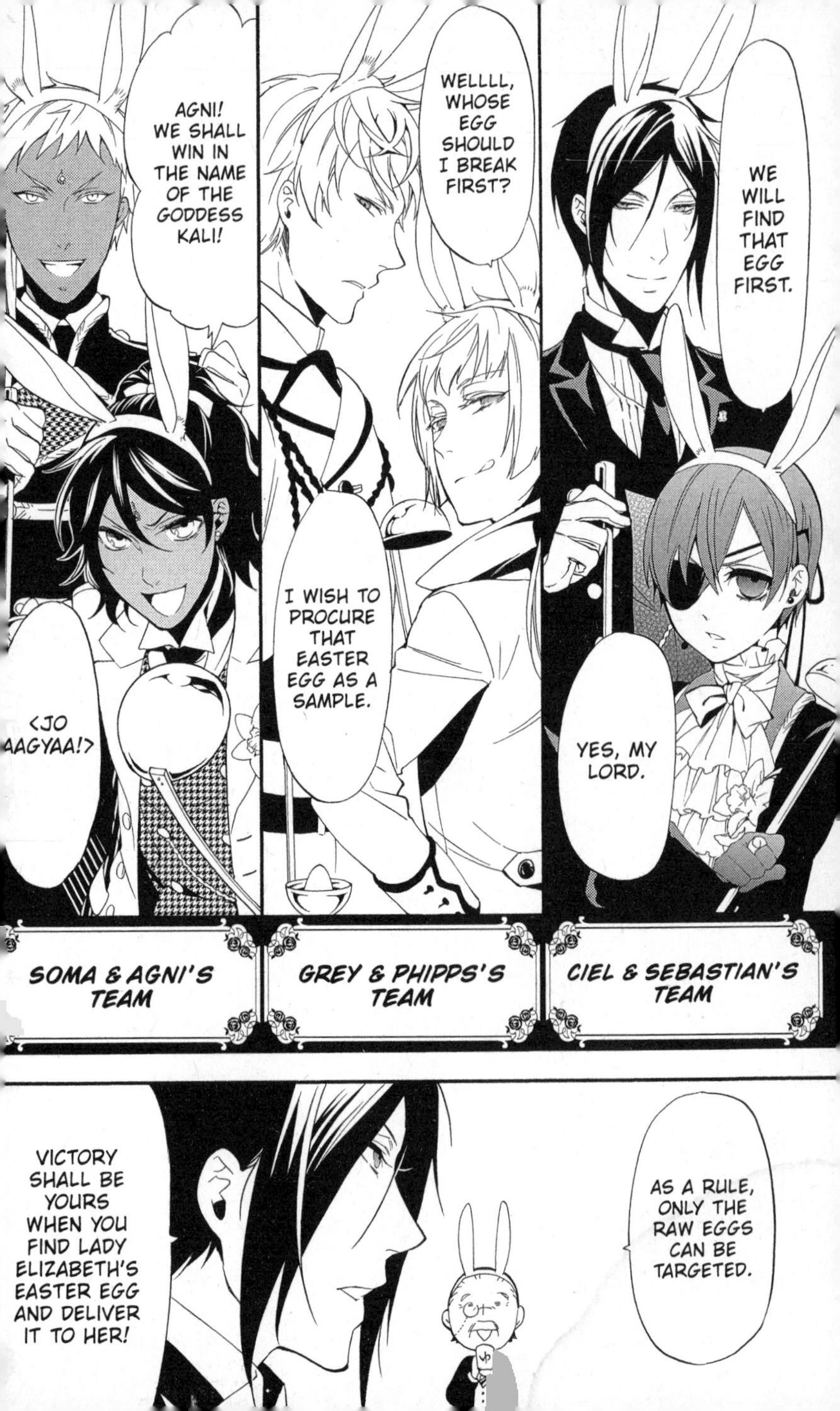
WE WILL FIND THAT EGG FIRST.
YES, MY LORD.
CIEL & SEBASTIAN'S TEAM
WELLLL, WHOSE EGG SHOULD I BREAK FIRST?
I WISH TO PROCURE THAT EASTER EGG AS A SAMPLE.
GREY & PHIPPS'S TEAM
AGNI! WE SHALL WIN IN THE NAME OF THE GODDESS KALI!
<JO AAGYAA!>
SOMA & AGNI'S TEAM
AS A RULE, ONLY THE RAW EGGS CAN BE TARGETED.
VICTORY SHALL BE YOURS WHEN YOU FIND LADY ELIZABETH'S EASTER EGG AND DELIVER IT TO HER!

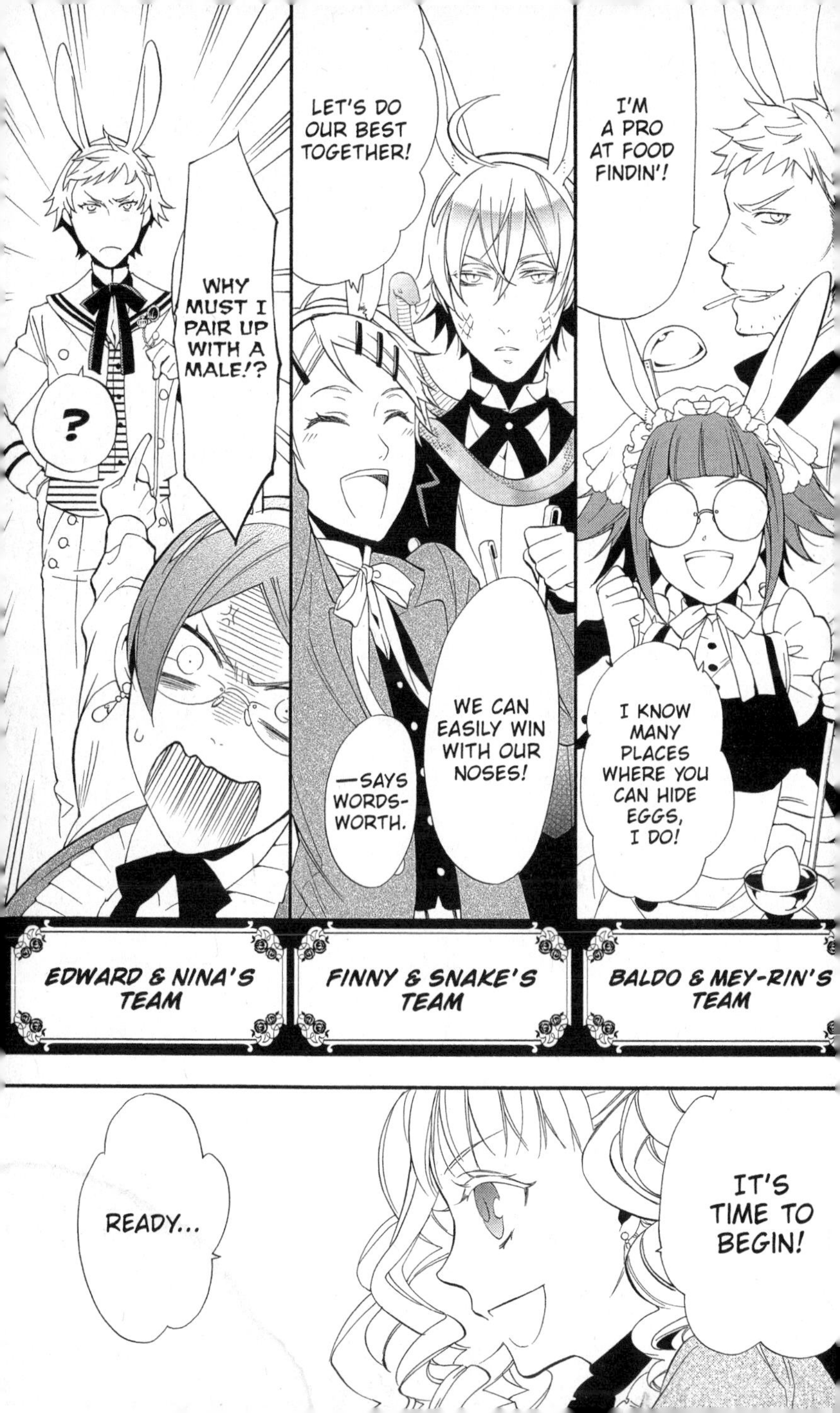
I'M A PRO AT FOOD FINDIN'!
I KNOW MANY PLACES WHERE YOU CAN HIDE EGGS, I DO!
BALDO & MEY-RIN'S TEAM
LET'S DO OUR BEST TOGETHER!
WE CAN EASILY WIN WITH OUR NOSES!
—SAYS WORDS-WORTH.
FINNY & SNAKE'S TEAM
WHY MUST I PAIR UP WITH A MALE!?
?
EDWARD & NINA'S TEAM
READY...
IT'S TIME TO BEGIN!

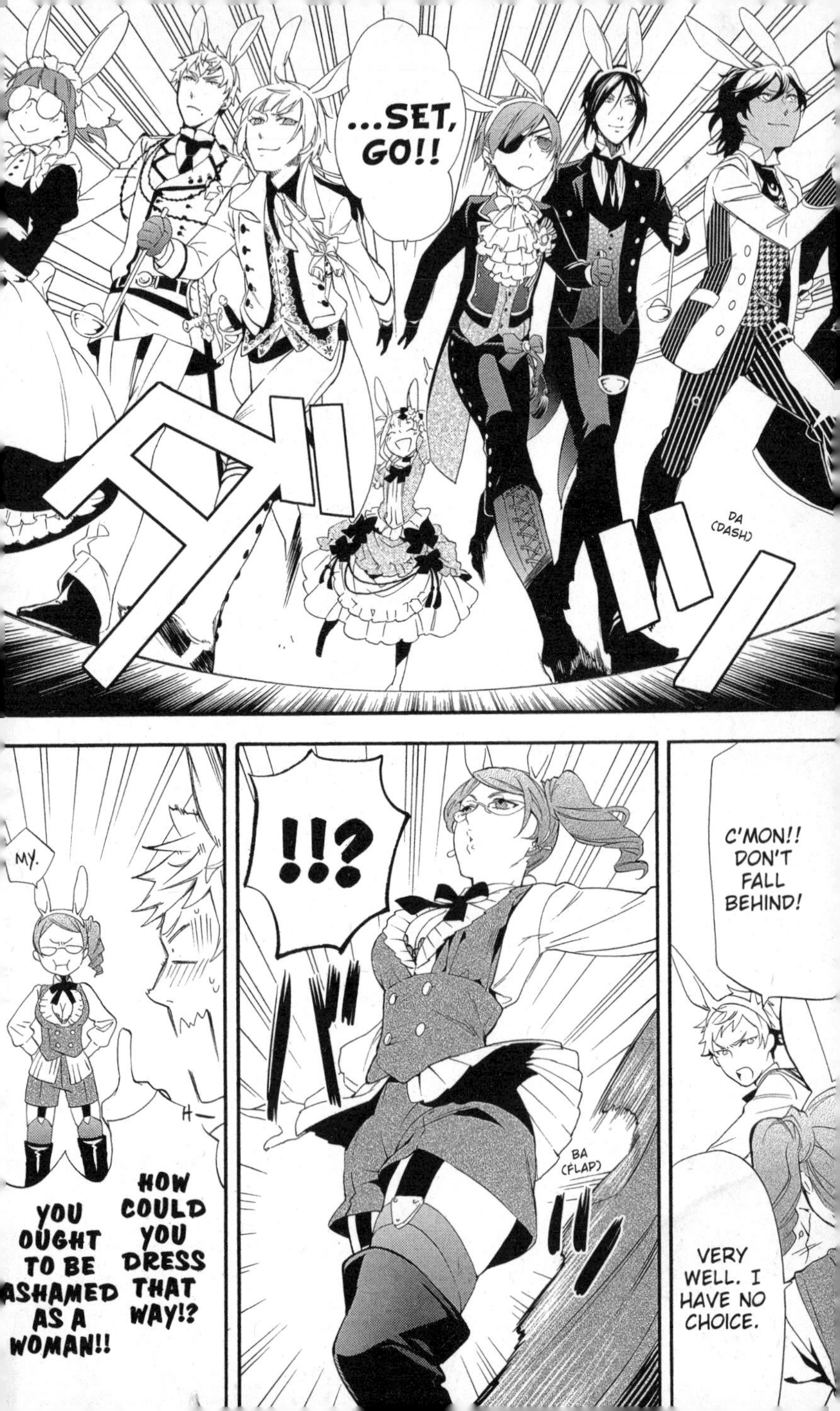
...SET, GO!!
DA (DASH)
C'MON!! DON'T FALL BEHIND!
VERY WELL. I HAVE NO CHOICE.
!!?
BA (FLAP)
MY.
H—
HOW COULD YOU DRESS THAT WAY!?
YOU OUGHT TO BE ASHAMED AS A WOMAN!!

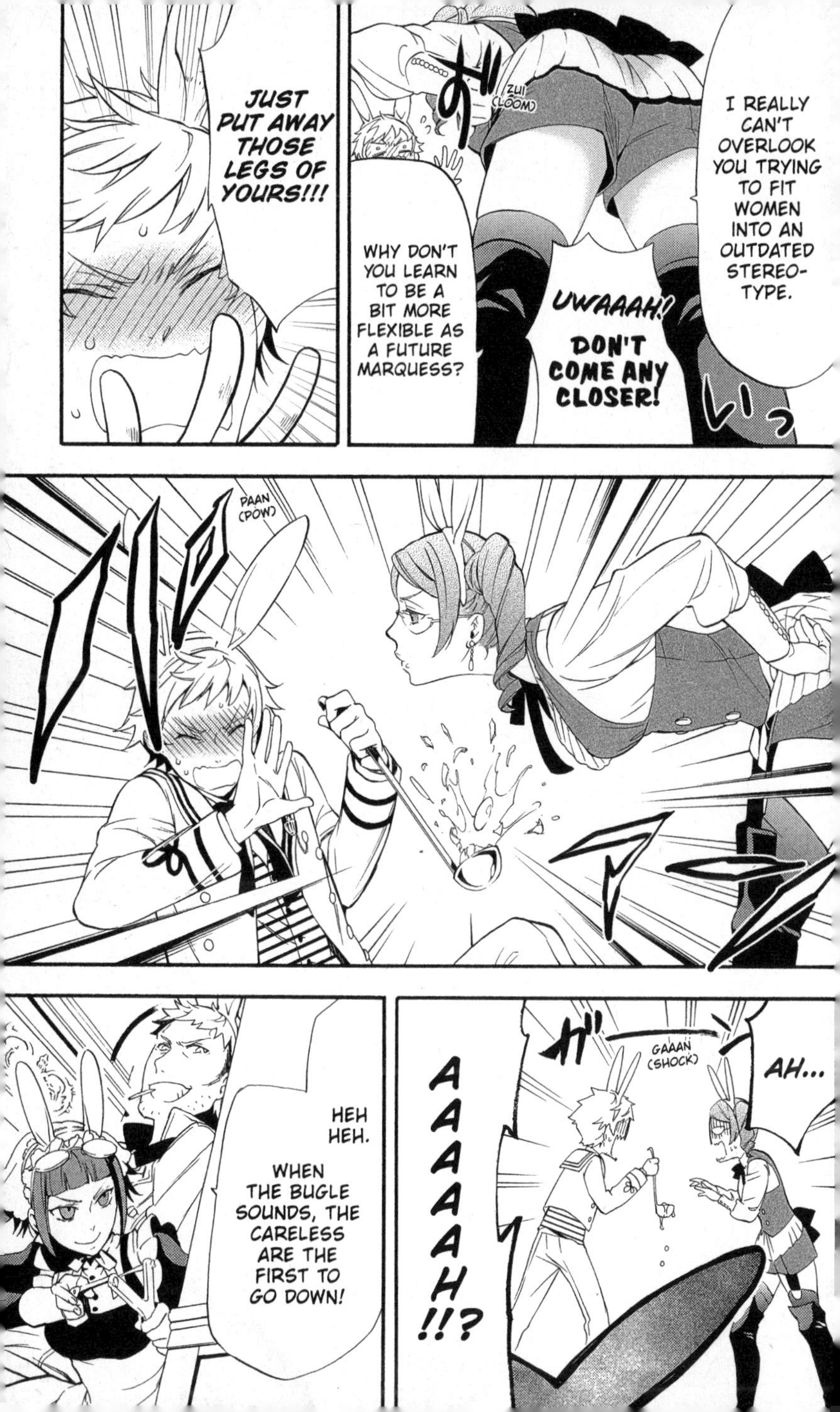
I REALLY CAN'T OVERLOOK YOU TRYING TO FIT WOMEN INTO AN OUTDATED STEREOTYPE.
ZUI (LOOM)
UWAAAH! DON'T COME ANY CLOSER!
WHY DON'T YOU LEARN TO BE A BIT MORE FLEXIBLE AS A FUTURE MARQUESS?
JUST PUT AWAY THOSE LEGS OF YOURS!!!
PAAN (POW)
AH...
GAAAN (SHOCK)
AAAAAAH!!?
HEH HEH.
WHEN THE BUGLE SOUNDS, THE CARELESS ARE THE FIRST TO GO DOWN!

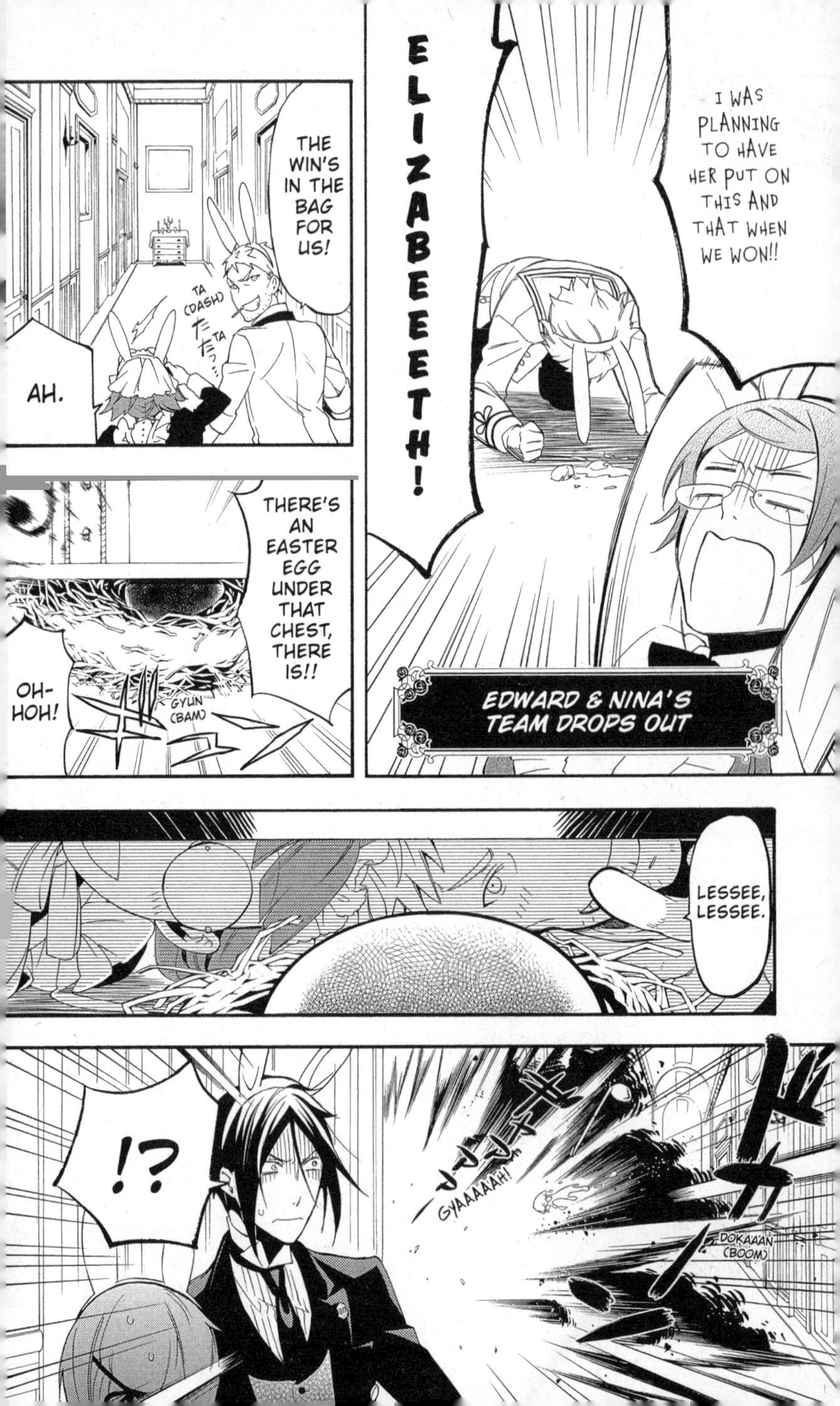

I WAS PLANNING TO HAVE HER PUT ON THIS AND THAT WHEN WE WON!!
ELIZABEEEETH!
EDWARD & NINA'S TEAM DROPS OUT
THE WIN'S IN THE BAG FOR US!
TA TA (DASH)
AH.
THERE'S AN EASTER EGG UNDER THAT CHEST, THERE IS!!
GYUN (BAM)
OH-HOH!
LESSEE, LESSEE.
DOKAAAN (BOOM)
GYAAAAAH!
!?

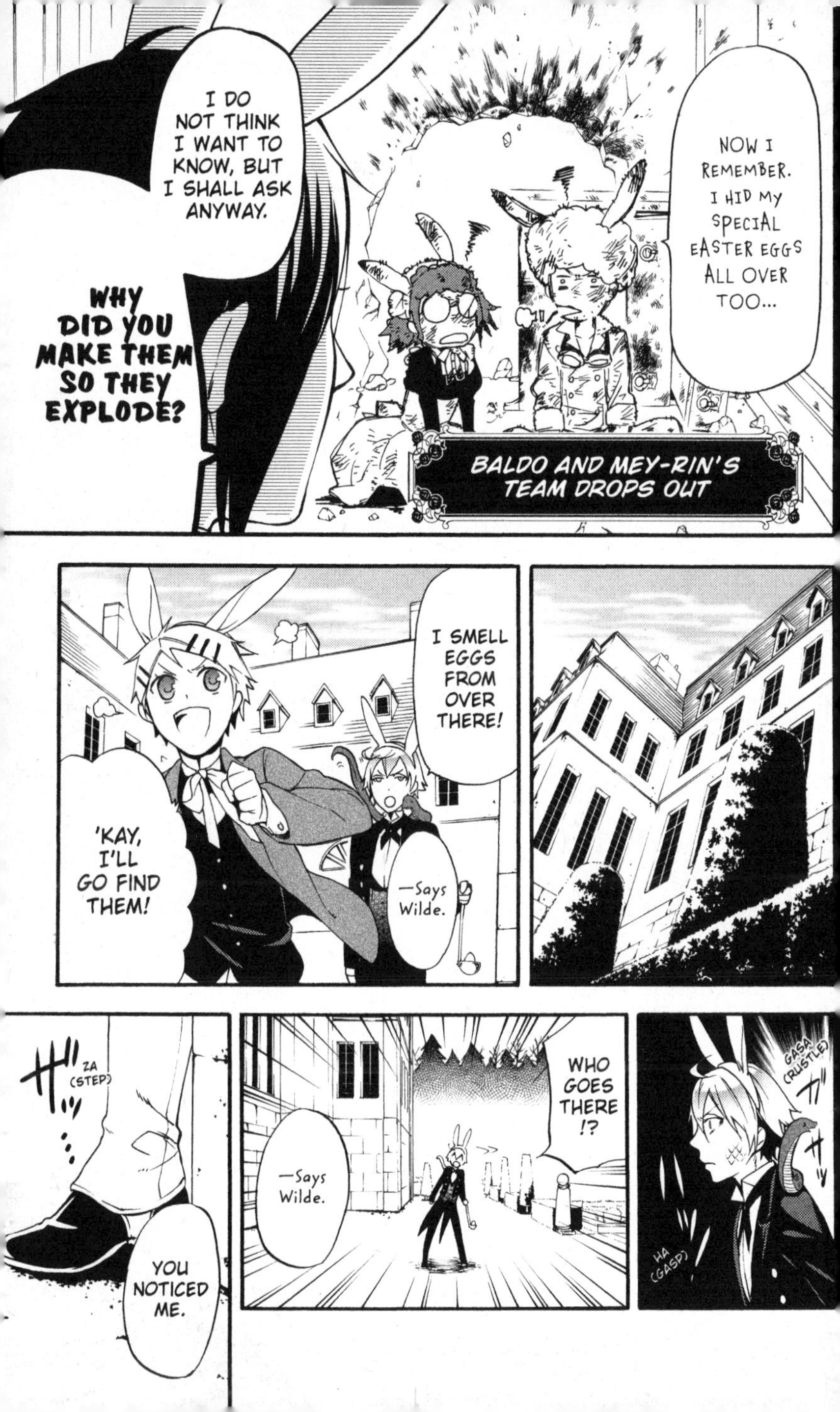
NOW I REMEMBER. I HID MY SPECIAL EASTER EGGS ALL OVER TOO...
I DO NOT THINK I WANT TO KNOW, BUT I SHALL ASK ANYWAY.
WHY DID YOU MAKE THEM SO THEY EXPLODE?
BALDO AND MEY-RIN'S TEAM DROPS OUT
I SMELL EGGS FROM OVER THERE!
—Says Wilde.
'KAY, I'LL GO FIND THEM!
GASA (RUSTLE)
HA (GASP)
WHO GOES THERE!?
—Says Wilde.
ZA (STEP)
YOU NOTICED ME.

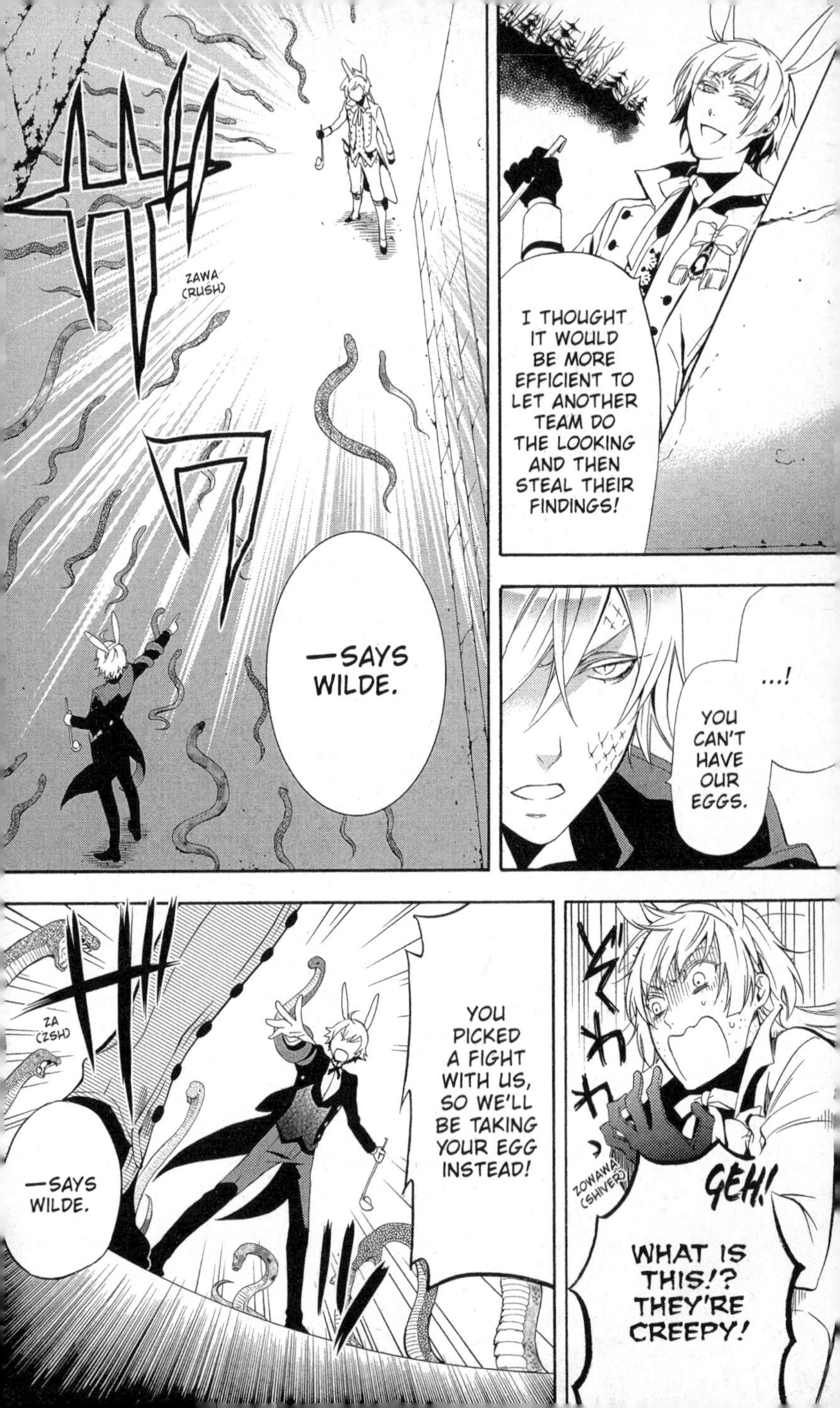
I THOUGHT IT WOULD BE MORE EFFICIENT TO LET ANOTHER TEAM DO THE LOOKING AND THEN STEAL THEIR FINDINGS!
...!
YOU CAN'T HAVE OUR EGGS.
ZAWA (RUSH)
—SAYS WILDE.
ZOWAWA (SHIVER)
GEH!
WHAT IS THIS!? THEY'RE CREEPY!
YOU PICKED A FIGHT WITH US, SO WE'LL BE TAKING YOUR EGG INSTEAD!
ZA (ZSH)
—SAYS WILDE.

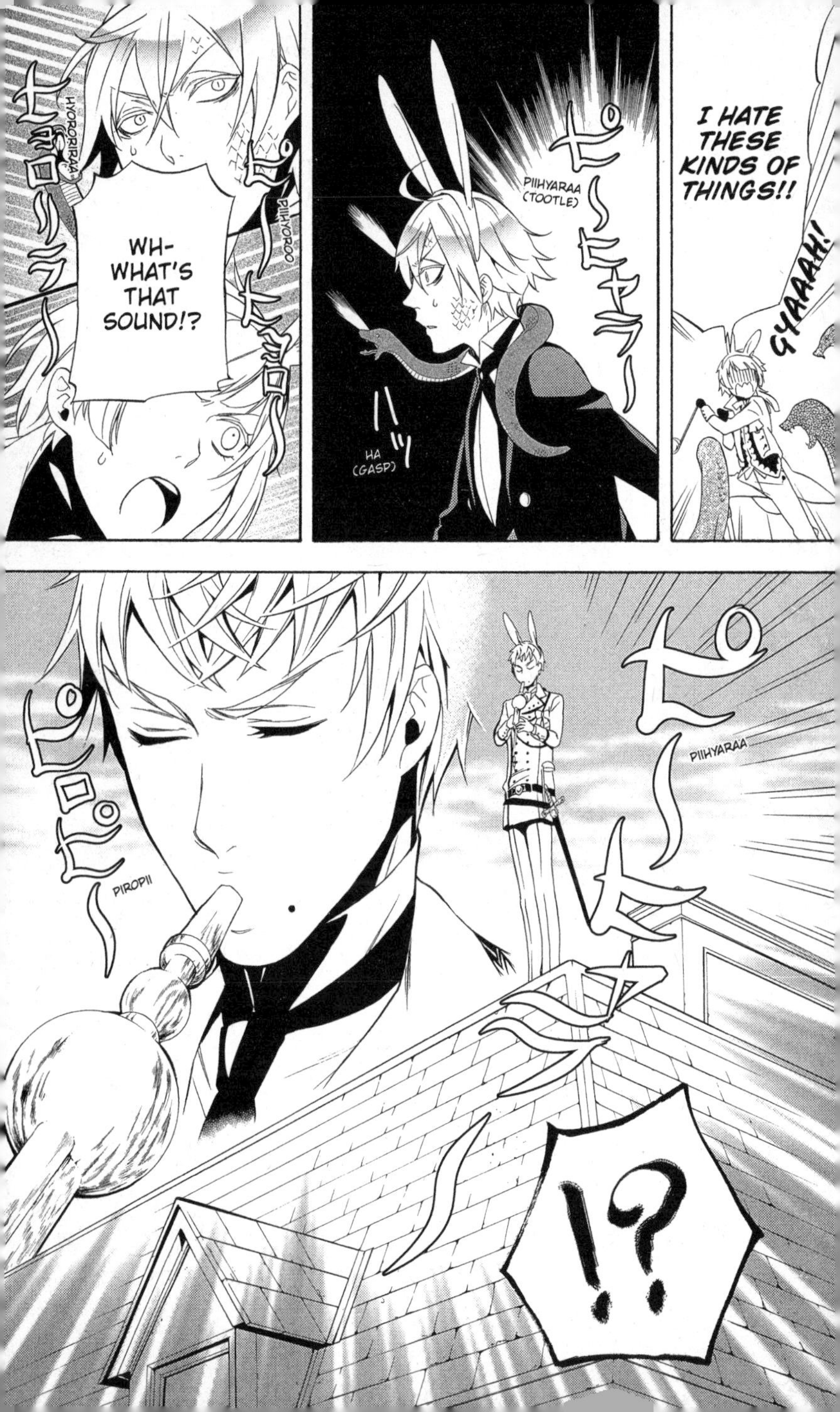

I HATE THESE KINDS OF THINGS!!
GYAAAH!
PIIHYARAA (TOOTLE)
HA (GASP)
HYORORIRAA
PIIHYOROO
WH-WHAT'S THAT SOUND!?
PIIHYARAA
PIROPII
!?

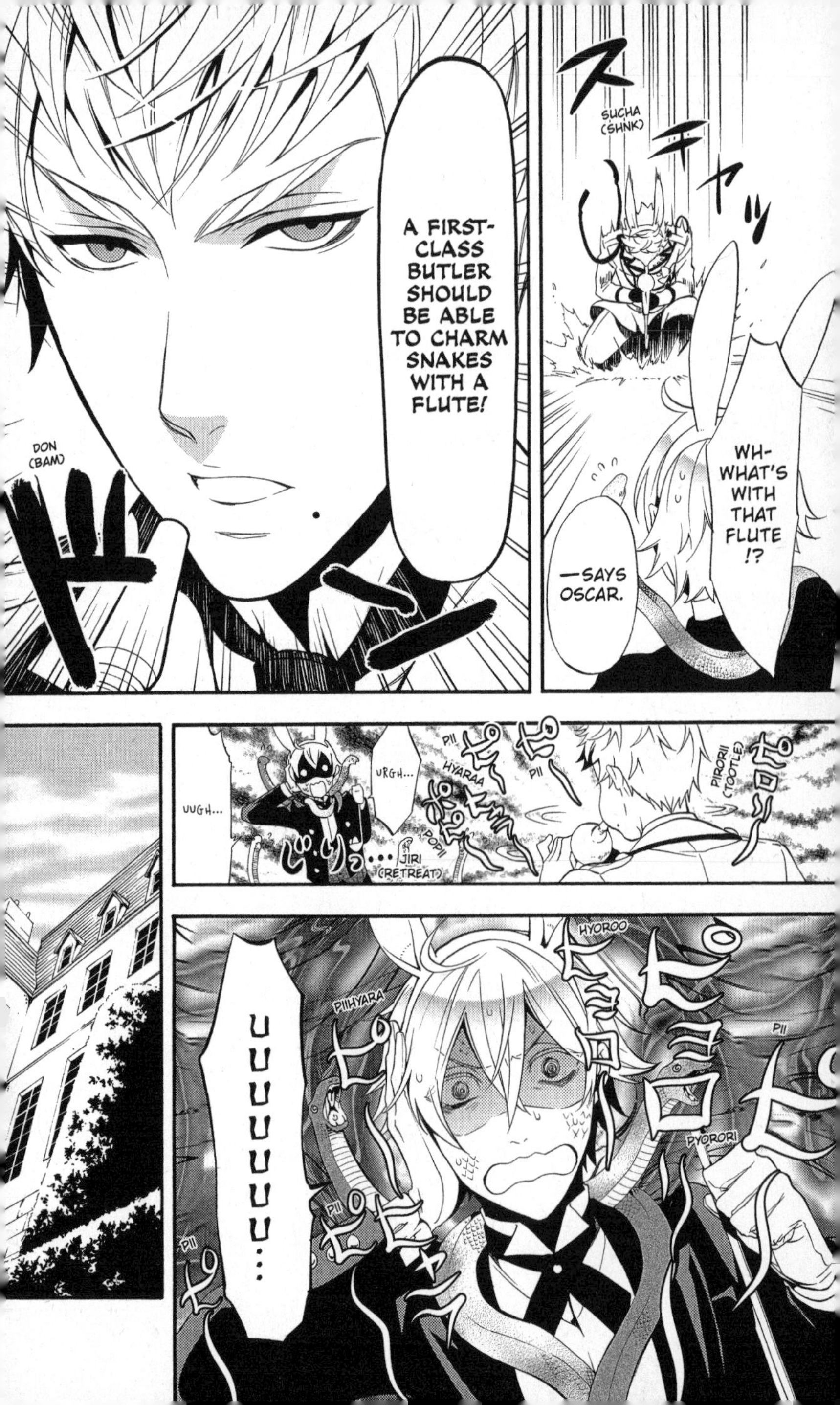
SUCHA (SHNK)
WH-WHAT'S WITH THAT FLUTE!?
—SAYS OSCAR.
A FIRST-CLASS BUTLER SHOULD BE ABLE TO CHARM SNAKES WITH A FLUTE!
DON (BAM)
PIRORII (TOOTLE)
PII
PII
HYARAA
POPII
URGH...
JIRI (RETREAT)
UUGH...
HYOROO
PII
PYORORI
PIIHYARA
UUUUUUUU...
PII
PII

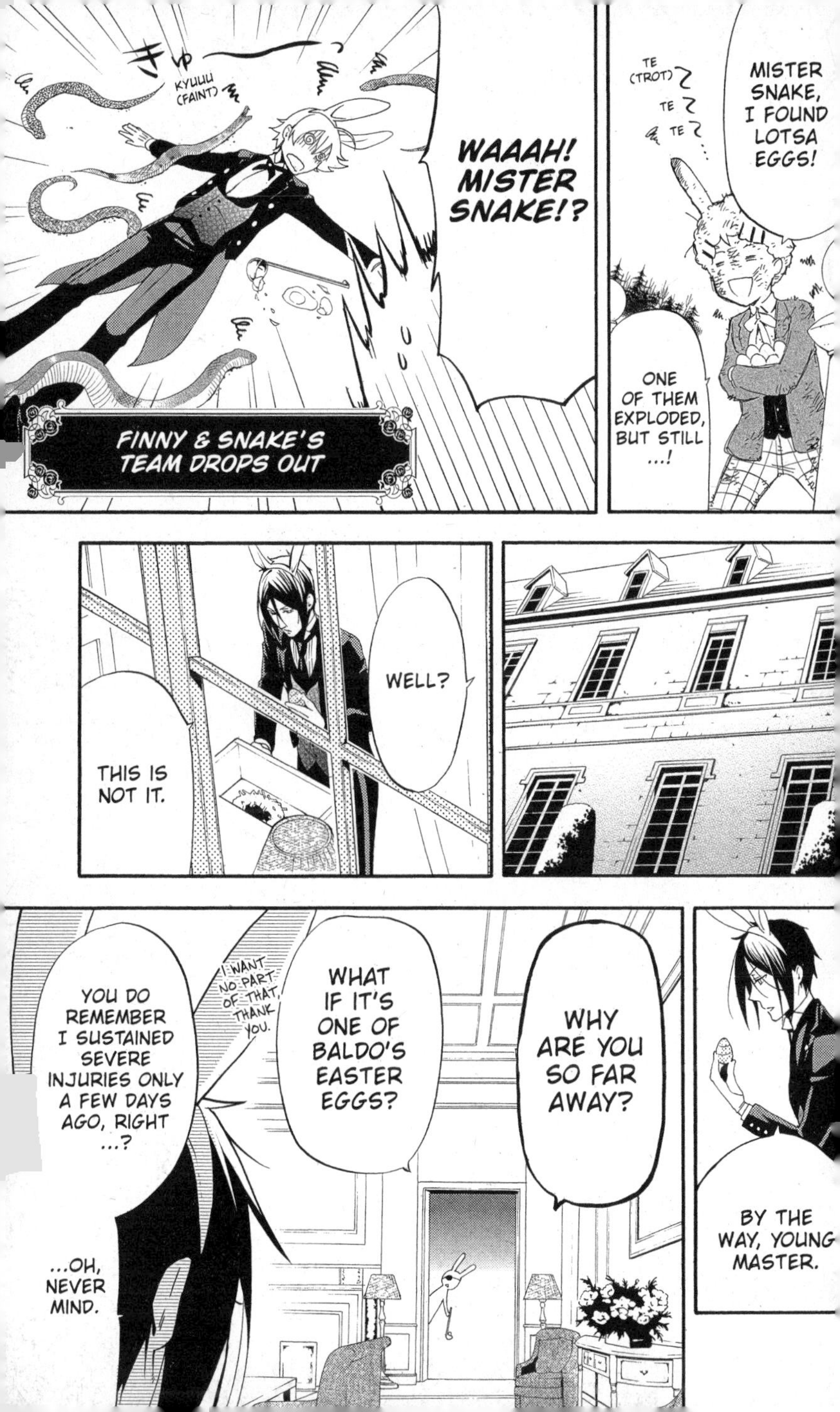
TE (TROT) TE TE...
MISTER SNAKE, I FOUND LOTSA EGGS!
ONE OF THEM EXPLODED, BUT STILL ...!
WAAAH! MISTER SNAKE!?
きゅ—— KYUUU (FAINT)
FINNY & SNAKE'S TEAM DROPS OUT
WELL?
THIS IS NOT IT.
BY THE WAY, YOUNG MASTER.
WHY ARE YOU SO FAR AWAY?
WHAT IF IT'S ONE OF BALDO'S EASTER EGGS?
I WANT NO PART OF THAT, THANK YOU.
YOU DO REMEMBER I SUSTAINED SEVERE INJURIES ONLY A FEW DAYS AGO, RIGHT ...?
...OH, NEVER MIND.

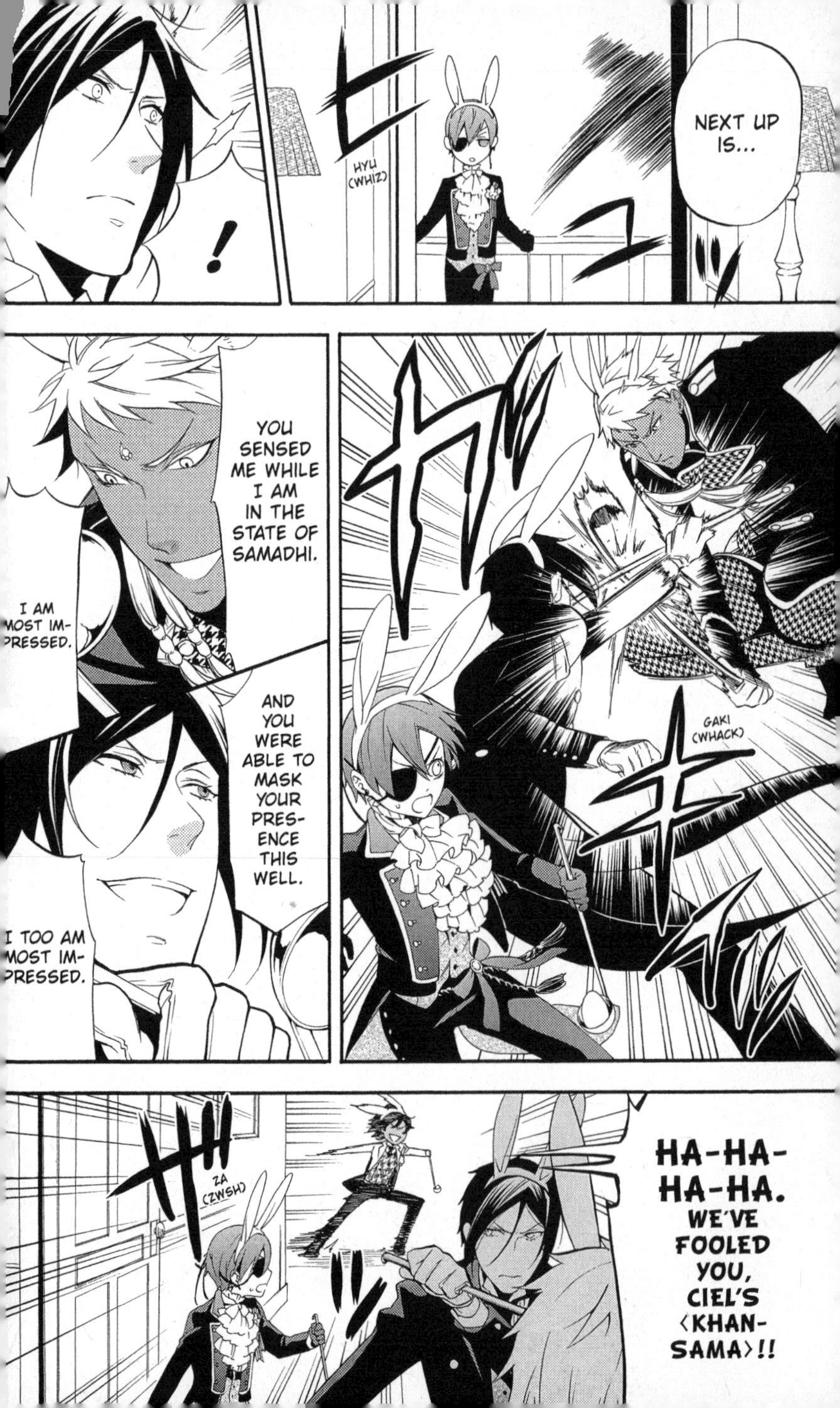

NEXT UP IS...
HYU (WHIZ)
!
GAKI (WHACK)
YOU SENSED ME WHILE I AM IN THE STATE OF SAMADHI.
I AM MOST IMPRESSED.
AND YOU WERE ABLE TO MASK YOUR PRESENCE THIS WELL.
I TOO AM MOST IMPRESSED.
HA-HA-HA-HA. WE'VE FOOLED YOU, CIEL'S ‹KHAN-SAMA›!!
ZA (ZWSH)

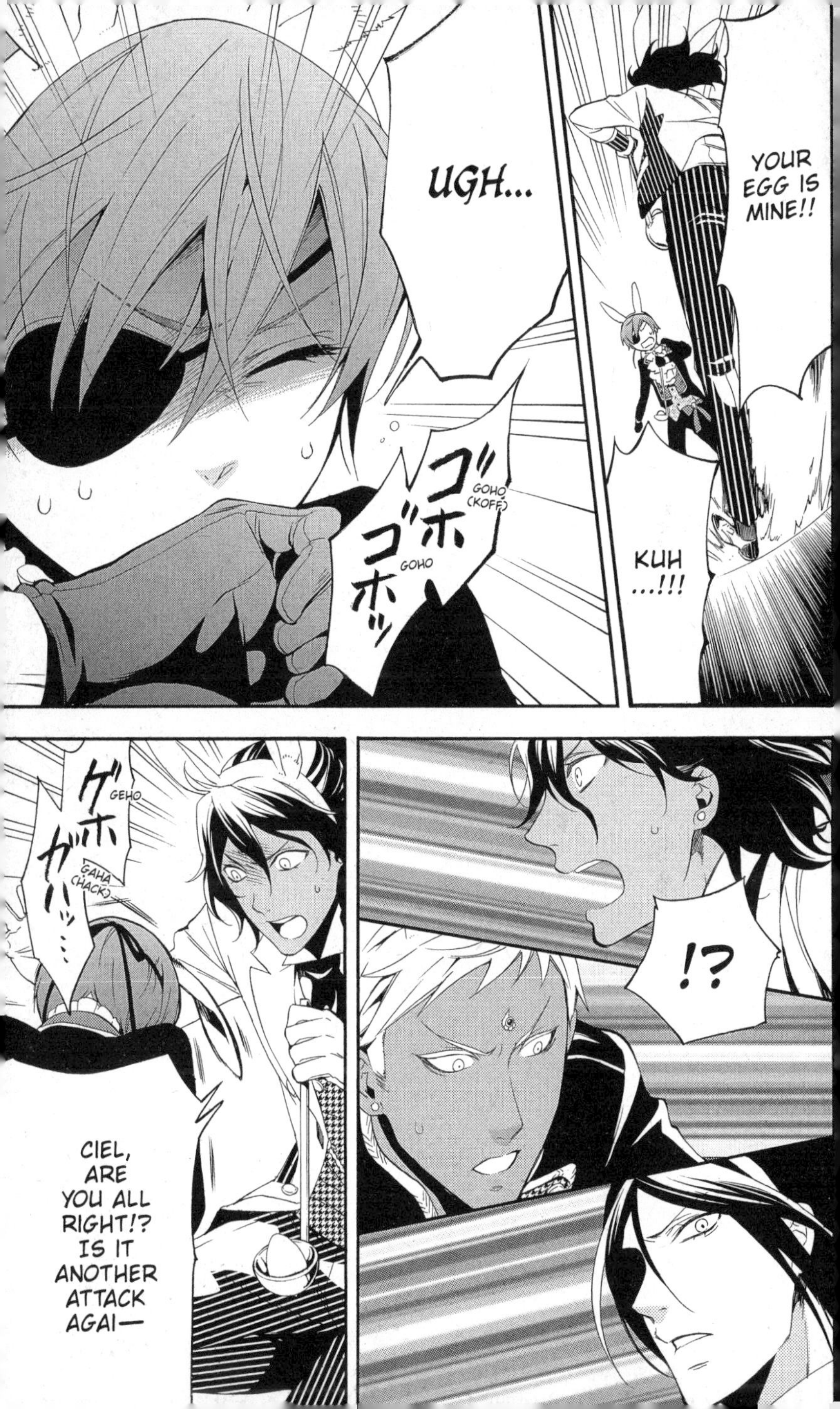

YOUR EGG IS MINE!!
KUH ...!!!
UGH...
ゴホ
GOHO (KOFF)
ゴホッ
GOHO
!?
ゲホ
GEHO
ガハッ…
GAHA (HACK)
CIEL, ARE YOU ALL RIGHT!? IS IT ANOTHER ATTACK AGAI—

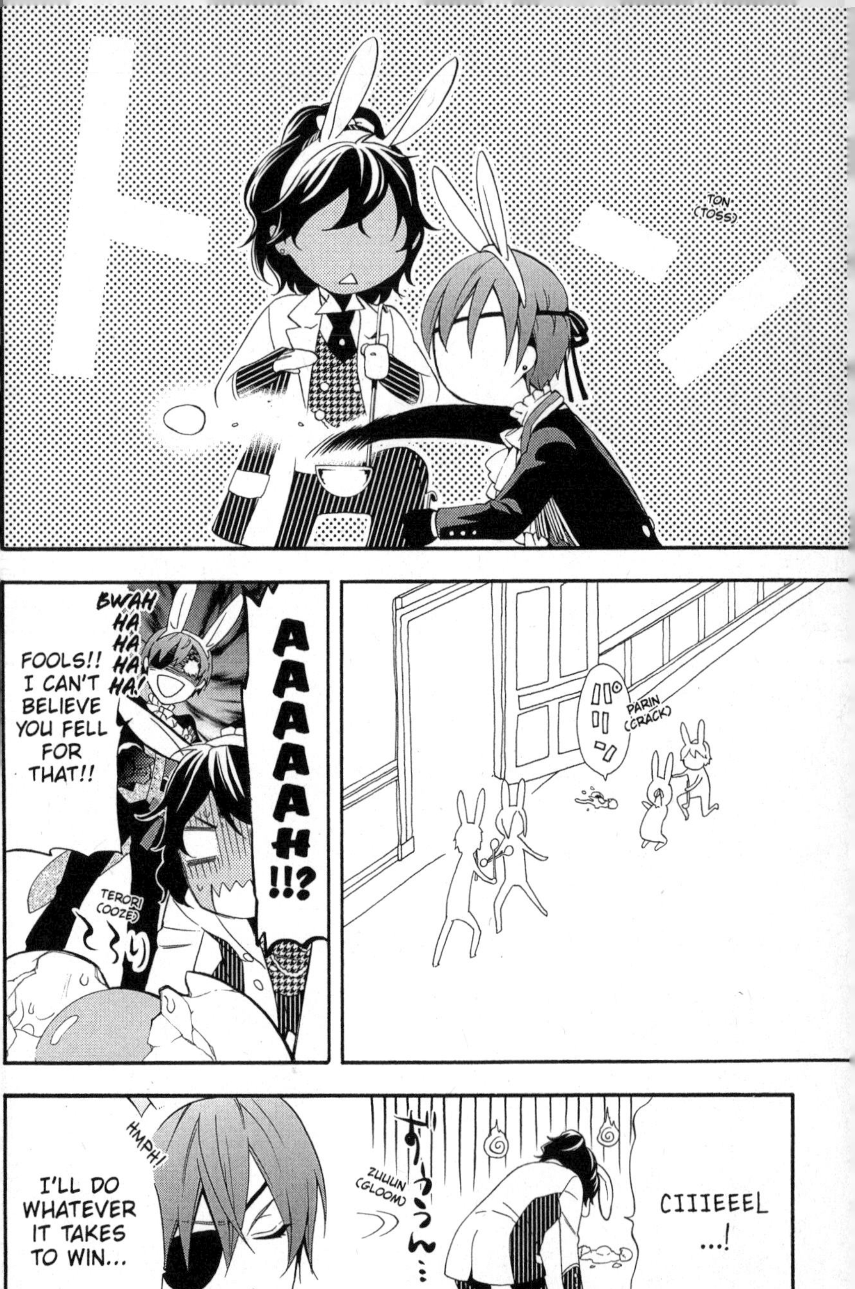
TON (TOSS)
PARIN (CRACK)
AAAAAAAH!!?
BWAH HA HA HA HA!
FOOLS!! I CAN'T BELIEVE YOU FELL FOR THAT!!
TERORI (OOZE)
CIIIEEEL ...!
ZUUUN (GLOOM)
HMPH!
I'LL DO WHATEVER IT TAKES TO WIN...

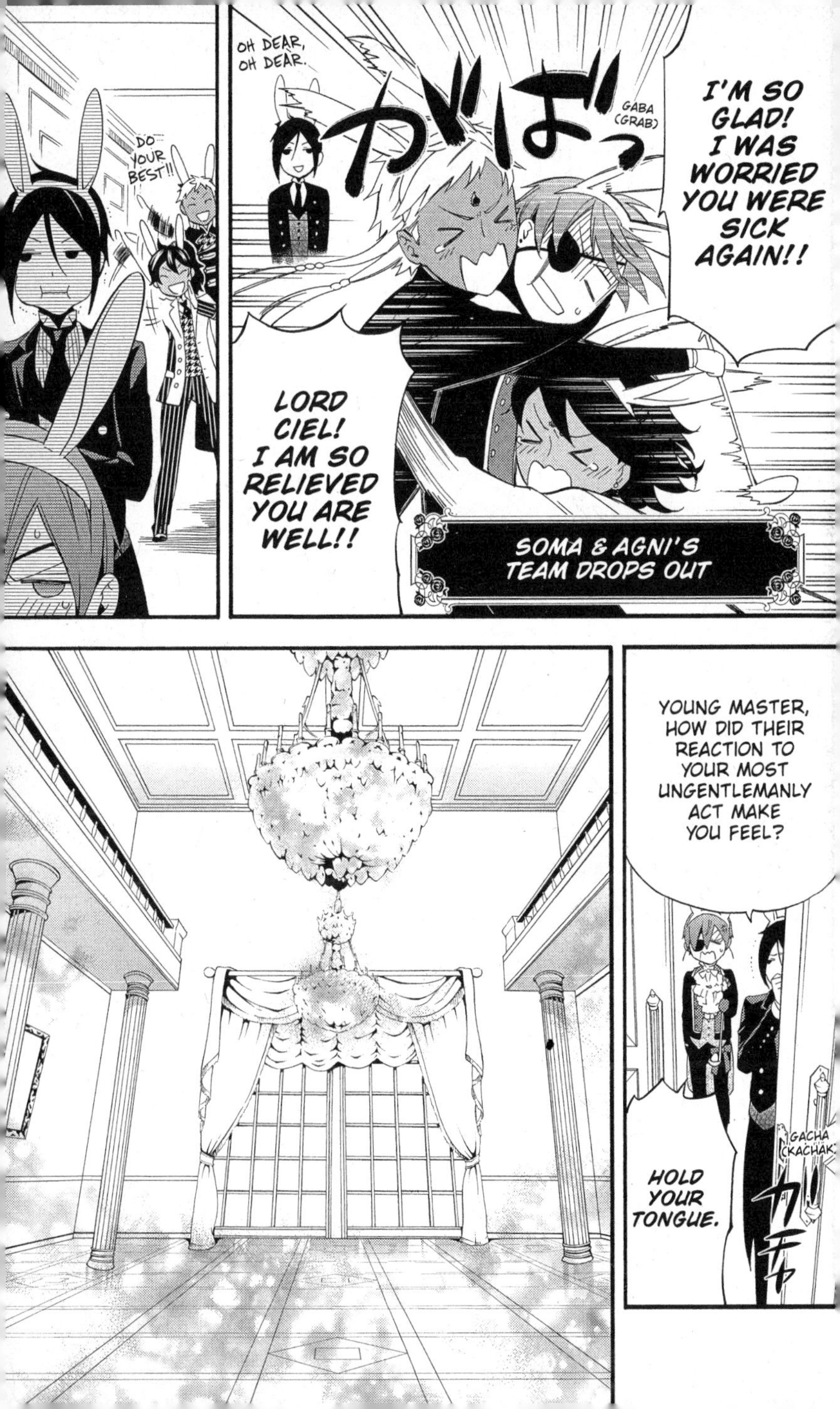
I'M SO GLAD! I WAS WORRIED YOU WERE SICK AGAIN!!
GABA (GRAB)
OH DEAR, OH DEAR.
LORD CIEL! I AM SO RELIEVED YOU ARE WELL!!
SOMA & AGNI'S TEAM DROPS OUT
DO YOUR BEST!!
YOUNG MASTER, HOW DID THEIR REACTION TO YOUR MOST UNGENTLEMANLY ACT MAKE YOU FEEL?
GACHA (KACHAK)
HOLD YOUR TONGUE.

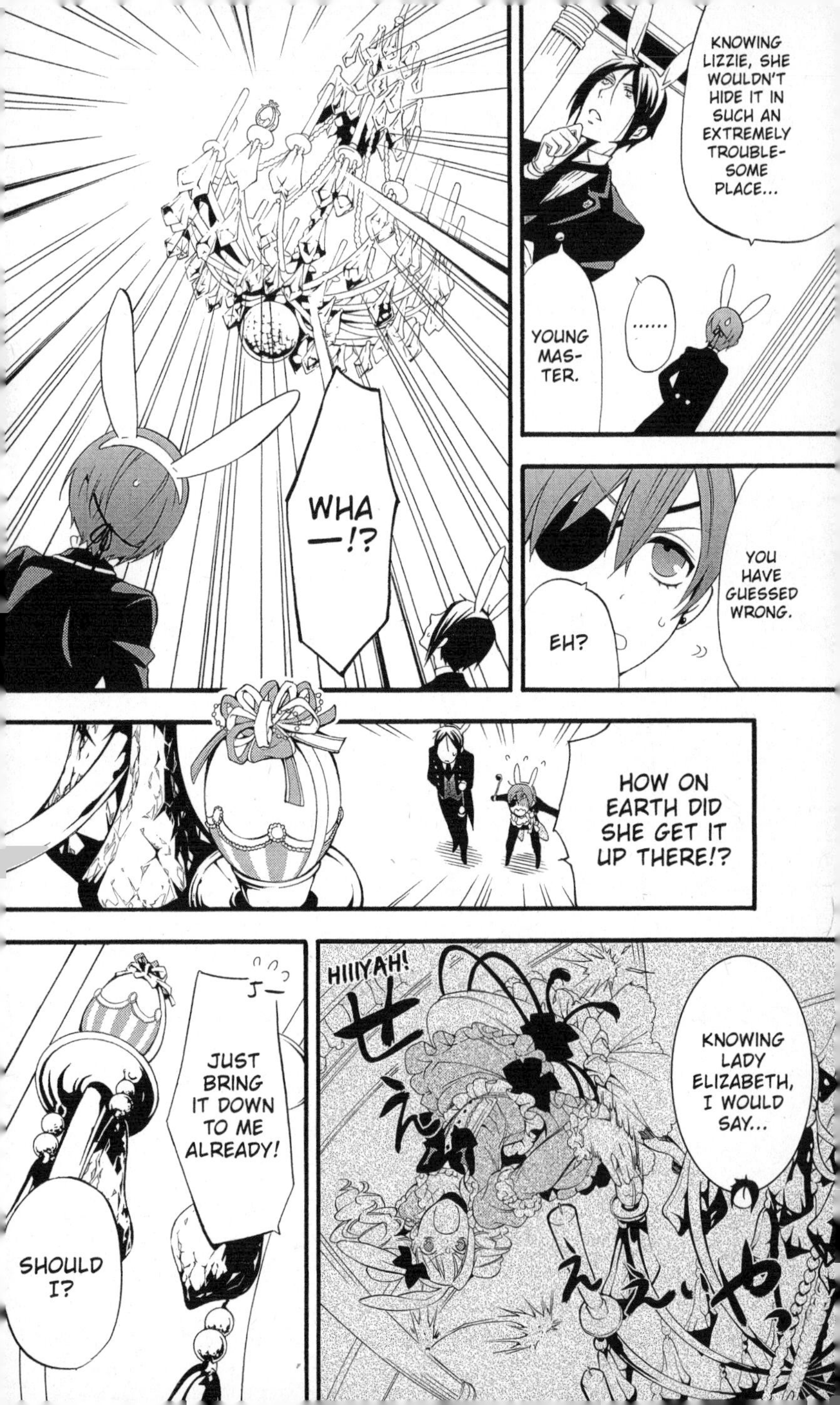
KNOWING LIZZIE, SHE WOULDN'T HIDE IT IN SUCH AN EXTREMELY TROUBLE-SOME PLACE...
......
YOUNG MAS-TER.
YOU HAVE GUESSED WRONG.
EH?
WHA—!?
HOW ON EARTH DID SHE GET IT UP THERE!?
KNOWING LADY ELIZABETH, I WOULD SAY...
HIIIYAH!
J—
JUST BRING IT DOWN TO ME ALREADY!
SHOULD I?

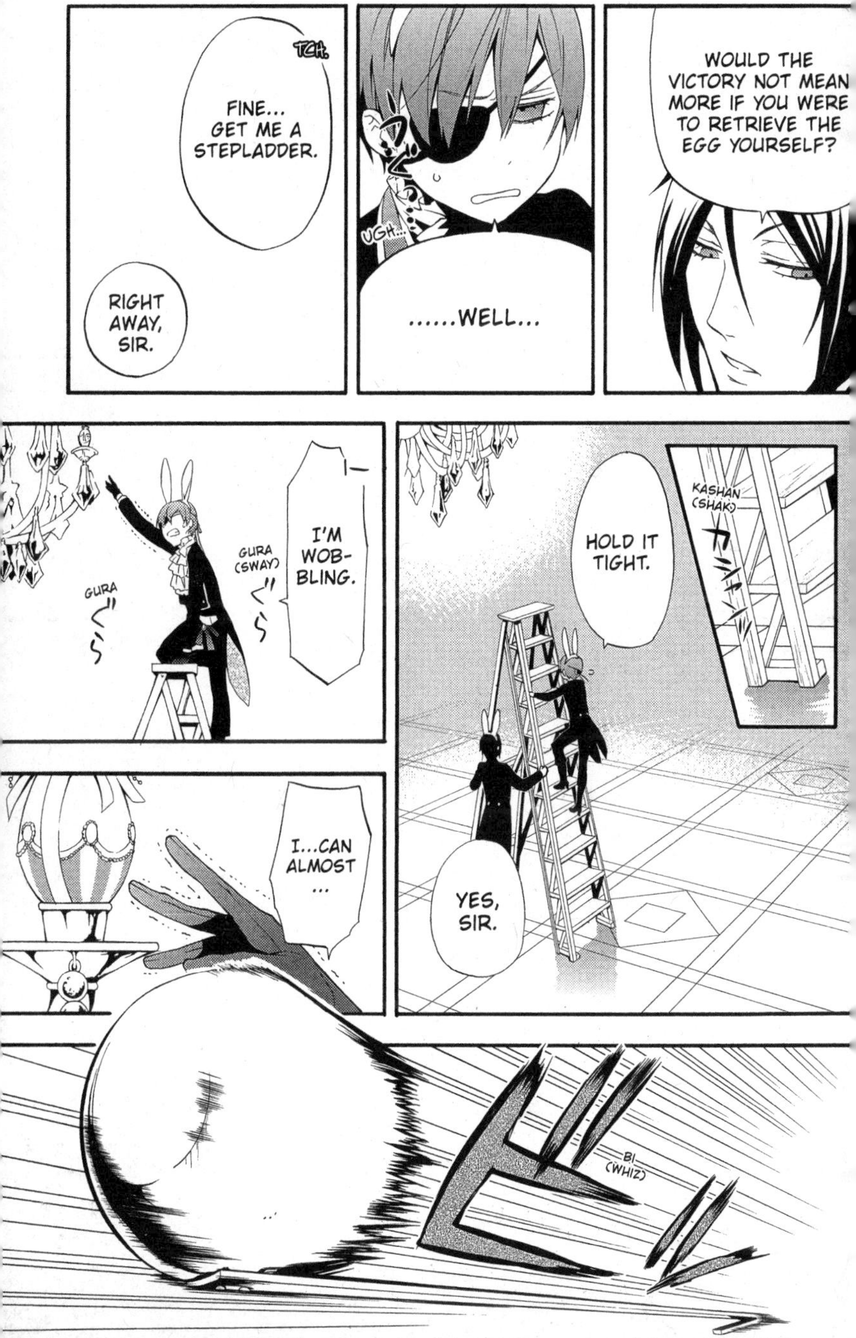

WOULD THE VICTORY NOT MEAN MORE IF YOU WERE TO RETRIEVE THE EGG YOURSELF?
UGH...
......WELL...
TCH.
FINE... GET ME A STEPLADDER.
RIGHT AWAY, SIR.
KASHAN (SHAK)
HOLD IT TIGHT.
YES, SIR.
I—
I'M WOB-BLING.
GURA (SWAY)
GURA
I...CAN ALMOST ...
BI (WHIZ)
...

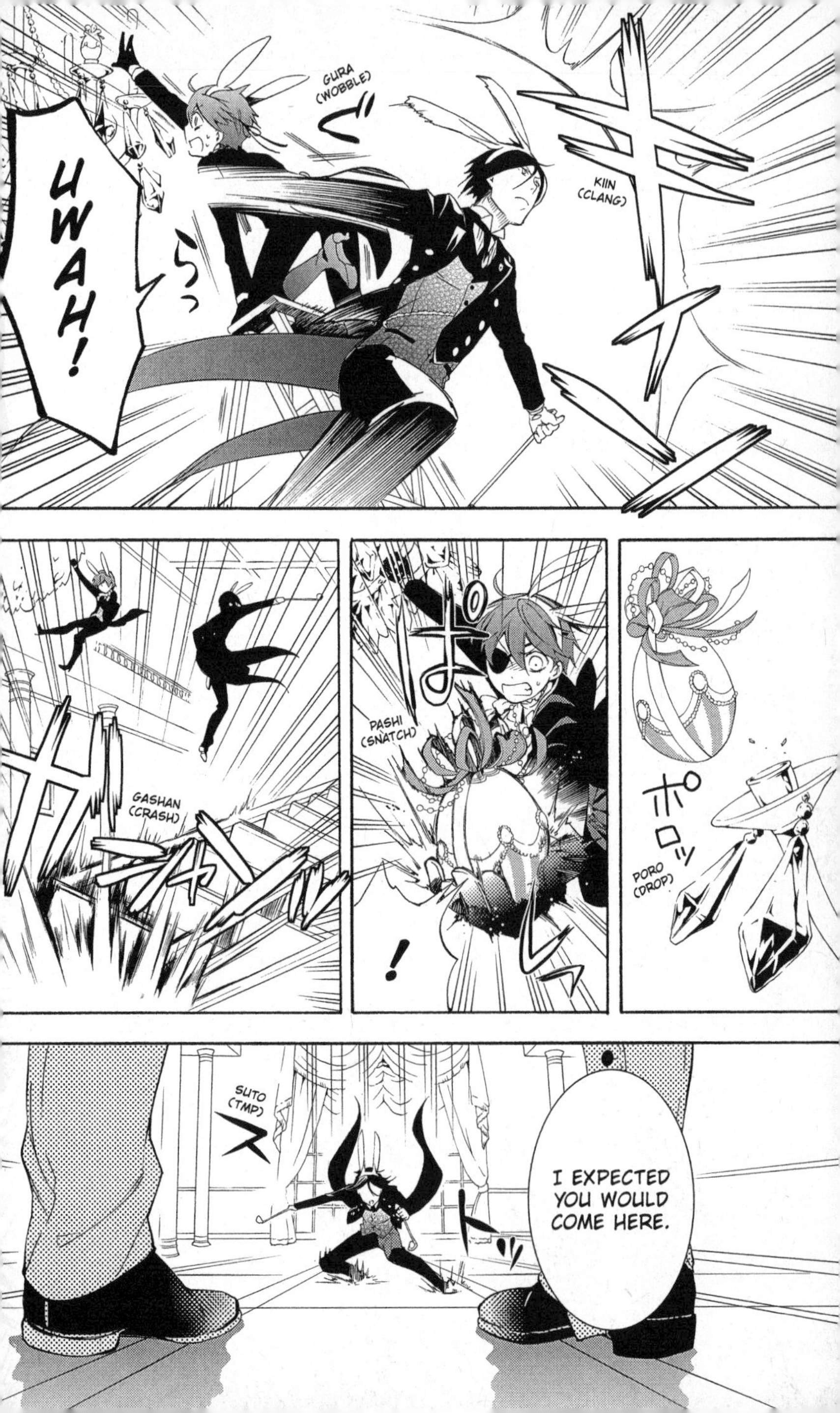
KIIN (CLANG)
GURA (WOBBLE)
UWAH!
PORO (DROP)
PASHI (SNATCH)
!
GASHAN (CRASH)
I EXPECTED YOU WOULD COME HERE.
SUTO (TMP)

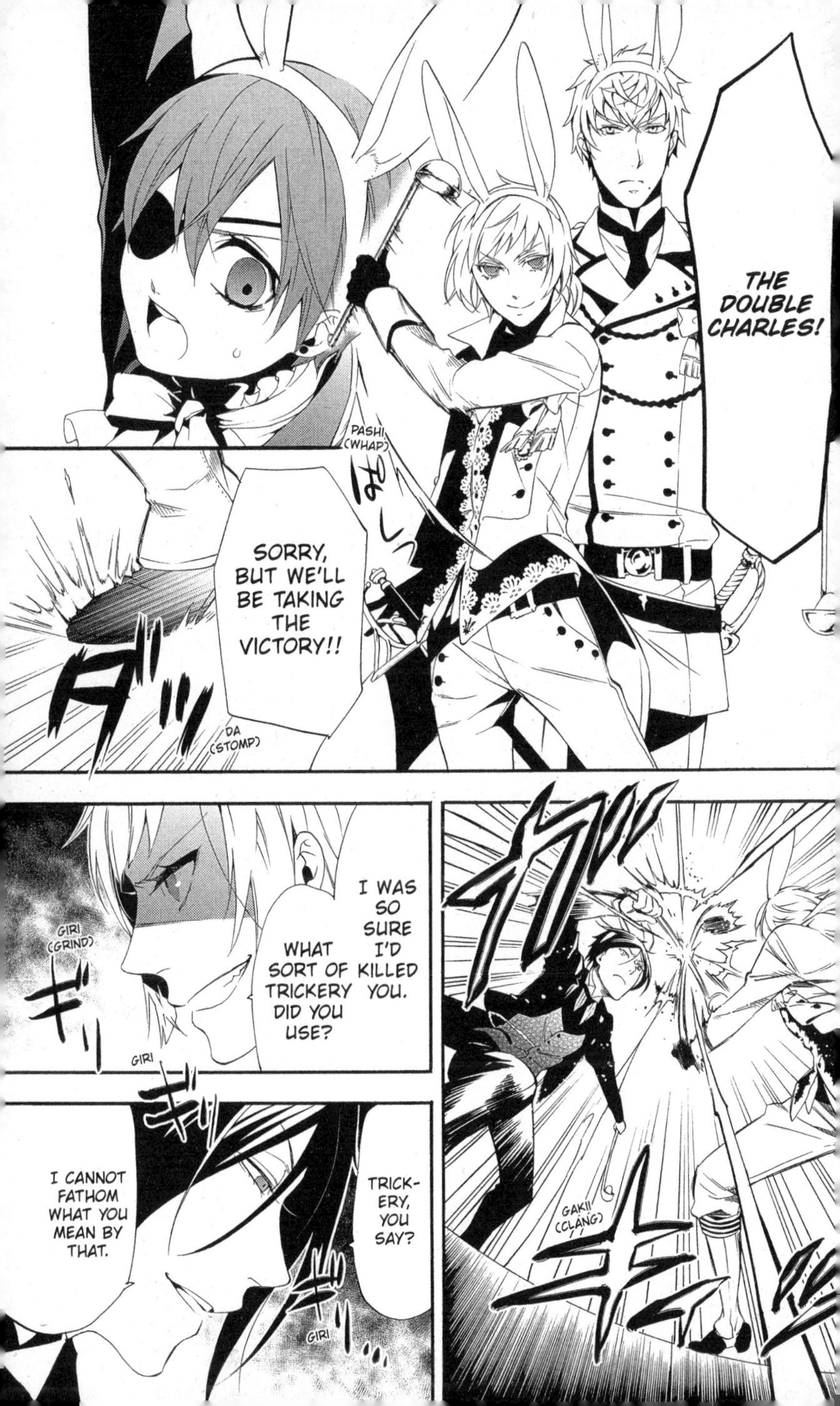
THE DOUBLE CHARLES!
PASHI (WHAP)
SORRY, BUT WE'LL BE TAKING THE VICTORY!!
DA (STOMP)
GAKI! (CLANG)
I WAS SO SURE I'D KILLED YOU.
WHAT SORT OF TRICKERY DID YOU USE?
GIRI (GRIND)
GIRI
TRICKERY, YOU SAY?
I CANNOT FATHOM WHAT YOU MEAN BY THAT.
GIRI

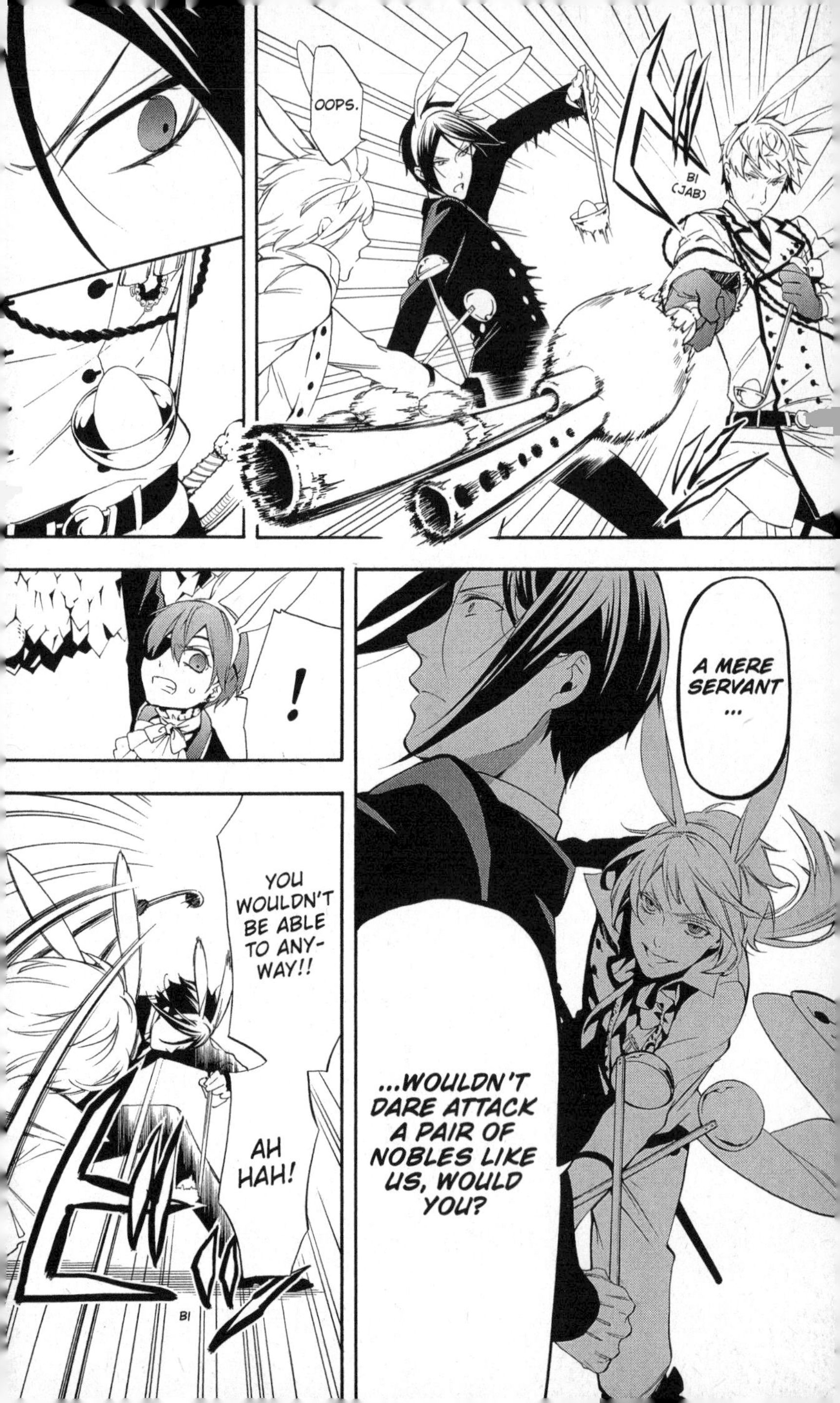

BI (JAB)
OOPS.
A MERE SERVANT ...
...WOULDN'T DARE ATTACK A PAIR OF NOBLES LIKE US, WOULD YOU?
!
YOU WOULDN'T BE ABLE TO ANY-WAY!!
AH HAH!
BI

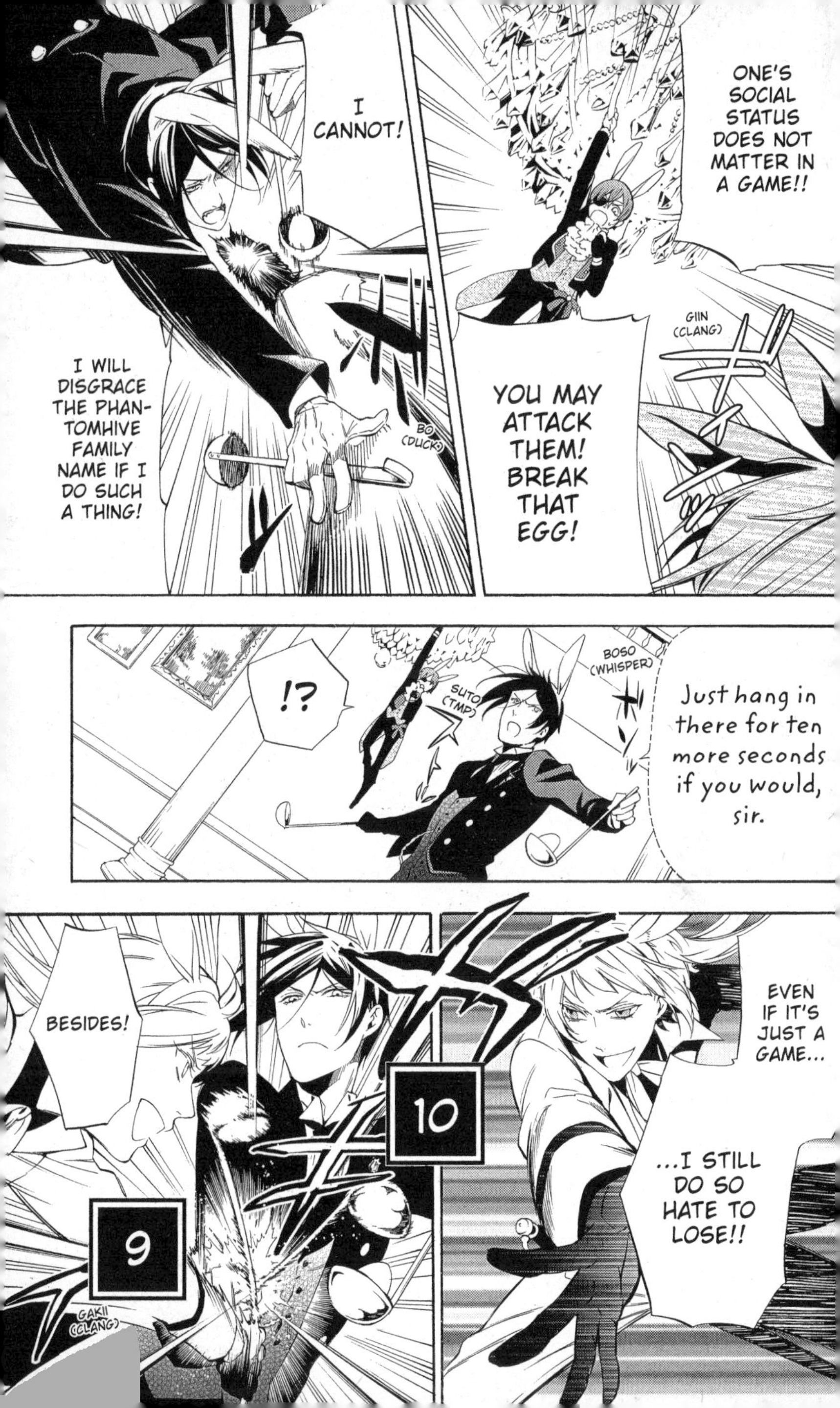
ONE'S SOCIAL STATUS DOES NOT MATTER IN A GAME!!
GIIN (CLANG)
YOU MAY ATTACK THEM! BREAK THAT EGG!
I CANNOT!
BO (DUCK)
I WILL DISGRACE THE PHANTOMHIVE FAMILY NAME IF I DO SUCH A THING!
BOSO (WHISPER)
Just hang in there for ten more seconds if you would, sir.
SUTO (TMP)
!?
EVEN IF IT'S JUST A GAME...
...I STILL DO SO HATE TO LOSE!!
10
BESIDES!
9
GAKII (CLANG)

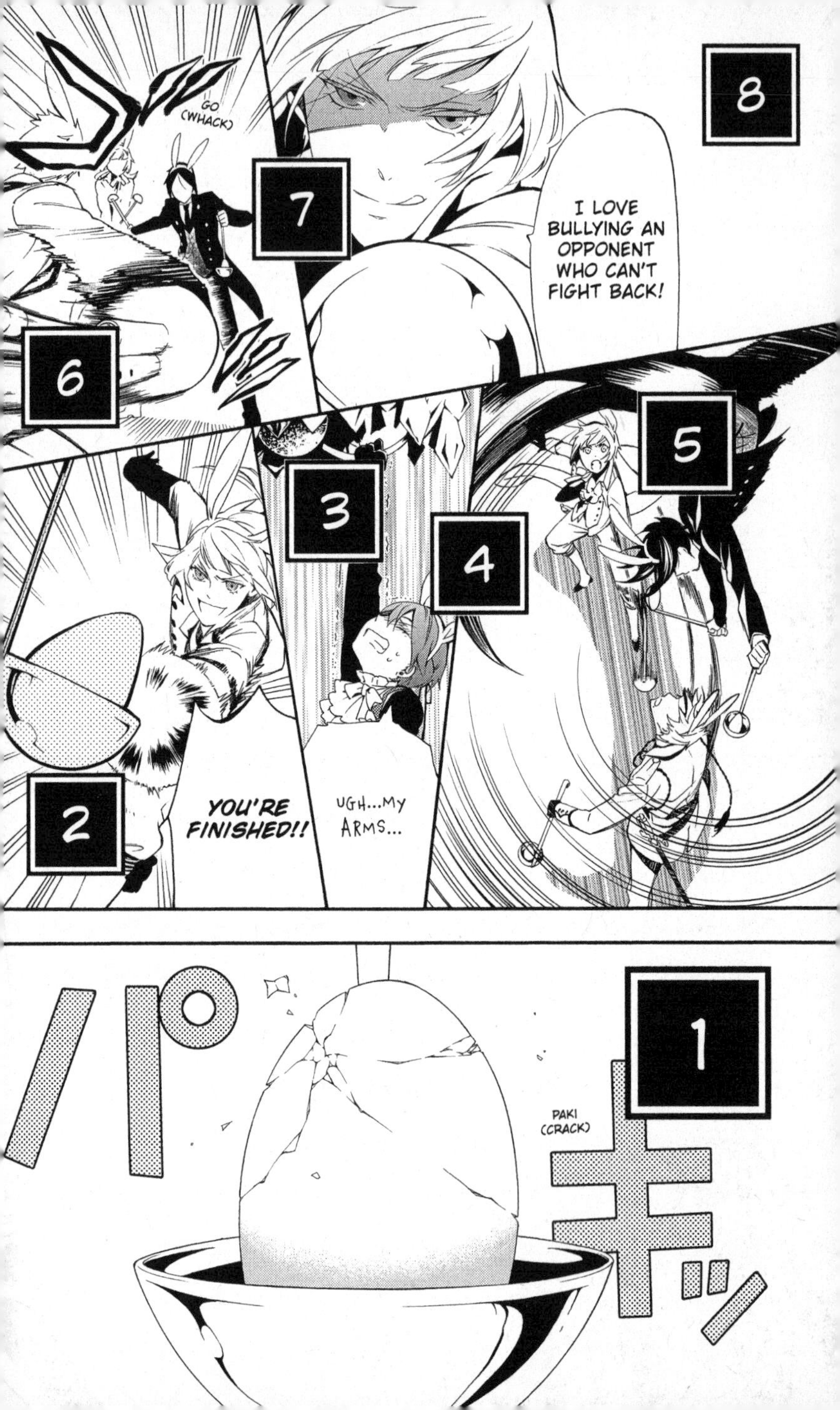
1
パキッ
PAKI (CRACK)
2
YOU'RE FINISHED!!
3
UGH...MY ARMS...
4
5
6
7
GO (WHACK)
8
I LOVE BULLYING AN OPPONENT WHO CAN'T FIGHT BACK!

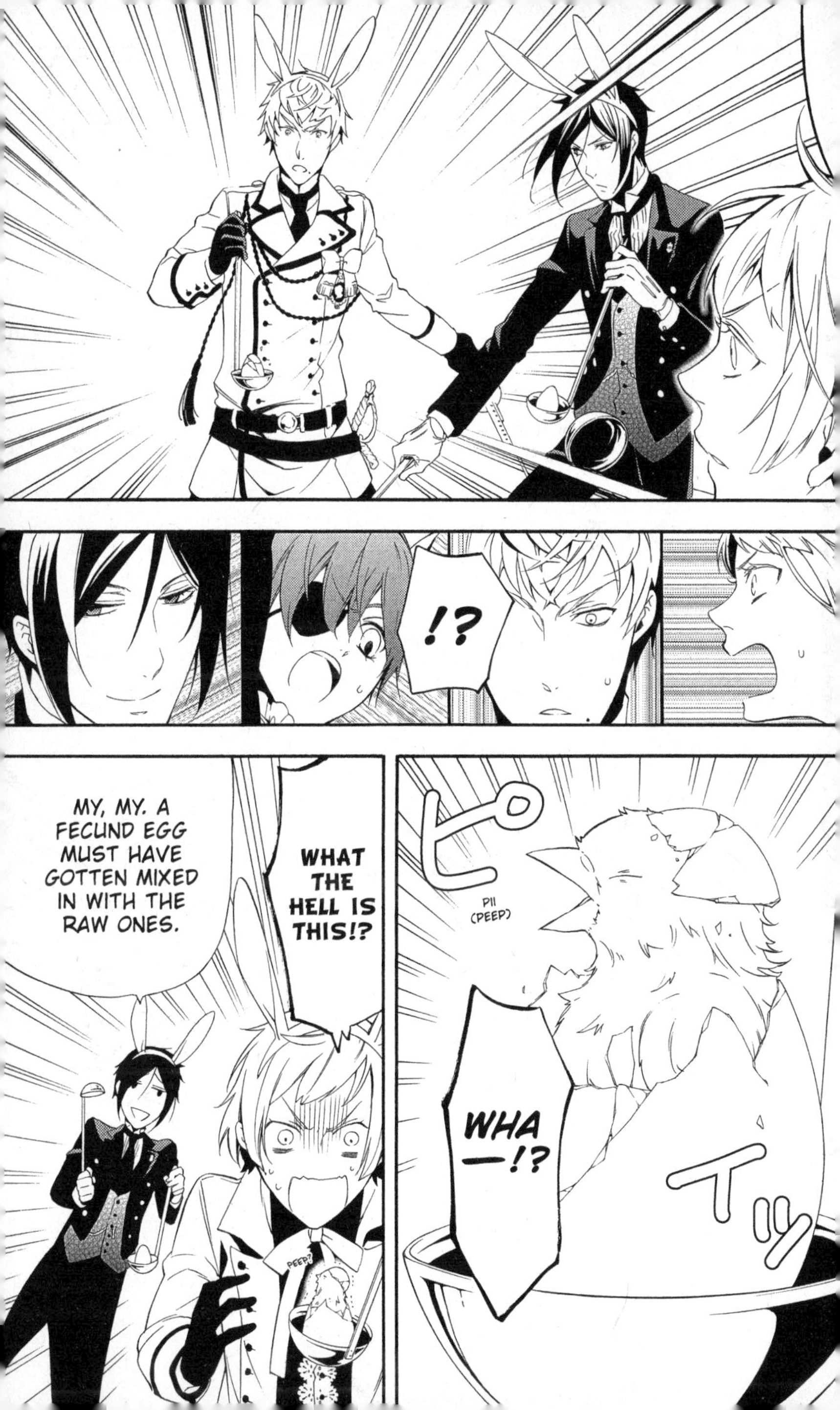
!?
ピ
PII
(PEEP)
WHA—!?
WHAT THE HELL IS THIS!?
MY, MY. A FECUND EGG MUST HAVE GOTTEN MIXED IN WITH THE RAW ONES.
PEEP?

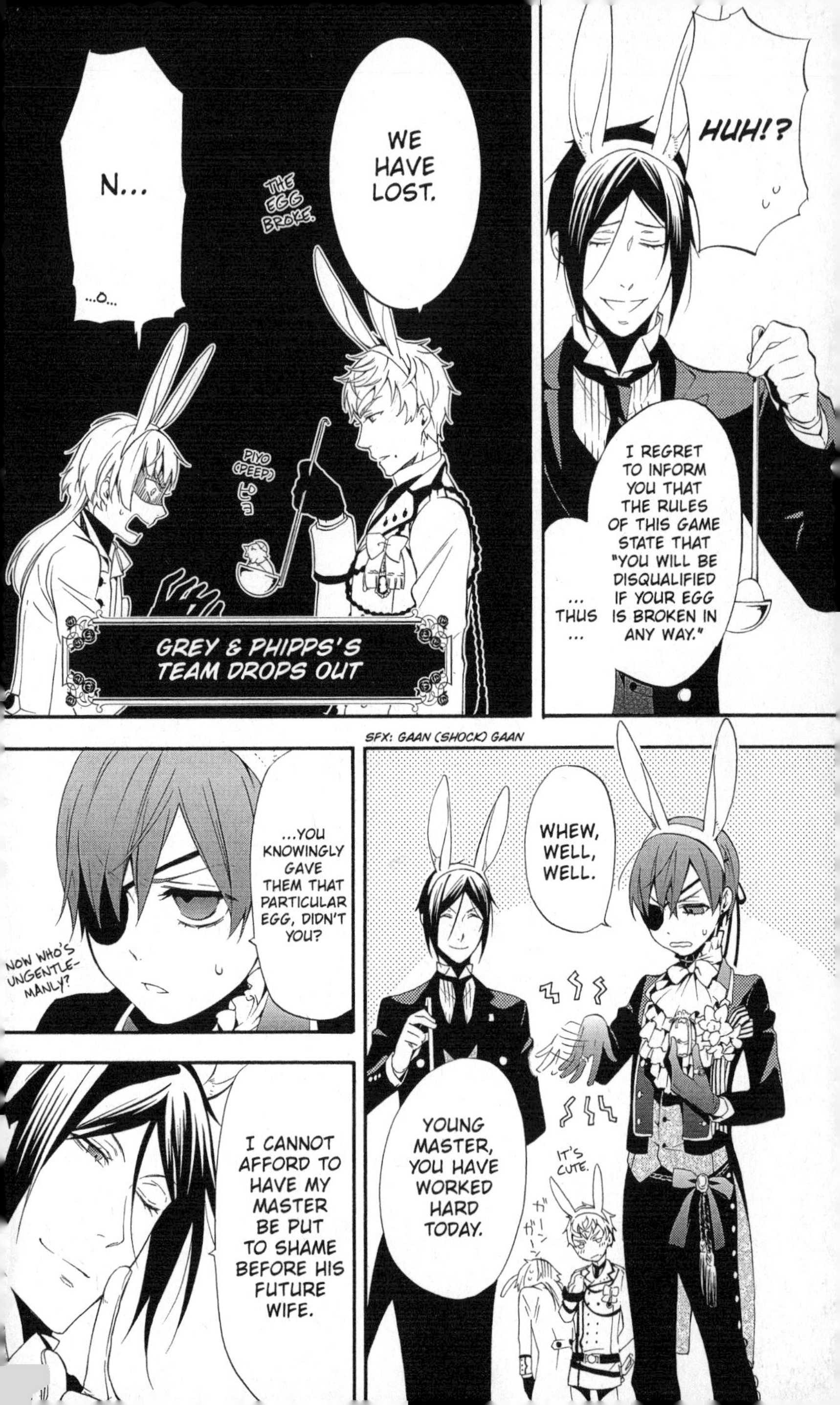
HUH!?
I REGRET TO INFORM YOU THAT THE RULES OF THIS GAME STATE THAT "YOU WILL BE DISQUALIFIED IF YOUR EGG IS BROKEN IN ANY WAY."
... THUS ...
WE HAVE LOST.
THE EGG BROKE.
N...
...O...
PIYO (PEEP)
GREY & PHIPPS'S TEAM DROPS OUT
SFX: GAAN (SHOCK) GAAN
WHEW, WELL, WELL.
YOUNG MASTER, YOU HAVE WORKED HARD TODAY.
IT'S CUTE.
...YOU KNOWINGLY GAVE THEM THAT PARTICULAR EGG, DIDN'T YOU?
NOW WHO'S UNGENTLE-MANLY?
I CANNOT AFFORD TO HAVE MY MASTER BE PUT TO SHAME BEFORE HIS FUTURE WIFE.

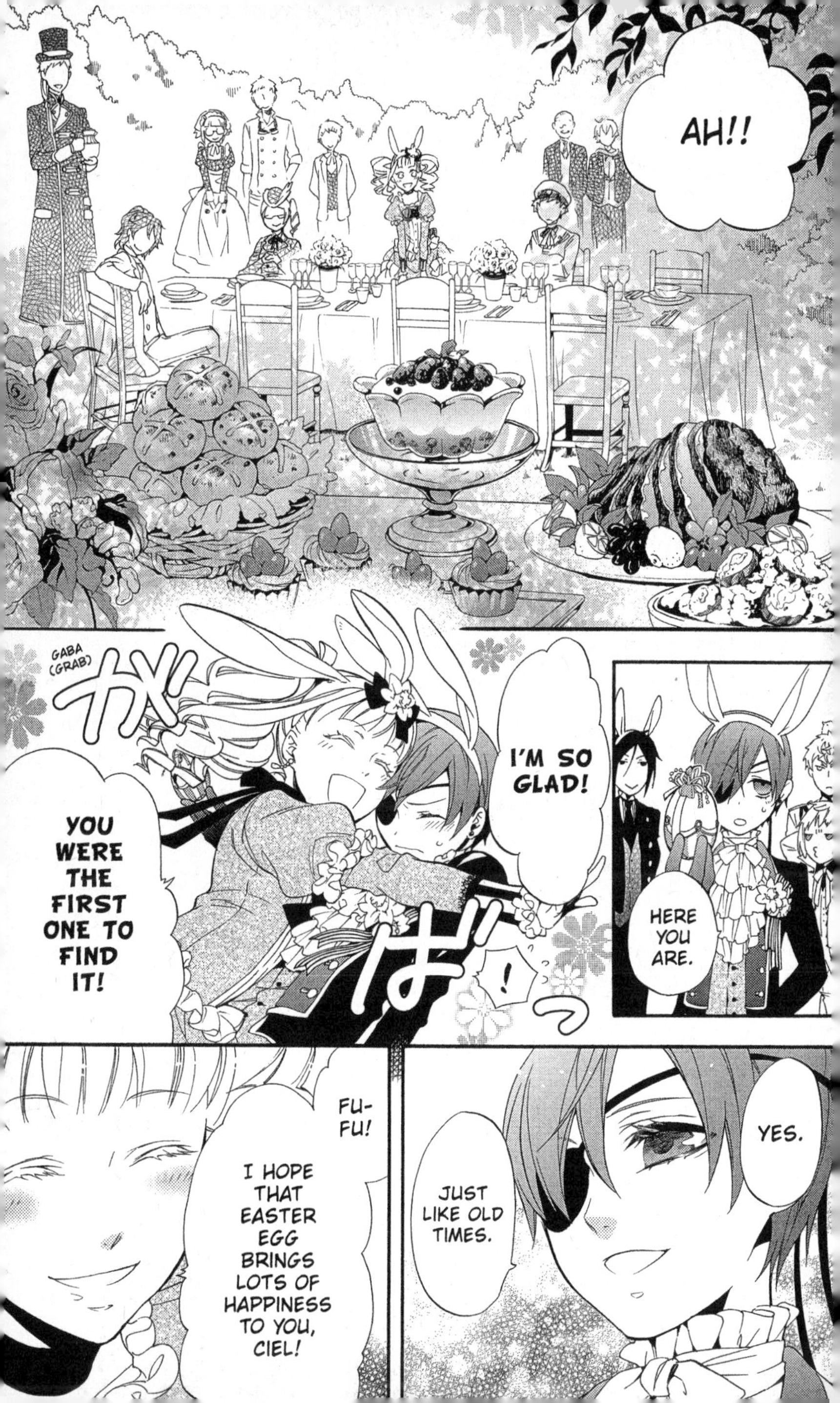
AH!!
HERE YOU ARE.
GABA (GRAB)
I'M SO GLAD!
YOU WERE THE FIRST ONE TO FIND IT!
!
YES.
JUST LIKE OLD TIMES.
FU-FU!
I HOPE THAT EASTER EGG BRINGS LOTS OF HAPPINESS TO YOU, CIEL!

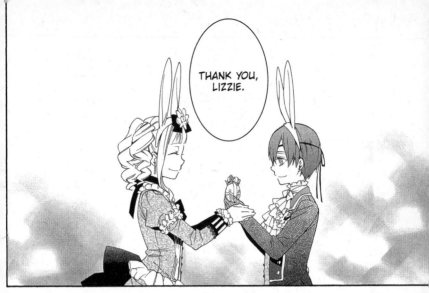

THANK YOU, LIZZIE.
OH, BROTHER. I'VE HAD ENOUGH. I'M HUNGRY.
MY BEST FRIEND DID INDEED WIN!
I WON'T FORGIVE YOU IF YOU BREAK THAT EGG, YOU HEAR!?
LOOKS YUMMY!
FIRST OFF, YOU DON'T EVEN COME CLOSE TO DESERV-ING MY SISTER'S HAND...
...
HEY, CIEL.

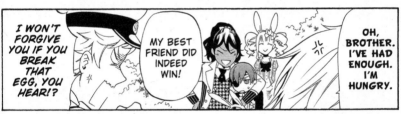

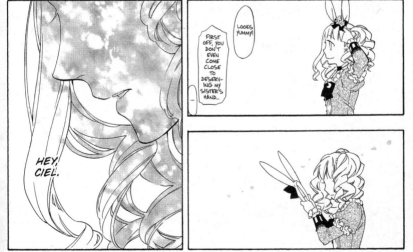

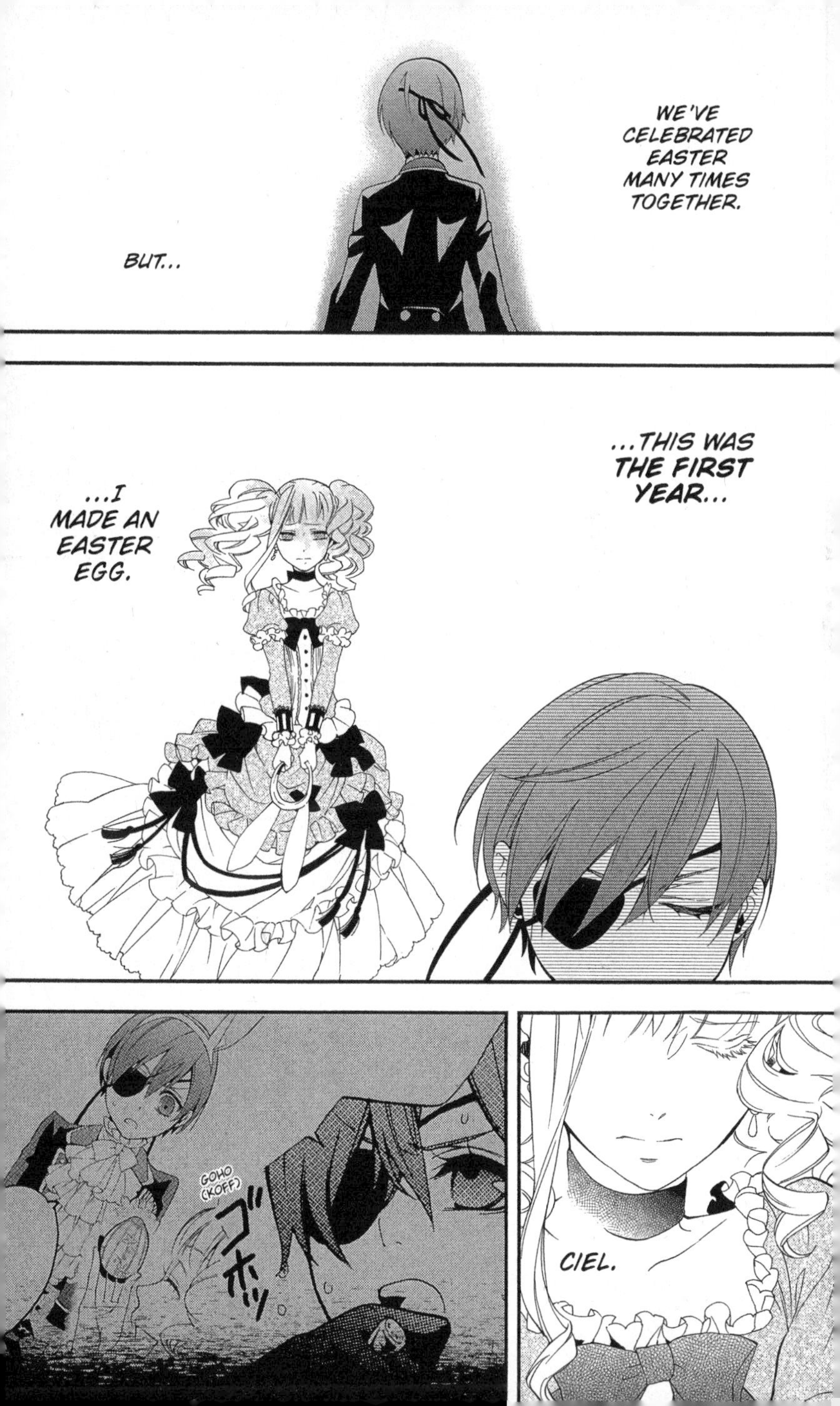
WE'VE CELEBRATED EASTER MANY TIMES TOGETHER.
BUT...
...THIS WAS THE FIRST YEAR...
...I MADE AN EASTER EGG.
CIEL.
GOHO (KOFF)
ゴホッ

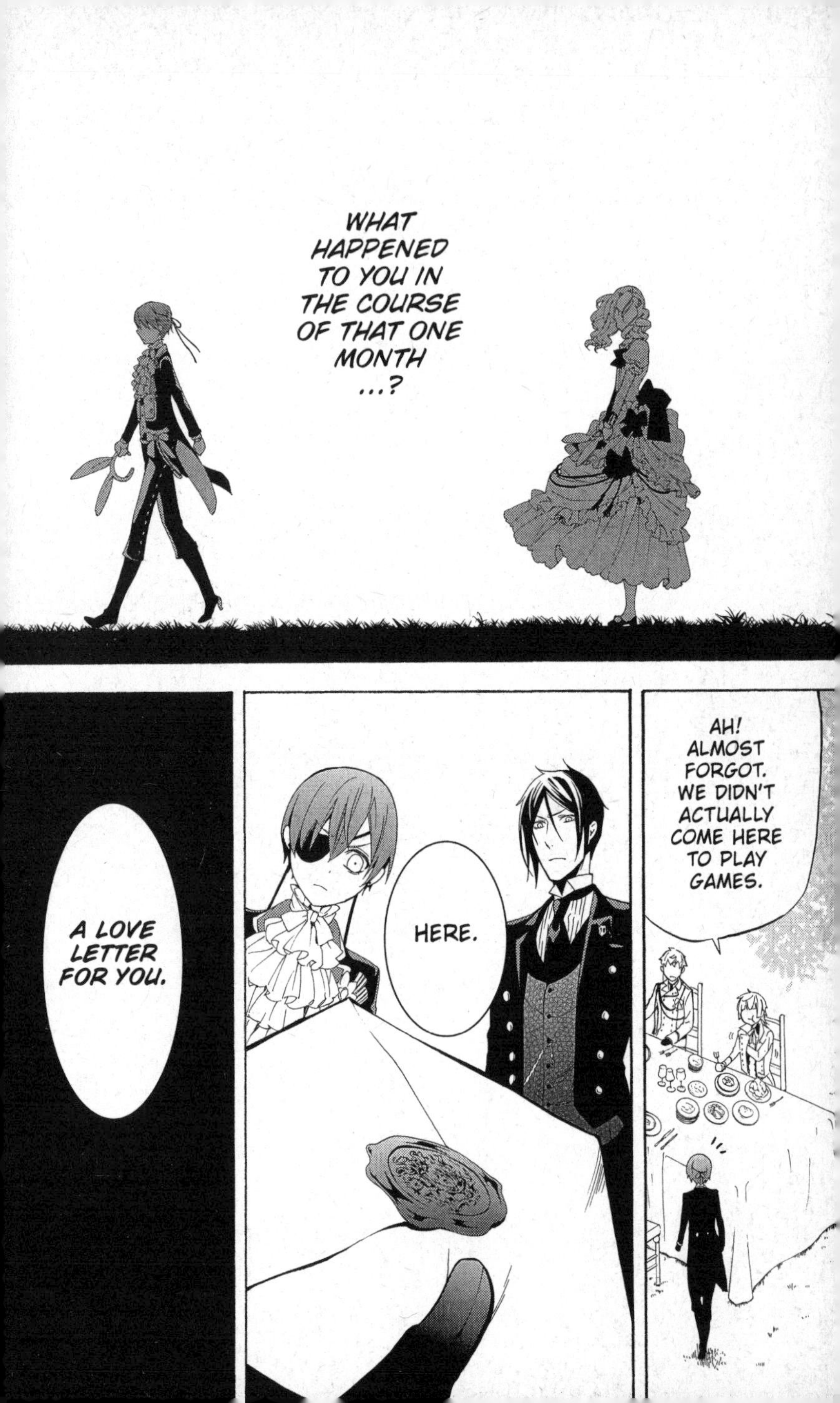
WHAT HAPPENED TO YOU IN THE COURSE OF THAT ONE MONTH ...?
AH! ALMOST FORGOT. WE DIDN'T ACTUALLY COME HERE TO PLAY GAMES.
HERE.
A LOVE LETTER FOR YOU.

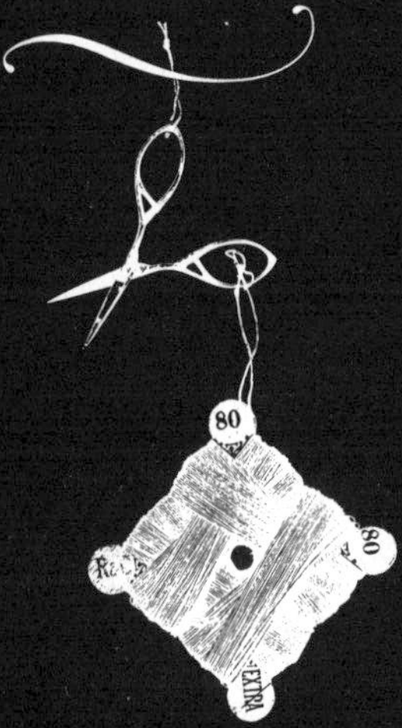
80
80
EXTRA

Black Butler

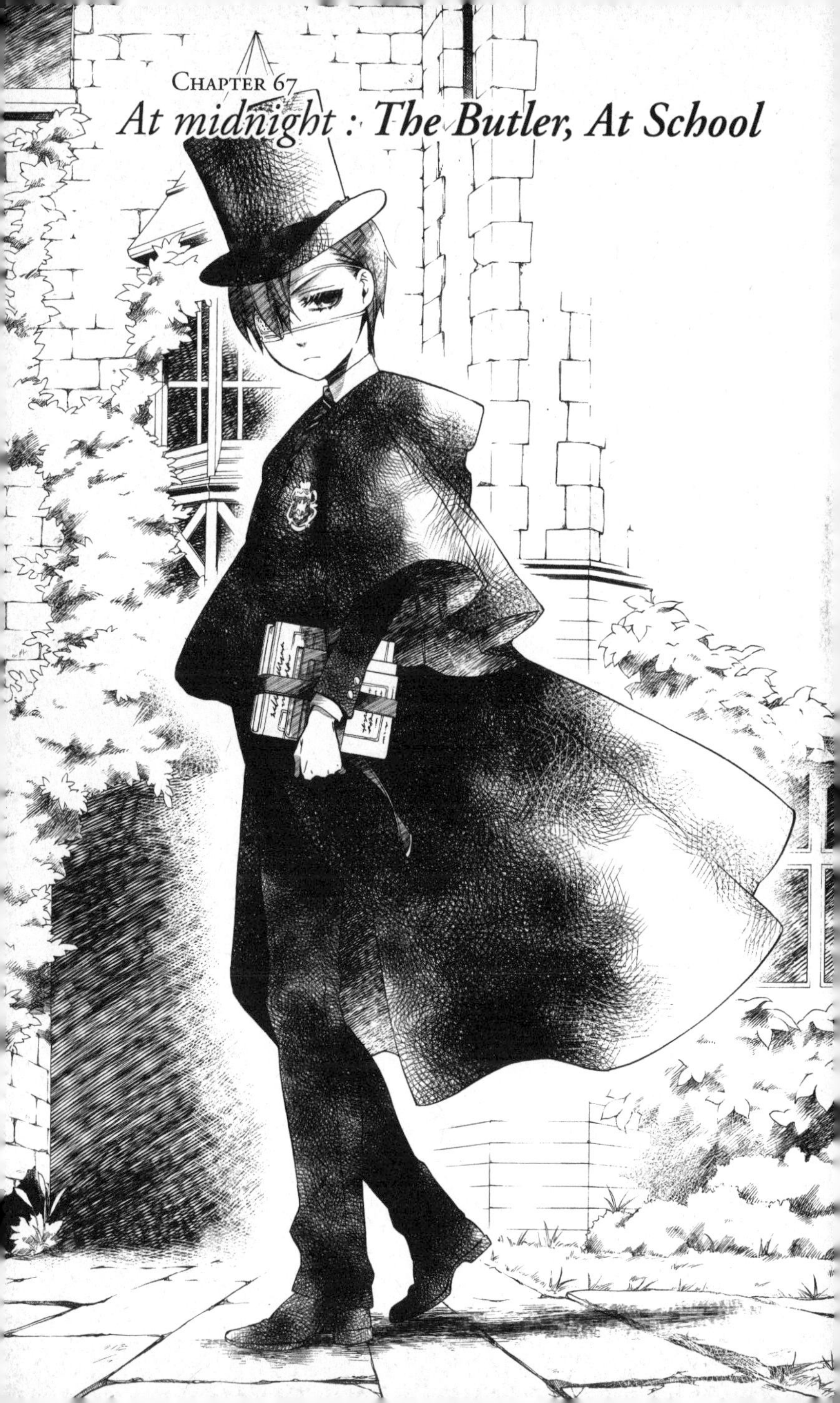

Chapter 67
At midnight : The Butler, At School

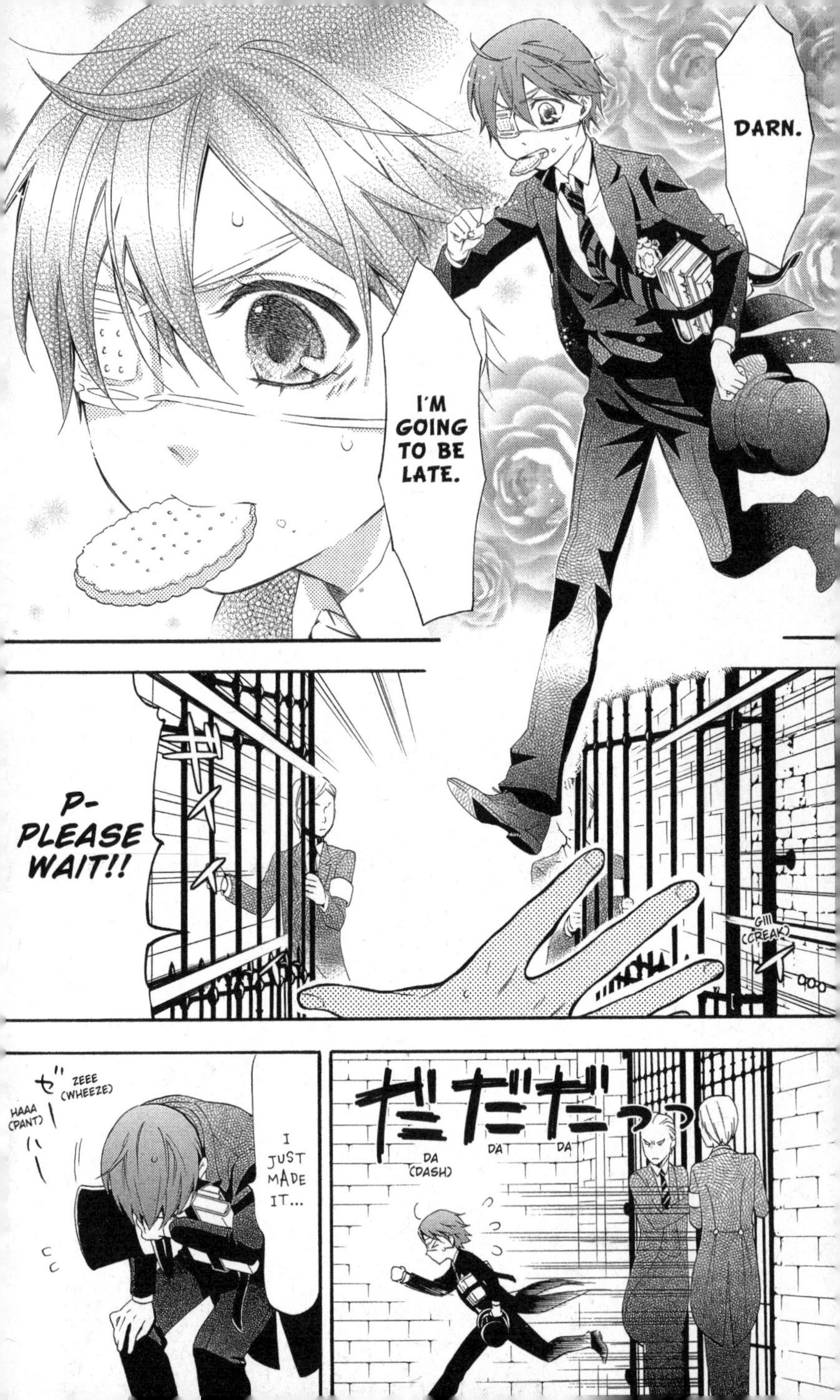
DARN.
I'M GOING TO BE LATE.
GIII (CREAK)
P-PLEASE WAIT!!
だだだっ
DA DA DA (DASH)
I JUST MADE IT...
ZEEE (WHEEZE)
HAAA (PANT)

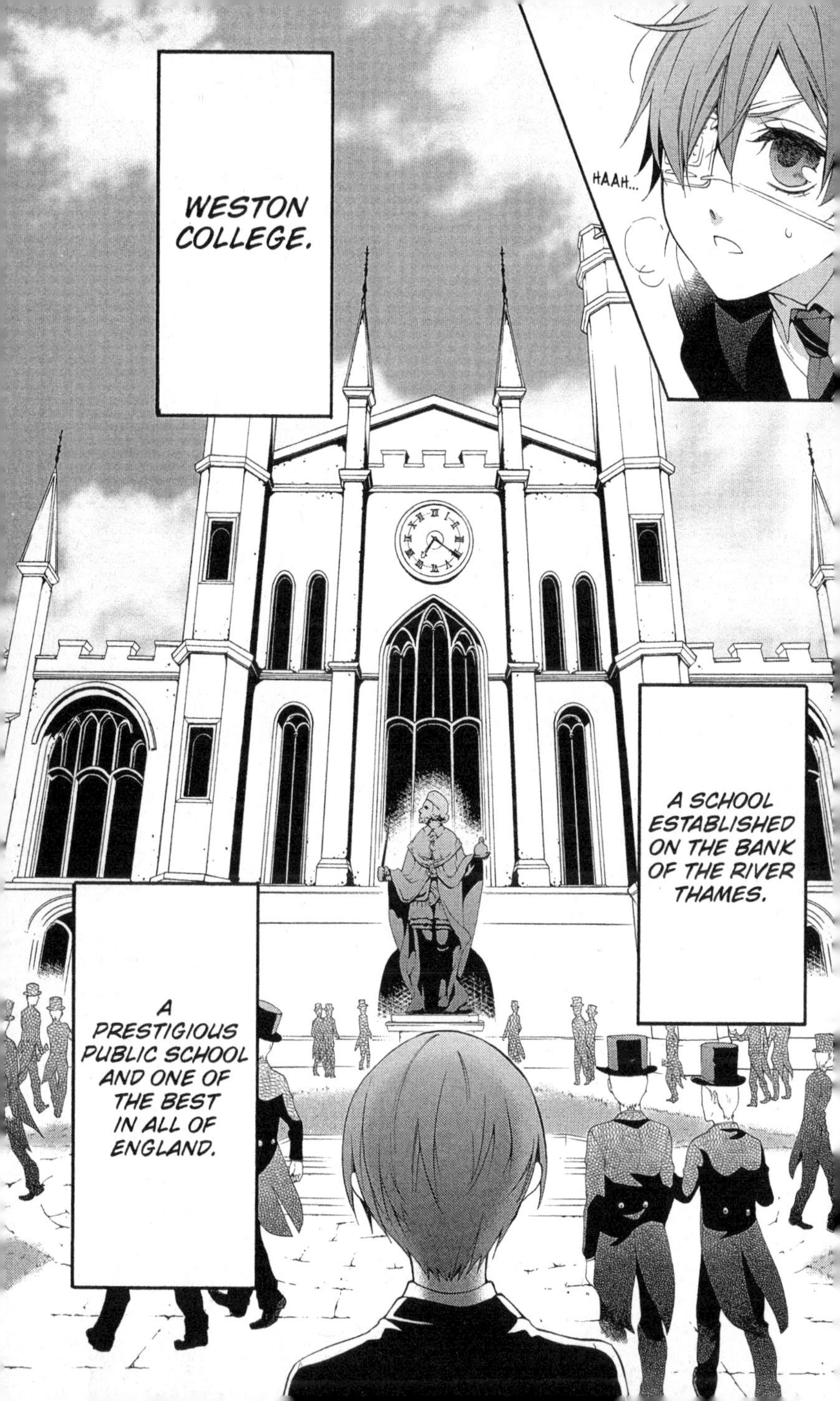
HAAH...
WESTON COLLEGE.
A SCHOOL ESTABLISHED ON THE BANK OF THE RIVER THAMES.
A PRESTIGIOUS PUBLIC SCHOOL AND ONE OF THE BEST IN ALL OF ENGLAND.

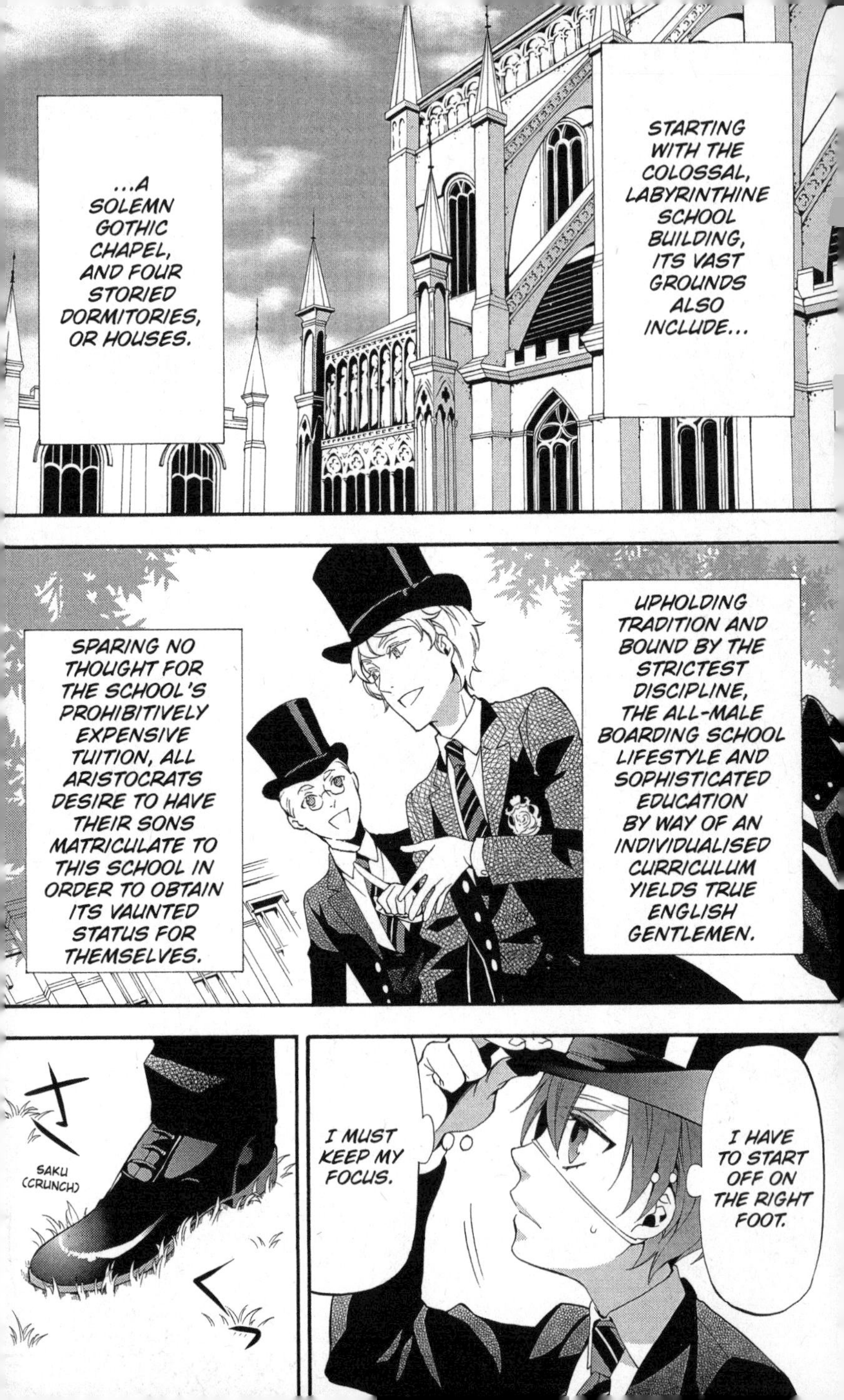
STARTING WITH THE COLOSSAL, LABYRINTHINE SCHOOL BUILDING, ITS VAST GROUNDS ALSO INCLUDE...
...A SOLEMN GOTHIC CHAPEL, AND FOUR STORIED DORMITORIES, OR HOUSES.
UPHOLDING TRADITION AND BOUND BY THE STRICTEST DISCIPLINE, THE ALL-MALE BOARDING SCHOOL LIFESTYLE AND SOPHISTICATED EDUCATION BY WAY OF AN INDIVIDUALISED CURRICULUM YIELDS TRUE ENGLISH GENTLEMEN.
SPARING NO THOUGHT FOR THE SCHOOL'S PROHIBITIVELY EXPENSIVE TUITION, ALL ARISTOCRATS DESIRE TO HAVE THEIR SONS MATRICULATE TO THIS SCHOOL IN ORDER TO OBTAIN ITS VAUNTED STATUS FOR THEMSELVES.
I HAVE TO START OFF ON THE RIGHT FOOT.
I MUST KEEP MY FOCUS.
SAKU (CRUNCH)

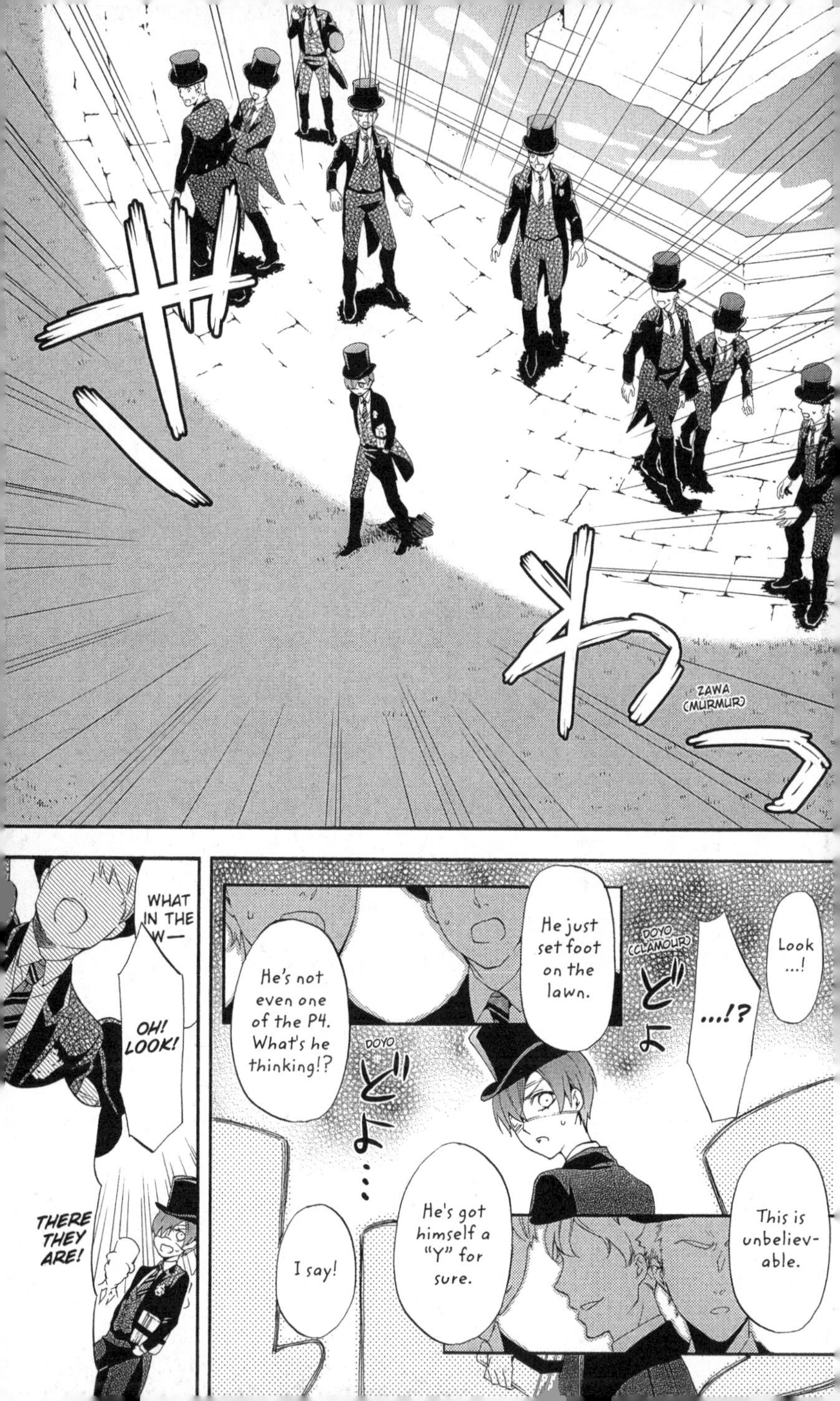
ZAWA
(MURMUR)
Look...!
...!?
DOYO
(CLAMOUR)
He just set foot on the lawn.
He's not even one of the P4. What's he thinking!?
DOYO
This is unbeliev-able.
He's got himself a "Y" for sure.
I say!
WHAT IN THE W—
OH! LOOK!
THERE THEY ARE!

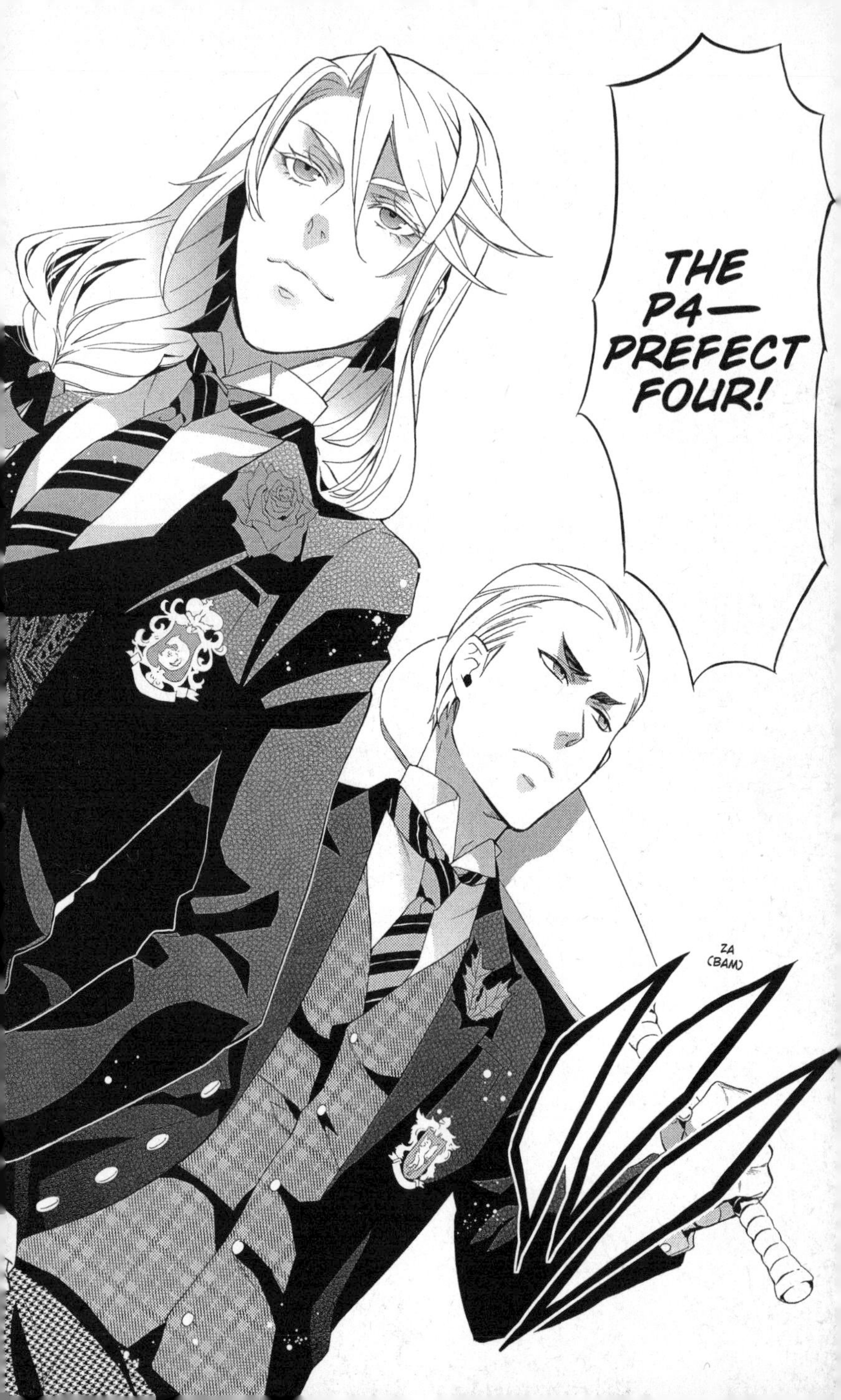
THE P4—PREFECT FOUR!
ZA (BAM)

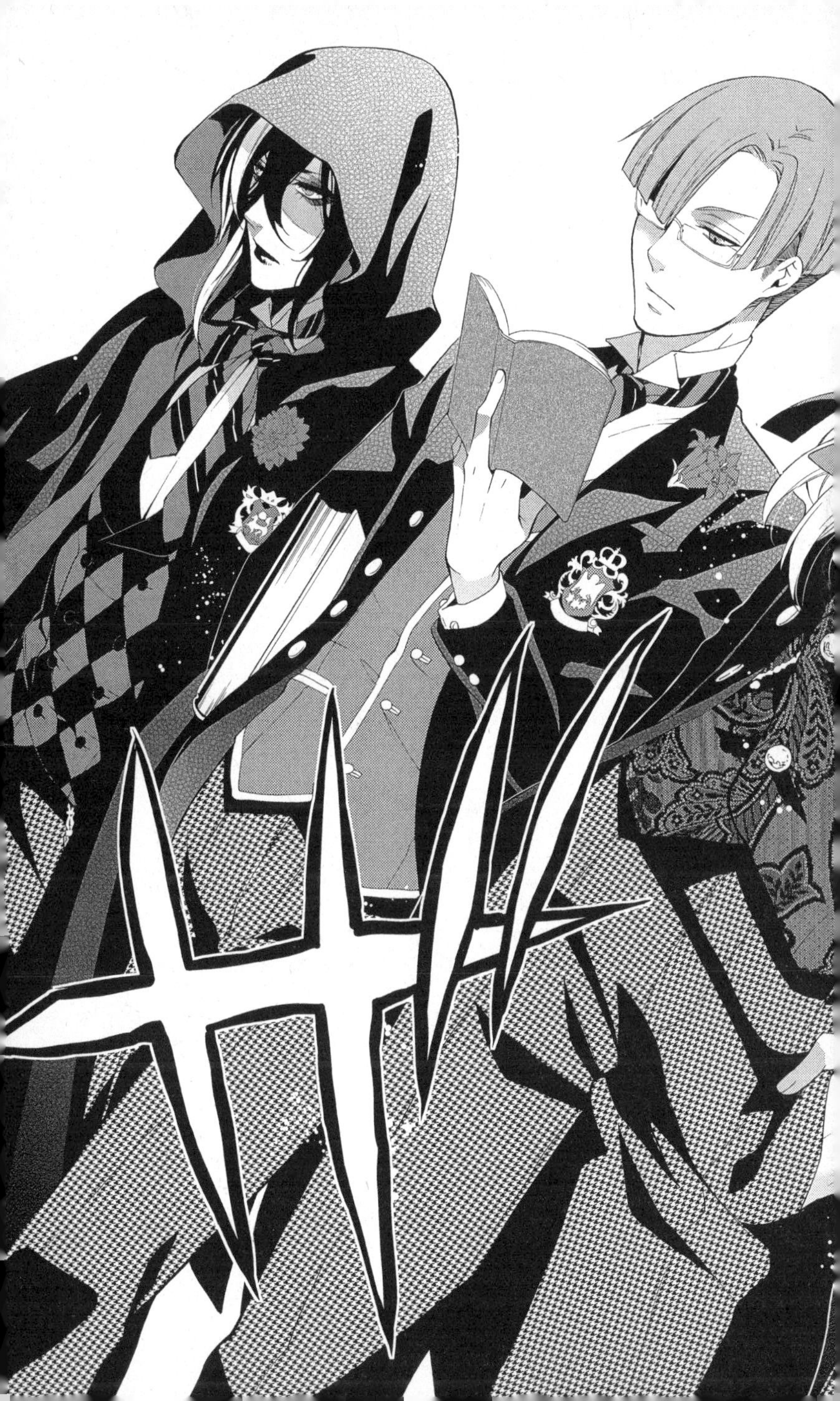

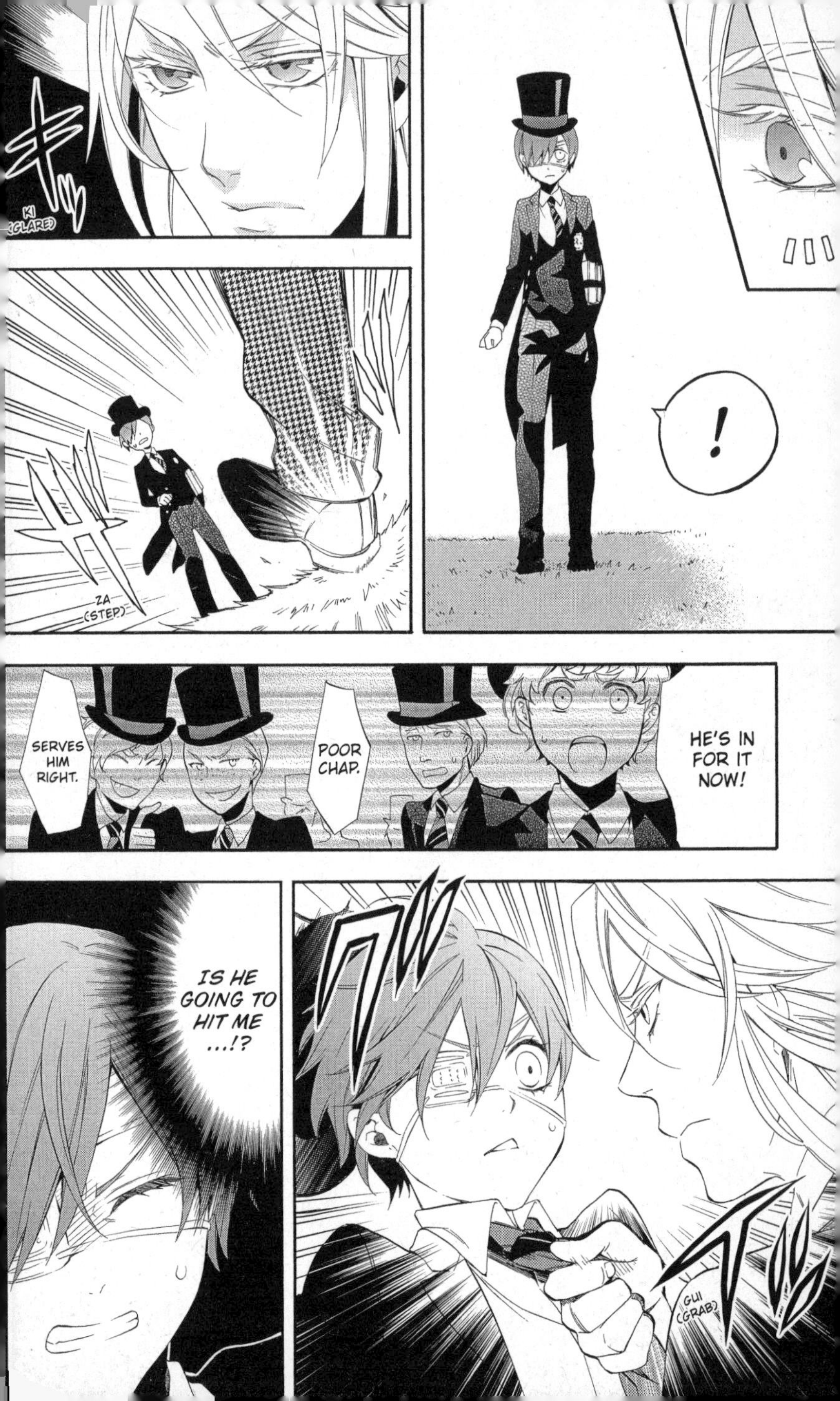

!
KI (GLARE)
ZA (STEP)
HE'S IN FOR IT NOW!
POOR CHAP.
SERVES HIM RIGHT.
GUI (GRAB)
IS HE GOING TO HIT ME ...!?

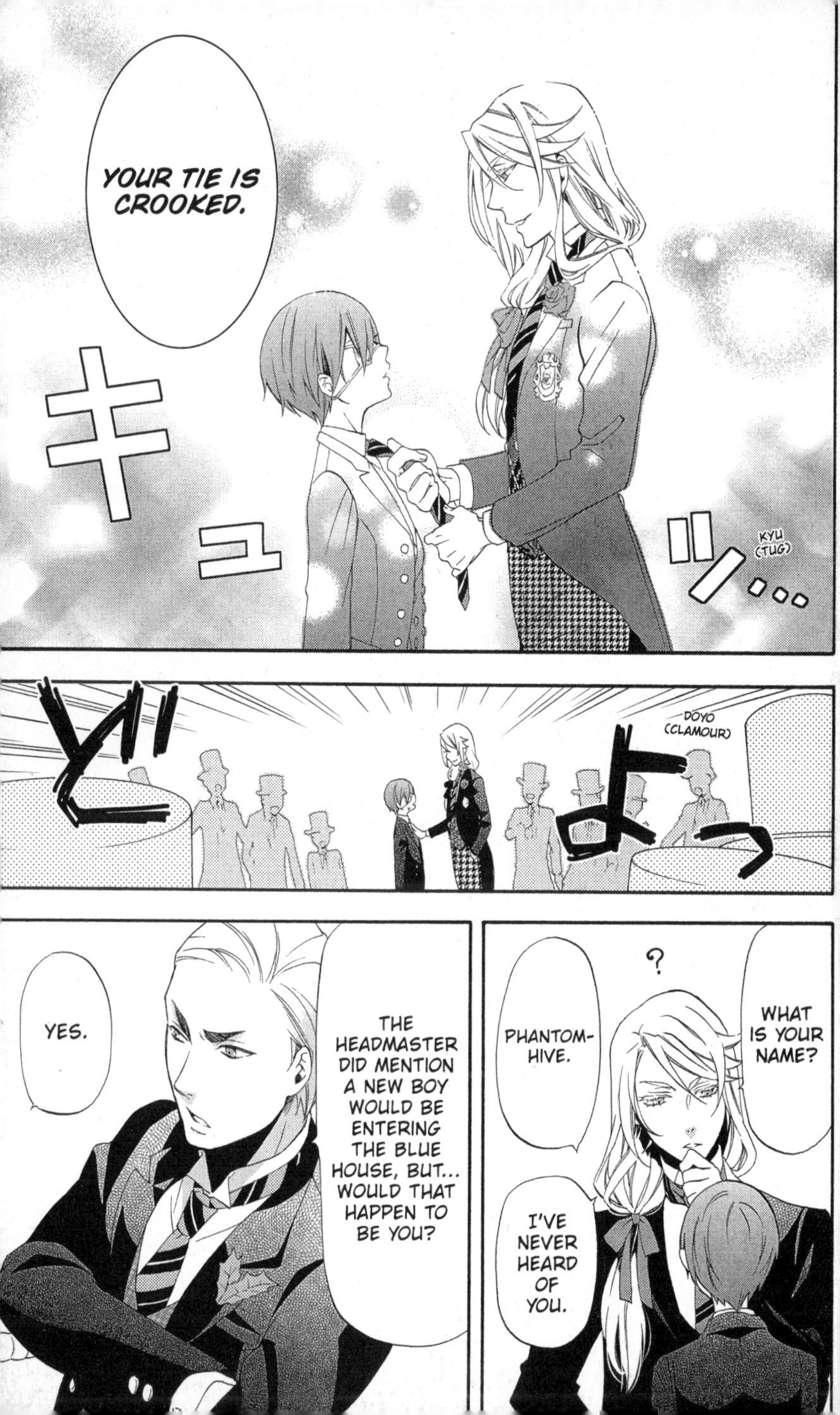
YOUR TIE IS CROOKED.
キュッ...
KYU (TUG)
どよっ
DOYO (CLAMOUR)
WHAT IS YOUR NAME?
?
PHANTOM-HIVE.
I'VE NEVER HEARD OF YOU.
THE HEADMASTER DID MENTION A NEW BOY WOULD BE ENTERING THE BLUE HOUSE, BUT... WOULD THAT HAPPEN TO BE YOU?
YES.

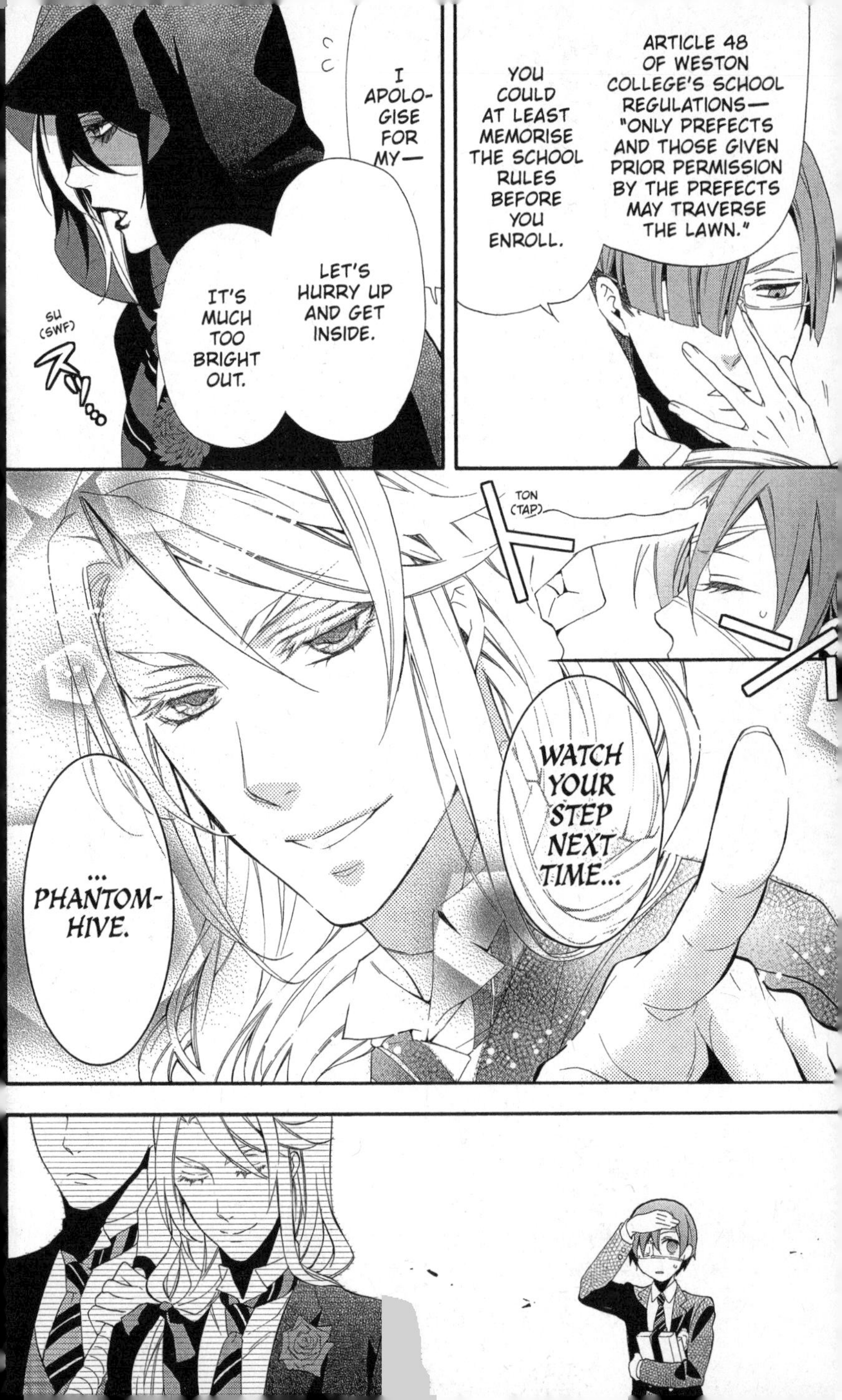
ARTICLE 48 OF WESTON COLLEGE'S SCHOOL REGULATIONS—"ONLY PREFECTS AND THOSE GIVEN PRIOR PERMISSION BY THE PREFECTS MAY TRAVERSE THE LAWN."
YOU COULD AT LEAST MEMORISE THE SCHOOL RULES BEFORE YOU ENROLL.
I APOLOGISE FOR MY—
LET'S HURRY UP AND GET INSIDE.
IT'S MUCH TOO BRIGHT OUT.
SU (SWF)
TON (TAP)
WATCH YOUR STEP NEXT TIME...
...PHANTOMHIVE.

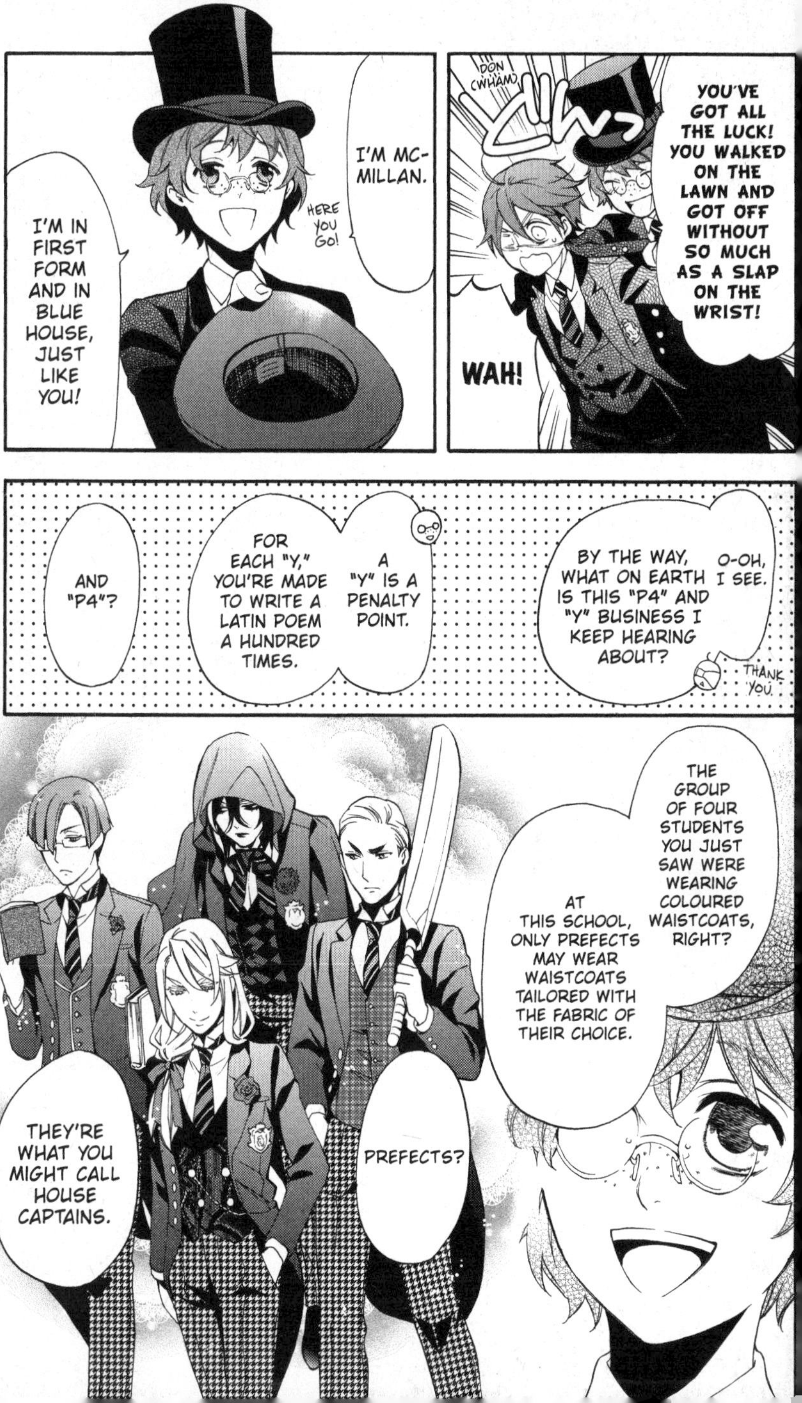
YOU'VE GOT ALL THE LUCK! YOU WALKED ON THE LAWN AND GOT OFF WITHOUT SO MUCH AS A SLAP ON THE WRIST!
DON (WHAM)
WAH!
I'M MC-MILLAN.
HERE YOU GO!
I'M IN FIRST FORM AND IN BLUE HOUSE, JUST LIKE YOU!
O-OH, I SEE.
THANK YOU.
BY THE WAY, WHAT ON EARTH IS THIS "P4" AND "Y" BUSINESS I KEEP HEARING ABOUT?
A "Y" IS A PENALTY POINT.
FOR EACH "Y," YOU'RE MADE TO WRITE A LATIN POEM A HUNDRED TIMES.
AND "P4"?
THE GROUP OF FOUR STUDENTS YOU JUST SAW WERE WEARING COLOURED WAISTCOATS, RIGHT?
AT THIS SCHOOL, ONLY PREFECTS MAY WEAR WAISTCOATS TAILORED WITH THE FABRIC OF THEIR CHOICE.
PREFECTS?
THEY'RE WHAT YOU MIGHT CALL HOUSE CAPTAINS.

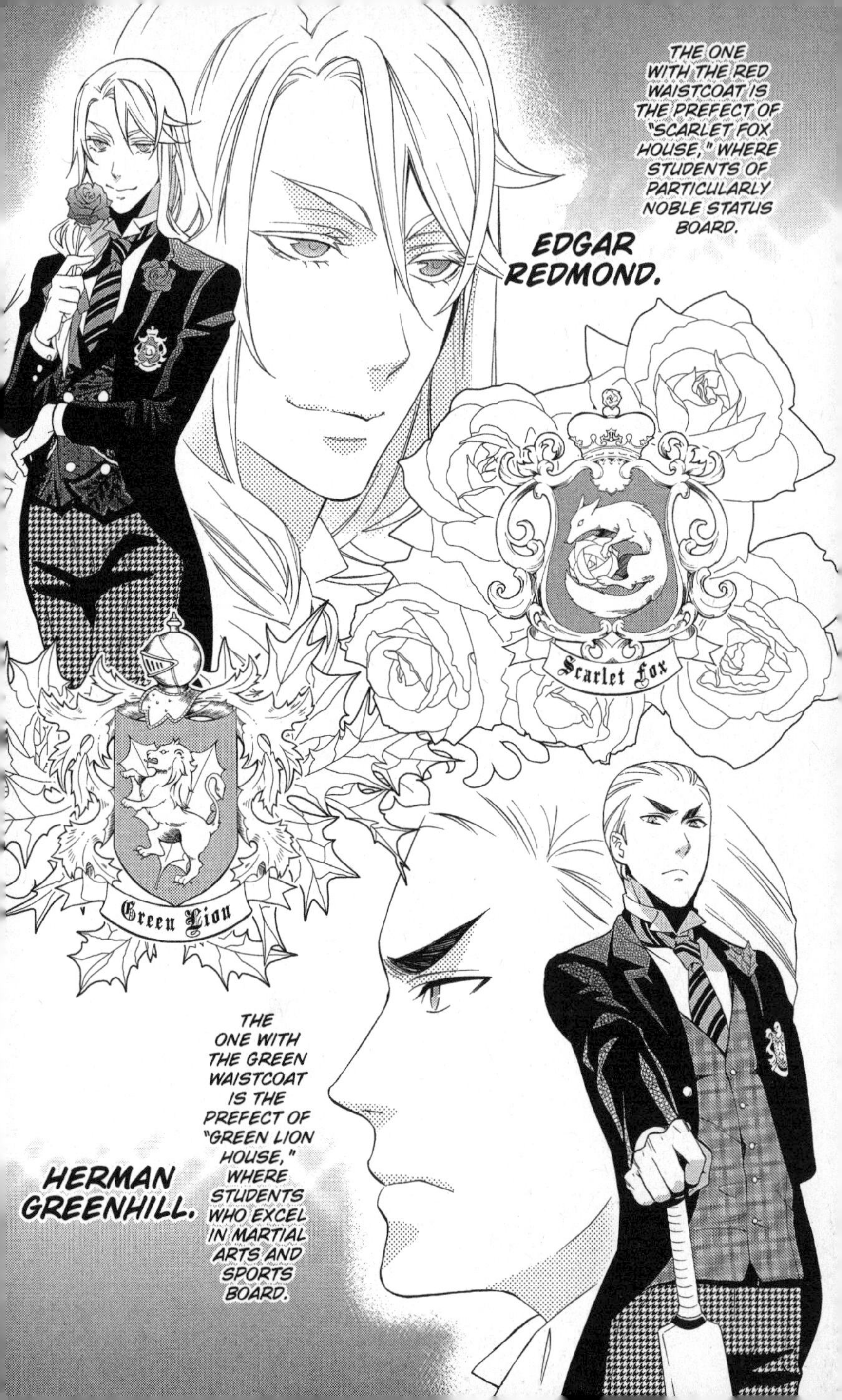
THE ONE WITH THE RED WAISTCOAT IS THE PREFECT OF "SCARLET FOX HOUSE," WHERE STUDENTS OF PARTICULARLY NOBLE STATUS BOARD.
EDGAR REDMOND.
Scarlet Fox
Green Lion
THE ONE WITH THE GREEN WAISTCOAT IS THE PREFECT OF "GREEN LION HOUSE," WHERE STUDENTS WHO EXCEL IN MARTIAL ARTS AND SPORTS BOARD.
HERMAN GREENHILL.

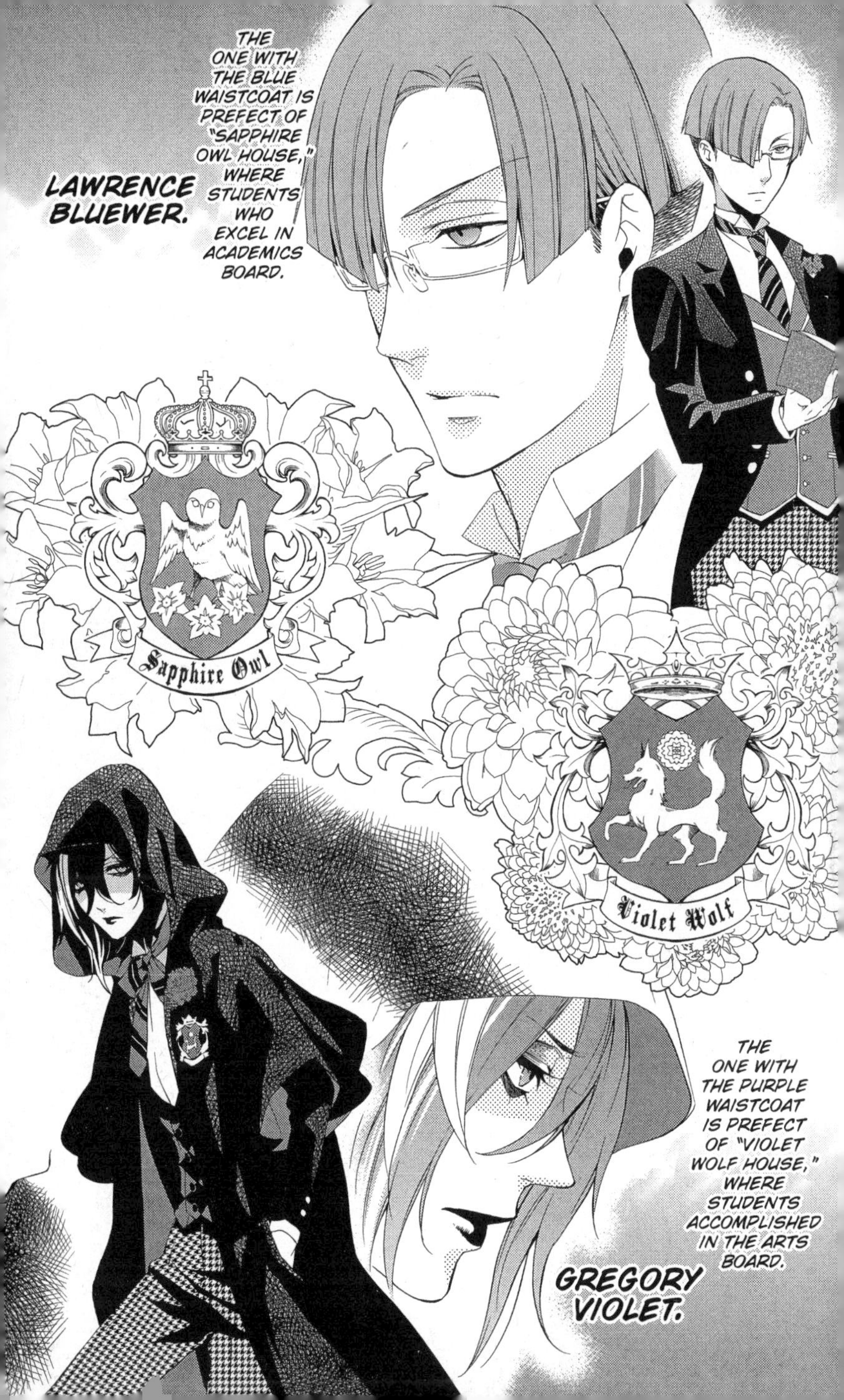
THE ONE WITH THE BLUE WAISTCOAT IS PREFECT OF "SAPPHIRE OWL HOUSE," WHERE STUDENTS WHO EXCEL IN ACADEMICS BOARD.
LAWRENCE BLUEWER.
Sapphire Owl
Violet Wolf
THE ONE WITH THE PURPLE WAISTCOAT IS PREFECT OF "VIOLET WOLF HOUSE," WHERE STUDENTS ACCOMPLISHED IN THE ARTS BOARD.
GREGORY VIOLET.

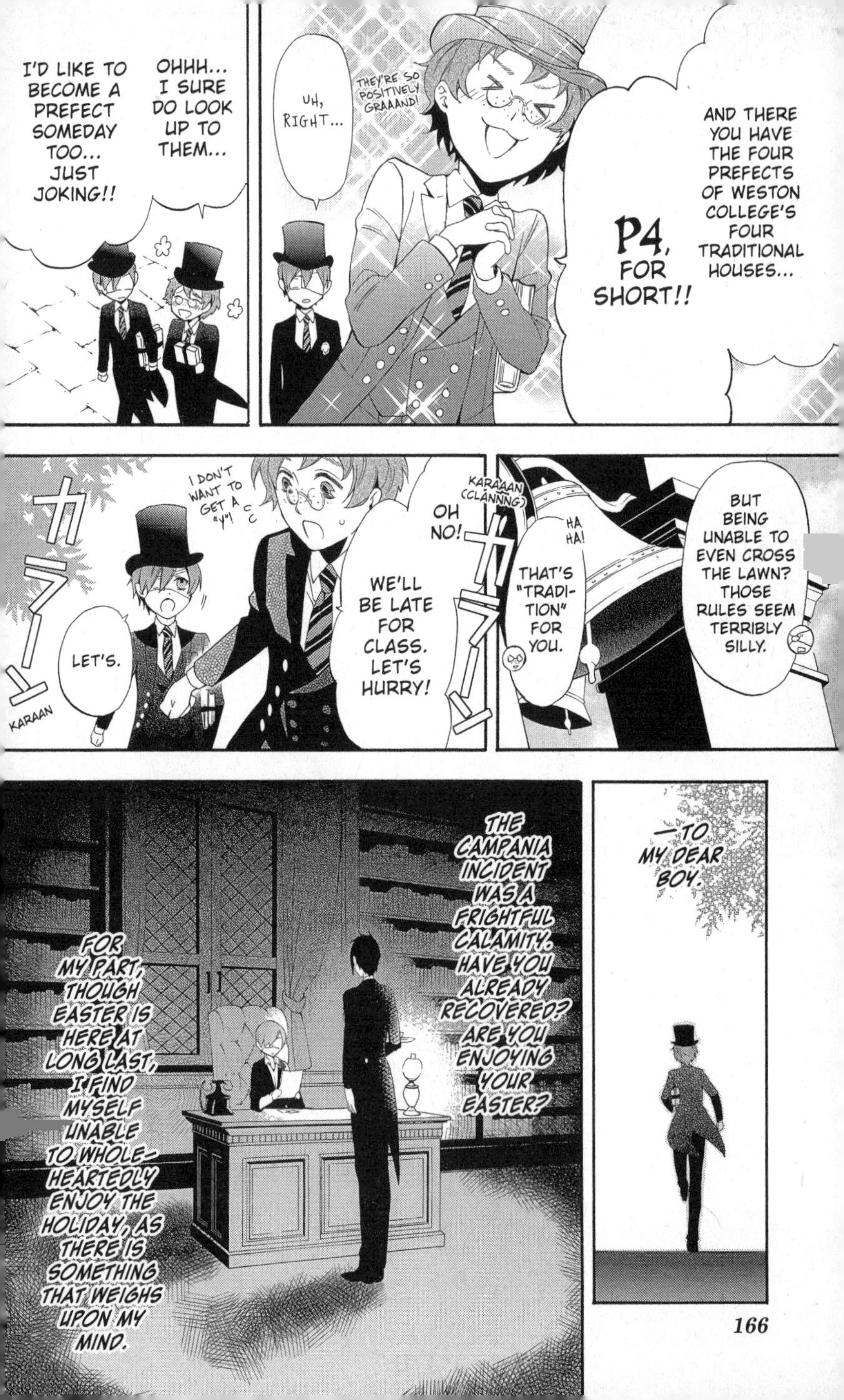
AND THERE YOU HAVE THE FOUR PREFECTS OF WESTON COLLEGE'S FOUR TRADITIONAL HOUSES...
P4, FOR SHORT!!
THEY'RE SO POSITIVELY GRAAAND!
UH, RIGHT...
OHHH... I SURE DO LOOK UP TO THEM...
I'D LIKE TO BECOME A PREFECT SOMEDAY TOO... JUST JOKING!!
BUT BEING UNABLE TO EVEN CROSS THE LAWN? THOSE RULES SEEM TERRIBLY SILLY.
HA HA!
THAT'S "TRADITION" FOR YOU.
KARAAAN (CLANNNG)
カラーン
OH NO!
WE'LL BE LATE FOR CLASS. LET'S HURRY!
I DON'T WANT TO GET A "Y"!
LET'S.
カラーン
KARAAN
—TO MY DEAR BOY.
THE CAMPANIA INCIDENT WAS A FRIGHTFUL CALAMITY. HAVE YOU ALREADY RECOVERED? ARE YOU ENJOYING YOUR EASTER?
FOR MY PART, THOUGH EASTER IS HERE AT LONG LAST, I FIND MYSELF UNABLE TO WHOLE-HEARTEDLY ENJOY THE HOLIDAY, AS THERE IS SOMETHING THAT WEIGHS UPON MY MIND.

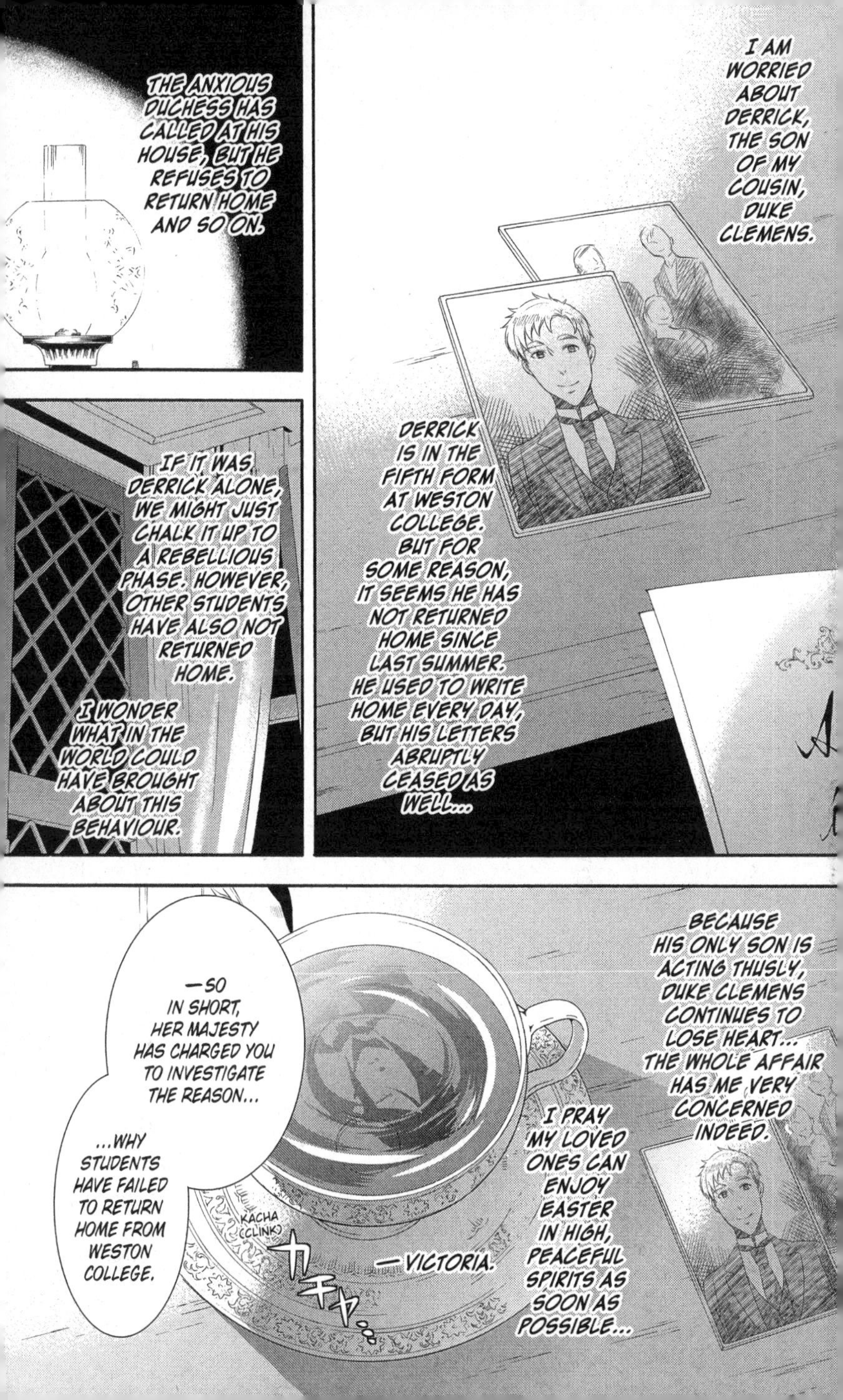
I AM WORRIED ABOUT DERRICK, THE SON OF MY COUSIN, DUKE CLEMENS.
DERRICK IS IN THE FIFTH FORM AT WESTON COLLEGE. BUT FOR SOME REASON, IT SEEMS HE HAS NOT RETURNED HOME SINCE LAST SUMMER. HE USED TO WRITE HOME EVERY DAY, BUT HIS LETTERS ABRUPTLY CEASED AS WELL...
THE ANXIOUS DUCHESS HAS CALLED AT HIS HOUSE, BUT HE REFUSES TO RETURN HOME AND SO ON.
IF IT WAS DERRICK ALONE, WE MIGHT JUST CHALK IT UP TO A REBELLIOUS PHASE. HOWEVER, OTHER STUDENTS HAVE ALSO NOT RETURNED HOME.
I WONDER WHAT IN THE WORLD COULD HAVE BROUGHT ABOUT THIS BEHAVIOUR.
BECAUSE HIS ONLY SON IS ACTING THUSLY, DUKE CLEMENS CONTINUES TO LOSE HEART... THE WHOLE AFFAIR HAS ME VERY CONCERNED INDEED.
I PRAY MY LOVED ONES CAN ENJOY EASTER IN HIGH, PEACEFUL SPIRITS AS SOON AS POSSIBLE...
—VICTORIA.
KACHA (CLINK)
—SO IN SHORT, HER MAJESTY HAS CHARGED YOU TO INVESTIGATE THE REASON...
...WHY STUDENTS HAVE FAILED TO RETURN HOME FROM WESTON COLLEGE.

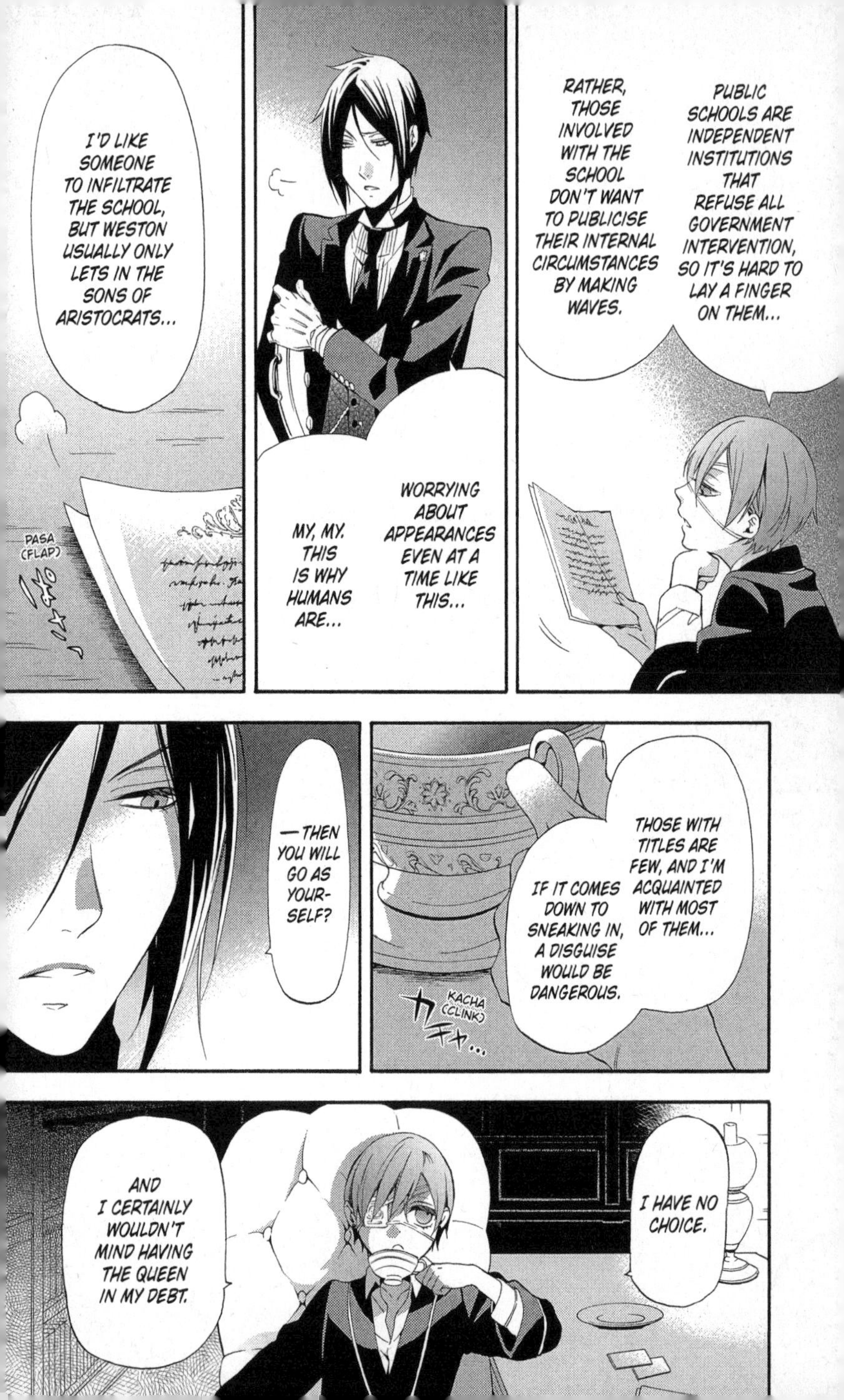
PUBLIC SCHOOLS ARE INDEPENDENT INSTITUTIONS THAT REFUSE ALL GOVERNMENT INTERVENTION, SO IT'S HARD TO LAY A FINGER ON THEM...
RATHER, THOSE INVOLVED WITH THE SCHOOL DON'T WANT TO PUBLICISE THEIR INTERNAL CIRCUMSTANCES BY MAKING WAVES.
WORRYING ABOUT APPEARANCES EVEN AT A TIME LIKE THIS...
MY, MY. THIS IS WHY HUMANS ARE...
I'D LIKE SOMEONE TO INFILTRATE THE SCHOOL, BUT WESTON USUALLY ONLY LETS IN THE SONS OF ARISTOCRATS...
PASA (FLAP)
THOSE WITH TITLES ARE FEW, AND I'M ACQUAINTED WITH MOST OF THEM...
IF IT COMES DOWN TO SNEAKING IN, A DISGUISE WOULD BE DANGEROUS.
KACHA (CLINK)
—THEN YOU WILL GO AS YOURSELF?
I HAVE NO CHOICE.
AND I CERTAINLY WOULDN'T MIND HAVING THE QUEEN IN MY DEBT.

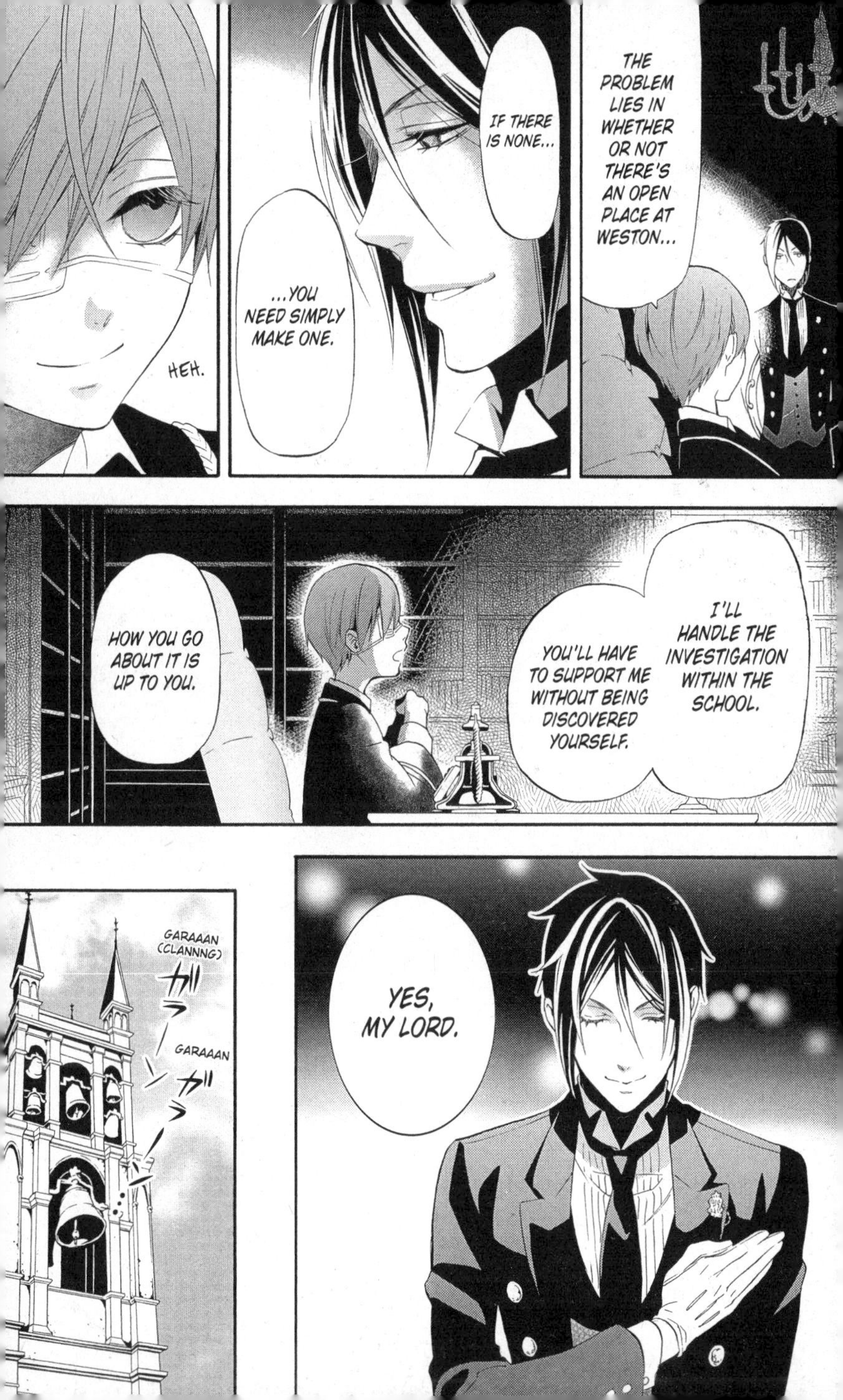
THE PROBLEM LIES IN WHETHER OR NOT THERE'S AN OPEN PLACE AT WESTON...
IF THERE IS NONE...
...YOU NEED SIMPLY MAKE ONE.
HEH.
I'LL HANDLE THE INVESTIGATION WITHIN THE SCHOOL.
YOU'LL HAVE TO SUPPORT ME WITHOUT BEING DISCOVERED YOURSELF.
HOW YOU GO ABOUT IT IS UP TO YOU.
YES, MY LORD.
GARAAAN (CLANNNG)
GARAAAN

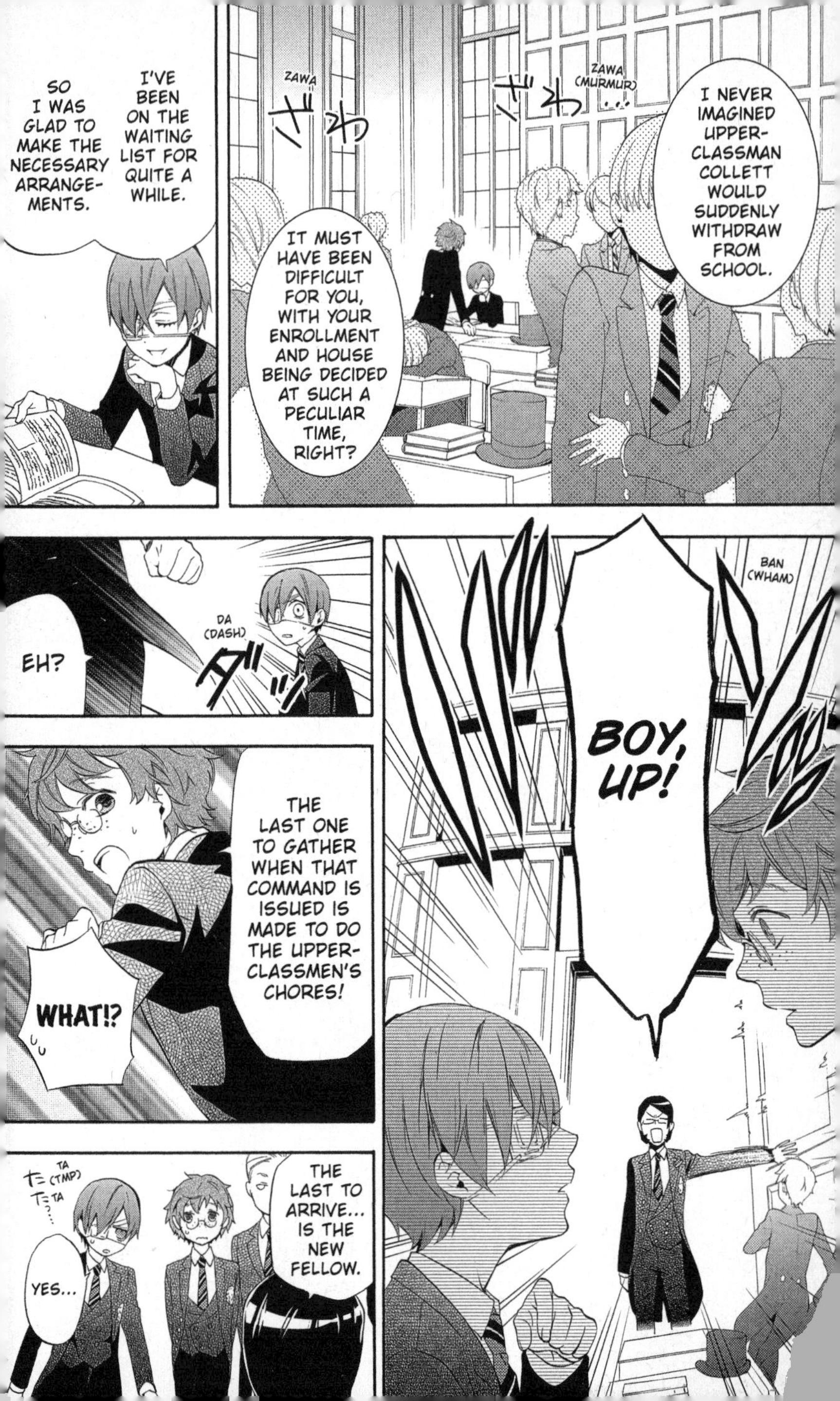
ZAWA (MURMUR) ...
ZAWA
I NEVER IMAGINED UPPER-CLASSMAN COLLETT WOULD SUDDENLY WITHDRAW FROM SCHOOL.
IT MUST HAVE BEEN DIFFICULT FOR YOU, WITH YOUR ENROLLMENT AND HOUSE BEING DECIDED AT SUCH A PECULIAR TIME, RIGHT?
I'VE BEEN ON THE WAITING LIST FOR QUITE A WHILE.
SO I WAS GLAD TO MAKE THE NECESSARY ARRANGE-MENTS.
BAN (WHAM)
BOY, UP!
DA (DASH)
EH?
THE LAST ONE TO GATHER WHEN THAT COMMAND IS ISSUED IS MADE TO DO THE UPPER-CLASSMEN'S CHORES!
WHAT!?
THE LAST TO ARRIVE... IS THE NEW FELLOW.
TA (TMP) TA
YES...

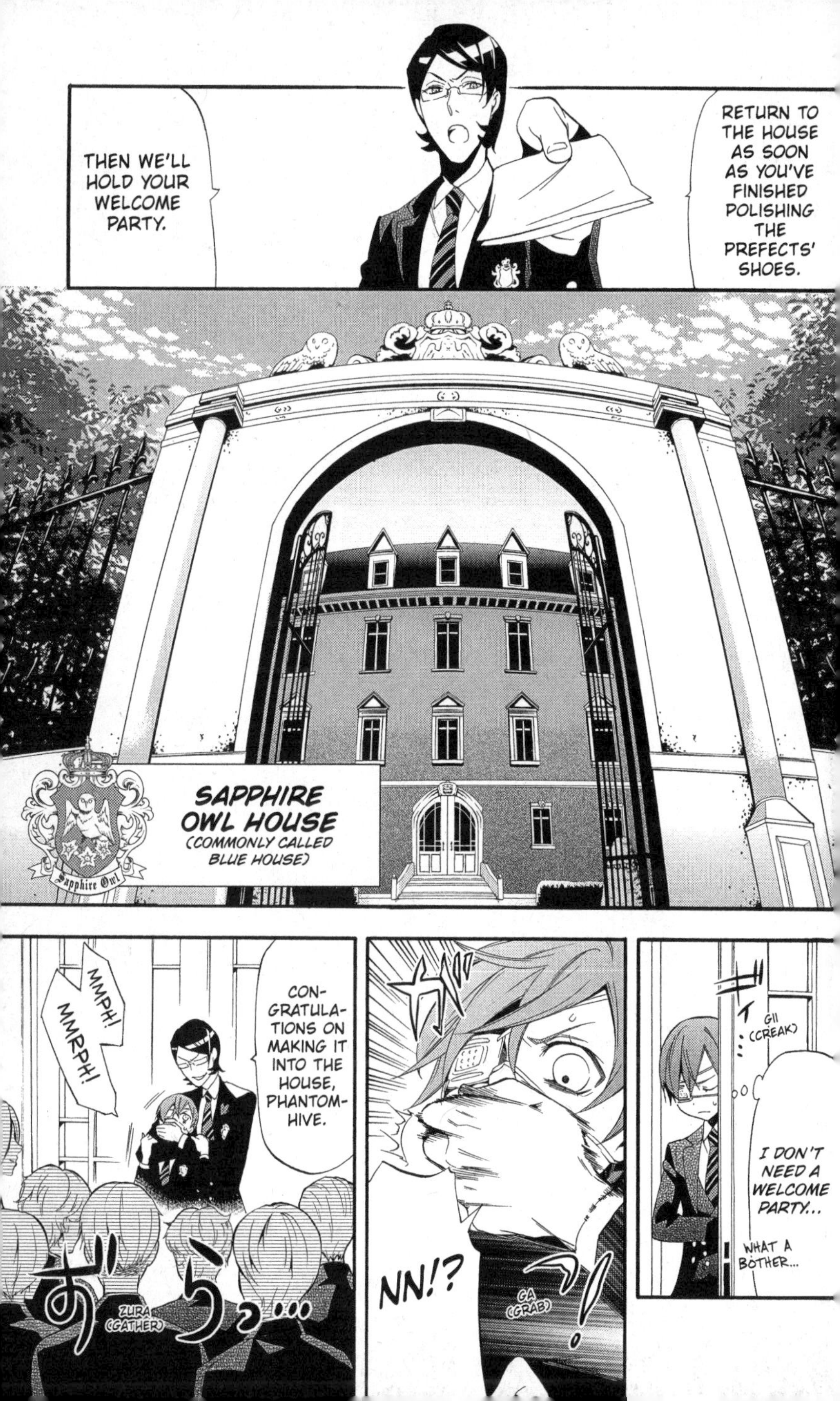
RETURN TO THE HOUSE AS SOON AS YOU'VE FINISHED POLISHING THE PREFECTS' SHOES.
THEN WE'LL HOLD YOUR WELCOME PARTY.
SAPPHIRE OWL HOUSE (COMMONLY CALLED BLUE HOUSE)
Sapphire Owl
GII (CREAK)
I DON'T NEED A WELCOME PARTY...
WHAT A BOTHER...
GA (GRAB)
NN!?
CON-GRATULA-TIONS ON MAKING IT INTO THE HOUSE, PHANTOM-HIVE.
MMPH! MMRPH!
ZURA (GATHER)

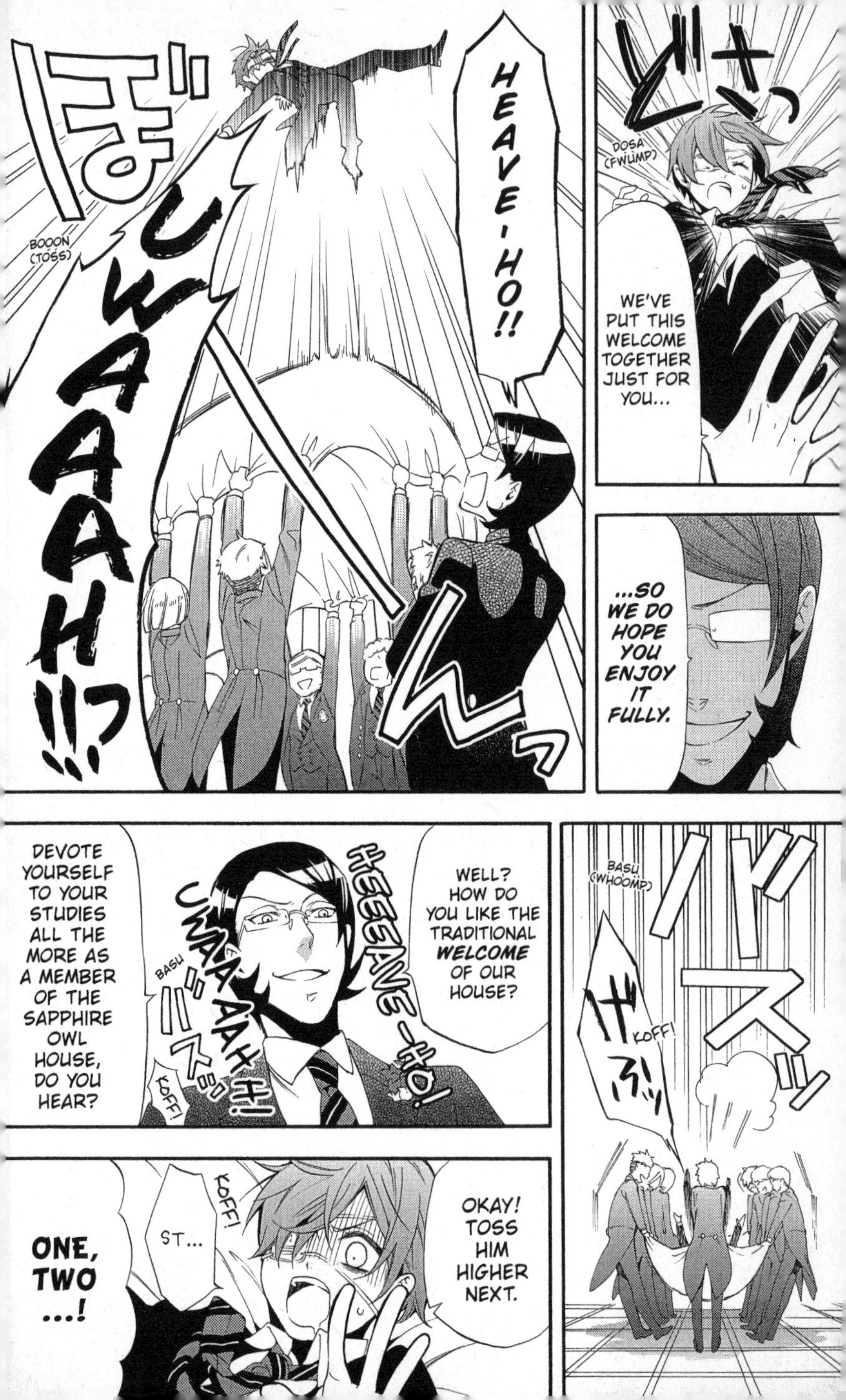
DOSA (FWUMP)
WE'VE PUT THIS WELCOME TOGETHER JUST FOR YOU...
...SO WE DO HOPE YOU ENJOY IT FULLY.
HEAVE-HO!!
BOOON (TOSS)
UWAAAAH!!!
BASU (WHOOMP)
KOFF!
WELL? HOW DO YOU LIKE THE TRADITIONAL WELCOME OF OUR HOUSE?
HEEEAVE-HO!
UWAAA AAH!
BASU
KOFF!
DEVOTE YOURSELF TO YOUR STUDIES ALL THE MORE AS A MEMBER OF THE SAPPHIRE OWL HOUSE, DO YOU HEAR?
OKAY! TOSS HIM HIGHER NEXT.
KOFF!
ST...
ONE, TWO...!

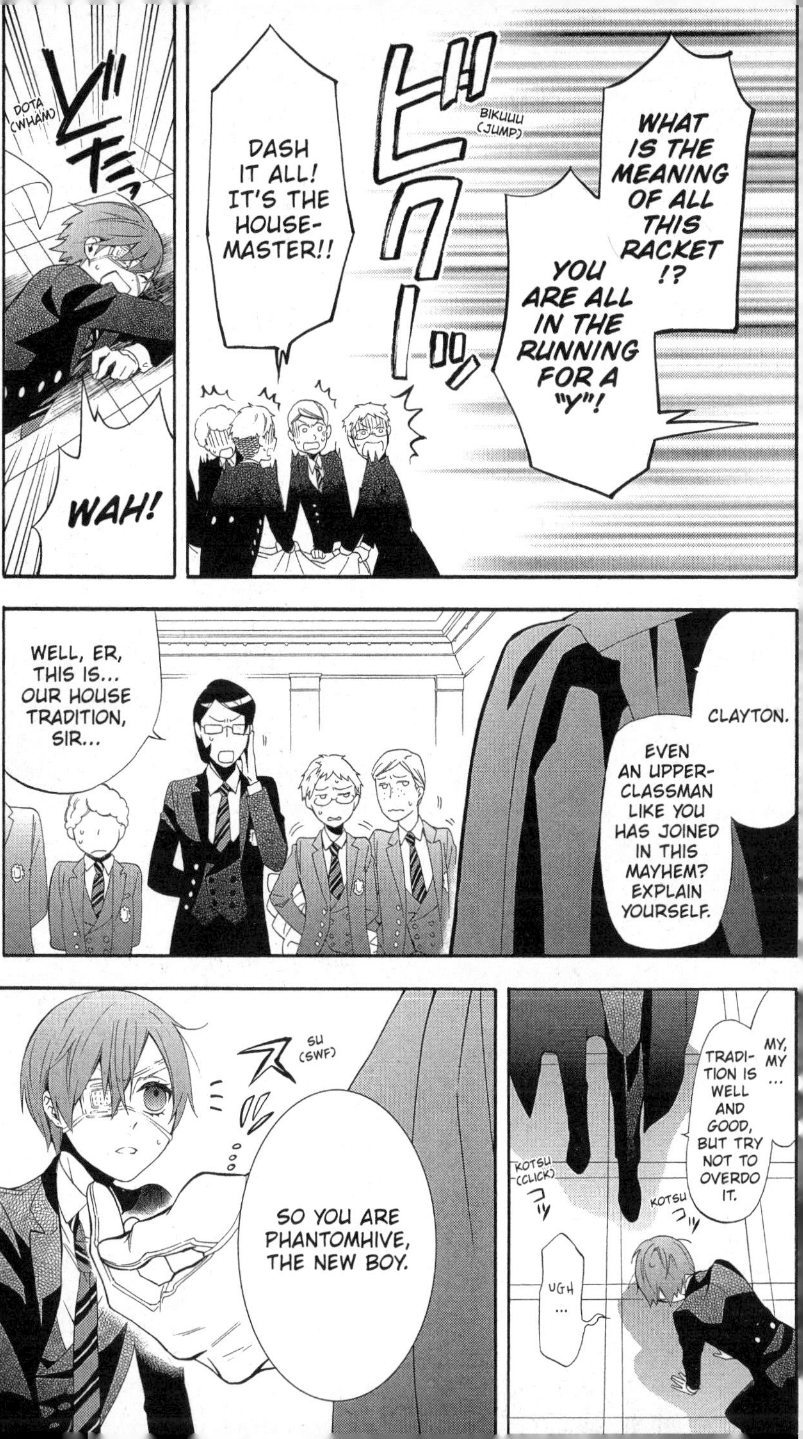
WHAT IS THE MEANING OF ALL THIS RACKET!?
YOU ARE ALL IN THE RUNNING FOR A "Y"!
BIKUUU (JUMP)
DASH IT ALL! IT'S THE HOUSE-MASTER!!
DOTA (WHAM)
WAH!
CLAYTON.
EVEN AN UPPER-CLASSMAN LIKE YOU HAS JOINED IN THIS MAYHEM? EXPLAIN YOURSELF.
WELL, ER, THIS IS... OUR HOUSE TRADITION, SIR...
MY, MY...
TRADITION IS WELL AND GOOD, BUT TRY NOT TO OVERDO IT.
KOTSU (CLICK)
KOTSU
UGH...
SU (SWF)
SO YOU ARE PHANTOMHIVE, THE NEW BOY.

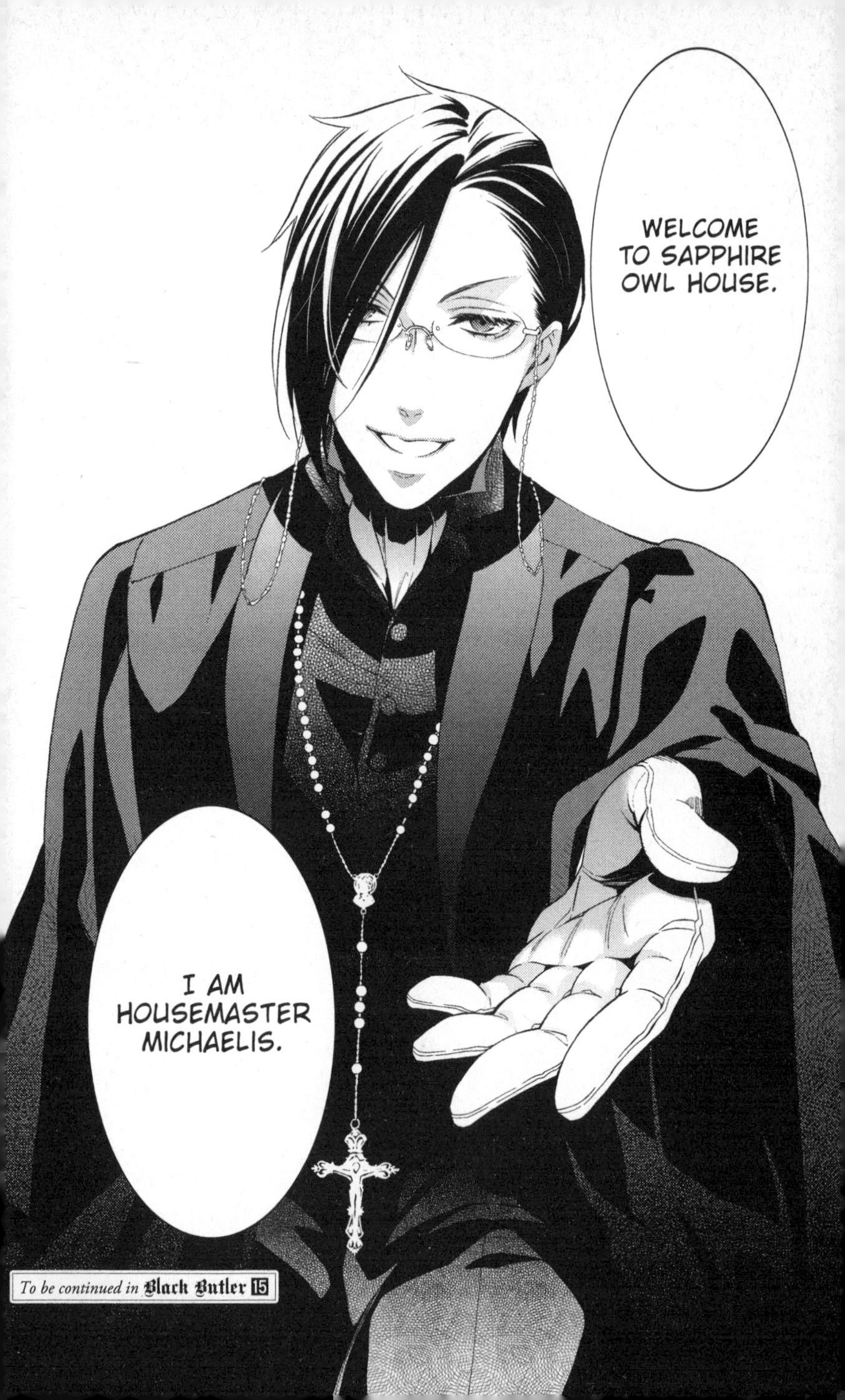
WELCOME TO SAPPHIRE OWL HOUSE.
I AM HOUSEMASTER MICHAELIS.
To be continued in Black Butler 15

⇒ Black Butler ⇐
黒執事

Downstairs

Wakana Haduki

7

Saito Torino

Tsuki Sorano

Yu Kamiya

Hashimoto

*

Takeshi Kuma

*

Yana Toboso

Adviser

Rico Murakami

Special thanks for You!

Translation Notes

INSIDE FRONT AND BACK COVERS
Koshien
A baseball stadium in Nishinomiya, Hyogo Prefecture, Japan. It is the home stadium of the Hanshin Tigers (a professional baseball team), but annual senior high school baseball tournaments are held there in spring and summer as well. Making it to (and winning at) Koshien is the dream of many young baseball players in Japan.

PH Gakuen
There exists a PL Gakuen ("school") in Osaka Prefecture, Japan, and its baseball club has won numerous Koshien tournaments.

PAGE 10
Mariage Frères Darjeeling
The Mariage brothers, Henri and Edouard, their family well versed in the tea trade for nearly two centuries prior, opened the Mariage Frères company in Paris, France, in 1854. Darjeeling teas are so named because they hail from the Darjeeling district of West Bengal, India, where tea planting was initiated by the British Dr. A. Campbell in 1841.

PAGE 19
Flower drawing
In Japan, a circle adorned with flower petals is drawn on an exam to indicate full marks.

PAGE 52
The bow is pitching upward from the weight of all the water we have taken on!!
When the *RMS Titanic*, the infamous luxury passenger vessel, sank in 1912, it was the stern that pitched up out of the ocean because the bow had taken on too much water and became submerged. Within minutes, the stern proceeded to break off and thunder down into the water below.

PAGE 86
They must have been unable to lower the lifeboats in time.
Unlike the *Campania*, all twenty of the *RMS Titanic*'s lifeboats were used during the sinking of the vessel, though approximately 1,500 individuals remained on the ship.

PAGE 98
Even in death, humans continue to attempt to kick others down to obtain that which they desire.
Another possible reference to Ryunosuke Akutagawa's short story "The Spider's Thread" ("Kumo no ito"); see Volume 4. One of the inspirations for this short story is said to be a fable from Dostoyevsky's *The Brothers Karamazov*, in which a sinner condemned to hell kicks at those who have latched onto a means of escape that she deems to be hers and hers alone.

PAGE 104
Chain of hair lockets
Hair jewelry was extremely popular in the Victorian Age as a durable and intimate form of personal memento, especially for individuals in mourning. Such mourning jewelry would incorporate hair from a deceased loved one as part of the jewelry itself or would be kept enclosed within the jewelry, like the lockets in Undertaker's chain.

Yana Toboso

AUTHOR'S NOTE

I always treasure reading letters and e-mails from my readers, as I can hear everyone's opinions directly.

"I'll surprise people here!" "I'll get people fired up with this!" I pick up my pens with enthusiasm and nervously wait for everyone's reactions when magazines and collected volumes go on sale. With Volume 13, the biggest response was not to Undertaker or Lizzie, but the talk about the pen nib at the end of the volume, and I have extremely mixed feelings about that. By the way, I'm still using the pen from before in the wrong way. And with that, here's Volume 14.

BLACK BUTLER ⑭

YANA TOBOSO

Translation: Tomo Kimura • Lettering: Alexis Eckerman

KUROSHITSUJI Vol. 14 © 2012 Yana Toboso / SQUARE ENIX CO., LTD. All rights reserved. First published in Japan in 2012 by SQUARE ENIX CO., LTD. English translation rights arranged with SQUARE ENIX CO., LTD. and Hachette Book Group through Tuttle-Mori Agency, Inc.

Translation © 2013 by SQUARE ENIX CO., LTD.

Yen Press
Hachette Book Group
237 Park Avenue, New York, NY 10017

www.HachetteBookGroup.com
www.YenPress.com

Yen Press is an imprint of Hachette Book Group, Inc. The Yen Press name and logo are trademarks of Hachette Book Group, Inc.

First Yen Press Edition: July 2013

ISBN: 978-0-316-24430-5

10 9 8 7 6 5 4 3

BVG

Printed in the United States of America